Famine Relief in Warlord China

HARVARD EAST ASIAN MONOGRAPHS 423

Famine Relief in Warlord China

Pierre Fuller

Published by the Harvard University Asia Center
Distributed by Harvard University Press
Cambridge (Massachusetts) and London 2019

The Harvard University Asia Center publishes a monograph series and, in coordination with the Fairbank Center for Chinese Studies, the Korea Institute, the Reischauer Institute of Japanese Studies, and other facilities and institutes, administers research projects designed to further scholarly understanding of China, Japan, Vietnam, Korea, and other Asian countries. The Center also sponsors projects addressing multidisciplinary and regional issues in Asia.

Publication of this book was partially underwritten by the Mr. and Mrs. Stephen C. M. King Publishing and Communications Fund, established by Stephen C. M. King to further the cause of international understanding and cooperation, especially between China and the United States, by enhancing cross-cultural education and the exchange of ideas across national boundaries through publications of the Harvard University Asia Center.

Library of Congress Cataloging-in-Publication Data

Names: Fuller, Pierre, author.
Title: Famine relief in warlord China / Pierre Fuller.
Other titles: Harvard East Asian monographs ; 423.
Description: Cambridge, Massachusetts : Published by the Harvard University Asia Center,
    2019. | Series: Harvard East Asian monographs ; 423 | includes bibliographical references
    and index.
Identifiers: LCCN 2018057670 | ISBN 9780674241138 (hardcover : alk. paper) |
    ISBN 9780674241145 (pbk. : alk. paper)
Subjects: LCSH: Food relief—China—History—20th century. | Indigenous peoples—
    China—Politics and government. | International relief—China—History—
    20th century. | China—Politics and government—1912-1928.
Classification: LCC HV696.F6 F855 2019 | DDC 363.8/83095109042—dc23
LC record available at https://lccn.loc.gov/2018057670

To Lucienne Gigout

Contents

Contents

List of Illustrations

Weights, Measures, and Currency

Unless otherwise specified, all monies are given in yuan (*yangyuan*) or (Mexican) silver dollars, each of which was equal at the time to 140–55 coppers (or cents). Reflecting local variations in measures, the Ministry of Communications converted both *shi* and *bao* into anything from 100 to 160 *jin* in its published accounting records in 1921. This book treats *shi* as equal to 120 *jin* and *bao* as equal to 160 *jin*.

liang = one-sixteenth of a *jin*
he = one-tenth of a *sheng* or one-fifth of a *jin*
bang (pound avoirdupois) = three-fourths of a *jin*
jin (catty) = 1 1/3 pounds
sheng (pint) = one-tenth of a *dou* or 2 *jin*
dou (peck) = 20 *jin*
dai (bag) = 50 *bang* or 37.5 *jin*
dan (*picul*) = 100 *jin*
shi (stone) = 120 *jin*
bao (sack) = 160 *jin*
dun (ton) = 1,680 *jin*

Acknowledgments

My words of thanks are inevitably as incomplete as any history can be. This project started in California, where I could not have had a kinder, more attentive, and more intellectually rigorous advisor than Kenneth Pomeranz, who waded through my work with the patience of someone with all the time in the world. Jeffrey Wasserstrom was equally a pleasure to work with over the years, generous with his thoughts and time and discussing all manner of things relating to my research and the wider field. I am also grateful to Guo Qitao for his insights and language training. Anne Walthall, Kate Edgerton-Tarpley, Robert Marks, and Janet Theiss gave helpful comments and advice early on, while Robert Bickers helped point the way to important collections in England. I am deeply indebted to the two anonymous reviewers who gave extraordinarily detailed and helpful advice, and to Micah Muscolino, Edward McCord, Pierre-Étienne Will, Diana Lary, Bertrand Taithe, Shirley Ye, and Georg Christ for their comments and conversations over the years. I also wish to thank Nick Scarle for producing the maps.

At Nankai, I could not thank Guan Yongqiang enough for his help in gaining access to materials on the mainland—and, most importantly, for his friendship over the entire course of this project. I would also like to thank Chuan Chen in Tianjin, Liu Yin in Beijing, Gong Chen and Liu Honglong in Xi'an, Shi Xia in Irvine and Sarasota, and Brooks Jessup in Berkeley for their help and camaraderie along the way. Colleagues in the history departments of the University of California, Irvine, and the University of Manchester have provided me with friendly home bases during years of research forays, while the charming faculty at Irvine's Department of East Asian Languages and Literatures and Manchester's Chinese Studies Division created ideal settings for me to hone my language skills and seek advice.

For financial support, I am indebted to Irvine's International Center for Writing and Translation, especially for a five-year Glenn Schaeffer Fellowship in Creative Nonfiction administered with cheer by Colette LaBouff; to the Harvard-Yenching Institute, the Department of History at Peking University, and the Fulbright Program for funding my time in China; and to the Shelby Cullom Davis Center for Historical Studies at Princeton University for offering me valuable time for working on the manuscript.

For their company and conversation over the years of research and writing, I would like to acknowledge Quinn Javers in my time spent in China and the Bay Area; Nicole LaBouff for the research forays to Europe; Kate Merkel-Hess, Adam Guerin, Romas Kudirki, Brock Cutler, Laura Sextro, Christina Ghanbarpour, and other dear friends and colleagues too numerous to name in California; Arnaud Orain for camaraderie and conversation in Princeton and Paris; and Mark Farha, with whom I have had the good fortune to cross paths at many times and places over the years. Then a shout must go out to the regulars at both of the Oscar's in Xi'an and to Simon and Dave in Tokyo for providing the music to get me through this project.

I write this with great affection and indebtedness to David and Isabelle Fuller, history enthusiasts and the most devoted of parents. I write this also in remembrance of Faruk Tabak, a scholar of the Ottoman Empire who, during tours together of the eastern Mediterranean in my undergraduate years, sowed the seeds for my turn toward China and academia in conversations that have stayed with me throughout this endeavor. My grandmother, Lucienne Gigout (née Fayard), born before the events described in this book, continues to provide those around her with the richest canvas of family life in Indochina, Morocco, and the Drôme over the past century, which has nurtured my fascination with quotidian history—something I have endeavoured to instill in my work. I dedicate this book to her. Finally, I complete this project with the most loving appreciation for my partner, Eleanor Davey, who entered my life as this book was written and has enriched it more than I can say.

INTRODUCTION

The Chinese Republic in 1920 was in many respects a failed state. The young successor to the Qing dynasty (1644–1912) had effectively split into military domains. The central government was at a historical nadir of fiscal solvency, in debt to domestic and foreign creditors by hundreds of millions of yuan. Only a year before, the Treaty of Versailles had rewarded Shandong to the Japanese, just as severe drought descended on the province. By the fall of 1920, drought would lead to partial or total harvest failure in more than 300 counties in five provinces ringing the North China Plain.

Of course any resulting decline in the availability of foodstuffs did not necessitate famine. Extreme and widespread poverty combined with rising prices to make grain inaccessible to millions.[1] In addition, continued deforestation, siltation of the river systems, and salinization of the soil exacerbated a long-standing ecological crisis that constrained productivity and reduced the supply of fallback sources of food. Limited irrigation meant that water tables went untapped as crops withered. Limited rail links meant that mule teams had to traverse hundreds of miles of rutted-mud roads to reach rural markets. Credit in the countryside dried up. In some places bandits swelled in number, while in others disbanded soldiers were unleashed on the public. Meanwhile the state, both at the central and the increasingly autonomous provincial or regional levels, bolstered the ranks of the military by spending vigorously to increase the capacity to wage war.

In the end, half a million northern Chinese would die of famine-related causes before the spring of 1921. Possibly more, it is hard to tell. There was no national census in the period with which to determine how many people perished or exactly how they died. The fact that starvation existed at all along the banks of the Yellow River in 1920–21 was a social and political failure, reminiscent of the drought and famine that had led to the deaths of 9.5–13.0 million people in the same five northern provinces in 1876–79.

But then, compared to what had transpired in North China half a century before, the splintering Chinese body politic in 1920 kept mortality in check in various paradoxical ways. Increasingly bellicose provincial regimes managed the movement between them of hundreds of thousands of people fleeing famine conditions. These same regimes mobilized and transferred millions of *shi* of relief grain into the districts afflicted with disaster. Charities and municipal authorities in Beijing and other urban centers expanded their shelter systems and clothing drives for people fleeing famine and soup kitchens for their resident poor. And afflicted communities themselves, many under the threat of pillaging by bandits and marauding soldiers, set up mutual aid programs designed to carry struggling villagers through to the spring harvest.

Accounts of early twentieth-century Chinese history have tended to overlook the domestic achievements behind the containment of famine, crediting relief at the time to international assistance. This stress on the global dimension of relief in 1920, however significant it was, obscures the interactions and transactions among Chinese during the crisis, and what this activity says about a particular moment in modern Chinese history: its social conduits and transit networks, the multiplicity and resilience of relief initiatives achieved amid war and social disintegration, and the value systems and poor relief methods from the Qing that continued to inform disaster governance at both the local and national levels well into the republican period. Taking the pulse of everyday society during severe crisis in China in the 1920s is what this book has set out to do.

Beyond Characterization of 1920s China

The term "warlord" (*junfa*) was relatively new to the Chinese lexicon in 1920, probably having been first employed, by way of Japanese, in the pages of a New Culture journal just two years before. It would take a few more years for the term to attain popular currency, not only among intellectuals but also among military authorities as a way to denounce foes as the country descended into civil war.[2] Whatever the term's original ideological uses, the warlord would become an analytical category through which early twentieth-century China was studied for the remainder of the century, becoming by the 1960s a field of academic study in its own right.[3] Concentrating on the factional struggles and machinations that characterized the politics of the 1920s, rarely did the field pay much attention to the civil dimensions of 1920s rule and their effects on the wider social life of the period. As a body of literature, these studies collectively presented the late 1910s and 1920s as a political drama performed on top of a downtrodden population. In more recent scholarship, one still finds these "colorful warlords" typecast as a class of their own, one that "tried hard to destroy the fabric of society," having "often decimated local communities and run roughshod over provincial governments."[4]

This book is not meant to be a formal study of warlordism, nor does it make claims about governance generally in this period. As a political system, the phenomenon has been capably studied by numerous scholars, most notably Edward McCord.[5] Rather, it is a study of an overlooked aspect of both formal and informal governance at a moment of contested political authority midway between the death of Yuan Shikai (1859–1916) and the rise of the Nationalists (Guomindang) later in the 1920s. It joins reassessments of the republican era (1912–49), both in the form of Western scholarship and the rise of revisionist histories of that era on the mainland.[6] These works have recast the period as remarkably open culturally and politically, especially compared to the Maoist period; as one of state building and strengthening of major fiscal organs of the state; and even as one of gains in agricultural productivity.[7] Historians have also acknowledged the role that war and the military played during the republic in determining the nature of modern Chinese society, from its full embrace by elites to its role in shaping Chinese culture and economy.[8] The sheer amount of armed conflict in China's modern period makes it unsurprising that violence has been a focus of scholars, especially China's struggle against the Japanese invasion and its great human destruction.[9] Although scholarship on disaster relief and philanthropy in China's past has grown considerably since the 1980s, especially in the last fifteen years, the literature on disaster experience and responses in the half-century between the last decades of the Qing and the 1930s and 1940s remains remarkably sparse.[10]

I aim to revisit early republican governance through famine for several reasons. First, relief administration was integral to the imperial ideology and rule of the dynastic system that had preceded the 1920 crisis by less than a decade. Welfare policy and practice to ensure the availability of sustenance—"nourish the people" (*yangmin*)—formed a fundamental basis of political legitimacy and cultural authority not only for the imperial house, but also for the empire's bureaucratic civil corps, the merchant community, and scholar-gentry concentrated among the general rural population.[11] The performance of poor relief and disaster management were key indices of the efficacy and priorities of both ruling elites and social organizations generally at any given moment in time.

There exist important works on famine relief and civic organizations over the *longue durée* in China, such as those by Lillian Li and the legal historian Karla Simon, respectively—both of which cover the republican era.[12] Yet however important these studies are, their scale of several centuries or millennia conceals dynamics over the short term that only a focused study can reveal. In historical accounts of the interregnum between the formal end of the Qing in 1912 and the consolidation of Nationalist rule after 1928, military authorities running the state are invisible in mentions of disaster, obstacles to its relief, or the root cause of a crisis. The assumptions remain that relief systems were close to moribund by 1920 and that the paternalistic ideology underpinning relief systems from the late imperial period had declining appeal to the early republic's military leaders and rural gentry, requiring a huge intervention from international relief actors for drought and famine in China to be contained.

Examining famine allows us to evaluate the extent to which the practices and values associated with political legitimacy and notions of virtuous rule continued to factor into formal and informal forms of governance in the republican period. Of the diverse range of political actors, some made bids for national or regional supremacy relying on modernization and nationalist drives, and others did so depending on brute force. But a surprising number of commanders at multiple levels of the military also staked the legitimacy of their authority on welfare initiatives. These efforts largely used the methods and discourse of poor relief and disaster management from China's late imperial Ming (1368–1644) and Qing periods in answer to the population's expectation of actions consistent with virtuous governance (*dezheng*).

This relationship between control and hierarchy with care for the most vulnerable is universal and certainly not unique to China or to any period. "Humanitarianism and paternalism overlap in various ways," notes Michael Barnett.[13] Or as Didier Fassin writes, "This tension between inequality and solidarity, between a relation of domination and a relation of assistance, is constitutive of all humanitarian governance."[14] It is these very contradictions and uncomfortable combinations that this study seeks to consider: how the military can intersect with relief matters, acts of compassion can underpin bids for authoritarian legitimacy, official roles can mesh with private charitable endeavors, graft can figure in largesse, and political and regional loyalties and rivalries can play out during periods of mass refugee movement and national crisis. The aim here is not to shoehorn any particular individual or class of military or civil administrators into humanitarian positions. Rather, the goal is to address the ways in which welfare measures in China's early republican period have been overlooked in narratives all too often dominated by strife, struggle, and disorder.

Broader Themes in Chinese History

There are numerous competing theories not only about the causes but also about the very nature and meaning of famine.[15] One marker of the phenomenon is the socially and culturally determined disruptions it makes in normal life. This approach is in keeping with how the existence of famine (*jihuang*) was customarily determined in China, through extensive canvassing of affected populations—which in 1920 identified acute subsistence needs in millions of households and surges in the consumption of famine foods, family flight, and other extreme measures. However, a more scientific marker of famine's severity in 1920s China is elusive. The line between normal—that is, socially tolerated—hunger and malnutrition and the physiological signs of starvation was a fine one. Limited demographic data offer little with which to assess rates of excess mortality.

Nonetheless, the documentary record attests to substantial loss of life to starvation and exposure over the winter of 1920–21 among the poorest strata of society, whose members were unable to pay the soaring prices for basic foodstuffs. How some twenty million destitute people in North China did not perish over the year is at the heart of this investigation.

Our knowledge of everyday social life in the decade before the Nationalist rise to power in 1928 remains remarkably sketchy, which explains this book's focus on the early 1920s. With the exception of studies of the labor movement, radical politics, and rural revolution that were popular during the Cold War, historians of the Chinese Republic writing on a variety of social subjects have produced far more on the Nationalist so-called Nanjing Decade (1928–37). The 1920s, a decade of great political, intellectual, and cultural ferment, remains flyover country for social historians, especially when it comes to the interior where some nine-tenths of Chinese lived.[16]

This book concentrates on famine responses in three related but rather distinct contexts: Beijing, the largest city in China to be fully administered by Chinese authorities in 1920; the rural districts of Zhili province (today's Hebei), which encircles the nation's capital; and the three north-eastern provinces known then as Manchuria, which abutted Zhili to the east. It does this for several reasons. After the 1980s, Western treatments of the Chinese past swung away from the inland, rural focus of Cold War scholarship and its search for the origins of Maoist revolution toward urban histories and global themes. Reflecting the growing dynamism of China since the end of the insular Maoist era, this scholarship also stressed China's transnational and global connections before 1949, and in these histories treaty ports such as Shanghai and Tianjin have loomed large as sites of intense interaction and exchange.[17] The field has been consequently enriched in many important ways, but this change in focus has also come with its costs.

The natural and man-made disasters of the early twentieth century that disproportionately struck rural, inland communities continue to be viewed through the perspectives of actors external to these communities, ranging from missionaries and cosmopolitan Chinese to prominent reformist journalists based in China's coastal cities. This is not to say the field is bereft of important studies on the Chinese interior in the modern period. We know a good deal, for example, about local inland communities, from village governance and rebellion to religious rituals and family dynamics.[18] But the scant attention to rural disasters in the 1920s risks casting stricken communities in China's hinterland as passive recipients of external initiative and largesse, largely from the cosmopolitan societies of the coastal treaty ports and from the United States.[19] Getting beyond the glare of treaty-port culture allows us to appreciate the social dynamics of inland society in a way that further dispels their past reduction to an inert historical specimen held up against a supposedly more dynamic and self-consciously modern social field—of, say, the Yangzi and Pearl River deltas. When histories overlook the relief aspect of 1920s governance, they both exaggerate ruptures with tradition in early twentieth- century China and privilege the revolutionary narratives that placed the cause of public welfare firmly in the hands of reformists and radicals seeking to jettison what they presented as a backward, bankrupt, or obsolete Confucian tradition. They also risk producing a narrow interpretation of Chinese disaster relief through the prism of state interests (in maintaining social order and a productive tax- or rent-paying agricultural population) and the nation-building project (among segments of China's mostly urban and coastal population responding to the foreign military, commercial, and missionary presence), when both rural and urban actors in early twentieth-century China had a far broader set of values, interests, and motivations.

Of course, we must not lose sight of the particular socioeconomic context in which disaster mitigation and acts of compassion were performed in China. This included the distributional hierarchies of petty capitalism, examined by Hill Gates among others, and the kinship hierarchies and transactional nature of family membership, particularly for females, explored by Johanna Ransmeier.[20] The limits and contradictions of relief activity and its role in maintaining social control and inequalities within this wider petty-capitalist and patriarchal context are ripe for debate. But such a discussion can hardly take place before the extent and variety of this Chinese charitable economy is fully appreciated.

Recognizing the resilience of governmental, charitable, or community relief measures in the early 1920s involves engaging with several key works on modern China. For example, scholars have noted the early twentieth-century abandonment of protective leadership roles traditionally played by rural gentry in North China in the face of heightened fiscal penetration by the modern state.[21] Yet, in at least one important respect—the willingness or ability to initiate, fund, or manage village or county relief—this transformation of village dynamics in many northern communities was far from complete a decade after the fall of the Qing. The inherited disaster relief repertoire in North China was in fact sufficiently multifaceted to withstand the social and economic stresses of the early republican period, and sufficiently embedded in social relations to withstand the collapse of China's dynastic system and the waning of its attendant ideologies. Similarly, the picture offered here modifies the extent of the breakdown of state capacities in China's interior over the late nineteenth and early twentieth centuries. It does so by questioning the assumption that in poor areas like North China there was an insufficient local elite presence to take on relief efforts in tandem with higher authorities when bureaucratic relief weakened, while also questioning how true it was that the republican state, which coordinated the smooth transfer of huge volumes of resources across the national infrastructure in the early 1920s, failed in its relief roles to begin with.

At a higher, official level, the relatively poor showing of formal, top-down relief institutions circa 1920 was both a sign of the breakdown of state capacities and the operation of a different, devolved dimension of the state. This involved an informal, parallel administration of semi-official (*banguan*) charities overseen by officials or prominent ex-military men or gentry. One factor behind the popularity of semi-official forms of civic organization was doubtless the pervasiveness of graft in the republic, with the attendant public reluctance to contribute to state-controlled initiatives. Throughout this study, one must of course keep in mind the staggering personal wealth of many of the republic's power brokers during a period of widespread immiseration and stratification, much of which was arguably due to corruption and exacerbated the effects of famine. The aim here is to capture the particular makeup of governance at the time during disasters, with military officials participating in both public and charitable realms simultaneously, operating municipal relief operations while putting their personal monies or the public monies they controlled into what were in effect quasi-governmental relief organizations jointly managed by the merchant gentry. Historians have identified the emergence of this hybrid mode of civic governance in the late Qing, and disaster relief in 1920 reveals the acceleration of this dynamic in the early republican years.[22]

The Global Perspective

If current events shape the interests of historians looking into the past, it is little wonder that the search for humanitarian systems in the past has become a budding field of history. In light of refugee flows from imploding Arab states, the resurgence of famine in the Horn of Africa, and devastating storms and tsunamis across the Atlantic and Pacific worlds, recent years have seen a flowering of studies of humanitarianism in historical perspective, often on a global scale. The bulk of this work is either institutional history—focusing on the Red Cross movement, pioneering nongovernmental organizations, or organs of international governance such as refugee commissions—or examinations of Anglo-American civil society or biographical sketches of Western activists.[23] Studies that make a point of locating modern humanitarianism beyond the geographic confines of the West, such as Keith Watenpaugh's work on the Middle East after World War II, still squarely situate the phenomenon in Western cultural space, defining it, in his case, as a "specific ideology of organized compassion that originated in Western Europe and North America." Non-Western actors and voices are brought into his study to "restore a measure of agency to the *objects* of the Western humanitarian agenda."[24] Attention to organized indigenous efforts to alleviate suffering in the so-called global South is lamentably scarce, to put it generously, in the field thus far.[25]

The aid sector is in crisis—and, some would argue, for many of the same underlying reasons of exclusivity. Over the past few decades there has been a narrowing of the definition and identification of humanitarian agents in the sector, to the point where humanitarian initiative has become almost the exclusive preserve of formal organizations and institutions of Western origin. As one student of the sector argued in a report issued in advance of the 2016 World Humanitarian Summit in Istanbul, the "centrality and indispensability" of formal Western-style humanitarian actors—"Western donors and non-governmental organisations, the Red Cross Movement and UN agencies"—have been, "if not an illusion, then at least a very partial picture of the reality of global humanitarian assistance."[26] The authors of the report, prepared by the Overseas Development Institute in London, seek a "fuller recognition of the 'complex heterogeneity' of the various existing forms of humanitarianism, as they are understood across the South as well as the North." They urge the adoption across the sector of "a new model of humanitarian action, one that requires letting go of the current paradigm . . . in favour of a diverse, devolved and decentralised model."[27]

Two experts on food security—former staff members of Save the Children and CARE International—second this assessment in the case of the recent famines in East Africa. They were tasked with analyzing what they described as a "mountain of information and data" on the 2011–12 famine in Somalia, information they stress was "mostly devoted to the formal, Nairobi-based, UN-led humanitarian response" to mass starvation in the region. The "whole category of analysis" thus employed, they realized, "did not address—and, indeed, often failed to ask—many questions about other aspects of the famine," one of which was the "large number of humanitarian actors engaged in the response to the famine who seemed unfamiliar to the established Western, OECD donor-funded humanitarian community."[28] In short, these analysts point to a disconcerting disconnect between members of the formal international relief system and the agents and networks of aid already in place in the societies the international system aims to assist—or what Claude de Ville de Goyet critiqued in 2000 in the *Lancet* as the "disaster myth" of helpless afflicted communities across the world awaiting rescue from Western aid teams.[29]

In this book I aim to examine a similar disconnect in the case of China's recent past. The parallels between current unknowns in the humanitarian sector and (mis)understandings of famine response in China a century ago are striking. The data on which histories of famine, and of disaster generally, in early twentieth-century China are based are heavily institutional and international in origin, generated by various chapters of the Red Cross or by such organs as the foreign-run China International Famine Relief Commission. Our perceptions of famine in prerevolutionary China are consequently skewed toward the activities of joint foreign-Chinese international agents or Western-style Chinese organizations based in major Chinese cities, when the majority of relief in early twentieth-century China was in fact provided by indigenous bodies working separately from and parallel to international ones.

The nature of indigenous efforts can raise questions about the various categories used by analysts to understand agency and expertise during disaster events, both past and present. The persistence of long-standing late imperial relief practices employed by, say, rural gentry, Buddhist groups, and other fleeting and temporary indigenous relief organizations in 1920 broadens the category of emergency relief practitioners beyond the members of formal international relief societies. Similarly, the fact that one can trace relief initiative and disaster management over the lifetimes of particular figures and generations in particular households complicates the notion of the professionalization of relief in this period. It is especially important to point this out as China's economic and political prowess increases again, yet its robust charitable and social welfare traditions are little known beyond specialists in the field of Chinese history. The 1920–21 North China famine rarely figures in academic studies more broadly, but when it does appear—in an examination of social welfare policies in the People's Republic (founded in 1949), for example, or an account of the rise of the American developmental regime—readers are left to assume that there were neither indigenous relief capabilities or know-how.[30] Yet the breadth and diversity of relief in China circa 1920 have broad implications for our understanding of both Chinese domestic politics and international relations at the time and may even have been a sign of the effectiveness of governance amid decentralization, countering any necessary correlation between social stability and a strong Chinese state.

While this study is meant to contribute to the growing field of worldwide humanitarianism, the use of the term "humanitarian" to describe actions or participants in events in China a century ago of course poses problems, either as an anachronistic concept or as an issue of translation. So the term will mostly be avoided in this study. Nonetheless, the organized nonstate efforts to alleviate suffering examined here, especially in a period of weak government and across a population and space as vast as those of China, should contribute to the wider field of humanitarian studies. Similar concepts to that of humanity, from which modern humanitarianism is derived, have long existed in both thought and practice in Chinese culture.[31] In 1920, the term *rendao* was perhaps closest to the modern meaning of "humanitarian," referring to moral law or a principle of humanity. In the Chinese press at the time, when *rendao* was mentioned at all (it appeared relatively rarely), it was generally used to refer to actions or conditions, as in "egregiously inhumane" (*can wu rendao*) or doing something "so as to respect humane principles" (*yi zhong rendao*)—to describe, in two representative examples, calls to lessen the overcrowding of refugees on ships or prevent plundering by disbanded soldiers, respectively.[32] Far more commonly used in the press was the term "warmhearted" (*rexin*), especially in descriptions of people who took personal initiative in performing or sponsoring charitable relief activities.[33]

The disaster that befell North China in 1920 was just one major humanitarian crisis among many in the wake of World War I, events that have attracted recognition collectively as a watershed in civic and humanitarian initiatives around the globe.[34] The Chinese famine of 1920 unfolded in the plains south of Beijing as the efforts of the American Relief Administration and other organizations were wrapping up in Belgium and the eastern Mediterranean; amid mass population exchanges between the former Ottoman domains of Greece and Turkey; and before a powerful earthquake on the Kanto Plain left Tokyo in ruins. Among all these crises, the 1920–21 famine appears in passing, if at all. This negligible imprint is, paradoxically, a function in part of the famine's successful relief—relative, that is, to the monumental Chinese famines of the 1870s, late 1920s, and 1940s–1950s, as well as to what transpired in Russia in 1921–22. There, amid mass crop failure in the Volga breadbasket a few years into the Bolshevik revolution, several million people died of famine-related causes, primarily typhus, despite substantial international relief—particularly from the United States.[35] A comparable number of Chinese were menaced by famine at the time, yet mortality in this instance would be a fraction of the dead over the border in Russia.

The famine response in China in 1920 resembled the "diverse, devolved and decentralised model" called for by critics of today's international aid sector. It was this very characteristic—the combination of contributions quite literally from people in all walks of life—that provided the resiliency of the collective response to what amounted to the greatest ecological crisis in China in nearly half a century. For this reason, this event and others of its type must be brought into closer dialogue with humanitarian studies generally, as it speaks to Abigail Green's important point that humanitarian action, however one defines it, must not be teleologically conflated with liberal, progressive, or democratic movements. Rather, organized efforts to alleviate the suffering of strangers must be recognized as stemming from a range of cultural contexts, ethical frameworks, and gender dynamics beyond the Anglo-American world.[36]

A recent flurry of major studies has shed light on the experience and extent of the Maoist famine of 1958–62, which involved tens of millions of deaths amid grain exactions from the countryside during the Great Leap Forward.[37] But until the field develops adequate knowledge of rural social relations and disaster governance immediately before the Maoist period (that is, under the Nationalist and republican regimes), our understanding of the developments leading up to the Great Leap and other Mao-era disasters will remain incomplete. In a recent reflection on famine and food security across cultures and time, for example, Steven Kaplan expresses frustration with Frank Dikötter's presentation of the Great Leap famine, remarking that Dikötter provides "a better grasp of the bludgeoning of rural society than its unravelling" over time.[38] Indeed, one of the least satisfying aspects of Dikötter's handling of the Mao-era famine is its decided ahistorical lens, together with its depiction of a 1950s Chinese populace fully prostrated before Party diktats, without any of the social texture of, for example, Ralph Thaxton's earlier work on the same event.[39] "Did peasant communities have no collective moral, historical and kinship resources?" Kaplan asks, referring to Dikötter's *Mao's Great Famine*. "Was the social bond particularly feeble in Pre-Maoist rural China?" In the following chapters I aim to shed light on practices of resource distribution and communal bonds at a particular point in pre-Maoist China by providing a biography of a postimperial, yet pre-Nationalist and pre-Communist subsistence, crisis. Ultimately, I aim to establish a benchmark of social cohesion and urban-rural relations with which to assess the unraveling of social ties over the course of the twentieth century—one that culminated in the rural catastrophe of the Great Leap.

Sources for the Early Republic

This study is primarily a social history, and social history demands a particular set of sources. Generally speaking, documentation of relief activity increases in proportion to the distance relief goods and monies travel and to the size of the agencies involved, due to reasons of publicity, logistics, and accountability. The documentary track of international relief that crosses oceans and frontiers is exponentially larger, often involving additional diplomatic, media, and banking channels. Since paper production rises with distance and size, leaving greater documentary traces behind, histories of disaster are more often viewed—both at the time and by later generations—through these institutional or international lenses, among them those of Western aid charities, Red Cross chapters, or agencies of the League of Nations or the United Nations. Local relief, running along social channels and provided on smaller scales, leaves fainter paper trails. This is especially true in the case of famine, which is by and large suffered by marginalized populations. And the relative paucity—compared to the earlier Qing and later Nationalist periods—of even official archival materials for the chaotic and fractured early republic makes it difficult to chart day-to-day matters of indigenous disaster relief and poor policy.[40]

With this in mind, the following account of the famine is stitched together, it is hoped, with a sufficiently broad set of source material to capture society in 1920s China in all of its diversity and complexity. To map the movement and timing of relief transfers into and across the famine zone, it relies on railway records published by various state ministries. For community dynamics within the famine field, it uses biographies, stele transcriptions, and other materials in district gazetteers (*difang zhi*). The Beijing Municipal Archives in fact offer remarkably little on the subject of the city's welfare administration over the course of the 1920–21 crisis. Fortunately, dozens of extant daily newpapers from the city at that time allow us to penetrate this documentary silence. They include broadsheets and tabloids published within walking distance of the drought zone south of the capital and even weekly (*Jiuzai zhoukan*) and daily (*Zhenzai ribao*) publications devoted to the unfolding famine. Republican newspapers were not only an essential conduit of information at the time on the extent and location of human needs across the city and the wider famine zone, but also a rare window for researchers today looking into the day-to-day workings of city governance a century ago.[41] Collectively, newsprint constitutes a rich vein of source material, what Timothy Weston has called republican China's "open archive" of journalist output, which, although "highly revelatory of social and cultural relations," has only recently been mined by historians.[42]

That said, the news print, stone stele, and district gazetteers used in this study were platforms for the educated, mostly elite—a distinct minority in the Chinese population. They shed very limited light on the experience or perspective of famine sufferers, which is unfortunately beyond the scope of this study. Instead, its more modest aims are to identify and chart the series and patterns of interventions and exchanges over a year that kept the vast majority of struggling residents of the Yellow River basin alive to the spring.

This book is roughly divided in two. Part 1, "Relieving Beijing," focuses on disaster governance, and the media and charitable activity in the capital over the first half of the subsistence crisis of 1920–21. Chapter 1 begins with the Zhili-Anhui War of July 1920 with the aim of sketching how relief to civilians affected by war transitioned in August into famine-fighting efforts in the drought-hit environs of Beijing. It also explores the republic's broad spectrum of printed news sources and the newspaper industry's relationship to the authorities at the time. Chapter 2 draws continuities between disaster relief administration in the late imperial period and the measures undertaken by the capital's municipal authorities in the autumn of 1920, while examining the increasingly ad hoc and spontaneous nature of official relief financing. Chapter 3 considers the intensity with which particular military figures engaged in poor relief at the time. It uses the examples of a former and a current commander of the Beijing gendarmerie, while considering their varied motivations, native-place sentiment, and bids for political and also religious legitimacy. Chapter 4 examines the broader field of charitable activity in the city. It reveals the considerable extent to which Beijing media covered suffering and death among the area's poor in 1920, while exploring how aid to the poor was connected to various aspects of city life, from commercial competition and growing nationalist fervor to the rise of religious sects and the capital's vibrant entertainment scene. Chapter 5 maps the social and professional networks behind the various temporary, crisis-specific relief societies that formed in the capital during the year to dispatch aid to the countryside. The chapter shows how urban interventions in the famine field took on a hybrid form of overlapping official and private efforts, a decentralized and multilayered state of affairs that possibly afforded the collective relief effort its resilience in a time of political uncertainty and anemic government.

Part 2, "The Famine Field," considers the various levels of disaster relief in the afflicted interior over the same time period, with a focus on

the hardest-hit province, Zhili, along with the relief role of communities
in neighboring Manchuria to which many people fled. One overlooked
explanation for the relatively low mortality during the year was mutual
aid at the village level, including loan and grant initiatives led by individuals or households in a given community—which are sketched in
chapter 6. Granaries and soup kitchens operated by local magistrates and
gentry in the winter of 1920–21, which constituted the lowest stratum of
the bureaucratic relief apparatus inherited from the Qing, are explored
in chapter 7. The chapter also touches on the issue of state finances and
corruption; the delayed famine loan brokered with the foreign powers;
and the limited role of the higher echelons of the state during the year, as
they were primarily concerned with the coordination of regional grain
transfers into the disaster areas. Chapter 8 charts migrant movement out
of the famine districts, predominantly to Manchuria—where the resources raised for the reception of refugees in communities there served
as an additional form of disaster relief over the year. Chapter 9 continues
the examination of famine responses north of the Great Wall by exploring the types of relief organizations in Manchuria for the famine field in
Zhili and Shandong (where many residents of Manchuria traced their
family roots), from theatrical fund-raisers to the docking of state salaries.
Chapter 10 examines the role of the joint Chinese-foreign international
relief societies, which, together with the Christian missions, have taken
center stage in the historiography of the 1920–21 famine. The chapter
shows how the crucial contribution of the international societies gained
significance only in the last two months of the famine—that is, after
the indigenous relief activity over the autumn and winter covered in
chapters 2–9. The conclusion charts the establishment of the China International Famine Relief Commission in the wake of the 1920–21 famine
through to the far more devastating northwest famine of 1928–30, suggesting that the republic experienced fundamental changes in governance and
social relations over the course of the decade as the country descended into
a near-permanent state of warfare from the mid-1920s onward.

Finally, the appendix describes the spontaneous establishment and
operation of the country's largest encampment of people fleeing the famine districts. The camp at Nankai, on the outskirts of Tianjin, was in
many ways a microcosm of the broader famine relief effort during the
year.

PART ONE

Relieving Beijing

CHAPTER ONE

War in July

The villagers of Xindiancun secured a statue from the Ma family tomb—stole it, some said—before summoning hundreds of other residents from their homes. With a likeness of the Dragon King (*longwang*)—a deity associated with bodies of water, large and small, and the life-giving rain—now in their possession, the men led a dozen girls in a procession under the dry summer skies, each holding up a vase in the style of Guanyin, the Daoist immortal and Buddhist goddess of mercy. An equal number of boys followed, each waving a small flag inscribed with words hailing the Dragon King, after which twelve widows marched holding brooms and winnowing fans. Two hundred men and boys playing the part of sea creatures crowded behind them, costumed as turtles or fish and with jars filled with willow branches balanced on their heads. Finally, a lone man brought up the rear, lugging a heavy metal shovel—a symbol of repentance to the gods. As the procession made its way past lifeless fields of wheat and millet, the marchers beat turtle shells with willow branches and sprinkled water on the passing ground.[1] But no rain fell from the sky.

The precariousness of farming communities in North China stemmed not only from how much precipitation fell from year to year, but also when it did. No rain at the wrong time led to shriveled seedlings, too much rain led to waterlogged crops rotting in the fields.[2] The survival of only sturdier, lower-grade crops meant even less income for people already struggling to exist on the thinnest of margins. When harvests failed completely, families turned to eating tree bark, leaves, and other famine foods; without even the dried stalks of threshed crops there was next to no fuel or material for roofs or fences for livestock. Variations on rain-seeking rituals, enlisting entire communities through an eclectic combination of popular Buddhist, Confucian, and Daoist symbols, had been performed throughout China's late imperial period, often with official patronage from the yamen, the seat of county government.[3] But our procession, snaking its way through parched fields in the northern outskirts of Beijing, was nine years into the Chinese republic. "A year ago today we had our last rain," a missionary wrote two months later from a Canadian Presbyterian mission in Anyang, hundreds of miles to the south.[4] It was the summer of 1920.

Skirting the mountains of Shanxi, the Yellow River spills onto the great alluvial plains of North China before taking its present course north of the Shandong peninsula to the sea. On the left bank of this eastward course lie some of China's oldest city sites, Anyang, in north Henan, and Xingtai in the south of Hebei province (known before 1928 as Zhili province), and beyond, the nation's capital, Beijing, and its twin city, the coastal treaty port of Tianjin. As if a celestial shower curtain had been drawn along the river from its Shanxi descent to its outlet into the Bo Hai, the Yellow River's left bank had not seen more than a splattering of rainfall in many places in the twelve hard months leading up to the autumn of 1920. Weak or disastrous harvests lay in store for thousands of communities across the North. Winter clothes would be pawned for seed and food, furniture and house beams sold off by weight, and children held up for sale in market squares, all over an area harrowingly similar in extent to that afflicted by the horrific drought-famine of the 1870s. That calamity had struck Zhili, Shandong, Shanxi, Henan, and Shaanxi. The same five provinces were set to experience full-fledged famine conditions again. But headlines in July 1920 hardly paid attention to the drought creeping into communities across the north, for war was under way.

The squat, walled city of Beijing sat on the northern edge of the North China Plain in 1920, connected to central China by two parallel rail lines. Each of these lines reached up from the hilly, terraced banks of the Yangzi and headed northward over the great floodplains of the Yellow River, where they met at the Chinese capital (map 1). On July 17, the trains running twice a day in both directions on the network's western line—covering 819 miles in thirty-three hours, and styled the *train du luxe* by the state-run railways, with their first-class carriages conveying international

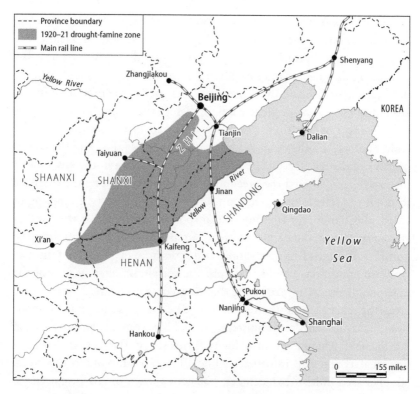

Province boundary
1920–21 drought-famine zone
Main rail line

Shenyang

KOREA

Zhangjiakou

Yellow River

Beijing

ZHILI

Tianjin

Dalian

Taiyuan

SHAANXI

SHANXI

Yellow River

Jinan

SHANDONG

Qingdao

Xi'an

Kaifeng

HENAN

Yellow Sea

Pukou

Nanjing

Shanghai

Hankou

0   155 miles

MAP 1. North China, showing the extent of the 1920–21 drought-famine.

tourists seated on sofas under crystal chandeliers—would not run as scheduled.[5] Instead, the rails were bearing the 11,000 soldiers of the Third Division commanded by Wu Peifu (1874–1939) from their base in central China, as part of a four-pronged assault on the capital. Wu's faction colleague, Zhili Military Governor Cao Kun (1862–1938), meanwhile pressed toward Beijing up the line from Tianjin.

The brief war that ensued, the Zhili-Anhui War of July 1920, was only part of a series of armed conflicts and limited wars that had occurred since the splintering of the central government at the death of President Yuan Shikai. But it was arguably the first with national ramifications—the first engagement of the era to be played out on a national stage—and it coincided with the start of the greatest subsistence crisis that China had experienced in nearly half a century.

This book begins with war in 1920 because the transition of war relief in the summer into famine relief in the fall was seamless. Neither crisis was a discrete event in any meaningful sense; disasters never are. The canvassing of war- or drought-afflicted communities, local and national fund-raising drives, and the delivery of relief goods were mobilized in and around the war zone of greater Beijing before the terms "drought disaster" (*hanzai*) or "famine" (*jihuang*) appeared in the headlines of the region's press. In other words, as the summer rains failed and the consequences of dismal harvests became apparent, warfare in the environs of the capital exacerbated the preconditions of famine among the destitute through the seizure or destruction of household property, trampling of crops, and temporary freezing of transportation links. But the conflict also spurred human energies to create a relief infrastructure to limit the numbers of deaths from starvation, and soon from exposure and disease.

Two conditions would underpin the speed and effectiveness of the relief mobilization in 1920—one that averted an even larger catastrophe, given the scale of drought over the year. The first was a generally responsive military leadership administering the Chinese capital and surrounding famine field, which is a central focus of this study. The second condition was an alert and well-informed public. The readership of North China, largely based in its urban centers, was kept abreast of growing needs in the surrounding drought-ridden countryside by a vibrant Chinese media that was diverse in authorship and perspective and that covered the unfolding disaster closely. In response, war relief campaigns, initially limited in size and scope, were transformed into agents of drought and famine relief with the arrival of autumn in 1920, when mobilization at a regional, national, and eventually international level shifted into much higher gear.

Newsprints and Authority

How reliable were reports of the war or the starvation of and assistance to the population? The extent to which China's press was subject to state interference in the early republic is debatable. The news outlets owned, or directly controlled, by the faction or regime in control of the government at any one time constituted a fraction of the hundreds in and around the capital. State control of the press in 1920 did not approach the level it had reached at the brief peak of centralized power under Yuan in 1914–15, when under repressive press laws the number of newspapers shrank, according to one count, from one hundred to twenty in Beijing by 1916.[6] The military leadership in 1920 was too fractured to exercise the kind of national stranglehold on news outlets and other channels of information that one might expect from authoritarian regimes, especially in times of war. After the closing of a press, a newspaper could easily be produced in a rival's domain, or in the protection of one of China's numerous treaty ports, and readily find its way into circulation elsewhere. Within a few years after Yuan's death, the number of daily newspapers across the country had rebounded to 550, with a fifth of them published in the Chinese capital.[7] Some were business oriented, while others were news digests of roughly four pages bankrolled by one of the myriad political factions of the day. Many papers were short-lived, and they varied considerably in size, scope of coverage, advertising, and even style of written Chinese— reflecting not only the contentious politics of the early Chinese Republic but also a moment of great cultural and literary flux.

Aspiring military leaders saw the press as equal to the battlefield in its importance for advancing their ambitions. They certainly tried to use the press for their own ends, but they did so in peculiar ways. The 1920 famine unfolded during the very birth of radio broadcasting: the world's first broadcast station opened in Pittsburgh, Pennsylvania, that November.[8] With radio in its infancy, the main conductor of news dissemination remained the telegraph, a technology that military men-*cum*-politicians in China used without fail, making the late 1910s and 1920s the highpoint of the political telegram in China, what Andrew Nathan has called the "equivalent of today's press conference or policy statement."[9] "No military commander moved in this period without public declarations," Edward McCord has noted, "usually in the form of 'circular telegrams' addressed to all leading officials and released to the press, justifying his action on constitutional, legal, or moral grounds."[10] These telegrams were often widely circulated in various media platforms, so a newspaper might serve as a space for political posturing and appeals for public support without necessarily serving as a mouthpiece for, or being in lockstep with, any particular regime, party, or faction. And circular telegrams revealed that a surprising degree of independence was possible in the period for individual military commanders willing to ignore the orders of their superiors—often in the name of the general good.

The print platforms used by these military figures were part of a broader discursive culture, one that frequently expressed concerns about the straits of common folk. Both for those in power and their rivals, newspaper coverage of the poor had political rewards. But coverage of such issues in the Chinese press took the form of straightforward news copy generated by commercial or official wire services—not merely party propaganda offices—and this included news organs owned by political cliques. Papers, often in formulaic terms, were vociferous in their condemnation of fraud and profiteering by so-called wicked merchants (*jianshang*) and detailed in their coverage of mundane matters of the grain markets, charitable handouts by often unnamed strangers in the streets, and soup kitchen policies and attendance. The local news briefs they ran were rarely, if ever, framed with any sense of class conflict; instead, their writers employed the language of pity and an ethical framework in which commoners' interests conflicted with those of profit-seeking opportunists—especially in times of scarcity due to war and calamity. The voicing by ruling elites of concerns for the downtrodden was nothing new, of course.[11] What is noteworthy is that a varied local press in early republican Beijing covered the affairs of the poor in a common tone through which public policy was assessed and openly critiqued.

The rate and extent to which publications across the political spectrum covered poverty at the time is also noteworthy. The major Tianjin-based broadsheet *Da gongbao*, bought by Yuan's Beiyang regime for 30,000 yuan in 1916, regularly ran news items and features about the welfare of the commoner strata of Zhili society, and rural counties in particular.[12] The Beijing-based *Shuntian shibao*, an equally prominent Chinese-language broadsheet that was Japanese owned, devoted entire two-page spreads to the subsistence crisis and to the general affairs of the poor and philanthropic activity in greater Beijing. As for the city's smaller, cheaper, and (from our vantage point, at least) more obscure tabloid-size papers, many paid especially intense attention to events and announcements of utility to people navigating the city and its institutions from a position of poverty and marginalization. *Aiguo baihua bao*, *Beijing baihua bao*, and *Xiao gongbao*—all heavily used in the social sketch of the capital here—were very similar to each other in the plainness and graphic-free style of their layouts. All three were presumably closely associated with the city's military authorities, given the volume of their coverage of the day-to-day running of the city. Using vernacular forms of the written language, or *baihua*, these smaller papers were perused readily by the lower classes, a surprisingly common sight in republican China. A Japanese survey noted that *Beijing baihua bao* had a working-class readership and daily circulation of 8,000, which would have included, for example, some of the city's many rickshaw pullers.[13] Rickshaw pullers regularly waited for fares on the streets of Beijing hunched over newspapers. (A Chinese journalist at the time went so far as to state that "reading a tabloid is [a Beijing rickshaw puller's] most common activity.")[14] *Aiguo baihua bao* was launched by a member of the city's Hui Muslim community in the wake of the 1911 revolution and offered extensive coverage of local philanthropy and the everyday hardships of ordinary people.[15] Both papers were apparently read also by members of the city's Chinese Christian community, as they appeared on a list of twenty-three newspapers subscribed to by respondents in an American academic survey taken of three Beijing parishes in 1919.[16] As for *Xiao gongbao*, founded in 1919, its name suggests that it served as a minor official report or bulletin for the capital community. Unfortunately, the men officially registered as its sponsors (*zhubanren*), Cheng Daoyi and Ji Shaoquan, are not easily identifiable (nor is the sponsor of *Beijing baihua bao*, whose name is given as Yang Dahong).[17]

If newspapers across the political spectrum participated in a shared discourse of advocacy for the region's poor in 1920, on another level their content positioned their audiences differently vis-à-vis the unfolding subsistence crisis. Newspapers were of course media of consumption, and they differed in their use of graphic design and photography and other technologies in their advertising and social events columns. The power of juxtaposition influenced how the famine crisis was understood by the various readerships served by the Chinese press at the time. In other words, various publics were consuming and responding to the northern famine of 1920–21. At the most basic level, two reading publics can be identified: the audience of local tabloids and that of national broadsheets. The facts that Beijing benevolent halls (*shantang*) were dispatching clothes to the famine zone or that members of China's military were active in both the municipal and the charitable accommodation of famine refugees in the capital were far more likely to find their way into Beijing papers with extensive local coverage than into larger, more prominent broadsheets aiming for a national scope and readership. So residents of China's coastal cities and inland treaty ports, where the vast majority of the country's press was concentrated, "read" the famine field and the movement of refugees in substantially different ways, depending on their choice or habit of news consumption and the social networks these reflected. In spite of newspapers' heavy use of wire news reports, which could appear in multiple newspapers on the same day, different editorials, advertisements, photographic spreads, or political cartoons presented a range of lenses through which readers consumed the crisis.

A comparative look at the various forums offered by Chinese dailies of the 1920s helps bring the parallel, if not entirely discrete, social universes operating in republican China into relief. On the one hand, readers of major broadsheets like *Yishi bao*, which had both Beijing and Tianjin editions, and Shanghai's *Shenbao* would take in events as they unfolded largely through a boardroom perspective on the crisis. These papers provided meeting notes, reports, and proposals from the international relief societies or from the Chinese Young Men's Christian Association or Chinese Red Cross; investigative reports by staff journalists or reformist student groups; statistics on crop failures and refugee movements; information about theatrical fund-raisers; and lists of donors—all printed between graphic ads for Nestlé's Milk Food ("perfect nutriment for infants, children and invalids"); China Ross Co. tablets for "vitality, health, energy, vigor" (with the image of a worn-out middle-aged Chinese man seated between a charging steamship and locomotive) and its competitor, Doan's tonic tablets ("The real Tonic for weak and rundown people," embodied by yet another Chinese); Jordan Silhouette and Velie Six motorcars; Pond's Vanishing Cream; Hennessy Cognac; or Cutex nail products.[18] And in some cases there were Western-style political cartoons lambasting traditional caricatures or a photo collage of famine victims juxtaposed with Chinese Boy Scouts celebrating the 1920 National Day in October with drilling and physical exercise.[19] On the other hand, through the fall of 1920 readers of the Beijing tabloids *Aiguo baihuabao, Fengsheng, Shihua, Xiao gongbao,* or *Zhongguo minbao* would see plain, print-only pages with image-free advertisements for native banks, booksellers, apothecaries, clinics, and native cigarette brands, while reading about grain distribution or shelter operation by Buddhist groups or charities like the capital's Society for Awakening Goodness (Wushan-she) or the Temporary Steamed Corn Bread Society (Linshi wowotouhui), along with street-level news of bulk grain handouts by individuals or the opening and closing of official or charitable soup kitchens.

The provenance and portrayal of products promoted in any given 1920s publication were largely correlated with its disaster relief coverage, presenting striking differences in social landscape within a city such as Beijing, not to mention between urban and rural areas: one replete with the new images and standards with which the consumer-citizen distinguished him- or herself from traditional or backward people, the other consisting of customary modes of consumption and social networking stretching from Beijing backstreets (*hutong*) south to the famine-struck Yellow River Plain. In short, as much as urban and rural communities were growing further apart both socially and culturally in the early twentieth century than had been the case in the imperial past, cultural spheres coexisted within urban centers as well. Thus, the citizenry of the Chinese Republic occupied alternative worlds within cities as well as between urban, coastal China and the hinterland. When re-creating an event as massive as a famine as it unfolded on the ground in China, then, the choice is not between using native or foreign voices, but between different native voices, which varied in terms of their social or geographical positioning, sociocultural distance from stricken communities, and so on. The implications of this for the literature on the period, and for disaster historiography in particular and its stress on cosmopolitan and international relief actors in early twentieth-century China, cannot be stressed enough.[20]

The Zhili-Anhui War

Cao and Wu, heading a political faction that controlled five provinces in central China, had mobilized some sixty thousand men for battle. Their goal was to dislodge Duan Qirui, head of a rival faction that controlled five other provinces and the capital, which it was defending with an equal number of troops.[21] If one includes Duan's reserves stationed in the capital region, the attackers were outnumbered and their southern domains left vulnerable to encirclement by the Anhui troops, who had been trained, funded, and covertly advised by an officially neutral Japan.[22] Leveling the field was the crucial support of the inspector general of the three north-eastern provinces forming Manchuria, the previously unaligned Marshal Zhang Zuolin (1875–1928). Zhang had joined Cao and Wu in declaring war on Duan, and Zhang's seventy thousand troops, moving over the provincial border from Fengtian, strengthened Cao's divisions on their push from Tianjin. Three armies were poised to fight for control of Beijing, where the republic's largely ceremonial president, Xu Shichang (1855–1939), was powerless to intervene.

The events that led to the July war involved a shift between four centers of power in the Chinese Republic. This involved Sun Yat-sen (1866–1925) and his Nationalist Party, which had formed a southern government in Canton in 1917; two rival factions, the Zhili and Anhui cliques, which had been founded by the two top protégés of Yuan at his death and controlled China's core regions; and Zhang in the Northeast. In 1918, Sun had been sidelined by a reorganization of power in Canton, and his departure for Shanghai temporarily removed a major claimant to leadership of the republic. Meanwhile, Duan, the head of the Anhui clique, had brokered the Sino-Japanese Joint Military Pact and won a loan from Tokyo worth fifty million yuan during his brief tenure as Chinese premier in 1918. Ostensibly to finance preparations for Chinese participation in World War I, the loan was formalized just a month before the November 1918 armistice, and the money—to be repaid to the Japanese through mortgaging of national assets ranging from railroads to mines and custom duties—was instead used to finance Duan's consolidation of power.[23] These maneuvers, along with the Treaty of Versailles's transferring of German concessions in Shandong to Japan the following year, led to a rising tide of public opinion nationwide against Duan's regime, which unleashed the student energies of the May Fourth Movement.[24] The founder of the Zhili faction, Feng Guozhang (1859–1919), died in December 1919 and was succeeded by Cao, who then formed an alliance with Zhang and moved against Duan.

In multiple ways, modern technology proved a mixed blessing to rural Zhili communities. Wars, including the July 1920 war, were often fought along, and for, rail lines, making the railway both a commercial boon and a scourge for the communities through which it passed, just as the imperial Grand Canal system had been during periods of unrest in previous centuries. The railroad had been introduced to China half a century earlier, but for various reasons, including its facilitation of foreign interests' penetration into the country's vast interior, its introduction was contentious.[25] While trains made possible speedy transfers of grain and other vital resources in times of scarcity—barring war or other disruptions—they also had the effect of increasing the cost of grain in producing regions relative to prices in the coastal entrepôts, tying rural communities ever more tightly to unseen and often destabilizing market forces.[26] The Qing government had thrown its full weight behind railroad construction only after the humiliation of the Boxer Uprising twenty years earlier: the burning of the railhead at Fengtai in May 1900 had been one of the first major acts of destruction by the Boxers in their northward campaign against the foreign community in Beijing.[27] With the Qing gone, infrastructure such as roads and railways were determining the flow and engagement patterns of feuding armies in the splintering republic.

Of course, war brought a range of consequences to communities near to and distant from the battlefield, including hampered communications and shortages of essentials. In July, with rail bridges destroyed in the early days of the war, the main arteries of mail, goods, and human traffic between Tianjin and southern destinations like Nanjing and Shanghai slowed considerably when switched from the rail lines to the canal system.[28] As a precaution, the foreign community, some of whose members had fresh memories of life in Europe during World War I, set aside a "siege provision fund" of 1,600 yuan in the summer seaside retreat of Beidaihe, in Zhili's northeast.[29] Trains to Beijing brought the wounded into the city throughout the night, and as Anhui troops encamped on its perimeter made daily forays through the city gates to purchase foodstuffs by the cartload, prices swelled for Beijing's residents and provided handsome profits for the city's grain dealers.[30] Meanwhile, the passing of tens of thousands of soldiers through communities in the vicinity of the capital during and following the engagements threatened far worse.

Early reports at the time of a setback and retreat of Wu's attacking forces on July 17 would prove false. In his move up from the south against the Anhui forces encircling the capital, the general had instead led a counterattack by one of his brigades under the cover of darkness, sweeping east from Zhuozhou and outflanking the enemy forces in a bold maneuver

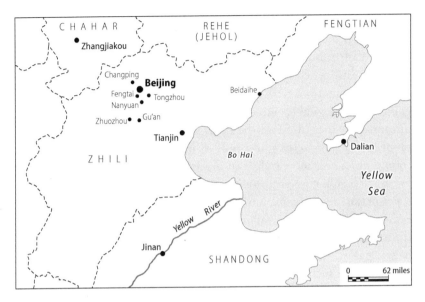

MAP 2. The Zhili war zone, with locations mentioned in the text.

(map 2). Caught by surprise, the troops at the Anhui division headquarters at Gu'an suffered heavy casualties and quickly pulled back toward Beijing. Six thousand troops fled north, some commandeering a train along the way and others stopping at Nanyuan, nine miles from the walls of Beijing, looting the town's outskirts when they found its gates shut. A second division in full retreat followed, after having been bogged down in the mud from a recent brief spell of rain. With Wu taking Gu'an and securing victory in the west, the eastern front, pressured by Cao and Zhang, quickly folded. Wu's maneuver alone did not seal the victory for his side, but it would establish his reputation as one of the more brilliant military strategists of the period.[31]

Handling Victory

The civilian toll from the Zhili-Anhui War does not appear to have approached levels reached in earlier outbreaks of civil war. In early 1920, a delegation representing Hunan communities called on Cao's headquarters in Zhili. Two years before, following the death of Yuan, northern armies led by Wu had been dispatched to subdue military forces in Hunan intent on breaking away from the Beiyang government in Beijing and aligning with the independent government in Canton.[32] The antisecessionist Hunan war of 1918 had produced an extraordinary amount of suffering and material loss for the people there: mutilations, looting and burning, and systematic rape and murder had received national attention in the press, prompting independent investigations and an outpouring of national outrage. As the delegation in 1920 recounted atrocities wreaked upon communities there in 1918, it "reportedly brought Cao's staff to tears."[33] Whether or not this episode is apocryphal, Cao and other leaders of the Zhili faction did apparently succeed in avoiding a repetition of those widely publicized horrors and the public backlash by, in part, taking steps to peacefully demobilize defeated divisions whose troops were languishing in the vicinity of Beijing. Nonetheless, violence against civilians and their loss of resources no doubt weakened the population's ability to weather future subsistence crises.

How does one explain the relatively low civilian toll in 1920? Suppression of news is a possibility. But despite the best efforts by authorities, including Duan, to shut down news operations, state control of information had its limits.[34] It is possible that in this instance training and discipline put a check on soldiers' excesses. Widely regarded for his tactical acumen, Wu's military success was also a function of the discipline he instilled in his men. Known for their goose-stepping and strict training regimen, Wu's forces were known for their relatively upstanding behavior in combat and among the civilian population.[35] In contrast, the troops under the command of the Anhui faction, while better equipped with Japanese-funded weaponry, were largely inexperienced, and their behavior in retreat reflected the lax and rushed recruiting process used to fill their ranks. Much of the extreme violence inflicted on the Hunan population two years earlier by the men under Wu's fellow Beiyang commander Zhang Jingyao (1881–1933) was attributed to his recruiting of bandits into his units to bypass the long and expensive process of training new recruits.[36] Pillage figured as part of some commanders' military strategy, or as recompense for their underpaying their soldiers, as it had for Zhang. However, Wu's men were not associated with the atrocities in Hunan, and postatrocity investigations singled them out for their good conduct.[37]

Of course, even commanders with disciplined men still risked un-leashing mayhem if they failed to promptly and properly disarm and demobilize defeated foes. With their command and pay structures dissolved, defeated troops were especially likely to join the ranks of bandits.[38] The victors of the ten-day war in 1920 faced the task of dismantling, or at least dislodging, a series of defeated divisions whose troops were roaming the environs of Beijing, and pockets of looting were reported the following day in areas beyond the patrols of the capital gendarmerie. On July 23, with hostilities formally ended, the western and eastern contingents of the Zhili and Fengtian forces linked up and camped at a village nine miles south of Beijing's southern gates. The same day, ten thousand Anhui troops passed by train into Zhangjiakou on the edge of Inner Mongolia, and the victors allowed Anhui forces to continue escaping beyond the Great Wall so they would not molest the capital region. Anhui troops were successfully barred from entering the town of Tongzhou, east of Beijing at the terminus of the Grand Canal, by the closing of the town gates, but they subsequently mutinied when instructed to disband and rampaged through the surrounding districts, prompting foreign missionaries there to request protection from the authorities.[39] The marauding soldiers were eventually absorbed into Zhang Zuolin's Fengtian army.[40] With at least one Anhui divisional commander seeking refuge in the Legation Quarter's French-run Grand Hotel des Wagons-Lits, and others in the Japanese Legation, disarming of the defeated divisions was effected at Nanyuan, south of Beijing, where the Zhili forces were camped on the horse-racing track. Meanwhile, Zhang's troops occupied neighboring districts, disarming Anhui troops and procuring much of their advanced materiel for themselves, but they were prohibited by Zhang from entering the capital itself.[41]

Toward the end of July, Cao Rui (1868–1924), the governor of Zhili and Cao Kun's younger brother, called a meeting with local officials and gentry from across the region to discuss relief needs stemming from the recent war. One of the defining characteristics of the period was a reversal of the civil-military relationship of late imperial governance, in which bureaucrats had been superior to military leaders in status.[42] Cao Rui effectively served as the civil administrator for Cao Kun. It is unclear what role, if any, Cao Kun played in his brother's disaster mitigation initiatives, which involved the creation of the Postwar Relief Society for the

Disaster Stricken (Zhanhou zaimin jiuji hui) tasked with assessing damage in the environs of Zhuozhou, where a swath of communities had been leveled by artillery fire. The society was also tasked with making appeals by telegram for funds from provincial assemblies, chambers of commerce, educational and agricultural associations, Red Cross branches, and other charitable groups (*ge cishan tuanti*) across the country, money that would be entrusted to three Tianjin-based banks.[43]

It is difficult to gauge the extent to which this appeal was heeded across the country. But evidence from Fengtian, Zhili's neighboring province to the east, suggests a broad response there. In September, a relief fund-raising office set up by official, educational, agricultural, industrial, and merchant communities remitted 5,000 yuan to the Zhili provincial government for distribution to communities that had been stricken by what was called calamity wrought by soldiers (*bingzai*) earlier that summer. The remittance was part of the money donated in response to a larger public subscription campaign that delivered funds piecemeal as soon as they were raised to avoid delays in their dispersal, so the total generated by this society over the year was likely considerably more.[44] Whether the cause was taken up by Fengtian communities due to the involvement of their own provincial army in the war is unclear. The crucial point to make here, though, is that this effort, initially for war relief, marked the beginning of a grain acquisition campaign through the fall by Fengtian communities for Zhili and neighboring provinces along the North China Plain.

Another continuity connecting the summer and autumn crises was a network of former and current officials involved in war relief whose members would reappear in famine aid mobilization in the fall. A prominent example of this involved the philanthropist couple Xiong Xiling (1867–1937) and Zhu Qihui (1877–1931), who in July formed a relief society for women and children (Furu jiuji hui) hosted at the Beijing headquarters of the Women's Chinese Red Cross (Nü hongshizi hui), which Zhu headed. Together with his wife, Xiong (who had held several prominent posts in his career, including that of prime minister of the republic in 1913–14) cabled thirty-two military governors and officials on July 22 to appeal for contributions (*juanzhu*). The Cao brothers heading Zhili responded with a 1,000-yuan contribution two days later, and similar contributions from the governments of Gansu, Jiangxi, Suiyuan, and other provinces across the country followed.[45] The couple's initiative eventually took care of more than 7,500 women and children displaced by the regional war at six shelters in and around the capital.[46]

Xiong, who made something of a career of charity relief management after his formal retirement from politics in the mid-1910s, had connections to other figures with similar patterns of relief involvement over their lives. They included Wang Hu (1865–1933), who like Xiong cropped up in a variety of disaster relief roles over the year. During his brief time as premier, Xiong had recommended to Yuan that Wang, a classically trained official who also had both military and formal agricultural training, be appointed civil governor of Xiong's home province of Hunan.[47] Due to a rival's objections, Wang never took up the governorship, and instead he worked in an office compiling official histories in Beijing before assuming the post of superintendent of the Beijing metropolitan region (*jingzhao yin*) in August 1920, in the immediate wake of hostilities across his jurisdiction—which encompassed two dozen counties ringing the capital.[48] Within days of assuming the post, Wang toured the war-ravaged districts and issued a formal appeal to the central government, which might account for the considerable funds his office dispensed in aid over the coming months.[49]

Civilian losses in the July war appear to have been predominantly financial or material, the results of cross fire and looting—which exacerbated the shortages that the harvest failure would bring. Back when war was imminent, the head office of the Chinese Red Cross in Beijing sent instructions out to begin fund-raising for war relief, and chapters in the region, such as Tianjin's, convened on July 11 to do so, a day before war was declared.[50] With hostilities over by July 23, reports of violence to the civilian population varied: a Beijing chapter of the Chinese Red Cross reported incidents of rape and massacre east of Beijing in the village of Yangcun, which had been in the heart of the battle zone.[51] Another Red Cross survey in the capital's eastern outskirts tallied one dead civilian and two injured from stray bullets in one village, along with three homes destroyed by stray shells and one destroyed in actual fighting; in addition, mounted soldiers had looted twelve nearby villages, and soldiers on foot another fourteen.[52] A report issued by the women's chapter of the Beijing Red Cross covered the northern outskirts of the city, including Changping. There in early August soldiers had arrived by train, robbing rich and poor families alike in villages near the station. But they apparently refrained from physical violence, since that is not mentioned in the Red Cross report. It ends by noting that the county police were set to distribute 50,000 yuan from Wang's office to Changping residents.[53]

Two examples of particularly distressed districts shed light on the nature, if not the overall scale, of war relief at the county level. In August, the merchant association and gentry of Tong county, east of Beijing, raised a sum of money to open four grain price stabilization offices (*pingtiao ju*) in the county, designed to counter the rising food prices ascribed to soldiers' ravages by sending agents to Zhangjiakou to secure a large shipment of grain.[54] These discount grain centers were continuations of an imperial method of relief in times of scarcity that was used by officials and local elites to sell grain at submarket prices to the poor.[55] In mid-September, again citing ravages of soldiers, Wang joined the county magistrate and gentry to coordinate the purchase of grain in Inner Mongolia for further subsidized sale to the public.[56] He inspected the wider region, in one case meeting with nine magistrates and assorted gentry in late August when it was decided that each county would raise and distribute a minimum of 2,000 yuan in additional emergency funds to those stricken by the recent war.[57] Around the same time a possibly related group, identified as the Temporary Relief Society of Tong County (Tongxian linshi zhenji hui), distributed relief (consisting of 5–7 yuan to each household), with a military escort and after canvassing the homes of the destitute, at points in and around the county seat.[58] And as late as the following January, the metropolitan office—then already long vacated by Wang, who had taken up the governorship of Jiangsu in September—sent 50,000 yuan in gold to the Tong magistrate, reportedly for distribution to the members of the business community who had been dispossessed there by looting the previous summer.[59]

Similarly distressed, the districts around Zhuozhou, southwest of Beijing, had seen Duan's forces defeated at the hands of Wu's men at great expense to local residents.[60] In early August, an aid agency called the Shunzhi Relief Support Office (Shunzhi zhuzhen ju), whose name suggests an official affiliation, was reportedly handing out emergency relief in nine counties, including Changping, Tong, and Zhuozhou.[61] This is corroborated by another news brief later in the month, which stated that the same office had, with a military escort, delivered 11,000 yuan to the area around Zhuozhou for distribution to those with losses from the fight-ing.[62] Many locals had taken to the roads in the wake of the July war, including 140 female refugees who arrived in Beijing in mid-August, where a local branch of the Women's Chinese Red Cross returned them to Zhuozhou with two sets of clothes and four or five yuan each.[63] But having been hit particularly hard by artillery fire, the trampling of crops, and the looting of its shops, Zhuozhou continued to experience hunger due to lack of food and clothes well into August, which prompted sev-eral members of the community to appeal for relief that month in per-son at the offices of Cao Kun and Zhang Zuolin in Beijing.[64] It is unclear whether these appeals were related to a reported distribution that same week, described as a personal donation by Zhang and handled by his staff, of 50,000 yuan to communities in the capital region menaced by marauding soldiers, bandits, and locusts.[65]

What were the total amounts of war relief and compensation for resi-dents of greater Beijing in 1920? A detailed investigation of districts af-fected by the fighting in Hunan two years earlier had put total property losses there at a staggering nineteen million yuan.[66] There is no compa-rable report for Zhili in 1920, but news reports suggest that the destruc-tion to communities around the capital—not to mention violence to the population—was considerably less, though still substantial. It is difficult to get a sense of the total losses, but compensation was presumably a small fraction of what the populace had suffered. What is nonetheless notewor-thy is that war relief, drawing on late imperial ideology and methods, maintained a long-established infrastructure of poor relief that would continue into the autumn of 1920, when failed or weak harvests had begun consuming household grain reserves and cash savings across the north.

War Transitions to Famine

In mid-July, as the armies of Cao and Zhang were preparing for their de-parture from Tianjin for the assault on the capital, some sixty miles to the northwest, the association of benevolent halls in the Chinese section of the treaty port met to discuss the implications of the severe lack of rain for the region's poor.[67] A few days earlier, President Xu had issued a call to all government ministries to prepare measures to "safeguard the people's food supply" (*yi wei minshi*), in the words of one news report, which noted skyrocketing grain prices amid the "extreme dearth of grain" (*mi-huang*).[68] Yet the Zhili leadership apparently did not formally acknowledge the prospect of famine until a joint communiqué was issued by the Zhili Provincial Assembly and the Tianjin Chamber of Commerce to the central government on August 23. With autumn harvests clearly set to fail due to "extreme drought" (*kanghan*) across the north for over a year, the two bodies formally "reported famine" (*chengbao zaihuang*), in the words of another report, a disaster that threatened an estimated ten million people in seventy to eighty counties across Zhili alone.[69]

Why had it taken so long for acknowledgment of famine conditions? Of course, farming communities were considerably more sensitive than city dwellers to the prolonged absence of rain, and raised the alarm earlier in the harvest cycle. For weeks already, the Dragon King—a "nearly universal feature" of Chinese communities from Inner Mongolia to Taiwan and the New Territories of Hong Kong[70]—had been hoisted on shoulders in community processions pleading for rain across the north, presiding over scenes of desolation not seen in most places since the 1870s. Part of the reason for any inaction by urbanites in the face of drought was its slow, creeping nature, which means that it has considerably slower effects on prices and subsistence compared, say, to a flood's immediate destruction of grain stocks and fields. Rainless skies had settled over many sections of the five-province drought zone as early as autumn 1919, which had led to weak or failed harvests of winter wheat the following spring. But it was not until late summer 1920, when it was evident that the north's primary annual harvest in the coming fall was also doomed, that alarm spread in the city press.

But there were also structural changes afoot that help explain the government's slow response to the onset of famine conditions. The health of the agricultural cycle was still of official interest in the republic, as it had been in the previous imperial period. This was, at the very least, because of its implications for the stability of the farming population along with those who relied on accessible prices for agricultural goods. One of the main tasks of officials at the lowest levels of government had long been to keep tabs on local prices and report them to the central government.[71] In similar fashion, Cao Rui sent out confidential investigators (*mi weiyuan*)

to look into drought-disaster conditions across the province at the beginning of July 1920.[72] And over the summer, an analyst at the Ministry of
Agriculture and Commerce predicted that there would "almost surely
be a widespread famine in the eastern provinces north of the Yellow
River" in the coming months.[73] But with the breaking up of the national
administration of tax collection at the death of Yuan in 1916, the provinces had stopped remitting land tax revenues to Beijing, making the
central government's fiscal health less directly tied to the state of agriculture nationally and increasingly reliant on more reliable revenues from
duties and other forms of taxation on foreign and domestic commerce,
which it received from independent and foreign-run institutions such as
the Maritime Customs Service.[74] It is telling that just before making its
bleak prediction of famine in August 1920, the department at the Ministry of Agriculture and Commerce that was charged with monitoring harvests and developing new crop varieties had just had its budget slashed.[75]

By the end of July, references to drought conditions had begun to
appear in press coverage of the war's aftermath. *Da gongbao* reported that,
despite pockets of freshly fallen rain in the capital region, several hundred thousand people were suffering from the prolonged and devastating drought conditions (*huanghan*).[76] While coverage of calamities
wrought by soldiers continued to dominate the coverage of the war's aftermath until the end of August, it was then—after twelve months of
rainless skies across much of North China—that the scale tipped toward
mentions of drought over those of war.

Conclusion

This chapter began with the battlefields of North China to shed light on
how a theater of war transitioned into part of a vast theater of famine
relief activity in 1920. This is not to say that war was a direct cause of
famine for tens of millions of North China residents. To be sure, militarization put great demands on state coffers and exacted a heavy toll on
the population. But the public toll inflicted by the July war was limited
in both intensity and scope, affecting an area dwarfed by the area of
drought, which encompassed more than three hundred counties by the

end of the year—in contrast to the few dozen districts traversed by fighting battalions in the summer. Extreme and widespread poverty would place millions of people on the brink of starvation after a year's drought, which was the result of the almost complete failure of the summer monsoons on which much of North China's agriculture depends. The lack of rainfall was in turn exacerbated by centuries of mass deforestation across the region, the salinization of the Yellow River floodplains, and other forms of ecological degradation that had long been unfolding.[77] The rudimentary and neglected nature of irrigation and transport infrastructures was also a major factor in the failure of the food system in North China.

As we chart the transition from war to famine, we should keep in mind that disasters—man-made or otherwise—were not experienced or handled as discrete events and should not be considered as such in hindsight. The basic needs of sheltering, clothing, and feeding the poor in times of war or famine, when dearth and violence both presented themselves in varying intensity, were the same. Governments and charities, with varying degrees of competence and generosity across times and areas, maintained mechanisms for relief that spanned the period between one weak harvest or major disaster and the next. With the onset of winter, an annual cycle of preharvest winter relief (*dongzhen*) was normal for society across North China, providing relief goods and grain subsidies to a limited number of the region's poorest residents. But the fall of 1920 presented an exponential increase in need in tens of thousands of communities on and alongside the North China Plain. At all levels of government and society, handling this required a minimum of peace.

Fortunately, in 1920 the northern half of the country enjoyed a period of relative tranquillity, the disruptions and violence brought in places by disbanded soldiers and bandits aside. Duan had "retired" to Buddhist studies in the security of Tianjin two days after Wu's maneuver precipitated the collapse of his defensive ring around the capital.[78] The French- and Italian-style villas of Tianjin's foreign concessions served as a refuge for defeated military men and ousted officials throughout the republican period—though Duan left Tianjin to take the presidency in 1924.

Even after Cao Kun's replacement of Duan as the head of the faction based in the capital, Wu exhibited the independence he had displayed already vis-à-vis his superiors in the Beiyang leadership by releasing to the press nationwide in early August 1920 a plan for what he called a National Citizens' Convention. By this time, Wu had begun to enjoy national acclaim. Two years before, against the orders of the Beiyang leadership in Beijing, he had made peace with the Canton government after the fighting for control of Hunan. Wu justified his return to the north as a bid to end hostilities between China's northern and southern military regimes and concentrate on the increased Japanese presence in the north—especially Shandong, his native province. For this and his condemnation of Duan's unpopular Anhui faction during the May Fourth Movement, Wu was celebrated as a unifying figure who stood for national interests. In May 1920, he had issued a nationally circulated telegram defending his decision to pull his Third Division back north from Hunan. In his August telegram to the nation, he called for civic groups around the country to elect representatives to temporary assemblies in Shanghai and Tianjin to consider establishing a new government, new constitution, and new election laws.[79]

But this rankled Zhang Zuolin, whose degree of open contempt for Wu at the time surprised even Zhang's own staff.[80] Cao Kun persuaded Manchuria's supreme commander not to denounce Wu's proposal, but Zhang left in Zhili roughly half of the 70,000 men he had deployed in the war, increasing his influence beyond his formal dominion in the Northeast.[81]

For the time being, Beijing, in Nathan's words, "hung in placid suspension between the poles" of two power bases: Cao's in Zhili and Zhang's in Fengtian, the heart of Manchuria.[82] The two men even became in-laws within a year through a marriage of their children.[83] Jin Yunpeng, a man also related by marriage to Zhang and close to Cao, was installed as premier. Xu remained in his largely ceremonial position as president, and the country's parliament would not convene for years.[84]

It was during this period of delicate balance that the threat of starvation would descend on millions of people across North China.

CHAPTER TWO

Municipal Relief

The capital of the republic and former seat of dynastic rule was no typical Chinese city. A multiethnic community of bureaucrats, clerks, and craftsmen, it was a city of men, who formed nearly two-thirds of the population within the city's walls. This huge imbalance, high even for China, was largely because Beijing drew students, who were overwhelmingly male, from across the country to its schools, as well as the estimated 100,000–125,000 "expectant officials" who were in the city awaiting government posts.[1] The high proportion of students and aspiring officials made Beijing relatively wealthy, a fact on display in the lavish funerals for which the capital was famous, often featuring bands and hundreds of paid mourners.[2] Roughly 800,000 people—China's fourth largest urban population at the time—resided within its walls in 1920. In the late 1910s, the police classified only 96,850 residents or around 12 percent of the population, as "poor" or "very poor," and these instances of destitution were relatively spread out, without the concentrations of poverty and slums that one might associate with a modern city.[3] In many Beijing neighborhoods, rich and poor shared lanes, if not walls.

One main exception to Beijing's relative prosperity was in the city's outskirts, where—in the shadow of the forty-foot-high ramparts—the incidence of poverty rose dramatically. There, along the suburban roads leading to the Western Hills, north toward the summer palaces, east toward the terminus of the Grand Canal in Tongzhou, and south to the main railhead at Fengtai, the impoverished constituted noticeably higher proportions of the population, and the clearest signs of destitution were visible. Throughout the drought and ensuing famine in 1919–21, these poorer stretches of mostly one-story homes and shops leading to the city walls were patrolled by gendarmes led by Beijing gendarmerie commandant (*bujun tongling*) Wang Huaiqing (1876–1953). A former Qing army officer, Wang presided over a centuries-old institution that had dual policing and military roles (fig. 1). Charged with maintaining the security of Beijing's perimeter to an average distance of six miles, Wang's men monitored the movement of people into and around the city and the entry and exit of goods. Among other duties, the military police searched for opium, cocaine, and other narcotics in the mule carts arriving from the region's farms; the caravans of Bactrian camels conveying coal from the Western Hills or tea to Mongolia, Russia, and beyond; and, increasingly, the city's cars and trucks. And they escorted valuables into the city—normally large transfers of silver specie or ingots, but also, in times of famine, precious grain.[4] On one representative day in 1921, Wang's office reissued bullets to the region's garrisons to suppress bandits; raised the fines for smuggling illegal goods; helped disband a defeated brigade of 2,500 troops in neighboring Suiyuan, in Inner Mongolia; and arrested a relief worker who had absconded with vouchers from a disaster relief society based at a city temple.[5]

But it would be remiss to reduce the gendarmerie's role to these military and policing duties. Its administrative jurisdiction over the poorest sections of the suburban and rural landscape ringing the capital reached far more deeply, into food security, welfare provisioning, migrant movement, and other areas of public concern. Of course, maintaining order in the aftermath of battle and seeing to the provisioning and management of migrants amid famine were two sides of the same coin. Villagers in Beijing's eastern outskirts, whose homes had been pillaged by soldiers during the July war, were arriving in crowds at the gates of the capital in late July. Within a week, Wang's office estimated their number at 2,500 and tasked garrison officers with returning them to their homes, with travel expenses covered by the gendarmerie.[6] Such a policy of returning fleeing farmers to their home districts followed the policy of Qing disaster administrators and was aimed at avoiding the concentration of migrants in urban areas and ensuring that farmers were near their fields in the event that favorable planting conditions returned. In mid-August, the gendarmerie canvassed the city outskirts to identify cases of immediate

FIGURE 1. Wang Huaiqing. John Benjamin Powell and Hollington Kong Tong, eds., *Who's Who in China* (Shanghai: Millard's Review, 1920).

need and released six hundred *shi* of rice and millet for its officers to distribute to households there over five days, at five *jin* a person.[7]

By September, the word on the street was drought disaster (*hanzai*) and famine (*jihuang*)—as opposed to calamity wrought by soldiers (*bingzai*), the term used earlier in the summer—as people arrived in the thousands and from as far away as Henan, mostly settling in the suburbs. Rather than continue returning masses of people over such distances, by the middle of the month Wang had begun sending out garrison officials to note the numbers and origins of those fleeing war and drought to prepare to settle them in the environs of the city.[8]

Why focus on the Beijing gendarmerie? The institution was, in many ways, the public face of the capital's military leadership, both in peace and in war. The intersection of military authority in the republic with the lives of the capital's poorest residents as famine unfolded over autumn 1920 is what this chapter sets out to describe. The authorities running Beijing were intensely involved in day-to-day disaster management, both in the reception of many thousands of people from the surrounding drought districts and in assisting city residents who would fall into destitution by the onset of famine in late summer 1920. The gendarmerie's suburban jurisdiction had the highest intensity of interventions in the lives of the poor over the course of the 1920–21 famine, and its commanding officer proved to be an energetic initiator of poor relief in the capital. Under the Qing, the duties of the capital gendarmerie had ranged from preventing sedition and repairing roads to operating soup kitchens and overseeing the local grain trade.[9] Over the course of his tenure, Wang, who was forty-four years old in 1920, fulfilled many of these functions with a force of gendarmes that was a fraction of the size of its predecessor under the Qing. Much of the relief mobilization and management Wang would involve himself in was done in an informal, quasi-official capacity, using ad hoc financing and resourcing while working with local philanthropists and charities. Wang also proved to be a micromanager of these efforts, visiting with residents at city shelters (*shourongsuo*), inspecting equipment at soup kitchens, punishing his troops when they neglected relief duties, and even posing for photographs with famine victims before they returned to their farming districts in the spring. A main point of this chapter concerns the semiofficial character of much of this state-sanctioned relief activity. By official, I do not mean merely state-sanctioned or state-recognized relief endeavors. All charities operating in the capital were required to register with the municipal police. By official, I mean government-run efforts, meaning those operating out of state offices such as police precinct headquarters or gendarmerie garrisons. In contrast, semiofficial operations were those run jointly by prominent local figures and the authorities and funded largely with donations from the public. In this way, when raising resources and recruiting relief personnel over the course of the year, the tasks undertaken by municipal authorities intersected with and complemented the work of charities in the city. This reflected the official-elite dynamic that was characteristic of relief efforts in the last decades of the Qing. Military men such as Wang and, as we will see, his predecessor as head of the gendarmerie, Jiang Chaozong (1861–1943; aka Jiang Yucheng), participated in the efforts of temporary societies that worked parallel with, and largely independently from, their formal offices. This fused much officially coordinated or sponsored aid work with quasi-charitable endeavors, creating a sector of relief activity with a strong civic character.

Qing-Republican Continuities

"A family of five can live in comparative comfort" on 100 yuan per year, an American researcher determined at the time in a survey of a community in suburban Beijing. This would have provided 35–40 coppers per day to spend on "simple and poor" food for the family, an adequate home, two suits of clothes for each person, sufficient fuel to make it unnecessary to scavenge for something to burn in the winter, and five yuan for such things as "meat on feast days and tea quite often," as well as the occasional trip to a temple fair in the nearby hills for medicine when required.[10] The line between this "comparative comfort" and the inability of entire families to feed and clothe themselves was one that increasing numbers of people would cross in the famine year. Police statistics indicated that by September 1920 the walled city of Beijing had experienced a tripling of its residents who were destitute (*jipin*): the number had reached two hundred thousand, or one in four Beijing residents, compared to the late 1910s.[11]

The rising cost of grain normally put the greatest stress on household budgets. Rent was relatively cheap in Beijing, accounting for merely 5–15 percent of household expenditures in 1920. In contrast, food normally accounted for the bulk of household outlays in the city and surrounding districts, from 68 percent in wealthier homes to 83 percent in poorer ones.[12] All but the wealthiest households were sensitive to the incremental increases in grain prices that occurred over the agricultural cycle in normal years—most notably in the weeks leading up to the spring or autumn harvests, when family reserves were usually at their lowest. Soaring prices accompanied failed harvests—760 cash (or 7.6 coppers) per *jin* of corn flour and 960 per *jin* for millet on one day in late August, which one paper described as "unprecedented" for Beijing—and would precipitate desperate and widespread measures in the countryside to liquidate assets to finance food purchases.[13] Weakening of the buying power of copper— the currency of the poor—in relation to silver exacerbated distress.

The republican state had inherited from the Qing a variety of measures aimed at reining in increases in grain prices when such signs of distress reached alarming levels. Under the imperial food security system, the first official move against unrest as food prices rose was price stabilization (*pingtiao*), the sale of subsidized grain at below-market prices. The purpose was both to make grain more accessible to the poorest people and to take the pressure off the broader grain market (when discounted sales of grain were sufficiently large, prices correspondingly leveled or fell for the general public as well). Subsidized sales of grain were normally conducted at particular points in the agricultural cycle: either in the run-up to the harvest, when prices were normally at their highest, or in the face of disruptions to the market, such as floods or bandit activity. These sales were conducted out of three types of granaries: So-called ever-normal granaries (*changpingcang*) located in the county seat and managed by the government were designed to stabilize or "normalize" the district grain market by buying up and releasing grain at strategic points over the year. These official institutions worked in tandem with community granaries (*shecang*) in surrounding towns, which were generally managed jointly by officials and local merchants and gentry, and charity granaries (*yicang*) in rural areas stocked and managed by local elites.[14]

In more normal years, subsidized grain sales would taper off or cease altogether as soon as a successful crop was available, having served their purpose in the lean, more expensive, months leading up to the harvest. But when major market disruptions contributed to famine conditions for a substantial segment of the general population, relief under the Qing took on several additional dimensions: First, subsidized sales generally remained in place across the famine field to benefit poor families with cash reserves or some income to spend. Second, for people who were already destitute and unable to benefit from discounted sales, Qing relief regulations provided a month's worth of emergency relief (*jizhen*) in cash or kind to carry the poorest over until the establishment of large-scale relief operations. And third, with the arrival of full-fledged famine conditions, dispensation of a main type of relief would begin, either in the form of porridge at soup kitchens (*zhouchang*) or allocations of grain, and this would generally last until the resumption of the agricultural cycle—which, in the case of a failed fall harvest, meant the return of warm weather and harvests in spring.[15] Since their official establishment with the consolidation of Qing rule over the empire in the seventeenth century, the stocking, state of repair, and general activity of these institutions naturally fluctuated with the changing local conditions and priorities of the state at the local, regional, and imperial levels.

The timeline of relief strategies used by authorities in 1920 closely followed this late imperial relief repertoire. At the beginning of the autumn, the Ministry of the Interior issued a temporary ban on the distillation of grain-based spirits in drought-afflicted counties, and Wang Hu, who, as seen in chapter 1, briefly took up the post of superintendent of the twenty-county metropolitan district, ordered all magistrates within his jurisdiction to enforce the ban.[16] The distillation of liquor from sorghum (*gaoliang*) and other grains consumed no small amount of agricultural production—"no country offers a wider variety [of] or cheaper prices" for alcoholic drinks, in the words of one foreign travel guide at the time—although it is unclear to what extent these bans were respected or enforceable.[17] At the central level, in mid-August 1920, the Beiyang government stationed an agent in Shanghai to manage bulk purchases of grain to import it into the capital region and stabilize the food supply. The first purchase consisted of one hundred thousand *shi* of rice, after which the government issued orders for all twenty counties in the metropolitan district to set up discount sales centers.[18] At lower levels, both the metropolitan government and the municipal police operated their own discounted sales centers from July into December 1920.

The largest discounted sales operation to be run by a government agency was that of the gendarmerie. By late August, Wang Huaiqing's office had set up twelve centers in the city's suburbs that were provisioned largely with millet from the region of Zhangjiakou, up the rail line (map 3).[19] At times throughout the winter, its grain selling activity slowed due to depleted stocks and then picked up again, such as when the gendarmerie's suburban centers brought in twenty thousand *bao* of millet (again from

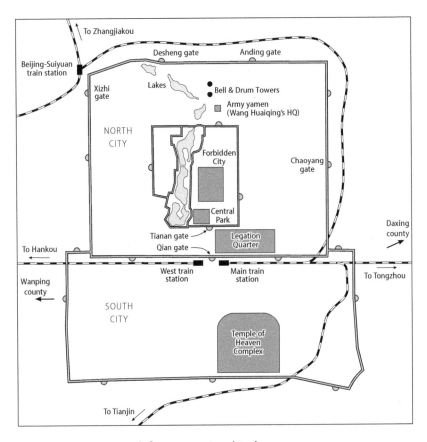

MAP 3. Beijing in 1920, with features mentioned in the text.

Zhangjiakou) in early February after shutting down temporarily the month before.[20] The operation then continued through mid-March.[21] The discounted prices ranged from five to six coppers per *jin* of millet, the most common grain sold at all discount centers, when on the Beijing market prices hovered in the area of seven to eight coppers per *jin*—a reduction of some 25 percent. The amount poor people could purchase at this price varied over the year from two to five *jin* per person per day.

The fact that agents of the Chinese government conducted such programs should not be surprising. The challenges that Wang Huaiqing and other Beijing authorities faced in 1920 were not unlike those of their predecessors during the great North China drought-famine of the 1870s, which was very much still in living memory.[22] In his relief role as gendarmerie chief, Wang was assuming the mantle of his Qing predecessors, who had monitored and recorded in detail the movement of grain by canal or road into city granaries and established relief centers in times of crisis.[23]

What is more noteworthy is that the gendarmerie chief divided his attention between the grain subsidy operation of his office and the establishment of an official charity that ran parallel to the official discount sales. The Grain Relief Society (Liangshi jiuji hui) was founded in mid-July by Wang and two other military men in anticipation of disruptions to the food supply by the military activity south of the capital.[24] Wang mainly served as liaison between the group and his formal office. One of his cofounders was another native of Zhili, Wang Hu—although his contribution was limited as he soon became governor of Jiangsu in September.[25] Leadership of the society fell to the third founder, Jiang Chaozong, an Anhui native and predecessor of Wang Huaiqing's who had served intermittently as acting or deputy commandant of the Beijing gendarmerie in the years 1912–17.[26]

Earlier in 1920, Jiang had been appointed head of the capital's yellow banner, one of the twenty-four banner divisions that had formed the core of the Qing army—which, divided by the color of their battle flags, had been stationed at various key points around the empire since the dynasty's capturing of the fallen Ming's domains in the mid-seventeenth century.[27] It made sense for a banner official to preside over charitable grain subsidies in the early republic, considering the acute destitution of the region's banner community. In the abdication agreements made at the fall of the Qing a decade earlier, republican officials had committed to paying banner stipends indefinitely. By the early 1920s, with a full quarter of greater Beijing's population still consisting of former bannermen and their families, these had become mere token grants of a handful of coppers at the main lunar festivals.[28] The Beiyang regime continued to fill top banner posts into the 1920s, but the bannermen's role was increasingly reduced to pressuring the leadership to honor earlier commitments that were met more and more erratically.[29]

Launched on July 20 with headquarters at Jiang's yellow banner offices and eight discount centers within the city walls, the Grain Relief Society soon expanded its operations in light of locust invasions west of the city and reached further into the outskirts in the fall, eventually having over twenty discount grain stations across the region.[30] The society was launched with 100,000 yuan in charitable contributions, including personal donations from various figures in the capital. For example, Wang Huaiqing contributed 20,000 yuan, another 1,000 came from Charles Crane, the Ohio businessman then serving as American minister to China, and there was a matching grant of 100,000 yuan from the central government. In addition, the society received tax exemptions and remitted transport fees from the relevant state ministries.[31] Its grain centers opened their doors for four hours each morning, selling a maximum of three *jin* of grain to each adult per day and one *jin* to each child. For the purpose of maintaining order after incidences of trampling and theft, men and women were separated at purchase time.[32]

Shipments of grain brought into greater Beijing by the society appeared to start large and grow exponentially as local fall harvests proved sparse or nonexistent, and as distant regions of the country like Manchuria and Inner Mongolia reported bumper crops.[33] Four months into the society's operation, multiple news sources reported an order for 500,000 *shi* of millet and 100,000 *shi* of wheat (*xiaomai*) from the district around Zhangjiakou.[34] This appeared to exhaust the group's funds—so much grain would have cost millions of yuan, and it is unclear how or whether the money or grain was ever sourced in full—prompting calls for it to cease operations.

Jiang's hybrid quasi-governmental program was distinguished in the press from sales of official grain (*guan mi*) conducted by the police, the gendarmerie, or other official agencies.[35] And there was a third, more clearly private, sector of grain relief distribution. These gentry operations appear to have been the first to act, when—in mid-July 1920—an informal group led by a local man with no apparent official position named Feng Gongdu launched what was referred to in the press as the Zhili Gentry Temporary Grain Discount Bureau (Zhi shen linshi pingtiao ju). Feng reportedly joined with nine other people informally united by what was called shared resolve (*tongzhi*) to establish the bureau, which sold discount grain at four temples around the city for two hours early every morning, using an initial loan of 50,000 yuan from merchants. By August, the bureau had eight locations in the suburbs, for a total of fourteen centers at temples, ancestral halls, and private residences in greater Beijing. It brought in grain under military escort from Inner Mongolia and later from Manchuria, including an October shipment of 1.5 million *jin*.[36] To put that in perspective, this shipment was equal to 7.5 *jin* for each of the 200,000 city residents officially recognized as destitute at the time.[37]

Grain firms and merchant associations responded to official incentives that ranged from tax exemptions to subsidized transport on the state rail system for relief provisions.[38] The Beijing Chamber of Commerce ran its own discount centers around the city starting in July, while more modest and apparently independent efforts to provide discount grain to particular Beijing neighborhoods operated out of storefronts.[39] Following official appeals for merchants to increase imports of grain from South China and elsewhere for storage in the Taiping granary complex that hugged the city wall outside Chaoyang gate, firms and individual merchants brought considerable amounts into the capital market.[40] In one instance 300,000 *shi* brought in from Inner Mongolia in mid-September reportedly served to lower the market price by 120 cash (1.2 coppers) a *jin*.[41]

Only in the depths of winter did discounted sales fully give way to free relief at soup kitchens and through home distributions. Feng's gentry-led operation closed its doors on February 1, 1921, around the time the Grain Relief Society disappeared from the news pages and presumably shut down as well.[42] During the autumn, such volumes of grain and cash changing hands in a network of crowded and often disorderly depots and sale centers provided ample opportunity for abuse and graft. In one case, investigators found that substantial amounts of grain were routinely snuck out the door by staff for sale on the market;[43] in another, buyers were reportedly shortchanged an eighth of each *jin* they bought;[44] and in still another, grain sales were inflated with "not a small amount of sand" at two locations, prompting investigations by Wang's office and unspecified disciplining of both station managers.[45] A week later, Wang banned the reportedly regular practice by discount center officials and guards of acquiring grain for home use, but with unknown success.[46]

As seen through the example of these operations in greater Beijing in 1920, there were no clear divisions at the time between official public efforts and those of privately run charities in Beijing. Beijing charities, the Qing historian Susan Naquin has noted, had "an intimate and complicated relationship with the state" in the late Qing that is "better captured by Bryna Goodman's 'partial autonomy, interpenetration, and negotiation'

than any tidy division between 'public' and 'private.'"[47] This dynamic
continued into the republic, when in the summer of 1920 various operations were started by military and municipal officials and by members of
the ranks of gentry and merchants acting as firms or individually. These
did not take the form of top-down state operations, nor were there dual
operations of state and extragovernmental actors working independently
from those in power. Instead, the responsibility of poor relief was met in
tandem by actors across the state-society spectrum.

Shelter

In addition to drawing rural residents to its grain markets, Beijing served
as a temporary shelter and transit point for hundreds of thousands of migrants over the year. This involved expanding a system of shelters that
municipal authorities had set up in mid-August on the city outskirts for
people fleeing the disruptions caused by the July war.[48] The influx of
threadbare migrants from the interior came in a period of increasing tensions over public hygiene and waste disposal in a city notorious for its
inadequate sewage systems. However, aggressive public enforcement campaigns as well as measures taken against the city's entrenched nightsoil
rackets did not come until 1928 when the city was under Nationalist control and a city Public Health Administration was created with the aim of
promoting "civility" and combating the spread of epidemic disease.[49]

The control of disease in 1920 was instead the responsibility of the
Beiyang Anti-Epidemic Bureau, an arm of the central government that
in September enlisted the Chinese Red Cross and other charities to help
construct epidemic prevention and treatment clinics for refugees. Over
the course of the year such groups worked with the state agencies in the
area to establish these facilities.[50] In the Beijing outskirts, the Hygiene
Bureau (Weisheng zongju) set up four medical clinics in November, following Wang's instructions to treat poor residents with varied ailments
in the area.[51] These were followed by charity dispensaries that were opened
in the city outskirts by local physicians and philanthropists over the year.[52]

Based on what made its way into the press, at least seventy-three shelters were established in greater Beijing over a nine-month stretch from
the onset of the famine in August 1920 to its waning in April 1921 by

twenty-five state agencies, charities, or lone actors. Some shelters could accommodate several thousand people, while others were designed for specific types of the needy, such as the old and infirm, orphan girls, children, destitute men or women, or a combination thereof.

In a bid to control and contain the bodies flowing into the city, garrison officers were tasked with counting the numbers of migrants in their districts so the gendarmerie could prepare for the reception of much greater numbers as the food crisis intensified in autumn.[53] By order of the chief of police, migrants were not allowed to set up their own encampments and were instead required to enter one of the fifty shelters set up by authorities in the city outskirts.[54] The scramble for sufficient and suitable space for settling tens of thousands of men, women, and children around the city led Wang in early November to send some of his subordinates to vacant mineral mines in the four suburbs to seek locations for shelter facilities, each with a planned two hundred rooms of packed earth. Within a few days, Wang reportedly secured permission from the association of Beijing gold dealers to construct temporary shelters on the grounds the association rented out to generate income for its own charitable activities.[55]

The fact that shelters were concentrated in the outskirts of the city did not mean that people fleeing famine were permanently barred from the city center. A tally conducted by the Beijing YMCA during an unspecified day during the famine counted 27,245 men, women, and children fitting the description of "poor" and "very poor" using one of nine city gates, 46 percent of whom were entering the city.[56] And while a group of 173 men and women from nearby counties were forbidden to pass through the city gates in early September and left to camp outside and roam the surrounding districts, within weeks there were reports of migrants who readily gained entry—including one group of 180 men and women from Hejian county who entered on foot through Qian (or Zhengyang) gate after having arrived by train at the west station.[57]

Soup Kitchens

Coming across suicide attempts was no rare occurrence for farmers, floodgate workers, or gendarmes patrolling the walls and city moat of Beijing. When individuals or even entire families were pulled to safety from well shafts or icy canal waters over the course of the famine year, they provided opportunities for journalists to ascertain the motivations of those driven to end their lives.[58] In this way, news reports offered brief profiles of men and women caught up in the unfolding food crisis, giving names, places of origin, and occupations of the distressed and often confirming that hunger was a main factor in their bids to end their lives.

Failed suicides could also offer a window into the network connecting authorities and relief facilities scattered around the city. In one such case two gendarmes patrolling the city walls pulled a sixty-year-old woman onto the bank of the city moat before taking her to the nearest sentry box, where she was questioned by the local garrison officer and then evidently by a reporter. The woman explained that her bannerman pension had long since ceased and, with no money left to live on, she had plunged into the city moat. The commanding officer then handed her a daily admission card to a soup kitchen at a local mosque, one that entitled her to double the normal portions there.[59]

The mosque soup kitchen in the eastern suburbs was one of a network of official and charity facilities offering free portions of porridge in Beijing over the famine year. In the winters leading up to that of 1920–21, authorities in the municipal gendarmerie, police, and metropolitan district opened seventeen soup kitchens in greater Beijing for the city's impoverished and those coming in from adjacent counties, usually starting on December 1. In light of the unusual levels of distress in late summer 1920, the heads of all three agencies decided to open the soup kitchens earlier than usual and add twelve municipal facilities in the two adjacent rural counties of Wanping and Daxing for a total of twenty-nine (or thirty, in some reports) official soup kitchens in the immediate environs of Beijing, plus thirty more facilities in the twenty counties comprising the metropolitan district encircling the capital.[60] The establishment of soup kitchens beyond the walls by city officials in the republic was a continuation of the gendarmerie's operations in the eighteenth and nineteenth centuries under the Qing, and many of the locations chosen in 1920 had been used for the same purpose as far back as the 1820s.[61]

The Ministry of the Interior, which supervised the municipal police, initially estimated that the city's expanded operations cost 300,000 yuan, compared to the average total of 20,500 yuan spent by city authorities—primarily the police—on soup kitchens in the preceding years.[62] In

September, President Xu Shichang instructed the ministry to release 10,000 yuan to get the operation off the ground immediately.[63] Two palace women, described in the press as former imperial concubines (*taifei*), followed with a donation of 5,000 yuan to the ministry for the purpose.[64] By mid-October, for both fund-raising and oversight purposes, the Soup Kitchen Provisioning Bureau (Jingji zhouchang choubanchu) was established with offices at a spacious family compound in the city staffed with members of the military, police, and gentry, and with Wang presiding as commissioner (*duban*).[65] A week later, seven municipal soup kitchens were up and running in temples, mosques, a teahouse, an artillery factory, and other facilities in the city, with another thirty-seven in the Beijing outskirts—and authorities would add more facilities in the following weeks as migrant numbers rose.[66] Daily attendance at municipal soup kitchens ranged anywhere from one to seven thousand, with some attracting people from as far as six miles away.[67] Following police instructions, a bell was tolled at facilities when serving time started, to limit the number of late arrivals who had to be turned away.[68] The bureau recorded 2,355,802 attendees in the month of December at thirty-seven facilities run by the gendarmerie, police, and metropolitan district, or roughly 76,000 people each day. This would indicate that three months before the official soup kitchen system's peak in March 1921, it appears to have reached three to four times as many people as the 18,000–23,000 served daily by city authorities in previous years, according to figures gathered by the American researcher Sidney Gamble.[69]

The bureau abandoned official policy, which had allowed anyone to enter a municipal soup kitchen, according to Gamble.[70] Attendance had been a sufficient sign of need in the past, but in light of burgeoning demand access in 1920 was "not so liberally given out as before," in the words of one news report.[71] Each facility instead received refugees and members of destitute households who had received colored entry cards from door-to-door canvassers, and anyone with cards could bring two children along with them.[72] When people deemed wealthy attempted to use such facilities and were discovered, they were apprehended and punished by Wang's office.[73]

In more normal years, municipal soup kitchens in Beijing had served exceedingly small portions, intended merely to supplement whatever food the poor were able to secure elsewhere. Each one-*jin* portion of porridge contained a mere 2.73 *liang* of grain, or roughly 380 calories, according to one report.[74] "One and all are carrying bowls, buckets, tin cans, baskets, anything that will hold a dipperful of hot porridge," Gamble observed in research he conducted in 1918–19 on such facilities (fig. 2). "As they crowd through the gate, each one is handed a small piece of bamboo which takes the place of an admission ticket and later must be presented to the man who is dishing out the food."[75] Throughout the first two months of the crisis, official soup kitchens across the city continued to serve portions as minimal as in previous years, which ranged from 350 to 400 calories per daily meal.[76]

With the appearance of full-fledged famine conditions in September, one local paper (*Xiao gongbao*, whose point of view appeared closely aligned to that of the authorities) had lamented the prevailing size of portions at city soup kitchens in previous years, calling for vigilance by philanthropists over the coming winter to better meet the needs of the swelling numbers of destitute people.[77] In mid-November Interior Minister Zhang Zhitan (1883–1946) ordered soup kitchens and refugee shelters in the city to increase the grain content of porridge portions to ten *liang* (five-eighths of a *jin*, or roughly 1,400 calories) for each adult and adolescent and to six *liang* (three-eighths of a *jin*, or roughly 850 calories) for children under the age of ten, dispatching inspectors to each station to see that the change was carried out.[78] This new ration closely matched the 1,350 calorie "adult famine ration standard" used under the Qing.[79]

As set out in the operation's guidelines, soup kitchen officials worked on a volunteer basis, and only hired staff members were paid.[80] Prompted in part by spot checks and chance discoveries of malfeasance early in the operation, Wang and his colleagues in the police kept close tabs on the goings-on at soup kitchens in the city and suburbs.[81] Using the surveillance system of secret investigators inherited from the Qing gendarmerie, Wang sent in undercover agents (*mitan*) by rickshaw and horse cart to check on management and conditions, and he called a conference of soup kitchen managers and inspectors in the autumn aimed at improving the performance of the unusually large operation.[82] During an inspection of one facility, Wang noted the pitiful attempt of an old man to get as much porridge as he could on a spoon—despite an earlier charitable donation of five thousand ceramic bowls to the bureau—which prompted him to issue a system-wide order to soup kitchen managers to purchase an

FIGURE 2. "Congee distribution, smoking boy and others," Beijing, 1917–19. Sidney D. Gamble, photographer. Courtesy of Sidney D. Gamble Photographs, Archive of Documentary Arts, Rare Book, Manuscript, and Special Collections Library, Duke University (222A__1243).

additional two thousand ceramic bowls for people who lacked suitable vessels of their own.[83] In one case of abuse, a grain supplier was disciplined for supplying a soup kitchen in a town west of the city with rotten rice.[84] In another, local gentry allegedly plotted to profit from the operation of a police-run soup kitchen in a town just south of the capital.[85] In still another, a garrison-run soup kitchen was condemned in a press report for continuing to issue only a half-ladle of porridge to each person as late as December, after the Ministry of the Interior had ordered that portions be increased.[86]

Consistent with the leading role that the government had taken in running soup kitchens in the capital since the 1600s, municipal operations, often run with gentry assistance, outstripped the handful of independent facilities run by charities.[87] Yet even efforts that might appear separate from municipal operations had official connections. For example, as official relief operations were getting off the ground in mid-October 1920, three members of the Chinese Hui Muslim community convened over tea at a mosque—one of forty in the city—outside Chao-yang gate and, in light of the unfolding crisis, decided to bring forward the opening date of the soup kitchen the mosque hosted every winter.[88] Other smaller soup kitchen facilities in 1920–21 were reportedly opened expressly for poor members of the region's Muslim community—which in 1919 numbered some 25,000 people in Beijing, or 3 percent of the population—as had happened during the late Qing. But this soup kitchen was opened to needy people outside the Chinese Muslim community. It was at times provisioned with grain and supplies from Wang's gendarmerie, which also sent inspectors to keep tabs on its operation over the course of the crisis. It also appears to have been the same mosque facility to which garrison officials referred the woman who had tried to drown herself in November. And consistent with the policy of the authorities of erecting sheds beside soup kitchen facilities in winter, the mosque added heated sheds for refugees and local homeless people this year.[89]

Beijing municipal soup kitchens normally ran until the end of February, but in light of the ongoing crisis, Wang, Police Chief Yin Hong-shou, and the new administrator for the metropolitan region, Sun Zhenjia (1858– ?), decided in January to keep them operating at least another month, financing the extension in part with money received for confiscated stolen goods and revenues from criminal fines.[90] Toward the end of March, since the continued freezing temperatures made it difficult for the poor to fend for themselves, the three men decided to extend operations for yet another month, for a total 195 days from October 15 to April 30—seventy-five days longer than in previous years.[91]

Financing

Not until 1927, on the eve of the Nationalist takeover, did the state begin collecting taxes in earnest on land or buildings in Beijing; until then, republican authorities had continued an exemption on real estate taxation in the capital inherited from the Qing.[92] With the exception of minor revenue raised from taxes on shops in the city, municipal agencies were funded by the national government, which in the case of the gendarmerie and police meant the Ministries of War and the Interior, respectively. The police budget grew steadily in the 1910s before plateauing at an annual amount of about 2.8 million yuan in 1919–22.[93] Thereafter, with the collapse of central state finances amid civil war during the 1920s, the police budget, along with the budgets of other city bureaus, became increasingly erratic, and city services were increasingly paid for in a hand-to-mouth fashion. With the approach of winter in 1920, even keeping the city's irregularly paid beat cops warm and fed as they patrolled at night became a challenge. In fact, the official solution did not differ much from the relief given the city's poor, whom the police were charged with managing, and Beijing precincts began providing hot porridge for their men on night patrol.[94] By 1922, the city was even paying police wages out of funds meant for city soup kitchens.[95]

Over its six and a half months of operation in 1920–21, the system of municipal soup kitchens and shelters was financed in a similarly ad hoc fashion, raising its operating income of 300,000 yuan from a motley set of sources.[96] In late September, Wang presided over a meeting at his office where it was decided that charitable donors who contributed at least ten yuan to famine relief operations over the year would have their names inscribed on a stone tablet displayed in the capital's Central Park, outside the inner walls of the Forbidden City.[97] Within a few weeks, the North China Relief Society (Huabei jiuzai xiehui) had provided Wang's gendarmerie with 100,000 yuan for its soup kitchen operations, money the Chinese relief group had raised in part at fund-raising events in the same park during the mid autumn festival.[98] In late October 1920, Police Chief Yin, concerned that additional soup kitchen funding from the Finance Ministry would not be forthcoming, reportedly succeeded in having an unspecified amount of leftover funds from Beijing flood relief transferred to the soup kitchen bureau.[99]

Monies also came from the lower ranks of the military, both as charitable donations and exacted through disciplinary measures. For example, an army patrol commander, representing the "full body of officers and soldiers" under the gendarmerie, told Wang that each would donate ten coppers out of his monthly pay to cover expenses for soup kitchens from their commencement in October to their day of closing.[100] Soon afterward, Wang docked half of the November pay of one of his garrison captains for failing to follow his directive to provide a group of thirty refugees with food and drink on their way by rail to Inner Mongolia, and the fine was used to cover soup kitchen expenses.[101]

Trade was another source of funds, either voluntarily or through special taxes. At times, managers of city grain shops made contributions to gendarmerie-run soup kitchens, such as a donation of three thousand *jin* of millet when the soup kitchens were first getting off the ground.[102] Later, the capital police announced a two-yuan monthly surcharge on cars in the city (on top of an existing monthly tax of four yuan) to cover soup kitchen expenses.[103] Afterward, monthly fees of one to three yuan were collected by the police from teahouses and apothecaries in the city.[104] In December, Beijing's court of law started selling off a backlog of stolen items unclaimed by their rightful owners to raise money for the reception of refugees.[105] Early in the following year, Wang proposed to the police and metropolitan district leadership that criminal penalties in the area be used to finance the extension of soup kitchen operations for another month.[106] Finally, grain was supplied from penalties placed on those accused of abusing the free relief system: reports in November that attendees of suburban soup kitchens were bringing back gruel to feed livestock were met with announcements of fines of between five and twenty *shi* of millet for those caught doing so, and within a week gendarmerie investigators arrested a villager west of Beijing for giving food from a local soup kitchen to his dog—Wang promptly fined the man a substantial fifteen *shi* of millet.[107]

Clothing the Threadbare

With the arrival of winter, exposure to the cold became as urgent a problem as malnutrition. Beijing's three main discount grain operators pushed their opening hours into midday expressly so "the poor would not freeze" when lining up for purchase: the gentry operations changed their hours in October, the municipal centers in November, and the Grain Relief Society in January.[108] Starting in mid-October, sheds were assembled from straw mats at each soup kitchen in greater Beijing so that, according to one report, the poor could eat "without being subjected to the freezing cold outside."[109] In addition to the system of shelters, the gendarmerie set up warming facilities (*nuanchang*) at twelve locations in the suburbs where people could escape the cold through the winter months.[110] Municipal shelters were heated in part by donations of coal from the public—for example, a city coal firm gave fifty thousand *jin* of coal to the gendarmerie in October—while coal warehouses provided bulk donations to poor households over the year.[111] But the needs of many people became increasingly basic with the approach of winter. In November, the Ministry of the Interior's inspectors noted an alarming number of the threadbare at the city's soup kitchens as temperatures dropped and the first snow of the year blanketed the city.[112]

Over the course of the year, clothing drives in Beijing would provide upward of 200,000 items or sets of clothes for the capital's destitute, who now accounted for a quarter of the population within the city's walls. Most of these clothing operations were official. While charities, aid groups, and individual donors conducted clothing drives of their own over the year—a cursory tally from news reports finds 39,749 items or sets of clothes distributed to the stricken by individuals and charities such as the Chinese Red Cross and the city's gentry-run grain discount centers— private drives were far outstripped by those of the authorities. The task of providing clothing was shared by state agencies at all levels and involved figures at the highest levels of the regime. Prime Minister Jin Yunpeng (1877–1951) initiated a project in October to procure clothing by cutting badges and insignia off army and police uniforms in storage around the city, after which President Xu ordered authorities to tally the numbers of needy households in their district for clothing distribution.[113] State workers arrived at soup kitchens in the suburbs to give out cotton suits to each elderly person and child found to be in need, while Yin ordered all precincts to send officers to local pawnshops—where the poor regularly used padded winter clothing as security for loans to buy seed, food, or other necessities—to repurchase (*caimai*) clothes for distribution.[114]

Other branches of the military were also involved. The navy brought twenty tons of clothes by rail to Beijing in December, after which the country's top naval official, Sa Zhenbing (1859–1952), launched a distribution at noon each day of "several thousand" coats and pants in front of the naval headquarters in the city.[115] Authorities also sent clothes from other regions of the country. For example, the military governor of Anhui, Zhang Wensheng (1867–1937), sent an escort of soldiers with fifty thousand outfits of clothing to Beijing in December, which followed a shipment of 500,000 *jin* of grain sent by his office to unspecified districts in the famine field a week earlier.[116]

Wang's gendarmerie appeared at the forefront of the region's clothing drives as well.[117] At the outset of the famine in September, he sent a deputy to a fabric market east of Beijing to "rush order" the production of three thousand sets of cotton clothing for distribution.[118] The following month, his office secured ten thousand old army uniforms for distribution in the suburbs.[119] In November, Wang released one thousand items of clothing from a warehouse of confiscated items, and he apparently donated his own money for the bulk purchase of cotton thread to be delivered to city and suburban soup kitchens for attendees to use to make clothes for themselves.[120] Within a few weeks the Soup Kitchen Provisioning Bureau, which was cochaired by Wang, procured thread in Tianjin for distribution at soup kitchen facilities for the same purpose.[121]

As one might expect, the circulation of such volumes of clothing fueled the black market and increased demands on policing. Authorities banned the depositing of relief clothes at city pawnshops over the winter.[122] Afterward, the city government announced fines of 10–50 yuan for anyone purchasing relief clothes from the poor or refugees.[123] Within days it was reported in the press that a policeman had apprehended a man for buying city-issued clothes from a refugee: the man was fined twenty yuan, but the refugee was not charged. Later in the winter gendarmes seized a stockpile of clothes tagged with the name of a charity at a clothing merchant's warehouse in the city and fined the business thirty yuan.[124]

Based on scattered news reports, military, police, and other official distributions in 1920–21 amounted to 178,651 items or sets of relief clothing. If we include the navy's twenty-ton shipment, whose 33,600 *jin* of clothing possibly contained another forty thousand items, official clothing distribution was enough to help cover each of the estimated 200,000 city residents considered destitute by authorities at the outset of the famine, plus several tens of thousands of refugees, suburbanites, or formerly middle-class residents who had fallen into the lower class due to the food crisis.

The lead that Beijing authorities took in clothing distribution during the 1920–21 famine was facilitated by a state-of-the-art uniform factory built in the city by the Board of War in 1912.[125] Still, the total number of clothing items given away was exponentially higher than in previous years. One account from the winter of 1916–17 put the number of city residents supplied then with clothes by the police and gendarmerie at 5,740.[126] Another estimated that in the more "normal" years leading up to 1920, municipal authorities had given away ten thousand items of clothing to the threadbare over the course of each winter.[127] Official policy in 1920 also departed from that of the late imperial period, when—according to the *Zhenji*, a seminal work about relief administration from the 1600s— grants of clothing were "strictly a matter for private charity," in the words of Pierre-Étienne Will.[128] Similarly, Gamble determined in a 1919 survey of the capital that while "the giving of clothes has long been one of the established methods of relief" in China, "most of the clothes are given away through private channels."[129] In the area of clothing distribution during the famine year, it appears that the military administration of China's capital in the early republic took on a more active relief role than its Qing predecessor had done—clothing hundreds of thousands in the capital area alone, while also distributing clothing in Shandong and other provinces through the winter.

State Paternalism

Who was to benefit from relief measures? Official manuals for relief investigators and administrators under the Qing had stipulated that the primary goal of state aid was to assist members of farming families generally, and especially those deemed most vulnerable to famine—a category of people normally identified as "widows and orphans," the "old and weak," and those otherwise left without support. This meant that transient farmhands and nonagricultural workers such as craftsmen were officially left to the care of their employers or private charity or to recruitment in work-relief projects run by the state.[130] Although scattered news reports are hardly the basis for a scientific tally, their patterns suggest that this gendered and paternalistic relief culture of the Qing period continued to inform decision making in the republic. For example, corpses found on the streets of greater Beijing of people reported in news briefs to have died from exposure, disease, or other poverty-related causes were around four times more likely to be male than female. Judging by the pages of newspapers from mid-November 1920 to the end of the winter in 1921, only males were perishing from the elements in the streets of the capital—and the dead were predominantly middle-aged men, although there were boys, teenagers, and elderly men among them.[131] Females were more likely to face the prospect of being sold to other families or human traffickers by their senior relatives to secure the survival of the remaining family unit, or for other motivations. Male autonomy, then, came with its risks, while controls imposed on females (in particular, girls) brought a degree of social mobility: the possibility of moving up into wealthier families as wives, concubines, or maids, or down into the sex trade—exchanged in what Johanna Ransmeier, in her study of family dynamics in the period, has called the "transactional nature of Chinese family formation."[132]

Neither of these observations is particularly surprising. In times of crisis, men and boys often left their families, following routes used in more normal years for seasonal migration to cities and regions such as Manchuria in search of work, and many of the migrants were vulnerable and without support if their search failed. And females in China had long been particularly vulnerable to entering the trade in people during times of famine, a fact lamented by activists and reformers as recently as the great North China famine of the 1870s.[133]

Perhaps more noteworthy is the fact that females and their offspring comprised a disproportionately high share of city residents served by public and charitable relief agencies over the famine year, which also helps account for the higher rate of reported male deaths on the streets of Beijing in 1920. News briefs over the year describing trampling and other newsworthy incidents behind the walls of relief facilities tended to focus on those in which women or children were involved.[134] The gendarmerie recorded 963 women, 469 children, and 376 men served at the mosque soup kitchen east of the city wall in November 1920.[135] A head count in early December at a police-run facility in the northern outskirts of the city found 1,380 women, 720 girls, 390 boys, and 170 men, plus a number of refugees, for a total of 2,815.[136] This breakdown was consistent with those of relief operations in previous nonfamine years. "First come the children, then the women, and finally the men," Gamble wrote about the operating procedure at Beijing's municipal soup kitchens in 1919, when adult males accounted for 3.8–29.0 percent of attendees.[137] District gazetteers present similar descriptions of soup kitchen protocol during the Qing—"women first, men afterward" (*xian nü hou nan*) in the case of Zhili's Wuqiang county.[138]

Prioritization of females in relief operations in the capital made numerical sense. As noted earlier, the capital was predominantly male, yet many of the men drawn to the nation's capital were of types not normally associated with dire poverty, such as officials in waiting and students. And the legions of male clerks and apprentices in the crowded stores and workshops downtown often lodged on the workspace floor while their wives and children remained on farms in the countryside. Beijing's females, on the other hand, were largely from bannermen families in the residential areas of the city and were disproportionately poor, accounting for 44.4 percent of those classified "poor" or "very poor" in the city, when females were only 36.5 percent of the city population.[139]

Still, this higher rate of female poverty in Beijing is not high enough to explain such high rates of female attendance at facilities across the city. It appears that able-bodied men were largely left to fend for themselves while those considered more vulnerable were prioritized by relief agencies. Idle adult males were seen as potential threats by authorities and were policed accordingly. As Janet Chen has noted in her study of changing policies toward the urban poor, "police files from the early republic indicate that the municipal authorities considered 'vagrancy' to be primarily a masculine crime of mobility and insubordination."[140] However, it must be stressed that official suspicion of vagrancy over the course of the 1920–21 famine did not necessarily translate into indignation toward the city's beggars (*qigai*). In light of the severity of the antivagrancy laws on the books at the time, which the Beiyang regime had adopted verbatim in

1916 from those written in the last years of the Qing—those found loitering in public were sentenced to fifteen days' detention—the city's head of military police in 1920 showed considerable accommodation to panhandlers.[141] With crowds of beggars streaming into temple fairs at the Lunar New Year, Wang wanted to ensure that Westerners (*xiren*) in particular were not molested by people in distress (*nanmin*) and the general poor (*pinmin*) seeking alms, who reportedly were "obstructing their view of the festivities."[142] As a result, he ordered that people were forbidden to beg at such fairs around the city, and instead soldiers were to have beggars—their condition "heart-wrenching," according to one report of the scheme—present themselves to the district garrison and register.[143] After the fair ended, the gendarmerie would reward each of those who had registered with 50–200 coppers, depending on their level of poverty. By the time of the news reports, over a thousand people had registered, and Wang funded their rewards with money raised especially for the purpose.[144]

Conclusion

The crisis that unfolded around Beijing toward the end of summer 1920 was hardly unprecedented. The influx of migrants into the capital region, the hikes in prices of daily necessities, and the establishment of aid programs would correspond to what had transpired in Beijing nearly half a century before, in the great drought-famine of the 1870s. City authorities had inherited a set of policies and practices from the Qing, which they used to orchestrate a broad civic response to the food crisis. Official reports at the end of the 1920–21 famine year stressed the "charitable nature" (*cishan xing*) of the citywide soup kitchen and shelter operation.[145] But relief responses also had new formulations and modes of expression, incorporating a discourse and attention to concerns about hygiene (*weisheng*), for example, while seeming to bridge the city's ethnic communities through the opening of mosque soup kitchens to the general public. Meanwhile, the capital gendarmerie and new police force "created models for public charitable activity," as Alison Dray-Novey has noted in her study of policing in the period, by expanding the social initiatives and interventions previously undertaken by city authorities.[146]

Both socially and institutionally, the Chinese capital was a city of contrasts and contradictions, a motley setting of imperial holdovers and modern innovations. By 1920 Beijing had become a city-sized museum of Eastern antiquity and market-stall curios for tourist consumption. The capital gendarmerie would last until 1924, when it was folded into the general army. In the same year Puyi (1906–1967), the last of the Qing emperors who had abdicated in 1912, would finally vacate the Forbidden City. The innermost part of the palace was still closed to the public in the early 1920s—although tourists could apply through their legation for permits to visit the outer sections of the vast complex.[147] Yet despite its touristic appeal of romantic decay, the city remained a fulcrum for events as the May Fourth Movement got under way and as the wider country descended into civil war. Beijing, in short, was a political arena in which power holders and aspirants based their legitimacy not only on newfound nationalist and socialist ideologies, but also on symbols and practices of paternalistic governance inherited from the imperial period—symbols that had persisting social currency and ideological appeal.

CHAPTER THREE

Military Men

W arlord" was popularized in the 1920s as a term for military figures who administered civilian government in an era of rampant militarization. It has since remained threaded into academic narratives of republican life. "Beijing was famous in the 1920s not only for its venal politicians, rapacious warlords, job-hunting officials, and idealistic students," reads David Strand's *Rickshaw Beijing*, "but also for its courteous but insistent policemen, rancorous mule drivers and night-soil carriers, polite but status-conscious shopkeepers, officious streetcar conductors, and artful pickpockets."[1] "Beijing in the Republican period was not only a city of warlords, protesting students, and literary figures," as Madeleine Yue Dong wrote in *Republican Beijing*, "but also a city of storytellers, wrestlers, snack vendors, and landscape architects."[2] I do not mean to question the significant contributions of either of these works to our understanding of early twentieth-century Beijing, especially the city's political and cultural dimensions. Instead, I mean to point out that the persistence of the warlord as a category saddles local rulers with a restrictive set of associations while preventing their immediate social milieu from acquiring the complexity and paradoxes that historians otherwise strive to confer on their subjects. Social welfare efforts by members of the period's military administration consequently remain something of an oxymoron. Many leaders of the period have been examined in their political and military capacities, and it is widely known that their personalities and policies varied enormously from models of progressive leadership in the form of supporting campaigns against foot binding to extremes of predation on the populace.[3] Yet historians have so far shown little interest in the social practices of these figures on a day-to-day level.

In this chapter I seek to flesh out, with the limited sources available, two leading figures in poor relief in the capital over the famine year: Wang Huaiqing and Jiang Chaozong, men with major roles in city administration and society who appear but rarely in historical accounts of the period. (Jiang appears in neither of the works quoted above, while Wang is mentioned in Dong's book only for ordering the destruction in 1926 of two statues of revolutionary fighters whom his troops had killed in 1911.)[4] In the process, I continue the discussion in chapter 1 on the nature of the news sources on which this and other chapters of this book are heavily based. While coverage of municipal relief could serve to burnish the reputation of city authorities, the news briefs filling the local sections of city tabloids were evidently the products of a relatively open market of information as opposed to party propaganda offices, despite the increased factionalism and partisanship of the period. As much as disaster coverage was infused with value-laden discourses rife with political implications, the empirical information the press conveyed about relief provisioning is often corroborated by other sources.

How does tracing the social activity of these figures alter our understanding of Beijing society in the early republic? Here we can draw a parallel between the role of the city's military authorities in civic and philanthropic campaigns and those of traditional *taitai* women, who have been similarly understudied. Xia Shi has shown how in this period of great social flux and ferment, particular types of women in Chinese society were well positioned to be effective conduits among multiple social spheres. These women—whom Shi classes as *taitai* (meaning Mrs.) due to their combination of modern education and civic prowess with homemaker roles behind their careerist husbands—were capable of bridging progressive and conservative circles, both foreign and Chinese, which was often necessary for the intense organization and fund-raising required of large-scale charitable endeavors.[5] Here, I aim to demonstrate how, in different but parallel ways, this hybrid positioning was shared by the likes of Wang and Jiang, men who served as nodes in an array of social networks, each holding together military, sectarian, native-place, charitable, and other spheres of activity.

Machinations and Motivations

Dotted throughout the documentary record of Beijing's famine year of 1920–21, as we have seen, is the figure of Wang Huaiqing, who served both as commander of the capital army garrisons and commandant of the gendarmerie over the course of the crisis. A Zhili native, he was in the higher echelons of the victorious Zhili political faction in the July 1920 war. His rise to the position of general began at the Beiyang Military Academy, founded by the imperial statesman Li Hongzhang (1823–1901) as part of Qing China's late nineteenth-century self-strengthening movement. The academy would have a far-reaching influence on Chinese war and politics in the half century between its founding in 1885 and the rise of the Nationalists to power in the late 1920s, most of whose leaders would be graduates of military schools in South China—notably, Huangpu (Whampoa) in Guangzhou (Canton). In the years leading up to 1920, graduates of the Beiyang Academy served as military governors in well over a dozen provinces across China, lending the academy's name to the Beiyang regime in power in Beijing during a period that later became synonymous with the warlord era.[6]

Many of these men became fabulously rich. The published recollections of Zhao Shixian, one of Wang's army yamen secretaries in the 1920s, describe a career of intrigue and self-aggrandizement at the highest levels of government by Wang, who rose through the ranks to work with Presidents Yuan Shikai and Xu Shichang. Zhao describes how Wang and his close associates acquired and then sold official property for handsome profits and in 1921 absconded with a trove of precious jades, calligraphy, and antiques from the Summer Palace in the city's northwest.[7] Another biographical sketch of Wang—by Li Lunbo, a staff advisor to Wang's Thirteenth Division—relates how Wang owned five pleasure gardens across the city, one landscaped with stonework and other features transported from the Summer Palace.[8] In this, Wang resembled Cao Kun, military governor and Zhili faction head, who was rumored to have used his private garden for security for a loan of 350,000 yuan to help cover his military expenses in the July 1920 war.[9]

Wang also profited from the same narcotics trade he was charged with stamping out as head of the capital gendarmerie. After being dispatched to the province of Rehe (Jehol) in Inner Mongolia in 1922, he managed to pocket two million yuan of revenue from the extensive tracts of opium poppy there, according to Zhao.[10] Part of this money must have been used to meet the enormous expenses of maintaining a division on alert in the rebel-contested area of Inner Mongolia as tensions increased between the Zhili faction and Zhang Zuolin's regime in neighboring Manchuria. As Edward Slack has shown, China's "narco-enonomy" was integrally tied to the country's militarization, which included the use of two million yuan from opium sales to pay for military expenses by General Ma Fuxiang (1876–1932) in nearby Baotou in 1923.[11] At times, the feeding and provisioning of troops were presented as a form of beneficence. Such was the case with the three million *jin* of rice Wang acquired from the south for the 130,000 men serving under him as famine unfolded in the autumn of 1920. With monthly pay for soldiers dwindling (*weibo*), headlines announced Wang's move as an act of "concern over the hardship of soldiers" (*tixu bing jian*)—one funded, presumably, from his various schemes in and around the capital.[12]

Various contradictory stances and dealings appeared to converge in the figure of Wang, unscrupulousness and concern, and misappropriation and largesse among them. A legal case recorded in the Beijing Municipal Archives offers a small window into the political dynamics in which he operated. It involved a night-time collision between Wang's car and a rickshaw on a main thoroughfare just to the south of Tiananmen Square. Police took the injured rickshaw puller to a state-run hospital after the incident on March 11, 1919. There he remained for nineteen days, after which legal papers were filed by the hospital for payment of the bill of 5.7 yuan by the financially liable parties, variously named in the file as Wang, the police precinct whose officers had admitted the patient, and the city's Bureau of General Affairs (*zongwuchu*).[13]

The case pitted the interests of a high-ranking general against those of a laborer from the ranks of the city's powerless.[14] Whether the funds were ever transferred by the city on the patient's behalf is unclear. The case nonetheless indicates tensions at the highest levels of city government, presenting a view of the factional and institutional divisions at play in the capital. Wu Bingxiang (1874–1930), then in his sixth year as head of the Beijing police force and squarely in the Anhui faction of the Beiyang government, was doubtless made aware of the collision handled by his men, especially as the case involved a leading figure in the rival Zhili faction.[15] It was in that same May, as the rickshaw case was still making its way through the legal system, that Wang became acting commander of the gendarmerie. Part of the Ministry of War, the gendarmerie had between a half and a third of its original Qing strength of 33,000 men. It compensated for this decrease in size by sharing duties with Wu's new police force of 10,000 men, a distinct institution under the Ministry of the Interior introduced as part of the New Policy reforms in the decade before the Qing's collapse in 1911.[16] Beyond the capital's main thoroughfares and city gates, which it patrolled and operated from sentry boxes, the gendarmerie's arresting powers overlapped with those of the city police, and this jurisdictional ambiguity led to occasional clashes that lasted into the 1920s.[17]

Right in the middle of the rickshaw affair, Wang and Wu found themselves dealing with a citywide maelstrom of student demonstrations against the terms of the Treaty of Versailles. Wang reportedly took a hard-line stance against what would become known as the May Fourth Movement, denying food supplies to more than a thousand incarcerated students around the city for nearly two days.[18] In contrast, Wu was nearly fired from his post for being comparatively soft on the demonstrators and was spared only thanks to the support of the Chamber of Commerce.[19]

Within fifteen months, the two men's personal rivalry came to a head at the end of the July war. Wang accused Wu of jeopardizing the safety of the city by "materially assisting" a prominent member of the defeated Anhui clique, in the words of the *North China Herald*, a prominent British mouthpiece in the international settlement of Shanghai, thereby giving the victorious Fengtian and Zhili armies an excuse to enter the city gates.[20] Weakened by the loss of his Anhui faction, Wu stepped down as head of police and fled with his family to the safety of the Legation Quarter. Wang then assumed dominance over the capital's military, taking the additional post of commander in chief of all army garrisons within the metropolitan district, and thereafter he worked closely with Wu's replacement, Yin Hongshou.[21]

The episode is characteristic of the period's dizzying rate of maneuvering among its power brokers, which was facilitated by the protection offered by the extraterritoriality of the country's many treaty ports, such as nearby Tianjin—where ousted leaders could wait in comfort until the political winds changed. But when we delve a bit deeper, Wang's denunciation of his foe appears to involve more than mere opportunism. Two stone steles erected in temples in Beijing's southern suburbs in the immediate aftermath of the July war suggest that Wang took the security of his jurisdiction seriously. Residents of Dajingcun in Beijing's southern outskirts raised the money by subscription for a "stone marker commending [the general's] virtue" (*song de bei li*) in his efforts to limit the chaos of the July war's aftermath in their village, after routed Anhui faction troops had fled there from the battlefields further south. Many of these troops arrived by train at the railhead in Fengtai, which was the southern limit of Wang's jurisdiction. There, the stone inscription explains, the disorder "emptied nine out of ten homes" before Wang "quelled the unrest" (*kanluan*), "freeing local merchants and other members of the community from worry" (*shang min dei yi wu yu*).[22] Wang had the military experience in the districts surrounding Beijing to execute such forays into the countryside from his gendarmerie yamen in the Inner City, having led imperial troops a decade earlier against revolutionary forces in the same districts of Tongzhou that were harassed by defeated Anhui soldiers in July 1920.[23] A second stele erected in a nearby temple in November 1920 lists the names of heads of eight villages around Fengtai, along with those of education officials from the capital's southern districts, who collectively "commended the virtue" (*song de*) of Wang for personally commanding his garrison troops in areas molested by retreating troops there as well, "quelling the unrest in the right way" (*kanluan youfang*), and enabling residents to live "safe and sound" (*anran wuyang*).[24]

The genre of stone stele inscriptions had a long history, marking events and public appreciation for the virtuous governance (*dezheng*) of local officials during their tenure. Wang's actions at the end of the formal hostilities in July 1920 were also consistent with the policies of his superiors, Cao and Wu Peifu, as discussed in chapter 1. And Wang's preoccupation with physical security would turn to a preoccupation with famine response in August, as greater Beijing transitioned from hosting a relatively limited series of battlefield engagements to becoming part of a much larger famine field.

The Press: Mere Mouthpieces or a Market of Information?

For a figure who served in major security roles in the capital for a sizable part of the 1920s, Wang has a remarkably limited presence in the collections of the Beijing Municipal Archives. Beyond what stone steles from the capital suburbs and a legal file might reveal, the archives hold little attributed to Wang. One text is the preface to the final accounting report of the Soup Kitchen Provisioning Bureau, produced at the end of the famine—which, Wang explains, he was asked to compose by his colleagues in the city administration. In it, Wang writes that "since ancient times there was no ideal disaster relief plan" (*zigu jiuhuang wu shance*), and erecting soup kitchens was the "absolute worst of them" (*you ce zhi xia zhe*). Nonetheless, despite an unrelenting flow of people to the city over the year, relief organizers "somehow used limited resources to meet an overwhelming situation," directly saving, in his estimate, the lives of eighty thousand people. He ends by extending credit well beyond those directly involved in the operation to officials at all levels, major philanthropists (*da cishan jia*), and workers who contributed to its success, adding that "even a good method cannot succeed without capable people."[25]

While these are presumably Wang's own words, they do not reveal much about the man himself.[26] For his actions, at least, I rely in these chapters on Beijing's press. The sheer intensity of press coverage of Wang is not immediately apparent when scanning newspapers of the time, since news stories used various forms of identification when reporting on him and his various offices. These forms included General Wang (Wang *jiangjun*), commandant of the gendarmerie (*tongling*), commander in chief of the capital army garrisons (*zongsiling*), and Wang Maoyi (his courtesy name acquired at adulthood), and he was also referred to with the term for his gendarmerie office, *tishu*. Once these references are recognized, though, it is clear that Wang was ubiquitous in local news, and readers can track his role in handling the minutiae of crisis management over the famine year.

The capital gendarmerie was headquartered on Mao'er lane (*hutong*), within earshot of Beijing's Drum and Bell Towers, used in the Qing to time the patrols of town.[27] There, due north of the Forbidden City, Wang left his offices one day in mid-September and rode by car through the city wall at Xizhi gate and into the western suburbs, heading for a shelter set up by the gendarmerie in Wuliucun. The reported purpose of his visit to the village was to "console" (*anwei*) the 380 people newly arrived there from the drought districts, and he handed fifty coppers to each person there, while depositing one hundred *shi* of rice for them to share—which, at fifty *jin* of grain each, was roughly seventy-five days' worth of famine rations.[28]

From the outset of full-fledged famine conditions and mass outward migration in September, it was clear that Wang would not be handling the unfolding crisis at arms' length. This, at least, was the message conveyed in scores of news items that appeared over the course of 1920–21. But who was behind the production of these vignettes? As a whole, the capital press was hardly admired for its quality or objectivity, and it was roundly criticized by the city's university students and foreign observers.[29] "Peking is unquestionably one of the worst propaganda-ridden capitals of the world," an American professor of journalism at Shanghai's St. John's University commented in 1922. The capital's news reporting, he explained, merely aimed to "accomplish some political or commercial aim by the dissemination of biased information."[30]

So were Beijing newspapers merely mouthpieces for the capital's military regime and its rival factions? This is a possibility worth testing. In late February 1921, *Yishi bao*, one of North China's largest dailies, ran a story headlined "Commandant Shows Concern for the Poor" (*tongling tixu pinmin*). "Fearing that any poor falling ill and seeking lodging in guesthouses might be denied admission," the story explained, "or that any who contracted illness inside were driven out," Wang had issued orders to all garrisons ringing the city to convey to inn managers that such actions were strictly forbidden (*jinzhi*). "Instead," the report continued, "authorities would cover the room and board charges incurred by all poor lodgers who had fallen ill," as well as the cost of coffins and burial for poor lodgers who died.[31]

The story is noteworthy for what it says about Wang's attention to housing policy. But equally significant is its appearance in a paper founded by a Belgian Catholic missionary in 1915.[32] Earlier in 1920 *Yishi bao* had been edited by Xu Qian (1871–1940)—a close ally of Sun Yat-sen and a "new type of 'Christian Statesman,'" according to his entry in the 1920 edition of *Who's Who in China*—who had written "several brochures in

English and Chinese upon the relation of Christianity to the National salvation of China." "Mr. Hsu states that his editorial policy will be directed toward the abolition of the Tuchanate system," the entry continues (referring to the system of military governors, or *dujun*), "and the establishment of the government on a constructive and constitutional basis."[33] There is a chance, of course, that with Xu's departure the self-described "liberal, progressive vernacular daily" took a more accommodating stance toward the Zhili faction in control of Beijing.[34] But its report is corroborated by a similar story in another city daily. "Out of respect for the lives of the people" (*yi zhong minming*), *Shihua* reported the following day, Wang had prohibited "guesthouse managers from intentionally creating difficulties" (*dianzhu guyi diaonan*) for lodgers. Anyone "thrown out of guesthouses into the cold to starve or freeze to death because they could not pay their bill would have their debts covered by authorities," or if need be, provided with coffins and proper burial.[35]

Two markedly different news platforms—*Yishi bao*, a national broadsheet with Beijing and Tianjin editions, and *Shihua*, a smaller local daily—produced remarkably similar accounts of the same event. Part of the reason for this may well be that Beijing's many newspapers relied on commercial wire services for much of their news copy (in one case at the outset of the famine in 1920, at least six city dailies—large and small, and some foreign-owned—ran the same news item about a charity in Beijing verbatim).[36] But for all the political jousting and intrigue that plagued the republic, it is difficult to identify overt propaganda for any particular faction or party in news items relevant to the famine in 1920, such as those about shelter policy or the provision of clothing. Although it was value laden and replete with ideological symbolism, press coverage of policy toward the poor over the famine year in the city evidently transcended immediate party politics.

The Question of Motive

But what is to be made of the personal touches in Wang's model of official charity? Is the maintenance of public security enough to explain his regular visits with refugees or personal dispensing of relief goods? One possible motivation was that Wang felt an emotional tie with people who fled to his jurisdiction, especially those from the hardest-hit area in south Zhili. Like most refugees, he and many of his peers in the military administration had humble origins. Born into a landlord family that was reduced to destitution by a profligate father, Wang minded sheep and cattle as a child before leaving as a teenager to join the army in neighboring Shanxi, having been instilled through his mother (*bingcheng zhe "muxun"*) with an understanding of the importance of loyalty in acquiring wealth and success in officialdom (*zuo daguan fa dacai*), according to his former secretary.[37] When writing his preface to the final accounting report of Beijing's Soup Kitchen Provisioning Bureau, Wang signed his name Ningjin Wang Huaiqing, in recognition of his native Ningjin county in the heart of Zhili's 1920–21 drought and famine field, where he had spent his childhood and lost his mother to illness when he was twelve years old.[38] A group of 130 refugees from Hejian prefecture—of which Ningjin was part—were lodged and fed with porridge by Wang's gendarmes one night in September before they continued to areas north of the Great Wall in the morning.[39] The fact that Wang docked half a month's pay from one of his garrison officers for neglecting to provide refugees with food and drink later in December takes on added significance when one realizes that the thirty refugees in this case also included some from Hejian prefecture.[40]

Some reports are more explicit about Wang's feelings for his native place. In December, Wang dispatched men with a sum of money to locate and redeem a baby boy who, he learned, had just been sold by the infant's mother at a location near his Beijing office: the boy's family was also from south Zhili.[41] And early in 1921, Wang was reportedly "moved by a sense of belonging to the countryside of his youth" (*nian xi xiang yi*) when he encountered twenty-seven refugee children from Daming prefecture in the extreme south of Zhili while inspecting shelters run by his system of garrisons in the suburbs. He promptly had the youths admitted to a primary school located on the same *hutong* as his gendarmerie yamen, and he covered all of their fees and teachers' salaries personally.[42]

But native ties could have played a role in only a fraction of the cases of people affected by Wang's overall policies and personal interventions. Unfortunately, the glimpses we have into the relief dimensions of his leadership throughout this chapter offer few conclusive insights into his thinking. When he crops up in political news or historical accounts, Wang occupies a reactionary or loyal position, thwarting a revolutionary insurrection by fellow officers in his rural Zhili district in 1911 or suppressing Mongol rebels in Chahar province two years later.[43] Wang was evidently conservative in his politics, and he performed his martial and civil duties in ways that would have been both recognizable and appreciated by many fleeing the countryside in 1920, as we have seen in the stone stele erected in his honor in the outskirts of Beijing. The protection of communities from brigands or marauding soldiers and the providing of relief from flood or famine were acts of equal importance in the annals, or gazetteers, of rural districts across Zhili during the Qing, and in biographies extolling local notables with virtuous or righteous conduct (*dexing* or *yixing*), bandit suppression and disaster relief were frequently performed by the same official, military officer, or member of the local elite.[44] Providing security and succoring the poor went hand in hand, with the maintenance of the social order being a primary aim.

A glimpse of the multiple personae that Wang presented to the public is given by a photograph of him taken by Sidney Gamble. In it, the recently appointed Beijing gendarmerie commandant presides over an opium burning in September 1919. To welcome the members of the International Anti-Opium Association who came to observe the destruction of opium and needles and other paraphernalia seized by his men in the city suburbs, Wang chose to don the type of cap and robe favored by literati (fig. 3).[45] Whether Wang opted for similarly refined but plain attire or for his decorated army uniform when visiting refugee shelters or soup kitchens the following year is unclear. Nonetheless, the substance of Wang's social interventions and the style of his self-representation during his tenure as head of the capital's military police suggest that he made claims of a higher authority than one founded on military credentials alone, employing the symbolic capital of a waning scholar-elite class.

Military-Religious Intersections

The character and range of Wang's policies and priorities over the famine year suggest a man operating in a wider ethical framework, one with values to which he evidently subscribed that had roots in the dynamics

FIGURE 3. "Opium burning, General." Wang Huaiqing (center) at a burning of opium and drug paraphernalia outside Beijing's Temple of Agriculture in September 1919. Sidney D. Gamble, photographer. Courtesy of Sidney D. Gamble Photographs, Archive of Documentary Arts, Rare Book, Manuscript, and Special Collections Library, Duke University (285A__1634).

of the civil or literary (*wen*) and military (*wu*) cultures of the late imperial period: above all loyalty, and a combination of martial valor and elite paternalism.[46] In this regard, Wang was similar to his predecessor as head of the city's military police. The example of Jiang Chaozong introduces an additional area of social overlap shared by the city's military and charity circles: sectarian groups. The capital's diverse range of religious communities was enhanced by the numerous spirit-writing groups and church-like syncretic societies that developed in the republic, which were lay offshoots of the city's Daoist clerical circles. Prasenjit Duara has dubbed these forms of association "redemptive societies," as they frequently combined a syncretic embrace of major world faiths with the promotion of "redemptive universalism and moral self-transformation."[47] The Society for Awakening Goodness (Wushanshe) was the most prominent of these groups in the Beijing media in 1920–21.[48] Founded as a spiritual community in the city in the mid- to late 1910s by Jiang and other former officials and Confucian scholars, the society embraced five major world faiths in a syncretic fashion, performing rituals before tablets to Confucius, Gautama Buddha, Jesus, Laozi, and Mohammed.[49] By the early 1920s, other branches would be established in cities around North and South China and as far away as Singapore, although the society's only following of note appears to have been the members of its founding Beijing chapter.

In the months leading up to and during the famine of 1920–21, Jiang's Society for Awakening Goodness served as one of the most active social relief charities in Beijing. One possible explanation for its prominence and social reach was Jiang's decorated military career. An army general under the Qing, Jiang enjoyed a role as power broker in the capital's politics that continued through the republican period. In the late Qing, military officers had frequently turned into the masters of religious sects, including spirit-writing groups. Jiang, who had taken on the Daoist appellation Dazhong, was heavily involved with Beijing's Daoist community in the 1910s and 1920s and with the capital's community of Daoist clerics and lay followers more generally (fig. 4).[50]

Although of quite different origins than Wang—Jiang was from an old and established family in eastern Anhui, just south of Nanjing—the two men had a good deal in common. Jiang served as caretaker of various institutions in the capital as power changed hands frequently in the 1910s. As mentioned above, he was one of Wang's predecessors as head of the gendarmerie, having served as commandant or deputy head of the capital's military police on and off from 1912 to 1917. And he enjoyed the briefest of appointments to the acting premiership of the republic in June 1917 when, under President Li Yuanhong (1864–1928), he took the post for the rather dubious purpose of countersigning a presidential decree dissolving the national assembly, which the dismissed premier had refused to do.[51]

Politically well-connected and known for his ability to help friends in trouble with the authorities, Jiang trod carefully between the factions

FIGURE 4. Jiang Chaozong in officer's dress (left) and ritual garb (right) around 1914. Courtesy of the Second Historical Archives of China, Nanjing.

of the period. He shared provincial origins with Wu Bingxiang, who had been deposed as police chief in late July for assisting members of the defeated Anhui faction in the war.[52] As head of Beijing's Anhui provincial lodge, or *huiguan*, a society for men from the province who lived in the capital, it was left to Jiang to oversee the disbandment of a meeting of forty-five men at the society's building in the capital when it was raided by police in the weeks following the Zhili-Anhui War.[53]

Nonetheless, Jiang managed to ally himself with the leaders of the Zhili faction that controlled Beijing in the early 1920s.[54] Moreover, like Wang, he combined a dedication to strong security measures with initiative and micromanagement regarding the concerns of the poor. Also like

Wang, Jiang was recognized in a stone stele inscription erected south of the capital for his efforts to safeguard communities there—in this case from bandit raids in the late 1910s. The stele, paid for by numerous small contributions, was erected in 1918 in Nanyuan, two years before the town's surrounding villages were looted by fleeing solders in July 1920. While the inscription has lost much of it legibility, the marker expresses the lamenting of members of a rural gentry elite about the rapid social and cultural changes brought by modernization and what some saw as the crumbling of an old moral order "at breakneck speed, sparing no town or village."[55]

In this ethical order, as described by the stele, for those who embodied virtue (de), "defense from calamity was their chief concern (shouwu), followed by fostering the people's livelihood and improving their welfare." Bandit raids brought not only violence and dispossession, but also the moral confusion that came with the destabilization or destruction of the Confucian family and the upending of social norms. It was in these terms that residents memorialized Jiang's antibandit forays into the capital's southern outskirts in the mid-1910s, expeditions in which he had accompanied garrison scouts and troops to Nanyuan, chatting with and "consoling" merchants he encountered on the roads. Afterward, communities in the environs of Nanyuan were able to "dwell in contentment and undisturbed security," which they commended with this stele to his "virtuous governance."[56]

After retiring from active military service, Jiang took leadership positions in a range of charitable and civic endeavors in addition to the Society for Awakening Goodness: the Grain Relief Society, which he founded with Wang Hu and Wang Huaiqing (discussed in chapter 2); the Temporary Steamed Corn Bread Society (Linshi wowotou hui), which he headed after the death in 1919 of its founder, Cheng Qiyuan, and which is discussed in chapter 4; a charity bank (cishan yinhang); and the Beijing Poor Children's Home (Beijing pin'er yuan) in the North City's Thousand Buddha Temple (Qianfosi), where he served as an honorary trustee (mingyu dongshi).[57]

Jiang and his charities were working in a changing culture of poor relief in which officials and charities increasingly sought to go beyond meeting the immediate needs of the destitute to longer-term strategies of poverty alleviation.[58] Credit often dried up in times of famine, even in urban centers where banks, pawnshops, and other lending institutions

were concentrated. In early January 1921, Jiang was behind the establishment of several low- or no-interest loan programs, efforts that both echoed
mutual aid practices of the past and anticipated the credit cooperatives
of the rural reconstruction movement of the late 1920s and 1930s.[59] Beginning in January, the charity bank "assisted families without means"
(*wu li zhi jia*) with small loans designed to help them "make a living."[60]
Police informed struggling households in their districts of the service—
the bank was open from ten o'clock to noon every day outside Qian gate
just to the south of Tiananmen Square—and "recently the poor," of whom
nothing was required to receive a loan apart from a guarantee from a shop-
keeper (*pubao*), had reportedly "come to the bank in an endless stream."[61]
Applicants could borrow one yuan with no interest, and repay the loan
in four installments over a period of fourteen days—after which, if their
debts were cleared, they could borrow again up to a maximum of ten
yuan. Interestingly, the purpose of half a dozen news reports on Jiang's
program was more to inform the public of the service than to draw attention to him as a charitable figure. Only one report mentions Jiang
by name as the initiator of the program; the rest identify the founder of
the bank only as a "major philanthropist" (*da cishan jia*).[62]

Similar credit programs appeared over the famine year around the
city, operating out of a fire god temple, a liquor and vinegar store, a middle
school, and other locations.[63] Some had lending capital of 10,000 yuan,
and most loaned money without interest.[64] It must not have been coin-
cidental that a majority of these microcredit initiatives had appeared in
January on the eve of the Lunar New Year, when debts were customarily
cleared and many financial institutions closed their doors. To solve this
problem, the Beijing municipal police issued a ban in early February 1921
on the closing of pawnshops across the city for the holiday so that credit
would be available to the city's poor through the remaining hard months
until the spring harvest—although it is unclear if or how this was enforced.[65] The timing of these microlending initiatives by the Society for
Awakening Goodness and others appears to have been designed to step
into the breach at a moment of tight credit.

Another cause Jiang took up was curtailing the mass slaughter or export of livestock in the surrounding famine districts by farmers who
were unable to feed their animals or in dire need of cash. During the fall
of 1920, the provincial and metropolitan governments issued orders to

magistrates to prohibit the export of livestock from their districts, while railway authorities along the Beijing-Hankou line reportedly enforced bans by the Ministry of Communications on the transport of livestock by rail.[66] Jiang began sending staff members into distressed villages in the environs of Beijing in October to buy up livestock and safeguard (*baoquan*) the animals over the winter in a pasture south of the capital so that they could be redeemed (*shuhui*) for working the fields in spring.[67]

One can only speculate about why Jiang took on these leading roles in charitable enterprises. The increasingly precarious position in which religious sects like his Society for Awakening Goodness found themselves may offer some explanation. Paul Katz has argued that social welfare programs served to legitimize religious organizations and their adherents in the 1910s and 1920s, when modern distinctions were drawn by Chinese political elites between "acceptable" religious faiths or ritual and "superstition" (*mixin*).[68] The charitable interventions by redemptive societies "secured them some degree of social and political acceptance" amid skepticism about their value to society and the nation, in the words of Vincent Goossaert.[69] While redemptive societies existed throughout the country, such bids for legitimacy were especially urgent in the north, where official destruction or seizure of temples in the preceding decade appears to have been more widely carried out.[70]

Conclusion

The amounts that these generals personally contributed to many of the relief acts above—in the case of Wang, 20,000 yuan to set up the Grain Relief Society and the money he provided to send twenty-seven refugee children to a nearby school—were often negligible in light of the riches they or their colleagues were known to have amassed at the time. So it would of course be misguided to overemphasize such contributions or initiatives in the lives of the struggling. But it is worth noting that, in his biographical sketch of a former boss whom he apparently knew for over thirty years, Zhao gives no indication that Wang did anything other than wage war, connive, and abscond with public monies.[71] Similarly, Li Lunbo, as staff advisor in Wang's Thirteenth Division, was in a prime position to observe any number of unscrupulous activities that his boss undertook, such as siphoning off salaries paid for troops that did not exist. But Li's essay on Wang pays no attention to any social concern or famine or welfare policy.[72] Zhao's piece appears in the same volume as an essay on Jiang Chaozong's career that is equally lacking any reference to the former general's charitable and civic endeavors, aside from a passing mention of his involvement in fighting a plague outbreak in Baotou through the Society for Awakening Goodness.[73] The *Cultural and Historical Miscellany* (*Wenshi ziliao*) collections in which these essays appear form part of an enormous corpus of personal memoirs and local knowledge of pre-1949 society that have been produced since the 1960s at all levels, from local communities upward. In this case, from the vantage point of the People's Republic, people associated in the 1920s Beijing press with a broad range of social and civic pursuits are reduced to caricatures—embodying, in Li's words, the "collective rotten breath of the Beiyang warlord clique."[74]

What is one to make of this? The few focused studies on the social programs of military figures in the republic have concerned cases associated either with Sun Yat-sen's republican experiment in Guangzhou in the 1910s and early 1920s or with the politics of the Nationalist Nanjing Decade. Alfred Lin has shown how such programs in 1930s Guangzhou stemmed from Sun's Three Principles of the People, in particular their emphasis on popular livelihood (*minsheng*), which had inspired a "new awareness" in Chinese politics of the connection between social policies and the modern nation-state.[75]

Recognizing the role of these two generals in the shift toward skills training and credit programs blurs any artificial dichotomy or distinction between traditional and reformist, progressive, or modern poor relief actors. Welfare provisioning and livelihood programs could just as readily be inspired by social visions oriented toward the past as they could by forward-looking modernization drives. Social welfare in the republic was of course not the preserve of reformists and modernizers, or of noted Confucian reformist intellectuals in the style of Liang Shuming, for example.[76] The personal interventions that we have seen the capital's serving and retired garrison commanders make during 1920–21 demonstrate the extent to which governance a decade into the republic could be informed by inherited models. While there is no doubt that succoring the poor and the resulting publicity could provide political benefits for any political type, the fact that these men devoted considerable amounts of time, energies, and resources to the commoner population does not square with understandings of military governance or even of society generally at the time. We now turn to the broader arena of charitable activity in which these men operated.

CHAPTER FOUR

Cigarettes, Opera, and
Religious Sects

In mid-September 1920, a couple from the southern environs of Beijing appeared in the capital's suburbs with their eight-year-old son and placed a wisp of straw in his hair—a sign used to indicate that a child was for sale. It had been seven weeks since the forces of Wu Peifu had routed the Anhui army in the family's home district of Zhuozhou along the rail line running up from central China. After that, persisting drought and a plague of locusts had further devastated their agricultural district. Their asking price was four yuan.[1]

Woodblock prints depicting the sale of children and young women had become iconic images of disaster as early as the Ming period. They had been used by scholar-officials in memorials to the throne on disaster policy or in booklets bearing witness to famine.[2] As recently as the great northern famine of the 1870s, which had struck in a period when the modern Chinese press was first taking shape, drawings of family members sold at doorsteps and the cruelties inflicted on those trafficked out of the famine districts circulated in China's coastal cities and as far away as London. Soon the exploitation of females in particular became a sign to some of the breakdown of the Confucian social order. To others, the exchange of people was a disgrace to a Chinese nation emerging from the waning Qing dynasty, in the aftermath of two defeats by Britain in the 1840s and 1850s and a series of catastrophic rebellions. Graphic reports and images of human sales and unspeakable suffering hundreds of miles away moved people to initiate or contribute to aid campaigns for the north.[3]

In Beijing in 1920, as poverty rates tripled at the outset of the famine in late summer, suffering was more immediate, even at times right next door. The dramatic reports of family bonds torn apart through sales in market squares served as repeated calls for action by the members of Beijing society with sufficient resources to weather the food crisis themselves. This mass distress presented opportunities for a wide array of responses. Some people in Beijing participated in the wider cause of disaster aid by publicizing the famine or making contributions large and small in response to fund-raising drives. As winter approached, buildings, their porticos, and restaurants around the capital boosted giving by hanging banners "arousing the charitable spirit" (*yinqi cishan xin*) in both Chinese and English.[4]

Fund-raising by small businesses and merchant associations for disaster victims elsewhere in China was of course nothing new. At least as early as the 1870s, the gentry and merchant communities in towns and cities of the lower Yangzi region had donated enormous sums to relieve drought-famine in the north.[5] Benevolent halls were another source of charity in the late imperial period that carried over into the republic. Historians have traced the emergence of these charitable associations to sixteenth-century Henan; their subsequent growth in the commercial centers of central China; and their appearance in Beijing in the late 1700s, where they were often founded by residents who had come from distant parts of the country.[6] In 1920, we find benevolent halls continuing to perform charitable services, generally in the modest volumes reflective of their local character. And they appeared to concentrate on so-called outdoor relief—doorstep distributions of clothing or tickets to redeem for grain performed outside the confines of charity workhouses, shelters, or other institutions.[7]

Here, our main aim is to sketch newer, different types of social welfare activism appearing within, or just beyond, the walls of Beijing in the early 1920s, as well as the forms of social or civic organization that underpinned them. This presents a range of possible subjects to cover, a number of which have already been capably handled by historians. There is the scholar-official turned professional philanthropist, a type most notably exemplified in Xiong Xiling (discussed in chapter 1), a member of the Hunan gentry who rose to prominence in national politics in the 1910s before turning to the management of flood relief and an orphan home in the Western Hills of Beijing in the 1920s.[8] Then there are new modern-style institutions that appeared in Chinese cities at the beginning of the twentieth century, such as the chamber of commerce, whose civic activism in republican Beijing and famine relief in neighboring Tianjin have been examined by David Strand and Ren Yunlan, respectively.[9] On the broader culture of charity in early twentieth-century Beijing, Wang Juan has shown how the increasing volume of activity in the city accompanied both a transformation in management style and professionalization and a shift from providing emergency assistance to targeting poverty's root causes through skills training and employment programs.[10] Taking this development a step further, Janet Chen has demonstrated how changing attitudes and policies toward the poor by officials and elites in twentieth-century Beijing and Shanghai led to a shift away from free "outdoor" assistance to methods that involved incarceration and criminalization of the poor.[11]

Building on these previous works, I turn to three additional, and less studied, areas of charitable activity in republican Beijing. First is the work of industrialist tycoons, the modern successors to the fabulously rich salt merchants of the imperial era who had been known for their lavish contributions to official relief efforts and their sponsorship of bridges, schools, and other public services. Here I look at the charities of big business through the role of the tobacco industry in times of famine. This offers the chance to consider disaster relief not only as a vehicle for social prestige for merchants, but also as an instrument of business strategy amid the fierce competition and economic nationalism of the republican era. I also touch on the role of the wife of the founder of the Nanyang Brothers Tobacco Company to see the ways in which the contributions of high-society women to the charitable sector were not only substantial but also readily obscured in the sources.

I then return to the Society for the Awakening of Goodness, the religious sect headed by the former gendarmerie commandant Jiang Chaozong, which worked with other charities and figures in the city's theater scene to hold relief benefit performances over the famine year. When studying social networking and civic activity in early twentieth-century China, Western researchers in particular have overlooked sectarian organizations and temple cults in favor of native-place, kin-based, or occupational forms of association. Paul Katz laments this neglect in the literature of what amounted to "one of the most important realms of public activity in late imperial and modern Chinese communities."[12] The fact that the Society for the Awakening of Goodness was one of the most active social welfare charities in 1920s Beijing reveals the considerable lengths to which sectarian groups went to adapt to the changing social and political climate of the republic, seeking legitimacy amid growing doubts about the utility of religious practice to society and the nation. I end by sketching aid activity across the city at the micro level, such as household and individual acts, capturing day-to-day assistance between neighbors or strangers at the street level. These local actions were remarkably varied in who performed them, and surprisingly large in scale, yet they are the most likely types of relief to be left out of historical accounts due to their informal and fleeting nature.

Who were the recipients of private largesse? Conventional wisdom at the time, at least among members of the influential foreign community, held that Chinese charity was limited to kinship networks. "Much will be done by a Chinaman to save his own family, but further than that his sympathies do not extend," a missionary in Beijing explained to his fellow Americans in 1926. "But let that son be another man's, and few will offer a copper to aid him, or even a cash to give him a decent burial."[13] The idea that personal connections were an essential part of China's culture of charity remains largely untested in scholarship. Until the 2000s, historians provided little in English on Chinese charitable codes and practices.[14] In the introduction to her 2009 monograph on charity in late Ming China, Joanna Handlin Smith notes that hers is the first book-length study in English of premodern Chinese charity since a thin academic volume was published in 1912.[15] The study of charity and disaster in China's past has advanced considerably, but not enough to truly test such a commonly held belief among foreign residents a century ago.[16] Of course, missionaries had particular motivations for depicting a native society bereft of certain values and modes of behavior. Yet the sources informing this chapter give little indication that native-place affiliation or other types of qualifications were criteria for charitable assistance. Instead, it appears that charitable assistance was generally given without condition beyond, in most cases, proof of need. Despite the intensity of charitable activity in and around the Chinese capital, the philanthropist (*cishan jia*) who appears throughout the pages of the Chinese press at the time has vanished from sketches of republican city life. Rethreading this figure into the period's social fabric is what this chapter sets out to do.

Big Tobacco and Famine

As in any crisis, famine was a chance for shops and larger firms to associate themselves with wider civic or humanitarian causes. Public welfare measures figured among the marketing strategies for cigarette firms facing the fierce competition in the tobacco industry in the early twentieth century. In the first stages of the famine, the manager of the Shanghai-based Dachang Tobacco Company sponsored the transportation of several hundred children from famine districts in Henan to Shanghai for skills training in workshops.[17] And a Beijing-based tobacco firm approached the police and gendarmerie leaders with a proposal to have refugees hawk its Longevity brand cigarettes as a form of work relief (*yigong daizhen*).[18]

But it was British-American Tobacco (BAT) and Nanyang Brothers, the two biggest players in the industry at the time, who were most directly involved in dispensing famine aid in greater Beijing. In the years leading up to the famine, the two companies had become significant influences on the cultural and social life of the country. The place of tobacco in modern China went well beyond serving as a mass-produced recreational drug. In the early twentieth century, cigarette advertising had come to serve both as a major source of revenue for the country's growing newspaper and magazine industries and as a medium for the dissemination of modern fashions, gender ideals, and symbols of budding Chinese nationalism.[19]

BAT, an alliance between American and British tobacco firms, had reigned supreme in the Chinese market for mass-produced cigarettes since its arrival in the country in 1902. Under its American director of Chinese operations, the company penetrated deep into the country's interior markets from its Shanghai headquarters. BAT was known for its aggressive and creative marketing strategies, which ranged from plastering communities with colorful advertising to stationing tellers of folktales in harbors along the seaboard and inland rivers, coached by the company's

Chinese employees to put product plugs in the tales they recounted to passing crowds as boats landed.[20] Since before the fall of the Qing in 1911, monthly camel caravans loaded with BAT cigarettes had trod the same routes to Zhangjiakou and other areas beyond the Great Wall from which relief grain would be sped southward in 1920–21. State-of-the-art printing presses imported by the company into China after 1905 produced thousands of posters and billboards destined for major cities deep in China's afflicted interior, such as Kaifeng and Xi'an, and would greet the thousands of people who fled famine and arrived in Manchuria by boat in the treaty port of Yingkou (Newchwang) during 1920–21, a flow examined in chapter 8.[21]

In October 1920, the manager of BAT's Beijing office, an Englishman named C. H. Page, began plans for the firm to establish its own soup kitchen facility in the eastern suburbs.[22] The firm was by no means alone in this private undertaking. Although they were major undertakings involving the management of crowds numbering from hundreds to several thousands of vulnerable men, women, and children, soup kitchens were set up not only by municipal agencies, as discussed in chapter 2, but also by a variety of group or individual private actors over the famine year. The relief group cofounded by Xiong, the Relief Society for the Five Northern Provinces (Beiwusheng xieji hui), established a soup kitchen and a shelter on the grounds of a shuttered glass factory, sending out canvassers to all parts of the city to hand out entry cards to refugees and the poor.[23] Village gentry in the southern outskirts of the capital collected small donations from 125 people to operate a facility through the winter there.[24] And a native of nearby Wuqing county, who had stepped down as deputy head of the army the year before, acquired 1,600 *jin* of rice early in January 1921 to dispense as porridge in the alley beside his residence in west Beijing, a service he apparently provided to the area's poor each winter.[25]

Despite the company's formidable resources and energies, however, the BAT operation would struggle to get off the ground. For a month the bricks had been laid for the kitchen set up on the grounds of a Buddhist temple east of the city, yet no food was being served—although hundreds of people reportedly came to check each day to see if it was open yet, which headlines deemed an "injustice to the poor."[26] When BAT's facility was finally operating on November 24, management kept to the old portions of 2.5 *liang* (roughly four hundred calories) for the thousand adults it served and turned away another thousand who had come from as far as three miles away.[27] Page had apparently complained to the official Soup Kitchen Provisioning Bureau about the time consumed by the daily personal inspections he was required to perform at the facility and dispatched instead a native comprador to oversee the operation in his place.[28] This move was followed by a widely published report on irregularities in accounting and procedures, and the discovery by Wang Huaiqing's soup kitchen monitors that graft by the Chinese inspector was behind the remarkably low number of servings.[29] When, a week after opening, the facility's 1,700–1,800 attendees were still receiving a mere two *liang*—a month after the Ministry of the Interior had stipulated a quadrupling of grain serving minimums at city soup kitchens—internal correspondence at the bureau determined that the operation was "very much against the idea of charity" (*shushi cishan benyi*), and one paper declared that the operation did "not merit the name" of a charitable organization.[30] On December 13, after three weeks of operation, BAT's soup kitchen shut down, and the gendarmerie took over its operation the following day.[31]

It is possible that BAT's operation was singled out for criticism in the local press due, in part, to its foreign origin. Yet the company had successfully weathered a boycott of American goods in 1905–6 that had targeted its goods specifically, and its sales had boomed since the last quarter of 1919.[32] More likely it was simply that the company's lackluster and half-hearted venture simply did not match its otherwise energetic marketing genius.

In fact, Nanyang Brothers, BAT's main domestic rival, was the target of more concerted bad press in Canton, Shanghai, and especially Beijing. And perhaps not coincidentally, Nanyang Brothers would also become considerably more involved in famine relief over the year. Founded by a Cantonese family, the company had cut its teeth in Hong Kong, where it built its first factory in 1905, and then extended into Southeast Asia before entering the mainland Chinese market in 1915 and quickly maturing into a full-fledged competitor of BAT.[33]

The negative press experienced by Nanyang Brothers was largely a function of the Japanese affiliations of its founder and director, Jian Zhaonan (1870–1923). Following the anti-Japanese boycott of 1915, and under renewed pressure amid the protest movement following the Treaty of Versailles's handing of German possessions in Shandong over to Japan, Jian had renounced his Japanese citizenship in mid-May 1919. Later that summer, Jian's license to do business in China was nonetheless revoked briefly, following a campaign by prominent politicians in Beijing who claimed the company's registration was invalid. Nanyang Brothers was still a newcomer in the North China market, having first had a real presence there only in 1916–17, and the company turned to charity in the drought districts of the north.[34]

Famine relief was one part of a larger field of intense commercial competition, but it clearly figured in the jousting between players in the tobacco industry, including younger firms eager to break into the market. In the style of super-rich salt dealers who had served as major contributors to official disaster relief initiatives in the imperial period, Jian, as a well-known tycoon and philanthropist, spent hundreds of thousands of yuan each year on flood relief, public health, and other charitable pursuits.[35] In September 1920, he decided to donate five yuan to famine relief for each box of cigarettes the company sold, up to a maximum of 100,000 yuan, and his company worked with a newly formed relief fundraising alliance of local merchants in the major market of Shanghai to keep track of the revenue from sales in the city.[36] Not to be outdone, the manager of the Shanghai-based Xingye Tobacco Company—an aggressive upstart that, according to Jian, had hired youths to distribute fliers and posters in the Shanghai region identifying Nanyang Brothers as a Japanese firm—donated 100,000 yuan for relief in Henan.[37] As if in direct response, the following month managers at Nanyang Brothers made it known they were devoting their annual mid-autumn festival banquet budget of 190 yuan to relief efforts.[38] Before long, as far away as Manchuria, the Nanyang Brothers' local office initiated a campaign that affixed famine awareness posters on doors throughout neighborhoods to "stir up the emotions" of the charitable so that they would send money to the famine field—doubtless done with a dose of marketing savvy.[39]

Nanyang Brothers used proceeds from its fund-raising drive to open a soup kitchen in the eastern suburbs of Beijing, in districts that had been ravaged by the war earlier in the year and the ensuing devastation wrought by drought and locusts, and the company added a second facility nearby in December that served several thousand people a day.[40] The firm had considerable experience in providing direct disaster relief, starting with highly publicized flood aid in Jian's native Canton in 1915 and including the distribution of rice vouchers to poor households in the Pudong district across the river from Shanghai earlier in the summer.[41] Soon the company expanded its operations, establishing a shelter and soup kitchen facility at the rail interchange at Fengtai, south of Beijing, where the lines south to Hankou and Pukou (via Tianjin) met. Both lines ran through the drought zone, making the suburb a major transit point for thousands of famine migrants a day. The facility hosted several thousand refugees, male and female, old and young, in a hundred rooms, starting in mid-November.[42] Members of the gentry and merchant circles of Fengtai issued a public notice announcing the opening of the facility and encouraging relief workers and officials in the famine areas to direct any famine migrants heading to unafflicted districts beyond the Great Wall to take advantage of the facility as they passed through, lest the penniless among them "roam about aimlessly" (*liuli shisuo*).[43]

The rivalry between China's two biggest tobacco firms of the era peaked in the early 1920s. The year before the 1920 famine, both BAT and Nanyang Brothers had spent enormous sums on advertising to associate their brands with the symbols of the May Fourth Movement and harness the protest movement's nationalist energies. Surprisingly, the Anglo-American company did so with greater success, experiencing a boom in sales later in 1919, while Nanyang Brothers' sales slumped.[44] But over the course of 1920–21, as ads for their respective iconic brand cigarettes, Hatamen and Great Wall, faced off in the pages of magazines published by major famine relief societies such as *Jiuzai zhoukan*, on another level the companies' fortunes reversed themselves.[45] BAT's venture into dispensing aid in the Chinese capital foundered, earning the more dominant company negative press, while charitable operations of the otherwise beleaguered Nanyang Brothers expanded and sustained thousands of people through the famine year, a fact spread by far-reaching publicity.

The example of Nanyang Brothers money going into relief does not end with its director. Jian was joined by his wife, Pan Jinong, who was evidently a presence behind the scenes in the company's philanthropic endeavors. Here the dynamic resembles that between the philanthropist couple Xiong and Zhu Qihui, touched upon in chapter 1—one in which female contributions to civic initiatives and enterprises are overshadowed by those of their male counterparts. As Xia Shi has shown, Zhu's instrumental role as mastermind and chief fund-raiser for the influential Mass Education Movement of the 1920s remains almost completely forgotten, while her male collaborators in the progressive movement received all the credit.[46] Remarkably, Zhu was able to achieve this while presiding over an extensive range of charitable and civic activities.[47] In the case of Nan-yang Brothers, Pan was similarly engaged with a number of charitable and civic causes at the time—although press sources offer only glimpses of her involvement, while her male collaborators' activities are easier to trace. Pan was approached by a man active in Beijing charities, Li Qing-fang (1879– ?), a native of Shanxi province who had earned a law degree in Japan a decade before.[48] The pairing of the two made sense, as it com-bined Pan's formidable wealth and connections with Li's experience in presiding over a portfolio of charity initiatives in Beijing, some of which were considered particularly innovative in the press. These included the creation of an "unemployment office" (*shiye jieshaosuo*) in the first few months of the famine crisis to advise and connect the jobless with poten-tial employers—a service that had reportedly helped forty to fifty people find "gainful employment" in its first ten days of operation.[49] And on the eve of winter, Li proposed to the Ministry of the Interior that it create a series of state-funded "public cafeterias" (variously named *pingmin shi-tang* or *gonggong shitang*) in the city's labyrinth of lanes and incoming highways where night soil carriers, street sweepers, and others among the city's estimated 100,000 outdoor laborers could eat in more salubrious and "hygienic" (*weisheng*) conditions than on the street.[50] While the fate of Li's proposal is unclear, a privately run "commoners cafeteria" (*ping-min gonggong shitang*), possibly related to Li's initiative, did appear in early 1921 in the western suburbs, selling steamed buns, corn bread, and millet porridge at half price to struggling peddlers and the general poor at three locations during daylight hours, reportedly at no profit—or, as some re-ports put it, "half sold, half given away" (*banshou banshe zhi yi*).[51]

Li had a different idea when he approached Pan in December: he re-quested that she sponsor the establishment of a shelter intended to pro-tect solitary refugee girls from human traffickers and the brothel system.[52] Institutions for girls and young women were widespread at the time, both due to the emphasis of progressive officials and missionaries in particular on increasing female education and industrial work and as a way of stem-ming the flow of females into the sex trade.[53]

Pan and Li's shelter joined a group of institutions for women specifically that were opened by municipal authorities and philanthropists over the famine year, including several in the capital and suburbs that offered classes in writing and handicrafts to solitary and jobless women with no means of support.[54] Many of these institutions shared characteristics with the work-houses or so-called industrial homes that increased in popularity through-out the first half of the twentieth century. Homes designed expressly for females at risk of entering the sex trade or those who had left brothels or other sites of prostitution were generally limited in capacity. For example, in August 1919, the Door of Hope, a police-run home in Beijing for "at-risk" females, had sixty-five residents, women mostly ages 16–25 who could leave only if they married or were adopted by relatives willing to support them.[55]

The shelter sponsored by Pan was somewhat larger, designed to house two hundred girls ages 6–13 on temple grounds lent by the Ministry of the Interior. Pan would provide the funds, and Li—a politically well-connected figure who would later head the provincial police bureau of Shanxi—would both handle relations with the local authorities and pro-vide experience for the day-to-day running of the shelter.[56] Initially the plan was to bring in forty refugee girls from each of the five affected prov-inces and house them for the eight months until the harvest in spring.[57] However, a report later described the shelter as housing 197 girls from south Zhili alone, the region hit hardest by the drought-famine.[58]

The modest numbers of girls taken in by such efforts, even together with police or private interventions, could not come close to preventing the circulation of young women and children, especially in the crisis econ-omy brought on by famine. The extent to which female refugees contrib-uted to the ranks of Beijing's estimated ten thousand legal or clandestine prostitutes or ended up at establishments beyond the city can only be left to conjecture.[59] Similarly, the extent to which Pan and other women were behind this and other initiatives discussed in this chapter, and lamenta-bly, elsewhere in this study is only occasionally hinted at by the sources.

Opera, Charity, and Religious Sects

One might assume that the women entering the brothels, cabarets, and teahouses of Beijing were insulated from the disaster unfolding in the surrounding districts. But conversation on current events undoubtedly went on between the women and their clients and among each other, leading at times into social interventions. A fund-raising collective of prostitutes, euphemistically named the Relief Aid Society of All Kinds of Flowers (Qunfang zhuzhen hui), publicized a series of musical performances of what a newspaper advertisement pitched as "old and new numbers" for the benefit of a relief fund at a large hall starting in December.[60] Similar events were held by prostitutes over the year in Shanghai.[61] The extent to which such endeavors were promotional affairs designed by management is unclear. But there is no reason to doubt that the women and girls who participated in them, whether or not they were the initiators, were combining their own experience of deprivation in villages in the region with a sense of contribution to Beijing society's wider effort against hunger.

The capital's art and entertainment scene had a record of supporting local charities stretching back into the late Qing, when in 1906 opera stars donated their fees for performances at a charity benefit to fund girls' education.[62] Over the winter of 1920–21, this custom continued as various parts of the industry provided charities with a regular flow of funds for efforts to help both the local poor and famine migrants, from ticket sales to acrobatic shows around the city to the capital's Beijing opera scene. As a recreational activity and spectacle drawing huge crowds to the city's twenty-two regular-sized theaters, most in the South City, staged dramas could generate substantial proceeds for charitable causes.

The No. 1 Theater, the capital's premier theatrical venue, could seat a thousand, and premium tickets ranged from eight yuan for a box to thirty cents for the cheapest seat. There in September, within a month of official recognition of famine conditions across the region, the Beijing opera star Mei Lanfang (1894–1961) organized two days' worth of opera fund-raisers for the relief of drought-famine in Zhili, Henan, and Shandong. Stars commanded 100–300 yuan for a performance and could generate considerable sums at the time.[63] Mei, the most influential figure on China's modern stage, was in a league of his own: four American bankers had paid him $4,000 for a half-hour's private performance the year before.[64] In September he was joined by Chen Delin and other actors in a performance before a packed audience, raising 3,015 yuan in ticket sales and an additional 1,500 yuan in donations for the benefit of an unspecified relief fund.[65] At the same performance was none other than Pan of Nanyang Brothers. Along with another female socialite, she raised 800 yuan in additional relief monies by selling cigarettes to those in attendance.[66]

Through the figure of Mei—who, then age twenty-six, was finishing an eight-month residency at a city theater—we can get a snapshot of various segments of Beijing society seldom considered together: the theater, the military, religious sects, and people struggling to survive a disastrous winter.[67] Mei continued to appear on the bill for fund-raising performances over the year, including a benefit with fellow stars Gong Yunfu (1862–1932), Tan Xiaopei (1883–1953), and Yang Xiaolou (1877–1938) for the City Poor Relief Society (Jingshi pinmin jiuji hui) at the No. 1 Theater in October.[68] (The society, led by Li Zhongkai, devoted monies to clothing and grain distribution over the winter, along with 2,500 yuan for the creation of a temporary credit assistance office [*linshi daizhu chu*] for small peddlers at the Lunar New Year.)[69] Later, in March, Mei performed at a relief benefit held by the association of Beijing residents who were from the three northeastern provinces, staged at the Fengtian *huiguan* in Beijing.[70] And his involvement with the fund-raising efforts of Jiang Chaozong's Society for Awakening Goodness reveals the intersection of the city's theater scene with its military and religious circles.

The stated goal of the society's periodical, *Lingxue yaozhi*, which it launched in September 1920, was the "encouragement of morality among all of mankind through showing mercy and compassion" to the downtrodden (*yi zai daci dabei, shi shiren daode*).[71] Fortunately, intense press coverage provides a glimpse into the group's varied activities. In January 1921, the society teamed up with the Temporary Steamed Corn Bread Society, a group, also led by Jiang, based in a city benevolent hall that had raised money each winter over the previous seven years for the distribution of corn meal to the city's poor. Together, the two groups secured the support of Mei, who gave two evening performances at the No. 1 Theater in January.[72] Proceeds from these shows went to support food distribution around the city, including meal tickets for 30,000 *jin* of corn meal to impoverished bannermen households in the western suburbs.[73]

On its own, the Society for Awakening Goodness had begun handing out corn meal tickets to destitute households around Beijing as early as the July war, and as the famine developed in late summer, the group intensified its activities and appeared to take the lead in what would become a citywide field of at least fifteen charity relief agencies operating in the city and suburbs through the winter.[74] With the arrival of cold weather in October, the society opened a warming facility (*nuanchang*) for refugees with ten rooms in a temple outside Desheng gate, which was reportedly "packed to the brim not long after opening," and by the end of the month construction was under way on three additional ten-room warming facilities outside other city gates.[75] In December and January, members of the society distributed clothes, coppers, and corn meal tickets on consecutive days outside half a dozen city gates; in one case, each person received two or three *jin* of grain and a set of clothes.[76] At times, the group entrusted its relief goods to the authorities, including 1,600 items of clothing it gave to the army in January for soldiers to allocate to the poor west of the city.[77] The group also provisioned privately run soup kitchens, sending 120 *shi* of grain to a member of the merchant gentry class who had set up a facility for the swelling numbers of destitute in his village west of Beijing in midwinter.[78]

Like many charities, the society continued to tap into the city's art and entertainment scene for funds, with a well-publicized campaign over several days in October at five locations around the city.[79] Included were the South City Amusement Park by the Temple of Heaven and the New World, "a sort of miniature 'Coney Island'" of Western-style complexes modeled on versions built earlier in Shanghai by Chinese merchants in the 1910s.[80] In places more accustomed to staging performances of comic cross talk and carnival-style games, the society hung drawings depicting the "various afflictions" (*suoshou zhongzhong ku*) suffered by famine victims over the counters as staffers solicited donations from passersby.[81]

Donors to the group's fund-raising campaign were later thanked in a central government weekly gazette, which printed a lengthy list of names that gave a good idea of the social, institutional, and regional diversity of the group's supporters.[82] From this it becomes clear that the society was able to draw support from a national network and various social circles. The fact that it had been founded and was led by Jiang, a former general, illustrates the degree to which military circles at the time overlapped with religious and philanthropic ones.

Individual Charitable Interventions

The winter of 1920–21 was no ordinary one, and it quickly stretched thin the capital's existing municipal services and charities. "Relief societies are too slow to rescue" those suffering on the streets, a Beijing paper lamented in November.[83] Afterward, calls for more vigilance in the giving of relief appeared in news stories covering the appearance of more dead in the streets.[84] "The great number of charities this year and their formidable distribution of clothes and grain have been overwhelmed by the sheer volume of the poor this year," remarked another paper when a "young beggar" (*xiao qigai*), aged seventeen or eighteen, was found dead from exposure in a west Beijing lane later in January.[85]

The numbers of corpses found on the street over the winter of 1920–21 made it clear that thousands were still falling through the cracks of the shelter system. It should be stressed that the gruesome presence of dead bodies in city streets was hardly absent from news accounts and was discussed more widely in the Beijing press around 1920 than existing scholarship would suggest. In his study of abandoned corpses in republican Shanghai, Christian Henriot finds that "the press, Chinese or foreign, actually rarely addressed the problem" and that coverage of the "high incidence of exposed corpses and abandoned coffins" began in the treaty port in earnest only in the 1930s.[86] Throughout the 1920s, by contrast, newspapers in the Chinese capital regularly noted the appearance of corpses on the streets, bodies that by law were to be inspected by the Beijing procuracy—an office that was a product of the New Policy reforms in the final decade of the Qing. However, close surveillance of deaths across the city and data collection about them by city authorities were not instituted until the mid-1920s, so the numbers of the dead were a source of debate.[87]

On the last day of 1920, the daily *Zhongguo minbao* reported a dispute between the daily *Yishi bao* and the central government over the numbers of deaths to exposure across the city since the onset of full-fledged famine. *Yishi bao* had put the figure at 4,200 dead by mid-November, or an average of roughly 1,400 each month since the famine had begun in earnest toward the end of August. However, the Ministry of the Interior disputed the figure as too high, based on information it received from the soup kitchen bureau, which was jointly run by the police and gendarmerie, but in its rebuttal, reported in *Zhongguo minbao*, the ministry did not offer an alternative estimate.[88] Continuing its Qing-era duties of tallying, identifying, and disposing of the capital's corpses, the gendarmerie appears to have taken the lead in burying those who died in public spaces in 1920, followed by officials from Daxing and Wanping, Beijing's two adjacent rural counties whose jurisdictions met within the city walls.[89] We can get a sense of how many bodies the gendarmerie was handling two months later, in the heart of winter, when the bureau issued a total of 467 wooden coffins for the burial of unclaimed or nameless disaster victims (374 who had died in the city's streets, and 93 who had died in the city's inns) over the course of a month starting in mid-January. Curiously, the report describes all the corpses as male.[90]

As official shelters reached capacity in midwinter, patrolmen were reportedly at a loss for places to send migrants they encountered in the streets.[91] Four relief societies and city charities had responded to the threatened shortage by opening eleven of their own shelters, most of them outside the city walls.[92] But shelters were also opened by individuals, including a woman who responded to rising rents and growing female homelessness by setting up a guesthouse for poor women without families in late summer with 800 yuan of her own capital. The guesthouse was to be located at the Temple of the Moon (Yuetan), and to stay there would cost a copper a night.[93] In addition, in mid-October a man described as a member of the city gentry gathered funds to establish a shelter for the poor at the city's Green Dragon Bridge (Qinglongqiao), offering coal-heated rooms and tea, although no food (residents were to fetch food elsewhere in the daytime and return for night lodging).[94] And in a village west of the city wall another member of the gentry established three temporary shelters, serving warm tea (also no food).[95] Finally, toward the end of winter, two philanthropists responded to the rising number of destitute on the capital's streets by establishing two shelters, one each for men and women.[96]

As the crisis intensified over the winter, city residents also engaged in outdoor relief of their own, appearing at soup kitchens with provisions and handing out cash to supplement what attendees received from the authorities. Lone donors spotted by news reporters over the course of one month included a Buddhist nun, an army officer, and the students at the city's No. 7 elementary school (using coppers saved from economizing with their lunch money).[97] At street corners and city gates, both men and women—refusing in some cases to identify themselves to reporters—offered coins or tickets for grain and coal to the crowds.[98] In city temples others gave bulk donations of coppers, clothes, and grain tickets redeemable at local grain shops.[99] In each case, distributions varied in volume, though many reached several thousand *jin* of grain or coal.

The scale of these private efforts could create havoc. One December afternoon, a servant and an escort of soldiers accompanied a woman, identified as the daughter of the director of the Beijing mint, into a temple in the eastern suburbs where, for three hours, they distributed corn meal tickets and coppers to more than 13,000 people. As people received three *jin* of flour each, or anywhere from two to ten coppers, the scene became so disorderly that one woman had a miscarriage and an older woman was trampled.[100]

Delivery of relief goods directly to poor households appeared to be more orderly than that in public locations. Some people entrusted distribution to the authorities, especially of large volumes of goods. This included one man who donated 8,000 yuan of his own money in late February and raised another 5,000 yuan, for a total of 13,000 yuan—which, while remaining anonymous, he passed on to Wang's office for distribution around the city by gendarmes. This was enough money to purchase, at discount grain center prices, a *jin* of grain for a full third of the city's population.[101]

Others chose to personally distribute goods to households in their community, though still with security details of gendarmes. One of the first of these visits to appear in the press at the outset of the 1920 food crisis occurred in summer in one of the city's more impoverished areas. The destitute comprised about a fifth of the residents in the district of Houhai, an area of small lakes just west of the Bell and Drum Towers, which was also in the heavily Manchu (or Tartar) northern section of the city (fig. 5). From Houhai, one could walk to the district's poorer suburban counterpart through Desheng gate, passing sugar shops, the stalls of a toy market (one of three in the city at the time), and a cluster of two prisons on the way.[102] It was there, just beyond the city's north wall, that in mid-August 1920 a man identified as a member of the local

FIGURE 5. A street scene in Beijing's North (Manchu /Tartar) City. Donald Minnie and Putnam Weale, *The Pageant of Peking, Comprising Sixty-Six Vandyck Photogravures of Peking and Environs from Photographs* (Shanghai: A. S. Watson, 1920).

gentry purchased 300 *bao* (or 48,000 *jin*) of rice and, escorted by gendarmes, handed out five *jin* of rice—equal to ten days' worth of relief rations—to 9,600 residents of his district.[103]

Some families instead dispensed goods straight from their home. In a suburban neighborhood outside Anding gate, a little over a mile to the east, the Chen household summoned gendarmes to their compound in November to oversee the distribution of 5,700 cotton outfits and 10,800 Beijing *diao*, or 108,000 coppers, to the area's poor, enough money to purchase 21,600 *jin* of grain at local grain discount centers. The Chen family, purveyors of Mongolian goods, reportedly handed out "huge sums" of relief items "every year" to the district poor: cotton clothes, coal, corn meal, and medicine, and they followed this distribution in 1920 with a distribution of 800 items of new cotton clothing to the poor in the vicinity of their home on November 24 and 25, clothes reportedly specially ordered for the occasion.[104]

There were also more spontaneous and impulsive gestures. In the imperial city at the very core of Beijing was the home of Yang Xiuqin, who a month later reportedly broke into the family safe while her father, Yang Tianji (1882–1958), a secretary at the State Council (Guowuyuan), was out on an errand, and took 100 yuan. Dashing outside to convert it to coppers, the girl handed out fifty coppers each to the nearby poor, potentially ten days' worth of relief rations for three hundred people, before returning home to a father "nearly vexed to death by it" (*chadianer qisi*).[105]

Conclusion

Beijing in the 1920s was a city in which both foreign and Chinese researchers in the new field of sociology were diagnosing social ills and root causes of poverty, laying the groundwork for the social engineering programs later under the Nationalists. The departure point for Janet Chen's important study of this development—the incarceration of the "most unproductive elements in society"—was a homeless boy picked up on the streets of Beijing in 1922 in the wake of the famine and sent to a workhouse. These institutions were a sign of what Chen identifies as a "major shift in approaches to poor relief" that had been under way since the last few years of the Qing, when in 1905 officials had moved to replace long-standing city soup kitchen and shelter institutions with a system of poorhouses. Chen sets this development against a "backdrop of expansive private charity after the turn of the century," into which "the Qing state (and its successors) also directed resources to new institutions that combined relief with punishment."[106]

The study of modern Chinese charity has tended to focus on such examples of institutional relief, performed by native-place associations or through so-called indoor methods, such as workhouses, orphanages, and homes for widows.[107] Part of the reason for scholarly attention to these methods is the fact that institutions tend to leave behind more detailed records of their operation than individual or temporary efforts do. This institutional focus has in turn shaped our understanding of the terms and values underpinning the administration of Chinese charity. While considering the relationship between native-place ties and personal connections and social welfare provisioning, Bryna Goodman has noted that it was a "common principle in the practice of charity" to provide "letters of introduction from guarantors" before being admitted or served in early republican Shanghai. This was evidently the case with particular types of charity, and with shelters and schools in particular, where admission was for a longer term. But Goodman's broader claim that "networks were necessary for charitable assistance" does not seem to apply to many of the Beijing cases examined here or in previous chapters.[108]

The food subsidy and outdoor relief practices of the republic's imperial predecessors continued to be a central part of welfare provisioning across Beijing in 1920–21, and judging by the volumes of people they affected, these practices were likely farther-reaching than the indoor relief provided by orphanages and other institutional charities. There is, of course, the possibility that a number of the charitable programs mentioned here came with conditions of native-place, bannermen, or other affiliations that were left out of the news coverage. Yet more often than not, the only condition to find its way into news stories on charitable relief in Beijing around 1920 was that recipients be considered vulnerable or unable to provide for themselves, however that might have been determined. In this respect, the capital was not necessarily different from Shanghai. In a survey from 1917, a professor at St. John's University in Shanghai noted that there were "over 40 native relief agencies and charitable institutions in this city," which "receive applicants without distinction of native place or trade," most of them using "outdoor" methods.[109]

Similarly, the shift that historians have identified toward more scientific poor relief aimed primarily at increasing productivity was indeed embraced by municipal and charitable agencies alike, including the Society for Awakening Goodness (which set up textile workshops for refugee and indigent children), as well as by Wang—who with colleagues in the city administration incorporated road maintenance and skills training into the city's poor relief operations over the famine year.[110] Yet these were a small minority of the programs used by Jiang and Wang's relief agencies, which were overwhelmingly on a free or noninstitutional outdoor relief basis.[111]

What, then, might have motivated charitable acts in Beijing around 1920? Of course, acts of relief were performed within any number of ethical and social frameworks. Religious injunctions to exercise compassion were motivations, as were bids for social prestige, traditions of keeping merit ledgers of good deeds, and a growing sense of national shame.[112] However, the most common motivation expressed or reported in the press was emotional in character. By and large, news articles were charged with pity and moral outrage, serving as appeals to readers of means to intervene in acts of injustice, contribute to existing aid programs, or initiate new charitable activities. Whether produced by staff writers or commercial wire services, news copy applied three categories to distinguish the types of needy in headlines and news briefs: the local poor, who often had fixed residences; *nanmin*, or people in distress—meaning disaster victims who had fled from nearby or distant districts, often for the duration of the drought crisis; and beggars (*qigai*), a term often applied to people who roamed and panhandled for longer periods. All three were covered in the local press with equally emotional language and calls for charitable action by people with means. More commonly, disaster victims were described as "pitiful" in local news coverage;[113] and scenes of suffering were "unbearable to witness."[114] Meanwhile, the philanthropic were often dubbed warmhearted (*rexin*).[115] On occasion, older stock phrases used to describe charitable figures in local gazetteers from the Ming and Qing periods crop up in 1920s reports of poor relief, such as when news writers acknowledged the contributions of charitable actors by describing them as people who "take pleasure in doing good and value giving away" (*leshan haoshe*).[116]

National shame over the plight of fellow Chinese was only occasionally invoked in local news items pertaining to the 1920–21 famine in greater Beijing. In some instances, stories involving charitable acts by foreigners on the streets ended with editorial remarks faulting the public for relying on the generosity of Westerners (*xiren*) to come to the aid of the poor and "shaming us Chinese" (*wei Zhongguoren xiu sha*), in similar ways that journalists in the 1870s had chastised their readers for allowing missionaries to take the lead in dispatching aid to the starving Chinese in the north.[117] While the 1920–21 famine occurred in a period of soul searching for many Chinese, who were trying to account for their country's weakness at the hands of foreign powers in numerous areas, acts of charity were of course reported on and encouraged in varied ways. Overall, though, nationalist sentiment and conscious comparison with foreign practices rarely played a part in quotidian coverage of famine-related distress in the city streets and suburbs, and any rationale for relief action, such as the maintenance of law and order or a sense of national duty, was either taken for granted or left unsaid in the newspapers read by tens of thousands across the region.[118]

The new forms that Chinese charity took in the early twentieth century may well also have been a function of the spread of republican ideals. The term *tongbao* (literally "of the same parents," or compatriot) was used on occasion to describe the suffering poor.[119] And parallels might be drawn between charity reorganization and the fate of the elite-dominated provincial lodges (*huiguan*) of the late imperial period, which were gradually replaced by more socially inclusive native-place associations (*tongxianghui*) in the early 1900s.[120] As Goodman has suggested, the support networks provided by these highly participatory associations also aimed at fostering the education and health of their members in a spirit of "democratic populism" meant to overcome established hierarchies.[121] It may be possible to consider the expansive networks of redemptive societies such as the Society for Awakening Goodness in similar terms, as they universalized sectarian religious practices of self-cultivation while presenting the broader community with welfare programs and skills training, credit, and other opportunities for social betterment.

Charity across the Chinese capital in 1920 may have been facilitated by the authority and resources of the state, but it did not wholly rely on them. Instead, it reflected the decentralized nature of Chinese government at the time, occupying a position somewhere between state activism and private initiative. In periods of strong central governance, the imperial state had looked with great suspicion on voluntary associations, going to the extent of criminalizing such activity in the seventeenth century.[122] In 1920, city authorities gave private poor relief endeavors around the capital plenty of space to operate. To relief actors, whether these operations were in the hands of bureaucrats or in those of gentry and merchants evidently mattered less than whether the job got done at all.

CHAPTER FIVE

City Charities and the Countryside

S urviving photographs make it difficult to view people fleeing the famine districts in 1920 as anything but an undifferentiated mass of desperation. News stories at the time, though, seldom failed to identify the
people in flight and where they originated. Names and places clearly
meant something to the readers hunched over newspapers in teahouses or
market stalls around Beijing. Origins and identities made relief easier to
execute than generic descriptions of refugee flight, providing news of kin
or precise points in the famine field where assistance could be dispatched.
Newspapers joined banners, notices, and meeting hall speeches in a broad
public conversation about afflictions in particular communities that lined
the roads leading south of the capital. Sifting through press reports over
the famine year brings to life such city connections to the countryside, if
only in partial and fleeting ways.

One evening in October 1920, Zhang Hong and two others lay dead
from knife wounds in a small temple in Beijing. Their hunger "unbearable," the man and his older sister had slashed themselves and a three-
year-old relative before police conveyed their bodies to a charity graveyard,
along with three coffins provided by the state.[1] That same month, Xie
Yutang and twelve other men and women freshly arrived in the city were
observed seated behind a temple by Xizhi gate exhibiting stoic patience in
the face of starvation, having gone without food for four or five days and
"waiting to die."[2] Soon afterwards, police encountered Wang Nimin
and her daughter wandering in the city "with no friends or relatives to
take them in" and checked them into a city workhouse for indigent women.[3]

A group of two hundred people appeared from the south in Beijing several weeks later, where they were met by gendarmes and escorted to a city shelter for refugees.[4] In a teahouse in January, a police detective—reportedly acting on an order that week from the Beijing police chief to bring refugee women found in local brothels to city shelters—collared a gangster (*feitu*) and the young woman he had "sweet-talked" (*ganyan youyin*) into prostitution after she had fled her home in the drought districts and failed to find relatives in the capital.[5] A few weeks later, when Wang Chenglin held up his seven-year-old son for sale on a city street, a passerby handed him five yuan, urging him to keep the boy and try to "make a living" with the money, after which the father thanked the stranger, hoisted his son onto his back, and left.[6]

The common thread linking these scattered reports is that they all involved migrants from a single corner of the famine field—drought-ridden Shen county, in central Zhili. Over the course of six months, these stories provide glimpses into the varied fates of men, women, and children making parallel journeys to the capital over the year. When a hundred Shen county natives convened in Beijing one evening in early October to form a relief society and pool money for their home district, there can be little doubt they were, in part, alarmed and driven by similar stories of distressed natives of their home district in the capital's press.[7]

This is not to say that native-place ties and bloodlines alone determined the form of city responses to distress in the famine field. The Shen county social network was but one type among many in Beijing that created their own fund-raising and delivery channels to the countryside. Beijing's organized providers of charitable assistance, such as benevolent halls and religious sects, did not limit themselves to activities in the immediate environs of Beijing, where (as seen in chapter 4) they canvassed neighborhoods over the famine year for the distribution of relief goods and monies. These groups were also agents of relief extending well beyond their vicinity, including the numerous rural counties that encircled the capital, and they operated independently of the state or larger relief groups. For example, a group of men assembled at west Beijing's Esteemed Goodness benevolent hall (Baoshantang) to form the Cotton Clothing Aid Society (Mianyi zhuzhen hui) that targeted all of the afflicted counties of the metropolitan region with distributions starting October 12.[8]

That same month, the Fellowship of Goodness (Tongshanshe) redemptive society dispatched members from its offices just inside the North City to acquire five thousand sets of clothing at a north Beijing market for delivery by truck to two stricken counties in mid-October: Gu'an, just south of the capital, and Ji, by the border with Shandong.[9]

Looking beyond these more established charities, this chapter provides a typology of the temporary organizations that were formed with the expressed purpose of projecting their activities into the famine field. By and large, these organizations took shape at the outset of the crisis and came from identifiable social circles in the capital, disbanding at some point during the crisis as famine conditions eased. Many were founded on religious and/or professional bases. Others stemmed from the above-mentioned native-place ties at the county, prefectural, or provincial level. Together, the groups examined in this chapter played a leading role in relieving the famine field. Only a modest portion of the relief goods heading to the Zhili disaster districts was financed by central state coffers, a fact discussed in part 2 of this book. Instead, relief was predominantly raised from extragovernmental sources ranging from local merchant gentry in the famine field, various types of small and large charity relief societies, and military officials in places such as Manchuria and central China charged by their counterparts in the Beiyang regime with raising relief funds piecemeal from their ranks and the public within their jurisdictions.

Native-Place Relief

Native-place networking was a major form of association that drove relief activity in the republic. As the longtime capital, Beijing attracted great numbers of officials, students, and merchants, many of whom lived there only temporarily and retained close ties with their native place—often intending to return there in life or for burial. These sojourners regularly organized themselves into provincial lodges, or *huiguan*, in the late imperial period. Often run by members of the elite, the lodges served as social and mutual-assistance institutions around the country and overseas for people of common geographic origins. By the 1920s, the term *tongxianghui*—or native-place association—was more commonly used for these organizations as their leadership became less exclusive, although *huiguan* was still widely used for the complexes in which these groups congregated.[10]

Huiguan facilities hosted meetings related to matters well beyond the concerns of particular native-place groups, serving as nodes of civic activity—especially in times of crisis. In *huiguan* halls across the city in 1920, natives of stricken sections of the country elected to form aid groups of varying scopes, from the county level on up. The hundred Shen county natives who convened in Beijing in October did so with the aim of providing discount grain, free relief, and interest-free loans to farmers back home with an initial estimated fund of 100,000 yuan, and a group of people described as merchant-gentry sojourners from central Zhili's Shulu county (today's Xinji section of Shijiazhuang) took similar action later in December.[11] At the prefectural level, groups formed with the intent of aiding multiple counties at once; this included the Henan natives who met in late October at a *huiguan* in Beijing to organize the canvassing and relief of nineteen western Henan counties, and the Beijing-Wannan Thirteen-County Relief Society (Beijing-Wannan shisan xian jiuzai xiehui) that was formed in January 1921 with offices at a family compound in the capital to coordinate relief for another section of Henan.[12]

Provincial groups were also formed. In mid-September, seventy-five Shandong natives met on a Beijing lane, and one put up 5,000 yuan for initial canvassing expenses to determine the extent of the Shandong disaster area. They formed the Shandong Disaster Zone Relief Society (Shandong zaiqu jiuji hui), headed by Zhao Erxun, a government official who was a Fengtian native and editor of the official Qing history (Qingshi gao).[13] (This organization was distinct from the Public Society for the Relief of Shandong [Shandong zhenzai gonghui], a quasi-governmental group founded in September by several prominent members of Jinan society. That was chaired by Lü Haihuan [1842–1927], a former Qing military official who had headed the Chinese Red Cross during its early years, with He Zonglian [1864–1931], a graduate of the Beiyang Military Academy, serving as vice chair.)[14] Later in the autumn other Shandong sojourners in the capital launched *Zhenzai ribao* (Disaster Relief Daily), a digest of famine reports and relief activities that was supported by advertisements of native banks and that ran at least through November, with the stated aim of both informing the wider public and "drumming up" (*guchui*) support for the unfolding famine relief effort across the north.[15]

Also in September, the Henan Relief Society (Henan hanzai jiuji hui) was founded at a Beijing meeting hall by sojourners in the capital, while the Shanxi Relief Fund-Raising Society (Shanxi chouzhen hui) was formed at a city villa, and the Sanqin Citizens Society for the Relief of Shaanxi (Sanqin gongmin jiu Shaan hui) was formed at Beijing's Guanzhong *huiguan*.[16]

Lastly, it might be noted that home ties might have worked in still other ways, allowing magistrates posted in the famine field to tap their own home districts for relief. This appeared to be the case, for example, with the magistrate of Wan county, who solicited a contribution of 800 yuan for relief of his Zhili district from a county in his home province of Anhui, in central China.[17]

Professional and Regional Affiliations

Another basis for the formation of relief committees in the capital was a combination of professional and regional affiliations that members shared. This involved major figures in the capital's military and civil administrations creating relief groups beyond the formal state agencies over which many of them presided. A prime example is Wang Huaiqing, the Beijing gendarmerie and garrison chief. In carrying out his responsibilities of securing the perimeter of the capital and policing its thoroughfares, Wang had headed various municipal poor and refugee relief agencies set up over the winter of 1920–21 (as discussed in chapter 2), as well as ones of more hybrid semi-official character, such as the Grain Relief Society. With 179 of its villages severely hit by drought and famine by mid-autumn, the leaders in Wang's native county of Ningjin had set up village-run soup kitchens funded with contributions raised by the county offices, along with grain discount centers, charity pawn offices, and children's shelters—operations that Wang helped with a modest shipment of "several hundred *shi*" of sorghum.[18] He also used his gendarmerie office to dispatch relief goods from Beijing to south Zhili—tellingly, to sections of the famine field that included Ningjin—sending twenty-one gendarmes to escort a shipment of 18,000 sets of new cotton clothes to Daming and Hejian prefectures in November.[19]

District gazetteers record similar acts over the famine year by fellow officers. Hubei Military Governor Wang Zhanyuan (1861–1934) sent two hundred *shi* of relief grain and a personal donation of 10,000 yuan for grain discount operations in his native county of Guantao, in Shandong.[20] The republican gazetteer of Zhili's Wei county recounts how one of its native sons serving as a military commander in Hubei sent men with relief supplies back to his native village repeatedly over the year.[21] And the gazetteer of Haixing county on the Zhili coast mentions the fact that Marshal Zhang Zuolin of Manchuria dispatched officials with free relief for the disaster stricken there in 1920—possibly due to the fact that Zhang could trace his ancestral roots to rural Zhili.[22]

More significant than these isolated acts is the fact that Wang Huai-qing joined with other Zhili natives in the Beiyang regime to form a relief society, which he headed, that complemented in important ways their existing roles in initiating and overseeing poor and refugee relief in greater Beijing over the year. The Shunzhi Drought Disaster Relief Society (Shun-zhi hanzai jiuji hui) was formed in mid-September by prominent natives of rural Zhili counties who lived in the capital and held official or military posts there, including Police Chief Yin Hongshou and Metropolitan Superintendent Wang Hu. Fund-raising was launched at a meeting at the Jiangxi *huiguan* that three hundred people attended. A general appeal for funds was made from military governors nationwide, and an initial gift of 100,000 yuan from Chinese president and Tianjin native Xu Shichang was followed by a well-publicized art and antique sale at Beijing's Central Park, inside the Forbidden City.[23]

The importance of the Shunzhi society—named after a secondary name for Zhili province—was not in the direct provisioning of relief, however; the group appears to have largely limited this to distributions of clothes and wheat seed across Zhili over the course of the autumn.[24] Rather, more significantly, it was in helping orchestrate the logistics required to speedily transfer the bountiful resources of Manchuria into the famine districts, a subject covered in chapters 7 and 9. At a series of initial meetings in September, Yin, a Tianjin native, took on the task of pressuring the Ministry of Communications to devote the rolling stock required for the volumes of grain needed to offset harvest failure across the North China Plain. Gu Zhongxiu (1874– ?), another member of the society and a native of Ding county, advocated the setting up of a relief lottery, which may have played a role in the multiple lotteries conducted nationally and touched on in chapter 7.[25] Meanwhile, Wang Hu, also from Ding, took on the task of facilitating the mass movement of sorghum, soybeans, and other crops southward from Manchuria, a role he was well positioned to play due to his experience in studying agricultural affairs in Japan and serving in military posts in Jilin and elsewhere in Manchuria on the eve of the fall of the Qing. Officials and the wider public in the northeast were clearly notified of the endeavour, as details of the meeting appeared within the week in the press in Harbin. By the end of September, Wang had also assumed the governorship of Jiangsu, from where he would be well placed to oversee the movement of relief goods northward from the Yangzi delta.[26]

Other groups of varying sizes were formed based on similar combinations of professional and regional affiliations. The Emergency Relief Society for the North (Beifang jizhen xiehui) was formed in the same week as the Shunzhi society, using the interest on the investments of a group of Zhejiang sojourners in the capital—all of whom served in the Finance Ministry or other financial positions.[27] Also in the same week, Beijing-based Finance Ministry officials from Zhejiang and Jiangsu founded the Poor Relief Society (Pinmin jiuji hui) to "follow the lead" (*fangzhao*) set by other recently created city charities and establish soup kitchens and distribute grain and coffins in the famine field using individual private donations—one man gave 18,000 yuan—as well as modest funding from the Ministry of the Interior and the Finance Ministry.[28] (It is unclear whether this group was the same as the City Poor Relief Society, mentioned in chapter 4, that worked with opera star Mei Lanfang.) And in the following month, two career army officers, Wang Zhixiang (1858–1930) and Li Zhangtai (1862–1922), natives of greater Beijing's Tong and greater Tianjin's Wuqing counties, formed the Capital Region Drought Disaster Relief Society (Jingzhao zaihuang jiuji hui) with the intent of setting up soup kitchens in districts around the capital.[29]

Groups with National Scope

As evidenced by some of the smaller groups mentioned above, the famine that afflicted the North China Plain in 1920 was not a concern of northerners alone. Despite the splintering of the republic with the death of Yuan Shikai in 1916 and what Edward McCord has called the "triumph of warlordism" in the North-South war of 1917, leadership and much of the sponsorship of the largest Chinese relief societies over the 1920–21 famine came from natives and residents of the south.[30] This prominent southern contribution arose in spite of repeated attempts by Duan Qirui's Beiyang regime to wrest control of Hunan in central China from rival southern regimes in 1917–18 in wars that had brought untold destruction and suffering to communities there.[31]

The first news items reaching Hankou and other Yangzi valley cities in September of the drought-famine to the north inaugurated the beginning of a regular stream of relief contributions from southern communities over the year. By March, *Shihua*, a Beijing newspaper, would report that with relief monies readily raised in places like Hunan, there existed "no north-south divide among the people" (*renmin shi bu fen nanbei de*) where famine relief was concerned.[32]

The launching of charity relief in 1920 in Beijing began most prominently with a mid-September meeting of various past and future premiers of the republic (Liang Shiyi [1869–1933], Wang Daxie [1859–1929], and Xiong Xiling) and one former president (Li Yuanhong). Liang, a Guangdong native and former chief secretary to Yuan Shikai and head of various financial institutions, had already formed a relief group that month called the North China Relief Society (Huabei jiuzai xiehui) which, together with members of the Chinese YMCA, aimed to provide both free and work relief (on the rails, roads, or canals) using grain brought in from Manchuria.[33] Liang's society served as a liaison with the joint Chinese-foreign international societies that were also forming in September (discussed in chapter 10), and it would also produce a major platform of intelligence and progress on relief across the five-province famine zone, *Jiuzai zhoukan* (published also as *Famine Relief Weekly*)—a journal of field reports, correspondence, photographs, and other materials—for the duration of the crisis.

Other relief societies formed that were also headed by former high officials, such as the Northern Provinces Emergency Relief Society, headed by Tian Wenlie (1861–1924), former head of the Ministries of the Interior and Communications, and headquartered at a railway office in Beijing.[34] And at the time of their September meeting with Liang, the two other former premiers mentioned above, Xiong and Wang, were working with

Zhao, head of the Shandong Disaster Zone Relief Society, to form a relief group headquartered at the offices of the Chinese Red Cross on a Beijing lane. The resulting Relief Society for the Five Northern Provinces (variously named the Beiwusheng hanzai zhenji hui or Beiwusheng xieji hui), also chaired by Zhao, was launched with a public drive for used clothing for the famine migrants streaming into the city.[35]

The figure of Xiong deserves special attention for the ease with which he moved among the capital's various social circles and their respective involvements in disaster relief, embodying the multifarious nature of civic activism in Beijing at the time. The fact that his group was headquartered at the Chinese Red Cross, where (as seen in chapters 1 and 4) his wife, Zhu Qihui, held several positions, is no coincidence.[36] Like Liang, whose relief society worked closely with the Chinese YMCA, Xiong combined an involvement in the city's foreign-style civic institutions with a classical education and intense involvement with Beijing's Buddhist community. China's most prominent high-level relief activist and facilitator at the time, he was a man with a foot in a remarkable variety of social scenes. Born in 1870 in Hunan, in central China, to a military father and given a classical education that led to his earning a *jinshi* degree in 1894, Xiong was active in late Qing and early republican politics, after which he served as director general of the Capital District Flood Relief and River Conservancy (Jingji yidai shuizai hegong shanhou shiyi). When hard rains and a rush of silt on five Zhili rivers flooded over a hundred counties in July 1917, however, it had been as an afflicted resident of a flooded Tianjin neighborhood that Xiong initiated and orchestrated relief for some six million people left homeless across the province that year.[37]

Xiong was also a devout Buddhist, organizing a series of lectures on scripture at the capital's Xiangfang Bridge Guanyin Temple (Xiangfangqiao Guanyin si) in the late 1910s, when he fraternized with two men, Ma Jiping and Wu Bihua (1877–1926), who would be central in the founding of what would become one of the largest famine relief groups in 1920–21, the Buddhist Relief Fund-Raising Society (Fojiao chouzhen hui). Members of the sutra lecture group at the Guanyin Temple formed the society on September 12.[38] Ma presided over the founding meeting of the relief society with a call for fund-raising in South China, where Buddhist monasticism and lay participation had been strongest over the centuries and was driving a Buddhist revival involving social and political engagement and associational and educational activity across the republic.[39] Ma appointed Zhuang Yunkuan (1866–1932), a Jiangsu native and Buddhist layman who was head of Beijing's audit bureau, to be the registered chairman of the society, which was soon collecting donations from the public at banks and temples for delivery along a monastic network to rural counties (fig. 6).

Conclusion

Some of the tell-tale technological and organizational phenomena of the twentieth century were present in relief operations in 1920, lending it— in hindsight—a modern character. Trains had penetrated further into China's interior, most notably with a rail line running through the mountains west from Shijiazhuang, in Zhili, to the capital of Shanxi, which had been worst hit of all provinces in the 1870s. Back then, woodblock prints of suicide and cannibalism in North China commissioned by philanthropists in greater Shanghai had mobilized donors as far away as Britain.[40] By 1920, professional advertisers in the form of the Advertising Club of China were submitting "proposals along publicity lines" to a relief committee "so as to put an appeal out more effectually before the public," and photographic exhibitions of the famine field made an autumn tour of Beijing to "press the public for donations" to charity.[41] Twenty-four car dealers in Beijing loaned vehicles for fund-raising parades in the fall of 1920, while an international relief society was reportedly in the process of securing the use of four airplanes from a government agency to send relief to the drought-afflicted districts.[42] The Dodge & Seymour car dealership in Shanghai meanwhile furnished seven specialized "Ford famine cars" for relief operations, sending them "into many localities where a motor car never before has been seen."[43] In 1920 both Standard Oil and the British-American Tobacco Company would also complement gentry and official relief efforts in parts of the 1920–21 famine areas with "self-financed and self-executed" food relief through their own networks of inland agents.[44] And cities as far from the famine as Guangzhou in the south, the metropolis of Wuhan on the Yangzi, and Shenyang in Manchuria saw uniformed

上海□□會賑□教佛京北月三年十國民華中
一之影攝賑散就有散賑□縣陸並會協賑界世

FIGURE 6. "Spring Relief Distribution by the Beijing Buddhist Relief Fund-Raising Society and the Fund-Raising Society of the Shanghai Merchant Association in Jingxing county, March 1921, Photo 1." *Jingxing XZ* (1934, reprint, Taipei: Cheng Wen Publishing, 1968), 2:939. Used with permission.

Chinese Boy Scouts drumming up donations in the streets for the relief of their famished countrymen on the North China Plain.[45]

But as we move in part 2 to the famine field itself, we should be careful about fixating on such signs of modernity and the so-called New China. Chinese society was too layered and fractured—culturally, socially, and politically—in this period of great transition for any single mode of life or emerging segment of society to justify taking the limelight. The task of feeding mouths and clothing bodies in over 90,000 square miles of parched earth (about the combined size of Pennsylvania and New York State) aroused a social response characterized by a remarkable complexity of forms and using a broad spectrum of older and more recent methods. Relief mobilization in the capital was organized along a variety of social, professional, religious, and regional networks, relying on parallel and independent channels of disaster intelligence and relief delivery to the affected districts. The regional disaster was also treated by many as a national crisis, despite the factionalism and regionalism that had been stoked by the onset of civil war over the year.

In the 1980s and 1990s, a debate took place among Western historians about the nature and origin of modern civic life in China. At issue was the degree of autonomy from the state achieved by the emerging associational forms in Chinese civil society in the late Qing and early republic—not to mention the applicability of Jürgen Habermas's "public sphere" to a Chinese context.[46] Where should the local and national relief societies and charities described in this chapter figure in this unresolved debate? Of course, commentary on and reaction to disaster governance and failures were pregnant with reformist or revolutionary politics—especially for a famine that fell between the May Fourth Movement of 1919 and the establishment of the Chinese Communist Party in 1921. But while the activities examined here were voluntary, they were not overtly political in nature. Their participants used the halls and newspapers for debate and discussion, but their aim was not to challenge the structures of authority in any Habermasian sense. However, it is clear that this mobilization supports the position that "associational life flourished" in the early republic, in the words of Karla Simon, and that the disguised involvement of officials and military officers in the diverse range of secular and sectarian charities of the day supports the definition of civil society offered by Timothy Brook and B. Michael Frolic, that frames it as a "formation that exists by virtue of state-society interaction, not something between, separate from, or autonomous from either."[47]

Generally speaking, formal state stewardship of relief in 1920–21 took a backseat to that carried out by hybrid organs run by officials, military men, gentry, Buddhist or Christian churchmen, or other members of the public. Consequently, unlike the recent 1917 Zhili flood relief directed by Xiong, the former statesman and philanthropist, no single Chinese figure or relief organ (public or private) would be associated with overall relief operations. Despite its efforts to document the crisis and serve as a bridge to the foreign community, Liang's North China Relief Society was hardly an umbrella group for the numerous native societies operating out of the capital—although that is what its foreign counterpart, the Peking United International Famine Relief Committee, considered it to be.[48] The overall aid effort to the North China Plain developed in a far too fragmented fashion, consisting of multiple layers of autonomous groups operating in parallel channels of relief into the interior, for any authority—official or otherwise—to supervise or even comprehend all of its parts. Relief efforts, remarkably decentralized, ran along layered webs of social and official networks at all levels and scales, connecting stricken districts with urban communities. This decentralized character likely led to inefficiencies, but they may well have been compensated for by the resilience offered by a multilayered and multifaceted operation. As we will see in part 2 of this study, the movement of relief goods, public or private, across the republic was facilitated and subsidized by a surprisingly willing, if weak, state apparatus, while mutual aid was practiced within afflicted villages as well.

PART TWO

The Famine Field

CHAPTER SIX

Village Mutual Aid

The aim of part 2 of this book is to investigate how the immediate survival needs of millions of impoverished residents in rural Zhili were met in 1920–21, limiting famine-related deaths to an estimated 500,000 across all five provinces, despite the high numbers of destitute people. Half a million deaths may be an exceedingly low bar for relief success, and proof that "relief fell short" (*zhenji youcha*) over the year, in the words of one district gazetteer.[1] However, the famine of 1920–21 must be placed within the broader trajectory of steadily increasing mortality due to natural disaster in China's modern period. Based on estimates by Xia Mingfang, there was a fourteenfold increase in the number of deaths to famine, flood, and other types of disaster from the first half of the Qing (1.2 million) to the second half of the dynasty (17.0 million), with even higher mortality in the republican period (21.0 million).[2] The question for us here is how events as they unfolded in 1920–21 bucked modern China's horrifically upward trend in disaster mortality.

As prices rose and household stocks were depleted, identifying and classifying calamity-stricken people (*zaimin*) across the field was an inexact science that used varied criteria. The drought that enveloped North China in 1919 varied in intensity across the five affected provinces and across districts. Surveys by state and extragovernmental relief agencies over the fall of 1920 put the total number of destitute (*jipin*), generally defined as those in need of assistance to survive until the anticipated spring harvest, at anywhere from twenty million to thirty million. Areas with the highest rates of crop failure, where the length of drought ranged from twelve to fifteen months, were concentrated in the section of the North China Plain where the provinces of Henan, Shandong, and Zhili converge. Estimates were that both Henan and Shandong had around four million destitute, with slightly more in the former than in the latter. Famine conditions in mountainous Shanxi to the west were less severe, with anywhere from 461,300 to 1,616,890 destitute people. As for Shaanxi, the province was politically isolated from Beijing at the time and generally left out of central government famine reports, but the Xi'an-based international relief society found 1,243,960 impoverished spread across seventy-two counties.[3] Our focus here will be Zhili, where across a hundred counties rising prices rendered between eight million and nine million people destitute; it was by far the hardest hit of the five provinces. In the heart of the drought-famine zone, in Zhili's central and southern sections roughly two hundred miles or more from Beijing, fifteen rainless months had rendered nine of every ten residents penniless in a dozen counties.[4]

The absence of a central clearinghouse of relief data for 1920–21 makes the question of how this crisis was met a particularly vexing one. There was, in other words, no accounting that came close to spanning official and charitable operations, both native Chinese and international, heading into the famine field in 1920–21, not to mention mutual aid at the local level. Thus, we have only scattered and spotty reports of the famine response in some three hundred afflicted counties over the nine-month crisis. Given this absence of information, railway records provide an invaluable window into movements both into and within the disaster field. No other institution in the republic was in a better position to centrally monitor the provenance, volume, and flow of relief goods than the state-owned rail network run by the Ministry of Communications, which moved these goods free of charge for the duration of the crisis over the system's thousands of miles of rail lines. And likely no single source sheds more light on this movement than a statistical table of relief freight transported into the drought areas in the month of December, midway into the famine.

This table, published at the end of the crisis in the central government's weekly gazette, relates that the total volume of relief grain transported over the last thirty-one days of 1920 into the districts of the north affected by drought and famine was enough to maintain roughly half of the destitute at that point in all five provinces. As for Zhili, a full third of this total freight was brought to railheads around the province, enough to sustain there, as well, roughly half of the eight million destitute.[5]

This month-long window onto the sponsorship and destination of relief shipments reveals several things. First, by the arrival of winter in 1920, food aid from all Chinese sources, official and extragovernmental, carried along the railways of North China totalled 170,457,191 *jin* for a single month.[6] At 75 yuan a ton, this had a market value of 8,144,869 yuan and was enough for daily rations of half a *jin* over thirty-one days for nearly eleven million people—or roughly half of the destitute at that point in all five provinces.[7] Formal agencies of the regime were only one sector, operating alongside at least thirty different native agencies and organizations behind the relief entering Zhili. In terms of volume, the central state—in the form of the Government Relief Bureau based in Beijing and agencies of the provincial government or military—is credited with sponsoring only a quarter of the relief entering the province by rail. The rest, according to the railway, was sponsored by private or quasi-governmental organizations, led by the Buddhist Relief Fund-Raising Society, which delivered enough grain to ten railheads in the province to feed 1,513,771 people for the month; the North China Relief Society, which brought in enough to sustain 322,560 people; and the Northern Provinces Emergency Relief Society, which brought in enough for 218,924 people.[8] Free freight transport for relief goods by the Ministry of Communications facilitated the entire movement, which by February 1921 amounted to 1,806,199.8 yuan in waived fees along the Shenyang-Beijing rail line and 1,211,874.55 yuan remitted on the line up from Hankou on the Yangzi.[9]

How accurate are these figures? There is, of course, the question of clerical accuracy regarding stated volumes: the Buddhist society's total includes a massive 120,000-*shi* shipment of assorted grain from Yongding, in Hunan, through the railhead at Fengtian, south of Beijing—a volume that cannot be readily confirmed by other sources. It is nevertheless broadly consistent with the spread of the society's activity, which delivered aid to ten railheads across the west Zhili famine field.

The fact that the state in 1920 occupied a backseat in a relief system driven by voluntary efforts is no surprise. It follows what Lillian Li has shown to be a gradual devolution of relief responsibilities by the once-activist Qing state over the course of the nineteenth century into the hands of local government, private initiatives, and foreigners.[10] What is noteworthy, however, is that, similar to what we have seen in Beijing in 1920, the forms that this devolution took continued to disguise official involvement in relief affairs. As discussed in chapter 5, members of the republican Beiyang leadership were instrumental in the formation and operation of many of these semiofficial relief societies and charities dispatching aid to the field. In other words, concealed in the republic's proliferating civic and charitable groups, official and military roles in relief activity continued in the informal, quasi-governmental fashion that they had during the final decades of the Qing.

Second, railway records are significant in what they say about the limits of the international role in addressing the 1920–21 famine. Only well into 1921 would the joint foreign-Chinese international societies based in Beijing, Shanghai, and the provincial capitals mobilize relief of any significance for the afflicted interior. The chart mentioned above offers a snapshot of the volume of Chinese relief flowing over the country precisely midway through the nine-month effort—that is, after four months of domestic activity but before these international relief operations got off the ground. And, as pointed out in chapter 10, only for a fraction of the crisis (the last two months of the famine) would the volume of international contributions come to rival native ones. From the vantage point of December, 1920, the overall relief effort takes on a much more native character, despite the stress on the international dimension in the literature.[11]

But then there is an area of exchange that railway records do not reveal: the traffic over the innumerable rutted paths that connected thousands of settlements in the interior. Ministry of Communications logbooks contain information about only a fraction of freight traffic within a famine field, where mule carts were still the predominant, and in places the only, means of bulk grain transport in the majority of counties— Zhili's included. Based on the fragmented sources available, this chapter sketches some of the loan programs and free assistance that arose within the field using local resources and transport networks. Surprisingly, one finds mutual aid efforts even in sections of the famine field classified by the international societies as nearly 100 percent destitute in the autumn of 1920 (fig. 7). This stratum of relief activity was largely independent of the assistance sent into the countryside by the array of city-based charities

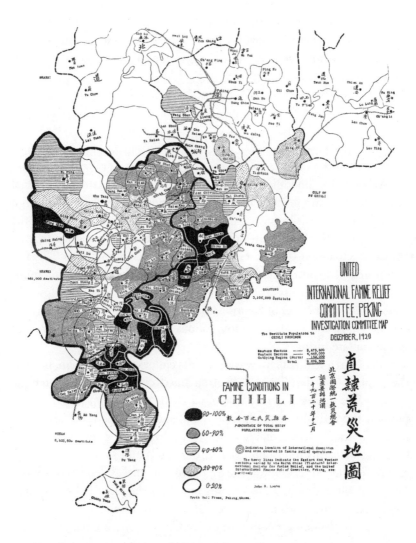

FIGURE 7. "Famine Conditions in Chihli [Zhili], Investigation Committee Map, December 1920." PUIFRC, *The North China Famine of 1920–21 with Special Reference to the West Chihli Area* (Beijing: PUIFRC, 1922), insert.

discussed in chapter 5. Village-level mutual aid was also distinct from the bureaucratic relief originating with the lowest echelons of the state bureaucracy, the county government. This bureaucratic relief, examined in chapter 7, involved state ministries' facilitating and subsidizing the transportation of aid into the famine field, where magistrates and other officials at the district level worked with local elites to set up distribution facilities. But before the interventions of outside charities and government, there were neighbors.

The Famine Zone

The Yellow River floodplain is marked by a broad and extremely gradual descent to the sea, a great expanse of flat agricultural districts cut through by slow-moving, silt-heavy tributaries originating in the uplands to the west. Despite the floodplain's temperate climate and its moderate total annual precipitation—about a third as much as that of southeast China—two-thirds of it normally falls between June and August.[12] This monsoon weather pattern is combined with cold fronts that sweep down in winter from the steppes of Central Asia, bringing clouds of dust that render the landscape a pale and monotonous yellow until the showers and sprouts of late spring.

The North China Plain was nearly devoid of wild vegetation, beyond the poplars and date trees that often lined communities and temple grounds. Centuries of deforestation, partly driven by imperial efforts to promote the agricultural production required to meet the needs of a growing population, were a major factor in the region's ecological fragility. Coupled with this monsoon cycle of dry spells and sudden heavy rain, chronic erosion and runoff in the highlands to the west led to epic flooding when the elaborate dike systems failed on the plain below, putting communities and fields under repeated threat of inundation.[13]

Some of the densest communities in China were situated in this setting, and the vast majority of them were rural—with more than 90 percent of the people living in small towns and villages sustained mostly by the intensive cultivation of wheat, closely followed by millet, sorghum, and corn.[14] Cropping patterns and techniques reflected the risks of working in such a climate. Depending on the weather in any particular year, drought-resistant millet could withstand modest drops in precipitation, while sorghum's tall stalks afforded the plant a degree of resistance to the waterlogging caused by mild flooding or heavy rain. These autumn crops were commonly followed by a spring harvest of winter wheat. (Used in steamed bread and noodles in the more affluent urban markets, the latter was considered a luxury grain, which ordinary farmers regularly sold to purchase greater volumes of millet, sorghum, and other coarse grains for home consumption.)[15] The region's ecological volatility was also reflected in tenancy arrangements: 15–25 percent of the farmers on the plain rented land, and landlords often shared their risk by collecting a portion of the crop as rent payment instead of cash, an arrangement more commonly practiced on the plain than anywhere else in China at the time.[16]

Other sources of income helped families get by. Well digging allowed farmers with land and ready access to the water table to cultivate walnuts, almonds, and dates as well as pears, hawberries, and other fruits. In some areas—particularly the piedmonts of western Zhili leading into Shanxi, where fresh water could be tapped several meters below the surface—irrigation was used for as much as 35 percent of the cultivated land.[17] While far from widespread, the rate of irrigation used to grow cash crops on the plain (10–17 percent of such crops, mostly legumes, in 1920) was nearly double that of the more intensely irrigated rice-growing regions of South China.[18]

The cultivation of cotton, an important cash crop in Zhili, expanded in the province by as much as five times in the first third of the twentieth century, covering as much as half of the arable land in some districts—mostly in the more-irrigated western sections along the foothills of Shanxi. Sold to the spinning factories in the nearby urban centers, cotton was also spun into yarn by the females of farming households in the winter as women had done for centuries, encouraged by the state as a cushion against lean times—while in poorer families females also wove mats and baskets from reeds.[19] In addition, for many families, one of the most reliable sources of extra income—earth salt—was readily available even in times of severe drought. The highly alkaline terrain was a mixed blessing for those residing on the alluvial floodplains of the Yellow River, which rendered soil infertile in places but also offered the opportunity to exceed daily subsistence needs through the production of salt for the market. By the time of the drought of 1919–20, salt production along the banks of the Yellow River had become a "big household industry," in the words of Ralph Thaxton, taken up by a majority of households in communities located in the heart of the south Zhili and north Henan drought

and famine field.[20] Interviews of survivors of the 1920–21 famine conducted by Thaxton revealed that residents had successfully turned to
earth-salt production for the cash they needed to survive the crisis. In the
case of a village in Nanle county, Zhili, a man who was fifteen in 1920
recalled that "few people in Qian Foji died because they relied on salt
making to buy grains to eat and sell in other places to get through the
famine." In the case of Qian Kou village, on the Zhili-Henan border,
Thaxton writes that salt making "became the principal means whereby
half of the village avoided long-term migration."[21]

However, the abundance of earth salt on the North China Plain was
of course a sign of systemic failure, the result in part of the nineteenth-
century breakdown of the dike system meant to control the Yellow River
and its tributaries, which led to periodic destruction of entire communities and their crops and the salinization of greater tracts of once arable
land. In the north, maintenance of this system had long been the responsibility of the imperial state, although in China's more affluent central
and southern regions local elites customarily assumed sponsorship and
management of water-control projects. The decline in official attention
to and investment in the vast inland Grand Canal and riverine infrastructure affecting the plain was part of an overall reorientation of state and
commercial interests toward the coast over the course of the late nineteenth and early twentieth centuries, leaving the population of the plain
with lost opportunities to benefit from passing trade along with increased
ecological vulnerability and the attendant instability of rising banditry
and social conflict.[22] Moreover, as Li and other scholars have argued, the
plain had experienced no changes in its overall cultivated acreage or per
acre yields for well over a century, despite a growing population over the
same period—leaving much of the populace teetering on the margins of
existence.[23]

How did these communities handle devastated harvests and soaring
prices for staples in the early republic? We are very much still in the dark
about this, a fact due in large part to the paucity of records. The northern agricultural regime had different social dynamics than in the double-
cropping, rice-growing regions to the south, where investment in land
led to high rates of tenancy and landlordism. The short growing season
and precarious ecology of the North China Plain meant that a large majority of its farmers were poor owner-cultivators working small farms that

were only several acres in size, residing in communities with less social stratification than in the more commercialized south. Historians have noted the existence of "various kinds of mutual aid groupings in North China villages, such as famine relief associations, credit associations, mutual aid groups," but rarely if ever in ways that flesh out how they operated at the village or household level in any particular crisis.[24] Compared to the rich corpus of writings left by the literati of Jiangnan, which informs Joanna Handlin Smith's remarkably detailed work on famine there at the end of the Ming, there are hardly any corresponding accounts of rural poor relief values and practices amid disaster in the early twentieth century, particularly in the disaster-prone north.[25] Instead, based in large part on the detailed village survey work performed by Japanese (Mantetsu) railway authorities in Zhili and Shandong in the 1940s, Western studies of northern village life have focused on questions of agrarian change and the heightened interventionist powers of the modern state. Leading into the modern period, the section of the North China Plain most affected by drought and famine in 1920–21 was marked by high land productivity (comparable in the 1930s, in fact, to that of the American Midwest) coupled with low labor productivity (leading to thin margins of subsistence), a case of severe "involution," in the words of Philip Huang.[26] Work by Chinese historians has provided considerable empirical detail on the increasing frequency and intensity of natural disaster in the republic and the disruptive effects on rural society and economy, but little on how these northern communities sought to mitigate these crises themselves.[27] In some respects, this lacuna in the literature is a function of scale: Li's examination of famine policy, markets, and the state in Zhili from the seventeenth through the twentieth centuries—an unsurpassed work that informs much of this study—thoroughly charts the downward trajectory of disaster governance in China over the *longue durée*, but it does so through a lens that inevitably overlooks short-term developments and the dynamics at play in any particular crisis, especially at the local level. All of these works make clear the immensity of the challenges faced in 1920, but not what ordinary people did about them.

The remainder of this chapter can offer only glimpses into the mechanics of mutual aid activity in rural Zhili around 1920, and the terms on which aid was granted. Its findings are therefore tentative. Mutual aid stems, in part, from the social obligations understood and practiced in

rural communities. Of course, the linkage of values to behavior is difficult to identify and depict, yet these values were expressed and performed
in popular art forms such as village opera, through which moral values
were transmitted, and were therefore widely known. As David Arkush
has observed in his study of village opera scripts collected in the 1930s in
Hebei (Zhili), these "obligations tend, unlike filial piety, to be based on
voluntary agreements rather than hierarchical position within the family,
and to be horizontal, in the sense of being between equals, rather than
vertical." One must avoid idealizing any such value system: in these village performances, Arkush points out, "it is frequently the rich who re-
fuse to recognize their obligations to the poor."[28] Instead, what is stressed
here is that community-wide mutual aid programs appeared at all despite
pillaging and other forms of violence across the famine districts.[29] Social
distress was exacerbated by the ravages of bandits in Henan especially,
but also in sections of Zhili, where at times they formed bands of seven
hundred men, plundering community coffers irrespective of local drought
conditions—at one point in the crisis extorting 40,000 yuan from large
counties and 15,000 yuan from smaller ones.[30] Of course, reports of "banditry" may well have concealed tensions brought on by the famine itself,
such as raids by desperate or opportunistic residents of neighboring, if
not necessarily better-off, communities—what Elizabeth Perry in her
study of rebellion in the region has called "predatory strategies" of survival.[31] What is remarkable is that considerable organized mutual aid measures occurred in this context, and that communities across Zhili remained
attentive to the welfare concerns of their residents into the 1920s, despite
escalating levels of violent conflict and civil war in increasing sections of
the country.

Village Responses

The arrival of famine in 1920 is most succinctly summarized by the gazetteer of Qinghe, a county of three hundred villages along the Zhili-
Shandong border (see map 4), where outside surveyors determined that
harvest failure had affected 90–100 percent of the population:[32] "In the
ninth year of the republic, severe drought prevented the sowing of crops

MAP 4. The Zhili famine field, with counties mentioned in the text.

for an entire year. A popular saying (*suyu*) for this is 'a year when the lid is torn off the pot' (*da jie guo nian*), and everyone in the district called it a year of famine (*jihuang*)."[33] With the failure of summer rains, farmers staked their survival on the harvest of winter wheat some seven months away, in May and June. Sowing wheat seed had its costs, supplanting the more lucrative cotton used for thread production; nonetheless, many chose to switch to planting winter wheat across the drought areas in autumn.[34] The limited cultivation of cash crops by farmers continued into the drought-famine of 1919–21, as farmers were spotted selling cabbages, sweet potatoes, and other produce—but not grain—at local markets in central Zhili even at the famine's peak.[35] Along with farmers, landless laborers, artisans, and peddlers turned to other fallback sources of income as household cash and grain reserves ran out, with varying degrees of success.

One option was migration. In times of dearth, able-bodied men in particular followed the seasonal routes they regularly traveled between harvests in search of work, to the mines of neighboring Shanxi, for example, or to open land for farming in expanses of Inner Mongolia and Manchuria further on. Entire families packed up and moved onto marginal, unclaimed lands on hillsides or sandy river banks nearby where they could cultivate hardier crops such as peanuts or potatoes, or south to the Yangzi valley or north beyond the Great Wall, to settle or eke out a living and return when conditions were more favorable again.

Those who stayed behind were often women, children, and the elderly, and many of them resorted to collecting tree bark, roots, leaves, husks, peanut hulls, and dozens of other types of famine foods. A tell-tale sign of famine conditions, such scavenging was especially trying as the already denuded landscape offered few wild plants. Many people turned to the consumption of mud cakes and fuller's earth.[36] The region's modest reforesting programs, designed to prevent drought and flood famine conditions in the future, suffered at the hands of residents who targeted saplings amid the general fuel shortage.[37] By the end of summer, the rate at which entire households (old and young, male and female) took to the roads by cart or on foot had escalated to crisis proportions. Prices for tools and carts plummeted as people jettisoned capital goods to buy grain.[38] In one section of south Zhili, three-quarters of the livestock owned before the famine were promptly sold.[39] Many people dismantled their homes, stripping the roof beams for sale; others sold their children—mostly girls, but sometimes young boys—to wealthier homes or human traffickers.

Significantly, one thing only a minority of owner-cultivators parted from was their land. A study of a south Zhili district found that 13 percent of land owned before the famine had been sold by the time of a mid-famine survey, despite the fact that somewhere between 60 percent and 90 percent of the district's inhabitants were reportedly stricken.[40] While those who did sell their land did so at rock-bottom prices, there was a steady rise in overall prices of land on the North China Plain through the 1910s and 1920s, which does not indicate a mass placement of land on the market.[41] If a majority of household heads chose not to sell their most valuable material asset, how did resident families survive until spring?

Varying in place and time over the year, mutual aid measures ranged from loans negotiated at village meetings, community-wide grants of vital items such as grain and winter clothes, and independent acts of largesse by local figures from middle-class or prosperous families. Using cases taken from local gazetteers, news reports, and provincial gazettes, we can make a few general observations about these measures. First, community members took on disaster management without holding formal office. The initiative behind village relief stemmed as much from individuals and local households acting in private, or what one might call microcivic, capacities as from village heads recognized by the state or occupying any formal position. Second, the funding or provisioning of aid measures was sourced from local families of means based on land ownership, successful crop rates in the recent harvest, or other determinations of their ability to contribute. And third, free assistance was limited to the poorest residents, often only the young, old, and infirm, as well as to females generally, and was designed merely to carry residents through to the following harvest expected in the spring.

Returning to Qinghe county on the Zhili-Shandong border, mutual aid measures were discussed with the onset of famine conditions in 1920 at village meetings across the district. Who was included in these gatherings? Presumably only those with membership in the community—that is, not hired hands, itinerants, and others with tenuous or temporary local ties, who were likely the first to move on in times of dearth. Yet village membership was relatively fluid in the north, and the criteria for it varied from place to place. Villages on the North China Plain were commonly nucleated settlements of 100–150 households of various surnames, in contrast to the single-surname villages common in South China, where kinship networks such as lineages were considerably stronger. Chang Liu notes that interviews from the mid-twentieth century relate that in some Hebei villages membership required owning both land and a house, and even burial of several generations of ancestors in the village—although the criteria were not always so strict.[42] Whether or not assistance was contingent on any form of village membership, Qinghe's gazetteer unfortunately does not make clear.

In Qinghe, relief plans were not uniform across the district, the gazetteer explains, as the county's three hundred villages varied in size and means. While free assistance may have been negotiated in villages with wealthy families, in the majority of villages there existed only destitute or, at best, fairly well-off (*xiaokang*) families. There, short-term loans with security were devised after estimating overall need in the community and determining the size and degree of need in each household.[43]

It is no surprise that loans were a common form of mutual aid, since by the early twentieth century credit was difficult to come by in rural China. While pawnbrokers and banks continued to send agents into rural areas, they and other sources of loans were predominantly based in urban centers. This was due in large part to the widespread rebellion and disorder of the nineteenth century, but also to the impoverishment of rural China as cities industrialized.[44] Of course, many people stood to gain from the opportunities famine conditions presented for profiteering and exploitation of various kinds, including of desperate neighbors and disaster victims on the move. But each community possessed its own normative codes of behavior according to which residents were expected to act in times of crisis, and that served to regulate individual and group responses. As Huaiyin Li writes of west Zhili's Huailu county, arrangements known variously as "'village regulations' (*cungui*), 'local regulations' (*xianggui*), or 'old regulations' (*jiugui*)" had "existed in local communities for generations and varied widely in different localities, reflecting the diversity of social ties, interest patterns, and power configurations in the peasant society." "Two basic principles stand out as common to these village regulations," Li explains: "reciprocity and the right to subsistence."[45]

In some cases, communities and individuals took steps to ease the process of getting back on their feet for victims of famine in the wake of disaster, settling on particular terms for the repayment of loans or writing off debts altogether. For example, amnesty clauses were written into the governing regulations of village-level charity granaries (*yicang*) active in the 1920 famine areas, stipulating that people who were genuinely unable to repay at the next harvest grain that had been apportioned to them earlier could be exempted from doing so.[46]

Cases of individuals turning down repayment by indebted neighbors after famines appear in gazetteer biographies, setting moral examples for future generations. One case involved a community in the central Zhili county of Nanpi, eighty-five miles from Qinghe, where in 1920 many in the countryside were struggling to carry on. Yang Chunting was quoted as saying, "With all my neighbors starving, how can I bear having a full stomach?" (*linren jie ji, wo he ren dubao*) before "exhausting his own millet stores for their aid" (*chu ji su liang wei zizhu su jin*). His brief biography, which says little else about him, ends with the fact that, after a "bumper harvest" the following year, when those he had helped came to repay him for his generosity, he refused to accept anything in return.[47] As exceptional as these cases may be, Pierre-Étienne Will found in local records from eighteenth-century Zhili that "charitable people" in times of strife "granted loans and burned the contracts afterward."[48]

Significantly, one also comes across incidents of debt cancellation at the village-wide level in places that had been almost completely impoverished in the 1920 famine. Bordering Qinghe county and as far from the railroad as any county in south Zhili, an estimated 90 percent of Wei's 163,000 residents were affected by the autumn harvest failure.[49] The gazetteer biography of a resident of Zhangjiazhuang, a village in one of the hardest hit areas of the county, relates that middle-class and poorer families (*zhonghu yixia*) took stock of their possessions and mortgaged or sold off land, clothing, and other resources as "temporary coping measures" at the onset of the food crisis, but were soon "filling the streets" in desperation. It was then that Zhang Jiusheng joined with the village headman (*cunzheng*) and others to "assemble those with shared resolve for a public discussion" (*yaoji tongzhi gongyi*) about the use of "all available grain for emergency relief" (*jun liang jiuji*). Several heads of wealthy village households, also surnamed Zhang, then "expressed unanimous consent" (*jun biao zancheng*) about drawing up a plan in which aid would be distributed to the poor on the following condition: all recipient households possessing less than forty *mu* of land that were later unable to repay the assistance given them would be exempted from doing so, while recipient households with more than forty *mu* would be required to repay within three years. At the appointed time of repayment in 1923, though, with many villagers still carrying debts from 1920 that they were unable to pay off, Zhang collected all the debt contracts drawn up in the famine year and, along with a second villager who had hatched the original plan with him, burned them in the presence of all "as a demonstration of charity" (*yong shi shishe zhi yi*).[50] So reads Zhang's biography in its entirety.

Unfortunately, the sources rarely offer so much detail. The entire biographical entry of one Wei native known for his "charitable spirit" (*xing cishan*) relates that with "every ferocious year that occurred" (*mei feng xiongsui*) in the early republic, he issued millet to people in the countryside (*xiangren*), "saving untold lives" (*lai yi quanhuo*). Another Wei resident is similarly introduced as having a "charitable spirit" after having distributed millet "in every disaster year" in the period. Still another is said to have "saved countless people" (*quan huozhe shenzhong*) in 1920 by "issuing a large amount of stored grain to village kin (*xiangzu*)."[51]

Sometimes one finds in a biography a pattern of relief acts over the course of a person's life. One Wei resident is said to have donated thirty *shi* to the local granary in the late 1870s, issued money to the famished in the 1900 drought, and in 1920 "issued capital to assist the poor through the famine."[52] In more dramatic fashion, another resident active in local relief in 1877 and 1900 was forced in 1920 to jump over his home's wall to flee from bandits to the next county, but not before exhausting his cotton supplies in handouts to the famine-stricken in the village, many of whom were reportedly saved by his act.[53]

Biographies of local notables and transcriptions of gravestones published in the district annals of some of the most destitute and remote sections of the Zhili-Shandong border region in 1920, including Wei, suggest that neighbor-to-neighbor assistance persisted despite the most trying of conditions.[54] What were the motivations for emptying stores of millet when it was at its dearest—when grain could readily be swapped for whole parcels of land? Intimidation undoubtedly played a role. As the compiler of the Qinghe gazetteer explained, the affluent families of each village in particular feared mass disorder from an outburst of the poor in 1920, and consequently "none of the capable households did not issue money and grain" from their private stocks when village meetings were called in autumn.[55] Pressure also played a role. In Guangzong county, which bordered Wei, drought victims as early as August formed groups of several hundred known as "teams of desperation" (*chiqiong tuan*), calling on the homes of local wealthy people to "estimate their available granary stocks" (*gu chi migu*), according to the account, and "demand that they fully grasp their plight" (*fei ba ta chiqiong buke*).[56]

And of course there were social and political rewards for offering largesse in times of disaster. Memorialized by members of the community and recorded on stone steles or in the local annals, anyone establishing a custom of issuing relief in times of crisis garnered a reputation for virtue (*de*) and benevolence (*yi*), Confucian values highlighted in gazetteer biographies, and set a standard—by word of mouth or in print—of generosity and initiative to which later generations could be held. The Qing had at times conferred official titles and positions on donors, and in the republic the state continued to award plaques and medals for such acts. Other motivations ranged from social esteem to the good karma or merit good deeds might provide the giver in the afterlife or confer on his or her progeny.[57]

Unfortunately, the Zhili sources are sparing in their insights into the decision making and values related to village relief in 1920. It might help, then, to cross the border into Shanxi, where the detailed correspondence and reports published in the provincial gazette, *Laifu bao*, include two documents that tell us a good deal more. The first is a public letter written in October 1920 by Feng Sizhi (1884– ?), a member of the rural gentry from the county of Pingding.[58] His mountainous district had experienced eight rainless months, after light rainfall and a weak harvest in autumn 1919—which had been half ruined by a locust infestation.[59] With the largest population in the province, the "land-poor and rock-heavy" county had a mere two *mu* of productive land per resident in 1920. Even in years of good harvest Pingding imported several hundred thousand *shi* of grain from Zhili, Henan, and Shandong, largely financed by the county's considerable mineral deposits and the remittances of some 80,000 of its native sons working in menial jobs or plying trades in those same provinces to the east.

In his published call to action, Feng explained that he and his brothers were "born and raised" in their village of Nan'aocun and to bear witness to the unfolding famine, he had returned home from the provincial capital where he headed an educational association (*jiaoyu hui*). Feng expressed frustration with official relief efforts and "all their talk of relief plans," explaining that "fund-raising remained a major problem." Two options presented themselves to Feng: what he called the "ordinary approach" (*putong banfa*), in which "each village manages its own relief affairs," and the "exceptional approach" (*tebie banfa*), in which clothes were distributed and porridge dispensed once the hardest hit areas were canvassed for their needs, and financing was sought from the state only when and where funds fell short.

It made sense that a man heading an educational society in the provincial capital would take up relief provisioning in his community. With the development of the modern school system under the New Policy reforms in the last years of the Qing, the education sector became a common destination for members of rural scholar elites and literati unable or unwilling to secure new positions of local governance such as the new village head.[60] What is noteworthy is that as Feng lays out his plan, he makes only passing mention of the state, and then in a dismissive fashion. He makes his plan out instead to be a family initiative. Laying the groundwork for the "ordinary approach" to famine response, Feng and his brothers took a head count of the stricken in their village. The men made this decision, Feng makes clear to his readers, only after "following the commands of their mother" (*feng wo muqin de ciming*). The brothers determined that 107 of the village's 300 households qualified as poor (*pin*), and Feng specified their criteria: only those widowed or alone and without support were included, a count that excluded homes with able-bodied men and addicts (presumably of opium).[61]

Feng might as well have said the "worthy poor." The social values behind such a notion were not new. In her study of early benevolent halls in central China in the seventeenth century, Joanna Handlin Smith identifies similar guidelines excluding the able-bodied in favor of the "sick and crippled," as well as preferences for "those who are filial, friendly, honest, and chaste, or who are living alone with no one to rely on."[62] And Feng left unclear how the able-bodied but jobless men no longer employed in the coal industry or returning from work in other provinces were to be assisted, if at all.

The brothers then drew up a plan designed, in Feng's words, to provide "enough to prevent death from hunger" (*bian ke e bu si*).[63] Each member of these poor households would be given a daily ration of two or possibly three (the source is barely legible on this point) *he* of millet porridge—that is, 900 or 1,350 calories a day—until May 1, as well as a set of winter clothes, putting total estimated expenses for the seven-month program in the village at 1,000 yuan.[64] (It might be noted that this ration used by Nan'aocun appears to correspond to those employed by relief administrators in the late imperial period.)[65]

The plan was then extended beyond their village, and a meeting was convened in the county seat in October with representatives of other villages. There, it was estimated that larger villages would have to spend 1,000 yuan on such a plan, and small villages several hundred yuan, using money pooled from all residents with the means to contribute. With "the proposal supported by all present," it was decided that "each village" would begin operation within the month of October. Anyone benefiting from the program was barred from begging in other villages, and it was decided that extra resources could not be generated to assist refugees from outside the county. Finally, in places where a village could not generate the necessary resources, appeals for assistance would be made to the state. Ending on the personal note that he would have to take on debt to go ahead with the village program, Feng appealed to wealthy gentry of the village and the county at large to "realize this plan in all villages and counties" of Shanxi, ending with the words, "How can we hinder (*fang*) a plan that is so much within reach?"[66]

Our source stops there. The extent to which Feng's blueprint for "each village to manage its own relief affairs" was adhered to is unclear—even in his own village. This is the limitation of a source from so early in the crisis, however detailed. To add to our picture of the mechanics of mutual aid at the village level, then, we turn to a second village plan outlined in *Laifu bao* that autumn: the plan for village self-relief (*cun zi jiuji*) drawn up and submitted to the provincial government by a village in Shanyin county, which lay on a well-worn route north to the fertile region of Datong along the Great Wall in Shanxi's borderlands with Inner Mongolia. Amid severe drought and a spike in prices in Anyingcun, a day's worth of handicraft work that had previously been sufficient to feed an entire family in the village was not enough to sustain even a lone worker. Using the same five-level categorization of residents employed by the Shanxi provincial government when determining its relief services, the village leadership (*cun zhang fu*) decided that its relief program should benefit families in the poorer fourth and fifth economic tiers of the village—the fourth tier defined as those with no agricultural work this year due to the drought and only handicrafts to rely on, and the fifth being the outright destitute.[67] In the presence of the head of each family, the village leaders would take an inventory of the grain reserves of every household in the village. Homes reaping over twenty *shi* of grain in the present autumn harvest would each contribute (*choujuan*) three *sheng* (pints based on the new peck measurement, or *xin dou*) per *shi*, with all types of grains accepted equally; homes reaping less than twenty *shi* that fall would not have to contribute anything; and homes reaping over twenty *shi* but with an exceptional number of mouths to feed would contribute less in proportion to the number of people and livestock in the household.[68]

"This famine year is an opportunity for wealthy families to do good for the community," read the plan. As for "stingy and mean types (*bilin deng bei*) who deliberately undercount their stocks, relief managers will enter, without contest, whatever amount householders wish to provide." But any such people were told to "hold their actions up to their conscience" (*liangxin shang zhuzhang ke ye*). For "charitable families" choosing to contribute grain above the three *sheng* quota, the market price of their donations would be recorded and their deed submitted to the county for due recognition for their act of charitable or "righteous" relief (*yizhen*), which traditionally often included an honorary plaque or banner from the state to hang at the family gate.[69]

Relief would be handed out to families in the fourth and fifth tiers in the following fashion: every ten days women, the widowed, orphans, those generally alone without support, and those either younger than sixteen years or older than sixty would each receive a daily personal grain ration of four *he* until the end of lunar April 1921—roughly 1,800 calories a day, or slightly higher than the ration in Feng Sizhi's village plan.[70] The village heads would write a donation order and stamp and seal it, and the recipient would present it to an assigned donor household for his or her grain ration. The submitted plan ended with a warning that no disputes, haggling, or disturbances would be tolerated.

Lying on a main north-south route through the province, Anying-cun was also beset by famine migrants from neighboring provinces heading north to the fertile expanse beyond the Great Wall. Concerns about the theft of ripening crops were especially acute in times of scarcity. Crop-watching associations were common features of farming communities, often composed of landowners who collectively hired watchmen to guard the sprouts of spring and autumn as well as protect the village trees.[71] In light of village fears that this traffic would "breed disturbances," the plan also allowed for the recruitment of thirty "able-bodied men" (*zhuangding*) from fourth-tier village families to serve on village patrols—a move doubtless also designed to occupy idle, down-and-out young males. The thirty would be split into three teams, and each team would serve one ten-day shift per month, basing itself in the village office. Oil, candles, firewood, and the same daily ration above of four *he* of grain per person would be provided by the village. By day the men would "tend to road maintenance," and by night they would take turns patrolling the area until their disbandment at the end of lunar February 1921.

We cannot be sure to what extent these village initiatives were carried out. But they offer insights into expectations, values, and the machinery of disaster response at the most immediate level. The village-level aid programs just described were not, in fact, the only form of assistance to the famine stricken in Shanxi over the year. The government, under Military Governor Yan Xishan (1883–1960), oversaw grain discount operations and low-interest loan programs to middle-class families unable to benefit from village mutual aid programs and those of relief societies. The relief bureaus of the provincial and central states supplied the province with clothes and millions of *jin* of relief grain over the year, and the American Red Cross provided extensive work relief projects. In the case of Feng's county of Pingding, five relief societies brought in 2.5 million *jin* of grain in December alone.[72]

This makes it especially noteworthy that Feng's public letter left out the role of outside relief agencies, since both those from the cities and those from overseas (in the form of missionary aid) had helped communities in Shanxi as recently as the late nineteenth century. A local man with Feng's level of education would surely have been familiar with the recent experience of external aid to Shanxi; moreover, Feng had experience abroad, having studied government in Japan in 1902–7, which may explain how his letter was also printed in the Beijing-based Japanese-owned newspaper *Shuntian shibao*.[73] Nonetheless, Feng focused on local potential.

Moreover, Feng's relief plan made no mention of the new formal structures of the state. In 1917 Yan's provincial government had instituted a four-tiered subcounty system of wards (*qu*), villages, and two subvillage units that increased official reach into village politics, a model that was later adopted by the Nationalist government for its local administration nationwide.[74] In the case of Shanyin county's Anyingcun, which dutifully reported its village relief plan to Taiyuan, relief appears to have been supervised by the men occupying posts in the village administration. By contrast, in Feng's case the initiative had a more voluntary character, taken up informally by a prominent household, and financed privately using, as he explains, their recently renovated family compound as collateral for borrowing to fund their share of the relief project. In similar fashion, across the North China Plain in Zhili, Zhang Jiusheng, the Wei county villager who burned the debt notes of his community, had no other community roles or accomplishments specified in his biography, despite being credited for taking the initiative and brokering a village-wide relief program before approaching the man formally administering the village—the village head. What was their authority? Only with the respect of their peers—who entrusted grain reserves to their plan when there was no way of knowing whether future harvests promised anything at all—could men like Feng and Zhang have carried out such plans and gotten their peers to agree to a debt amnesty afterward. The two men clearly had an informal authority—a cultural, moral authority—in the village, which stemmed from the "cultural nexus of power" conceptualized by Prasenjit Duara and was largely illegible to outsiders accustomed to formal institutions of order and social welfare provisioning.[75] Providing a layer of aid parallel to that administered by officials at the subcounty level and higher up, Feng's plan continued the multilayered relief practices active in the late imperial period, when local elites, if able and willing, acted in tandem with agents of the central state yet outside the formal *baojia* structures of village policing, census, and surveillance.

Attuned to suffering and couched in emotional language, elite decision making was doubtless wrapped up in concerns for family standing and the maintenance of order.

Evidently, the initiative and perseverance required for conducting relief efforts in such challenging conditions also involved personality and the duty prescribed by faith. This is illustrated by the recollections of Margaret Barbour, an American missionary stationed in Ding county over the famine year, where "a Chinese Mohammedan" surnamed Bai—"rich, benevolent, with a heart and mind in keeping with his splendid, six-foot physique"—"opened in his own house a soup kitchen at which he fed seven or eight hundred people for months before other relief came," according to Barbour. "And when relief did come, in the form of an Englishman sent down to investigate, this Mohammedan said: 'I have just built a new home. Take it—take all of it. I will go back to the old one. Anything to save the people.'" As Bai's home was converted into an international relief station, Barbour noted she had gained a "new respect for the followers of Mohammed."[76]

Upbringing certainly also played a role. It should be noted that women only rarely figure in gazetteer and other local accounts of the famine, but when they do appear it is in ways that suggest women were instrumental in crisis decision making at the community level. Surveys of two northern Zhili communities taken later in the decade found that the number of households headed by a woman ranged from 4 percent to one-third.[77] In times of crisis, as men were lost to migration, conscription, or violence, it was even likelier for impoverished, shrinking families to be publicly headed by a woman—one sign of a Confucian family in disarray, indicating the vulnerable families that were the main recipients of aid during disaster.[78] But interestingly, in the cases when a specific parent is singled out in print for inspiring acts of charity relief, more often than not, it is the benefactor's mother. When Feng and his brothers decided to take charge of famine affairs in their village of 300 households, he twice made a point of mentioning that it involved consultation with their mother. Elsewhere in gazetteers one comes across mentions of how male residents of the famine field "followed mother's instructions" (*cheng mu xun*) when donating to relief efforts in 1920.[79] In another case, a grave inscription printed in the gazetteer of Qing county, south of the port city of Tianjin, was composed by a son for his mother after her death in 1927.

Qian Chongkai (1881– ?), a military official, explains that his mother had instructed him to "balance ambition with frugality, living as if in times of poverty and giving away whatever surplus the family had in the form of clothes, gruel and coffin handouts." "Accordingly," the inscription follows, "in the great famine year of 1920, with the granary stocks insufficient for relief, [the family] purchased several thousand *shi* of grain for the stricken."[80]

By emulating even the most quotidian of charitable practices of one's parents—showing kindness to the poor, guarding against greed, or providing medicine to a neighbor—one becomes a good son, a custom of crediting one's mother for relief efforts that was practiced in the late imperial period.[81] It was a moral exercise that Henrietta Harrison describes, in her study of the diaries of a member of the Shanxi gentry who lived through the 1920–21 famine, as the "transformation of . . . filial piety into a general justification for doing good."[82]

Conclusion

The logistics required to mobilize and allocate resources within and between communities in a famine field beset by banditry and other risks were formidable, regardless of their scale.[83] Unfortunately, for outside observers, the social and communication channels over which mutual aid was conducted are largely ephemeral and opaque. While the new industry of journalism might have played a crucial role in informing China's major urban populations about the disaster unfolding in the interior, newspapers were not essential to the transmission of news along great distances: rural informational currents included letters sent home from sojourning students and merchants and the oral news network moving along the social landscape of the typical Chinese villager, one largely set by the paths to market over which appeals could be transmitted or assistance delivered. "Surprisingly detailed accounts were also passed on by word of mouth," Harrison observes in a study of newspapers and rural nationalism. In one instance, a bookseller in 1901 visiting a Shanxi village from a nearby market town reported to a prominent villager the "numbers of people attending a famine relief station there on three different dates that month." "Newspaper news did not simply replace oral reports," Harrison explains, "but became a part of the existing network of communications" over which news of war, bandit raids, or aid measures traveled.[84]

Rural relief activity, then, remains an elusive phenomenon for the researcher, since communities in the famine epicenter of south Zhili evidently generated relief among themselves under the radar in 1920, running on channels greased as much with personal trust, word of mouth, and traditional modes of transport as they were with publicity and the well-documented rail system.[85] While south Zhili was, as a whole, more densely populated than the north of the province, the vast majority of its population was scattered in rural districts or cities of fewer than 10,000 people, and anyone tapping into granary or household reserves to administer village- or town-level relief in 1920 would have done so far less visibly—that is, in terms of provincial or national gazes—than their coastal counterparts sending grain in from great distances, with all the publicity and paperwork that involved (long-distance relief agents applied for provincial passports, or *huzhao*, to have their nonprofit goods pass tax-free to the famine zone).[86]

What volumes of relief could have been moving beyond the railheads? Hardly obsolete, cart traffic competed vigorously with trains: "In the period between 1916 and 1920, quantities of grain shipped over the C.E.R. [Chinese Eastern Railway] ceased to give a correct picture of the effective grain surplus in North Manchuria," explained a report by the Chinese Eastern Railway in Manchuria, "owing to the tremendous growth of native cart traffic exporting cereals directly to Changchun, or to the Kirin-Changchun Railway."[87] This flow of cart traffic was not confined to Jilin or the northeast. One foreign resident in 1920–21 described a scene of "long caravans of grain-carrying carts" in front of his home just north of Zhili, in Fengtian (today's Liaoning province), with "big freight carts pulled by seven mules, and smaller carts pulled by three . . . escorted by government troops. . . . The carts came by the hundreds, passing our front gate for days on end," headed for districts in Zhili to the south.[88] Finally, China's extensive, if decaying, canal system acted as a third artery of movement in 1920 on top of carts and rail cars. A young Philadelphia Quaker en route to an extended stay with Chinese family friends in south Zhili described "a continuous line of boat sledges piled high with country produce" in her journey on the frozen Grand Canal in December 1920.

She recorded passing "bushels of hulled rice. Red corn. Golden millet. Peanuts in hull" as "small boys and girls darted through the more serious traffic on small sledge boats, pushed forward in the same way as ours, miraculously escaping accident by fractions of an inch."[89]

The cases in this chapter suggest that village elites taking on informal or peripheral roles in the political life of their communities were, in numerous places across the 1920 famine field, still active in mutual aid tasks at the most local—village or household—level. This happened even as village governance was reconfigured in late Qing reforms and during the republic with the creation of village heads, police officers, and other formal agents of the state. The continued viability of neighborly aid efforts in sections of North China's drought districts in 1920 led to aid that flowed out of sight of most outside observers that year: below the view of railway records and of most news accounts in city papers, and unrecognizable to outsiders accustomed to church, civic, or police-like institutions of social welfare and order.

However, one must not exaggerate the reach or capacity of relief measures at this most local level. Famine conditions were of course incredibly destructive to families and communities and deleterious to household resources.[90] Scarce population data for the period make it difficult to determine exactly how destructive the famine was to particular communities, and how mortality or flight played themselves out. The detailed popular register provided by the gazetteer of one central Zhili county, Wuji, suggests that in places gender composition was radically altered by the famine. Half of the county population was afflicted by harvest failure in the autumn of 1920.[91] The gazetteer records a decrease of some 5,000 female inhabitants between 1920 and 1921 (67,163 down to 61,992) but an increase in males of some 6,500 over the same period (from 86,475 to 92,995), while the number of households remained stable at 30,000.[92] Any paradoxical rise, or at least retention, of the male population may have been due, in part, to the attraction that American Red Cross relief work presented, through which 540 wells were dug in the county during 1921—albeit by local families.[93] But the stark contrast suggests a considerably higher rate of female mortality and/or dislocation through trafficking or flight at least in one central Zhili location. The source offers no breakdown by age, and thus no indication of whether this reduction was disproportionately in infant girls, young women, or daughters-in-law—

who customarily had weaker claims on household resources than males and elders, especially during times of adversity.[94] Whether or not this rare data set is representative of the famine field at large, it suggests the great social violence and disruption visited by such events. Eventually, assistance beyond the village level in 1920–21 would arrive in the form of modest emergency relief and soup kitchen operations, an added layer of disaster mitigation conducted by the official bureaucratic administration in tandem with local elites in the countryside—a subject to which we now turn.

CHAPTER SEVEN

Bureaucratic Relief

Over the years the role of the Beiyang regime during drought and famine has received little attention. The rare depiction of the Chinese leadership in 1920–21 paints a picture of neglect. "The Ministry of the Interior was important because it was in charge of parliamentary elections," Andrew Nathan notes in his political study of Beijing in the years 1918–23. "Its duties in public health, famine relief, and local administration were neglected."[1] Marie-Claire Bergère also charges it with negligence during the 1920–22 crisis: "No one would think of denying the complete ineffectiveness and profound corruption shown by the warlords."[2] And in a study of Canadian missions in China, Alvyn Austin accuses it of outright obstruction: "In the drought of 1920–1, the inability of the warlords to move food and their diversion of relief supplies to their own armies caused more suffering than the drought itself."[3] More recent works limit the military to a destructive role in the famine or ignore the military entirely, leaving the reader to assume that such matters were, at best, left to civilian officials or to the philanthropic to handle, if military men did not exploit or exacerbate the situation.[4]

The Beiyang regime in fact appears to have coordinated a sustained transfer of resources into the North China famine field in 1920–21. Closely following the timeline of relief by the military administrators in Beijing, this transfer of surplus grain stabilized prices across the Zhili famine field over the course of the fall, and with the soup kitchen operations into the winter indicated the existence of a still viable bureaucratic relief system operated in the capital and the surrounding famine districts. A major obstacle to the system was financing. This chapter considers how, as relief planners scrambled for funds over the first half of the famine, joint control by the foreign treaty powers over the Chinese customs administration prolonged negotiations over Beijing's proposal of a surtax on customs duties to finance a famine loan. With limited capacity to directly fund relief, the various levels of the Chinese state pieced together relief funding and resources in a variety of ways, including reducing state salaries and imposing surcharges on the state rail system. The majority of relief activity in the famine field was administered by district officials in tandem with local elites (examined in this chapter) or by Chinese and foreign charities (examined in chapters 5 and 10). In their structure, if not in their volume, relief operations at the district level in multiple sections of Zhili in 1920 would roughly match what had existed in the eighteenth century at the height of imperial relief capabilities, with one main difference: the central and provincial levels of the state played secondary roles, serving mainly as facilitators for the procurement and transportation of relief goods from beyond the Great Wall and the Yangzi valley. The bulk of existing relief financing and management was sourced jointly by officials and gentry at the district level. To students of disaster policy in the late Qing, this symbiosis between the organs of the state and local elites would be familiar. Here we sketch how Qing disaster policy carried over into postimperial administration.

Qing-Republican Continuities

Starting in July 1920, magistrates of Zhili counties facing the prospect of weak or failed autumn harvests oversaw the resumption of the annual cycle of discount grain sales, just as their counterparts administering Beijing were doing. In some cases this involved adding rooms to existing public granaries in county seats or setting up centers in temples in surrounding towns.[5] In some areas satellite charity granaries appeared in rural districts. In this way, the three-tiered system of granaries at the county, town, and village level promulgated in the Kangxi period continued to inform defense against famine in the republic.

Funding for below-market-price sales (*pingtiao*) from granaries was most commonly sourced from local merchant and gentry households, with the prodding of the magistrate.[6] In most cases, the sources do not specify the terms on which monies were raised. One representative example simply states that the magistrate borrowed 12,000 yuan from local businesses to finance the district's discount sales bureau.[7] For a more detailed accounting of how funds were raised by local governments to finance grain subsidies, we return to Wei county, the hard-hit Zhili district along the border with Shandong whose village and individual relief we discussed in chapter 6. Facing unfolding famine that threatened an estimated 90 percent of the 163,000 residents in his district, the Wei county magistrate received permission from the provincial government, finance bureau, and prefect at Daming to offer a public bond in November, the terms of which the magistrate determined in consultation with gentry in the district. Bearing interest of 8 percent per annum and with a limit of 20,000 yuan on the capital that could be raised, the loans were "voluntary" (*suiyi*) as opposed to the "mandatory" (*qiangpo*) bonds issued at times by the state. People who purchased 1,000 yuan in notes would receive an inscribed board from the county; those purchasing over 3,000 yuan would receive recognition from the province. All interest would be repaid by the time the bonds matured in autumn of 1921, but the bondholder had the option to extend the loan period so the monies could be devoted to bandit defense.[8]

Charity granaries were, in some cases, stocked through a system of community contributions based on household land ownership. One documented case is that of central Zhili's Ding county, whose magistrate met with gentry in the autumn and formed the Ding County Drought-Disaster Relief Society (Dingxian hanzai jiuji hui).[9] As part of this wider effort, residents of each village gathered together to discuss the formation of charity granaries (*yicang*) across the district, according to the district gazetteer; households owning over twenty *mu* of land—or roughly three acres, the average family farm size in North China at the time—were to contribute two *he* (one-tenth of a liter) of grain per *mu*; households owning less than twenty *mu* and those in possession of only homes and capital (such as carts or beasts of burden) were to provide transportation for grain. As for the interest or income the charity facilities earned from the loaning out or sale of grain, it was to be reinvested in the purchasing of additional granary stocks.[10]

Price-stabilization efforts across such a wide field of activity doubtless varied in integrity and zeal, while presenting ample opportunity for graft. By November, at least three-quarters of Zhili's counties had opened discount operations in some form or another. For the counties that lacked rail lines, which was the majority of districts in the case of central and south Zhili, the operations involved millions of *jin* of grain changing hands as they traveled by mule cart into the interior.[11] In one metropolitan county—Fangshan, due west of Beijing—county-run granary sales were reportedly few, amounting to "several dozen *shi*" over two autumn months, and at parity with market prices.[12] Unfortunately, far less news coverage in the interior than in the capital makes it even more difficult to gauge the extent of neglect or malfeasance in granary operations in the interior.

Description of the inner workings of these facilities is also hard to come by in the sources. Two particularly detailed dispatches from just south of Zhili's border with Henan shed some light on organizational and other operational techniques. In Wu'an county, the endeavor involved thirty-three teams in both the city and countryside, each with a discount branch that sold each *jin* of grain at 40–50 *wen* (4–5 coppers) below the prevailing local market price, a reduction of roughly 50 percent.[13] In nearby Weihui, the discount center was set up in the temple of the god of war, where the local agricultural association held its meetings. Weihui's magistrate put "gentle (?) pressure on every well-to-do family in the county to contribute according to ability for famine relief," and in "all" the surrounding districts, the correspondent added, magistrates and local gentry "contributed capital" to establish these centers.[14] Pigeons and sparrows were kept from the wheat, which sat in woven reed bins eight feet high and nine feet wide, by mats on top. Coarse sorghum was added to the grain portions on sale to, in part, put off the well-to-do who were accustomed to finer grain varieties, such as wheat or rice. Doors opened each day at nine in the morning, and with a purchase limit of 70 *jin* a day per visitor, 70,000–140,000 *jin* were sold daily. The proceeds were used to acquire more grain from an unafflicted part of the province.

Discount grain operations in at least seventy-four Zhili counties brought in anywhere from 318,243,800 to 467,641,200 *jin* of grain for discount sale in the three months between mid-August and mid-November 1920, according to records of the Ministry of the Interior, using monies raised locally and 500,000 yuan of diverted central state funds.[15] As we will see below in this chapter, much of this mobilization was stimulated by tax exemptions and facilitated by reduced or remitted freight fees, which the provincial government and agencies of the central state in Beijing conferred on condition that the grain be sold at reduced cost to the poor, generally 10–50 percent below prevailing prices.

To put Zhili's province-wide discount grain project of 1920–21 into perspective, it would have amounted to a half-*jin* famine ration of grain every day from August to November for 8,732,055 people, or 52 percent of the estimated population of the seventy-four afflicted counties with grain discount programs.[16] This number of people exceeds the population of Zhili estimated to be directly affected by the drought-famine, which stood at 8,076,500 as of mid-November (according to Tianjin's international relief society), the moment our data for volumes of province-wide discount sales end.[17]

Pierre-Étienne Will and R. Bin Wong have argued that the Qing civilian granary system was more effective and lasted longer than scholars have previously recognized. Tracing its operation up to the start of the devastating Taiping rebellion, Wong points out that the system consumed anywhere from 0.5 percent to 2.0 percent of central state annual revenue from 1700 to 1850, and that in one stretch of the eighteenth century it "fed as much as 5 percent of a provincial population for more than 15 percent of the year."[18]

It appears, then, that despite the breakdown of central government oversight in the early years of militarism and during the intermittent outbreak of civil war in the late 1910s and 1920s, the civilian granary system was still able to feed a similarly substantial segment of the rural Zhili population in a time of crisis. While the centuries-old system undoubtedly had periods of neglect, corruption, and destruction—particularly amid the rebellions, wars, and extreme instances of drought and flood in the late nineteenth century—civilian granaries were sufficiently robust and culturally embedded in Chinese communities not to simply disintegrate with the decline of the Qing imperial system.

Emergency and General Relief: Soup Kitchens

Of course, offers of discounted grain by definition benefited only those with available cash. Sources of cash in troubled times, as discussed in chapter 6, included the pawning of clothing, tools, and other property;

gifts or loans from extended family members or village mutual aid programs; income earned from basket weaving, producing earth salt, and other pursuits; the sale of land or family members to neighbors or traffickers; and relief monies from outside charities. Those bereft of such resources and unable or unwilling to flee the famine areas could, at times, look to emergency grants of aid in cash or kind from the state.

Here the record of activities of the central and provincial levels of government in 1920 is far more limited. Instead, the burden of providing the second stage of official relief under the Qing—a month's worth of emergency goods to sustain the most vulnerable until the start of general relief operations—largely fell on local semiofficial or private efforts. In some places, emergency relief was dispensed through mutual aid negotiated at the village level or by outside charities and resident missionaries. In others, the afflicted presumably had to fend for themselves by begging or foraging until general relief got under way in November and December, largely in the form of soup kitchens.

Members of the gentry such as Feng Sizhi in Shanxi, as we saw in chapter 6, publicly criticized officials at the central and provincial levels for failing to come up with anything like sufficient funds to meet the monumental crisis at hand in mid-autumn 1920. These failings were no less evident in Zhili. As of October, provincial authorities had set aside a total of only 288,500 yuan for emergency relief (*jizhen*), even though by their own count 15,950 villages in ninety-two counties across the province were severely stricken, resulting in emergency allocations to ninety counties of 1,000–10,000 yuan each that month.[19] In each recipient county, then, provincial emergency relief could sustain somewhere between two thousand and twenty thousand people for a month, when Zhili counties had populations of up to 250,000.[20]

As these initial palliative supplies were quickly exhausted, starting in November magistrates around the famine field met with local gentry to raise funds locally for the opening of soup kitchens. As was the case in the Qing period, in addition to the official relief apparatus set up during any particular crisis, mainly in county seats and towns, there were any number of informal, gentry-run relief stations in the interior. How many depended on the particular crisis, immediate local conditions, and the social dynamics within communities. In 1920, these relief stations varied in capacity from several hundred to several thousand attendees a day. They also varied in their density and distribution which often reflected decisions made locally based on the severity of crop failure and the size of the affected population.

There is no reason why soup kitchens had to be chosen as the main relief method over the winter of 1920–21. As recently as the late nineteenth century, communities in many of the same counties had handled drought and famine in their localities with distributions of grain instead, while others had used soup kitchens.[21] Each method had advantages and drawbacks. Soup kitchens offered more control over the provisioning of relief resources, yet this benefit was offset by the dangers—including disease and disorder—presented by the movement and concentration of famine victims at relief centers. Perhaps for these reasons, the numerous international relief societies overwhelmingly chose to distribute relief in the form of grain and money in 1920–21.

A concentration of news and gazetteer accounts about two sections of central Zhili offer at least a sense of the scale and circumstances in which county-wide operations were launched over the famine year. Located on the edge of the rail line running south from Beijing to Hankou, central Zhili's Wan county (today's Shunping) had received a mere 1,000 yuan in emergency relief funds in October. This minimal allocation from the province may have been due to earlier lower official estimates of the scale of the disaster there, since the Ministry of the Interior had recorded only nineteen "heavily-hit villages" in the county and seventy-nine "lightly-hit villages" in October.[22] In December, though, an international relief society based in Beijing estimated that the proportion of Wan's population affected and made dependent on relief by the drought-famine was 60–90 percent.[23] It was then, in early December, that 3,000 yuan in contributions were raised locally to establish a soup kitchen in the southern section of the county seat. The magistrate then tasked "fair-minded and upright scholar-gentry" (*gongzheng shishen*) with dispersing themselves among the county's afflicted villages to set up thirty soup kitchens funded with money raised in communities throughout the county that had been "spared disaster" in one way or another.[24]

A similar arrangement of soup kitchens funded and managed by the merchant-gentry class appeared in five districts adjacent to Wan. As winter approached, operations in Mancheng (population 102,000) included one facility for every four to five villages, or one for every seven to eight smaller villages, in addition to six shelters for those deemed old and weak; Ding's (population 310,000) had a soup kitchen for every two villages and a shelter for the elderly in the county seat; both Anxin (population 148,000) and Tang (population 230,000) counties were establishing one soup kitchen for every two villages, with plans to operate through March 1921 in the case of Anxin; and Yi (population 268,000), whose autumn crop had been over 60 percent of normal, was running six facilities in its western and southern districts.[25]

Similar endeavors appear to have gotten under way in November in a cluster of three counties further down the Beijing-Hankou rail line, with each reflecting the county's population size and degree of destitution. With fewer than 20 percent of the 65,000 residents of Gaoyi estimated to be affected by the drought-famine, the gentry there joined with the magistrate to set up five soup kitchens in the afflicted districts.[26] In neighboring Zhao, also relatively lightly hit by crop failure but with a much larger population of 215,000, Chinese Red Cross investigators sent from Tianjin reported that wealthy gentry had assembled at the county offices and begun pooling donations for the establishment of soup kitchens in each afflicted village.[27] Abutting both counties but harder hit, Yuanshi had at least 90,000 out of its population of 140,000 stricken by late autumn. There, the Red Cross reported that village leaders raised monies from among merchant-gentry to fund soup kitchens in each village in the county.[28]

Was the density of soup kitchen activity sketched above representative of the Zhili famine field? These counties in western and central Zhili sat astride the Beijing-Hankou rail line, which certainly facilitated their provisioning and lowered transport costs through the autumn and winter. But there is the issue of source bias: proximity to the railway could also result in more frequent or thorough canvassing by investigative teams and city reporters, on whose work much of this section is based.

There is no easy answer to this question. Sources are too scarce to attempt to map the existence of rural efforts that were so remote and atomized. But their existence, at least in districts along the Beijing-Hankou rail line in west Zhili, caught the notice of at least one foreign relief agent in the region: "Chinese *in many places* have organized independent societies for relief," a field worker for an international relief committee reported to his superiors in early February 1921, from southwest Zhili's Shunde (Xingtai) county. "They finance them *without aid from other than local sources.* They have established soup kitchens and are giving excellent grain rations. In some places they give one and in others two meals a day. Whatever the number of meals, the ration is large. The man who gets it has all he wants. One of these chow *changs* [*zhouchang*] in Shuntefu cares for two thousand refugees a day and on a festival day 2,700 were fed."[29] Railway records indicate that the Xingtai self-government assembly (*zizhi hui*) brought in half a million *jin* of grain in December, possibly to provision such an operation, although it appears that others were active in the same vicinity: the city's modern gazetteer states that in 1920 a city resident (*yi ren*) "initiated and managed a soup kitchen serving over 9,000 people a day" there as well.[30]

As much as the above soup kitchen activity maintained stricken communities and passing refugees through the winter, none of our examples so far involves villages in the hardest-hit sections of the famine field, which was centered in north Henan and south Zhili. This raises the question to what extent locals in 1920 were able to sponsor soup kitchens in the sections of the North China Plain where nearly entire districts were deemed afflicted by outside investigators. It is hard to say, but two final examples suggest that even in areas of utter destitution the possibility of local soup kitchen operations cannot be discounted.

Xinhe was one of the hardest-hit counties in 1920. It was reckoned by missionary investigators to have been 100 percent impoverished, due in part to back-to-back crises in the years leading up to the drought.[31] Small in territory but with a sizable population of some 183,000 residents, Xinhe was also especially isolated from the railroad, equally distant from the Beijing-Hankou line to the west and the Tianjin-Jinan line to the east. The region had been submerged under the floodwaters of broken dikes in 1917, and with the arrival of full-fledged famine in 1920, "countless" perished, according to the district gazetteer, "weary of the prolonged drought" that pushed "previously honest and good-natured people" to roam far away or "loaf about without decent occupation and assuming cunning ways," with bands of thieves "tempting model workers and the young to follow their ways." In the winter of 1920, county authorities and police were reportedly helpless in the face of plundering bandits, with several surprise attacks occurring each night—leading even the wealthy to "live in fear" and flee to the county seat. Furthermore, in the months leading up to the 1920 drought, the county magistrate was dismissed from his post and was replaced because he had inadequately estimated the scale of the looming disaster.[32]

All of this suggests that it was impossible for Xinhe communities in 1920 to aid each other. Yet forty-five pages later the same source offers details about a soup kitchen set up in that year in a town well south of the Xinhe county seat, a facility that was by all appearances locally initiated and funded. According to the gazetteer's section of "filial and benevolent" (*xiaoyi*) biographies, eight managers, two of whom were also on a list of twenty-five charitable figures (*shanshi*), administered donations of 1,580 *diao*, which was enough to purchase grain to give 260 people in the town of Sutian daily rations for six months. All but four of the thirty-one people listed as participating in this charitable endeavor were surnamed Zhang, and judging by their given names, the operation was dominated by four sets of brothers along with one female donor surnamed Mao.[33]

A similar situation occurred to the south of Xinhe, along the border of Shandong. There, meetings between magistrates and local members of the merchant-gentry class in Guangzong failed to come up with sufficient funds for soup kitchens on a county-wide scale. Of the county's 90,000 residents, some 78,000 were deemed fully afflicted by famine. And when community meetings in the fall determined that at least one soup kitchen for every ten villages had to be set up throughout the county for four to five months to feed 42,000 destitute residents unable to survive without help, not even 3 percent of the minimum funds needed to do so—1,040 yuan out of an estimated 40,000–50,000 yuan—were raised, leaving the magistrate to lament this fund-raising failure in a written appeal to a major Beijing relief society for emergency relief.[34] The Tianjin Red Cross investigators who reported active county-wide soup kitchens elsewhere in the province affirmed that Guangzong had no coordinated local relief effort beyond discount grain operations at five gentry-run locations around the county and a charity loan center (*huojie suo*).[35]

Here too reports of failure to set up relief centers in a section of the famine field must not be taken as absolute: the Guangzong district gazetteer contains a biography of a native of the county seat who was, it relates, entrusted with the management of a soup kitchen in 1920 that saved "a multitude of lives" there—this in a county that by other accounts had failed to establish any such facilities at all.[36]

Detailed descriptions of the operation of relief stations are also frustratingly rare, although one did make its way into the pages of Shanghai's *North China Herald* in February 1921, when the English-language weekly printed a dispatch from a relief station in the suburbs of Guide (today's Shangqiu) in eastern Henan. There, where famished refugees were converging from the west and north of the province, the reporter found four to five hundred destitute sheltered and fed daily at a soup kitchen "entirely run by local Chinese." The "four local gentry" running the operation had "themselves largely subscribed" to the money and grain contributions, the latter "kept in large matting baskets . . . all sealed by having a board with carved characters pressed on the flattened surface. This raises the characters in bold relief on the top surface of the grain and not a handful could be abstracted without detection." Donations were posted on the walls, the reported explained, "and "none of the grain is taken for the daily feeding, we were informed, unless the full committee of four were in attendance . . . everything seems very open and above board." Such rudimentary theft-prevention techniques and the posting of accounts on the premises were indicative of a locally financed operation, accountable chiefly to the members of the surrounding community. It was exceedingly rare for such news to find its way into the treaty-port press in 1920–21, especially into a generally critical British publication whose correspondent deemed it "a great satisfaction" to find "benevolence instituted and carried on entirely by Chinese without graft attached as far as one can see." The headline read: "Real Charity in Kueiteh: Merciful Undertaking without Any Squeeze."[37]

State Finances and the Maritime Customs *"Famine Loan"*

So what was the role of the Beiyang regime in relief provisioning? At the beginning of November, the Ministry of the Interior reportedly issued orders to all counties in the region with surplus wealth or fair harvests earlier in the autumn to finance multiple soup kitchens in their districts in light of the coming winter. Included in the ministry's instructions were orders for county officials to investigate needs in areas of drought and erect shelters to shield refugees from the cold; tally and report the numbers of residents fleeing to neighboring districts; and ensure that there were sufficient grain discount centers in the famine districts.[38] The Zhili government followed in December with orders to all magistrates in the province to form relief societies with local gentry and, in light of the scarcity of available relief funds from the province, collect donations from wealthy gentry, for distribution in kind or for the construction of soup kitchens.[39]

Relief operations shifted into higher gear in central and south Zhili in November and December, and closely in line with the ministry's instructions. Does this mean that district-level officials and rural gentry were in lock-step with directives from the central leadership? That is doubtful. Printed correspondence in official publications, such as the Shanxi provincial government's *Laifu bao* and the central government's *Zhengfu gongbao*, indicate the existence of active communication channels between top levels of the state and the district and village levels over the crisis year. But it is far more plausible that district magistrates and local elites setting up soup kitchens and taking other measures in the countryside were simply turning to a common cultural playbook of relief practices, inherited from the late imperial period, that they shared with the national and provincial leaders who issued such directives from Beijing and Tianjin.

If the higher echelons of the state played a role in the overall relief effort, it was to coordinate the nationwide movement of resources. The central relief operation was launched with the establishment of the Government Relief Bureau (Zhenwuchu) in September, for which the government was reportedly successful in raising an initial million yuan. The organization of a Disaster Relief Council (Zhenzai weiyuan hui) followed, with Cao Rui, the Zhili governor, as chair and the outgoing superintendent of the metropolitan region, Wang Hu, as vice chair.[40] Despite his imminent departure, the choice of Wang nonetheless made sense, as he was an experienced relief administrator (as shown in chapters 1 and 5) who was, moreover, taking up in that same month the governorship of

Jiangsu—which, together with the wider Yangzi River valley, would become the second largest regional source of relief grain over the year, after the northeastern provinces.

Public money, not grain or the rail cars and carts to deliver it, was the most pressing need in 1920–21. The unseated regime of Duan Qirui's Anhui faction had used roughly fifty million yuan in loans from Tokyo in its efforts to defeat its enemies, much of which merely resulted in the considerable volumes of materiel that were seized by the victorious Zhili and Fengtian armies.[41] By one accounting, the Ministry of Finance's cash debts alone would reach nearly 300 million yuan by September 1921.[42] Meanwhile, provincial tax revenues controlled by the central government were steadily evaporating. Although the foreign-managed Chinese Maritime Customs Service continued to transfer customs income to whatever regime was in control of Beijing, the central government, now effectively controlled by Cao Kun and Wu Peifu, had only piecemeal funding for its day-to-day operations.

At the provincial level, anticipating a major shortfall in land tax revenue in the fall, Zhili announced a supplementary set of tax regulations stipulating that three *mao* be collected for each yuan normally collected in grain tax; however, magistrates were also instructed to assess the hardships of residents in their districts due to the drought and put off tax collection accordingly.[43] It is unclear how widely tax exemptions or postponements were granted to disaster districts, but they presumably had a negative impact on provincial revenues. In the case of hard-hit Wei county (whose local relief efforts were examined in chapter 6), tax remissions were granted on the basis of the rate of harvest failure in the particular section of the county where a farm was based. Remissions were 20–70 percent of assessed taxes, payment of which was put off until autumn 1921.[44]

With the central government failing even to meet its payroll, a handful of prominent former officials involved in relief planning turned to international financing. A week before holding an inaugural joint Chinese-foreign (*huayang*) international relief meeting in late September 1920 at his Beijing residence, former premier Xiong Xiling drew up a proposal for a foreign loan on behalf of his newly formed Relief Society for the Five Northern Provinces. For this, Xiong approached the official representative for negotiations with the foreign treaty powers. At the time this was the Spanish minister to Beijing, Don Luis Pastor, who held the rotating post of dean of the Diplomatic Body, the collective of foreign powers in Beijing. Noting that it was a "common practice in foreign countries" to raise funds through surcharges on transport fares, Xiong, along with his colleague Wang Daxie, another former premier and cofounder of Xiong's relief group, proposed a loan of fifty million yuan from European and American financiers, using the transport surcharges as security. Most of China's state railroad construction was underwritten by foreign loans, the men noted, and the country's shipping lines were also foreign-owned, so any "agreement for imposing such surcharges can only be arrived at by our Government by taking up the matter with the Diplomatic Body."[45]

The men were promptly rebuffed and instructed to go instead through the "proper channel of communication, that is, the Ministry of Foreign Affairs," and Pastor noted that "personally" he was "somewhat doubtful whether, in their present form" their proposals "would prove acceptable to the Diplomatic Body."[46]

A week later, the head of the Chinese Ministry of Foreign Affairs, Yan Huiqing (aka W. W. Yen, 1877–1950), submitted a new loan proposal to the heads of the foreign legations. The son of an American-educated Episcopal pastor and a Christian mother, a graduate of the University of Virginia, a professor of English at St. John's University in Shanghai, and lately Chinese envoy to Copenhagen, Yan had a considerably narrower social bridge to cross in his dealings with the legations than many of his counterparts in the Beiyang government.[47] Explaining that "contributions" to the Government Relief Bureau were "inadequate," he proposed a 10 percent surtax on both maritime and native customs for one year. Although import duties were capped at 5.0 percent by treaty agreements, Yan sought to increase them to 5.5 percent. All surtax revenue, he affirmed, would remain "under the effective management of the Inspector General of Customs," a post that was in foreign hands, and would be "utilized exclusively for famine relief purposes." Acknowledging that the duty, which Beijing had managed to increase to 5.0 percent just a few years before, was "explicitly sanctioned by Treaty arrangements," he requested that an exception be made as a charitable "extra-treaty action."[48]

Concerns over unequal application of customs surcharges, among other things, held up the loan agreement. "You will recall that this Government's acceptance of the surtax was conditional on its being imposed on all countries alike," Washington cabled its minister in Beijing, Charles Crane, at the New Year, alluding to a dispute among the foreign signatories.[49] The same day the British consul general informed Pastor that it remained the "unanimous opinion" of his "colleagues" that out of fear of Chinese mismanagement, "some measure of foreign control over the proceeds of the surtax is eminently desirable."[50] "Conditions of all legations must be met before surtax can be levied," Crane wrote in a follow-up telegram to Washington in early January, three months after the initial proposal to the powers by Yan.[51]

Privately, the British minister to Beijing, Beilby Alston, cited different reasons for the delay of the famine loan of four million yuan. Beijing's formal access to the powers was at the time orchestrated by a man who was "slowly drinking himself to death," Alston confided to Earl Curzon, the British Foreign Secretary. "Last year [Luis Pastor was] nearly dead of cholera, and he now frankly says that, though he escaped death at the hand of cholera, the *décanat* [deanship] will surely kill him. He is totally unfit for the post, and the delays, owing to his inability to attend to business in the transaction of the affairs of the Diplomatic Body, are becoming a public scandal."[52]

However, Beijing was precluded from going through other international channels for financing. One of the reasons for the continued recognition of whichever faction's regime was in control of the republic's nominal political capital through the late 1910s and 1920s was to ensure the servicing of debts and Qing-era war indemnities, which continued to be met through Maritime Customs revenues through the famine year.[53] After the recent world war, the treaty powers, pursuant to a proposal from the United States, had formed a united front for the purpose of offering loans to the Chinese government. This consortium of banking concerns from the United States, Britain, Japan, and France was intended, as Akira Iriye explains, "to be given a retroactive and current option on all loans to China. By this means a new system of international cooperation to assist China would replace competitive disorderly arrangements."[54]

Meanwhile, correspondence from the Chinese side took on an even more desperate tone. Around the New Year, Beijing's Government Relief Bureau had redrafted its proposal for the control and distribution of the pending loan monies, a key concern of the foreign governments, which the Ministry of Foreign Affairs forwarded to Pastor. "I request Your Excellency to be so good as to transmit [these proposals] to the Ministers of all the Powers resident in Peking," Yan wrote, "and to quickly obtain their assent and to send me a reply as soon as possible, so that relief may be granted to the poor Chinese suffering from famine. Such is my hope."[55]

Yan's motivations, writing from an arm of the Chinese government that "carried out China's foreign policy virtually independently of the factional rivalries in Peking," in the words of Andrew Nathan, were not questioned.[56] Instead, the foreign diplomatic and press corps voiced concerns about the possible fate of any funds entrusted to the central government. Fears over the diversion of relief funds to military uses were most vocally expressed in relation to North China's main power brokers, Cao Kun and Zhang Zuolin. Yan's proposal to the powers had been submitted "within a few days of the announcement that Generals Chang Tsolin and Tsao Kun have intimidated Peking into promising each of them a grant of three million dollars per annum," the *Peking & Tientsin Times* noted, "to enable them to raise and maintain additional Army Divisions."[57] The paper argued that China had enough millionaires—former statesmen and military officers among them—to provide money equal to the sought-after loan from the powers, and there was no "guarantee" anyway that such a loan would not be "calmly requisitioned by the militarists for the use of their Armies."[58]

With the central government operating hand to mouth, banks were becoming increasingly careful to protect their assets from state borrowing or outright seizure. In the 1910s, regional branches of the Bank of China in Guangdong, Shandong, Sichuan, and elsewhere became easy prey for military authorities demanding or otherwise making off with bank reserves of more than a million yuan at a time. In 1920, top managers at the bank devised a system of safeguards by keeping its note issuance capabilities and cash reserves at foreign-run treaty ports so that bank branches in the interior were less vulnerable to seizure—a strategy that apparently worked, according to Linsun Cheng.[59]

Further complicating the picture, though, were reports in the foreign press that substantial sums for relief were coming from the country's leaders: 1.6 million yuan from three commercial sources and the estate of a deceased man in Shanghai; 500,000 yuan bequeathed by the late military governor of Jiangsu, Li Chun (1875–1920), for relief efforts in his hometown of Tianjin;[60] and two million yuan from Zhili's Governor Cao Rui, Cao Kun's brother. If Cao Rui's contribution "comes out of his private pocket," an editorial in Shanghai's *North China Herald* remarked, "it is indeed a munificent gift," although its existence is difficult to corroborate.[61] This would have amounted to 10 percent of the 20.0 million yuan in assets that Cao Rui had owned at the time, according to a Japanese historian cited by Gavan McCormack, who also estimated that Cao Kun was worth 4.0 million.[62] How the uneducated sons of a Tianjin cloth peddler and, in the case of Cao Kun, the onetime drinking partner of President Yuan Shikai, were able to amass one of the largest family fortunes in Zhili of course says much about the scale of self-aggrandizement by the powerful at the time.[63] There is little doubt that corruption and absconding with public funds were scourges in republican politics. One reported case involved leftover relief funds for the vast province-wide relief effort during and after the Zhili floods of 1917, which were cited as a possible source of relief funds when drought and famine loomed in the summer of 1920. But of the eighteen million yuan originally raised for relief, twelve million had been spent and, according to one report, three million had since "vanished," leaving another three million sitting in a Tianjin bank as of August 1920.[64] Follow-up coverage offers no hint of the fate of this large sum. The ever-present drain on public funds by the military was another reason to resist contributing to government relief campaigns—presumably even on the part of officials.

Over a hundred days passed before signatures were finally put to the loan of four million yuan, at 8 percent interest, on January 19, 1921, sourced in equal parts from four foreign banks.[65] Nonetheless, the imposition of the surtax—which would produce 750,000 yuan monthly for the Chinese government—was actually delayed until March 1 "in deference to the views of the Diplomatic Body," which had been pressured to delay tariff collection by Tianjin's American Chamber of Commerce and general Chamber of Commerce.[66] A further condition stipulated that the entire four million yuan remain under foreign control and in the hands of the six provincial international relief societies.[67] Beijing's Government Relief Bureau would handle none of the money.

Alternative Financing Schemes

At the onset of famine in the autumn, with their coffers empty and revenues limited, central government leaders had presided over a scramble for relief monies, starting with contributions from official salaries. Premier Jin Yunpeng proposed that all officials beyond the capital earning salaries in excess of fifty yuan a month contribute 5 percent of their pay for two months, estimating that the move could raise more than one million yuan per month.[68] A month later, with projected funding needs skyrocketing, Jin donated 20,000 yuan and set aside an additional 20 percent of his monthly salary in the last three months of 1920 for relief, and he then encouraged officials throughout the government to follow his example by "making, at will, an accurate estimate of their own ability to contribute" in the same fashion.[69] The Ministry of Justice had already responded to the premier's September appeal, ordering all ministry personnel along with officials of all courts and inspection bureaus beyond the capital to deduct 5 percent of their pay for disaster relief funds. The ministry added that courts and jails in the capital were already carrying out the order.[70] The Finance Ministry responded to Jin's October call by deducting 20 percent of the salaries it paid to staff members for three months, ending in December.[71]

But it is unclear how these deductions were realized: even the Finance Ministry was struggling to pay its staff, and salaries there had already been in arrears at the start of the year.[72] Following the Ministry of Foreign Affairs, in October the leaders of the Ministry of Education ordered all schools to devote 20 percent of their staff members' monthly pay to disaster relief; the directive was in fact 20 percent of the pay that staff members actually received, since pay there too was already well in arrears—reportedly setting off an outcry among teachers and others at the lower ranks of the educational system.[73]

Realizing in October that approaching individuals for relief monies would not be enough, the Ministry of Agriculture and Commerce began contacting business firms around the country to "beg for relief funds" (*qi zhen*), as one headline put it.[74] It was almost immediately announced that the Beijing-based Bank of Communications and Bank of China had each contributed (*juanzhu*) 100,000 yuan to the official relief bureau.[75] This was on top of the 890,000 yuan that the central government had managed to borrow from six banks (half from the Bank of China branch in Tianjin) in August.[76]

To fund famine relief in the north, the Ministry of Finance increased stamp duties on milled flour in Shanghai and, together with the Ministry of the Interior, raised 500,000 yuan through the sale of lottery tickets to the public in Tianjin, Harbin, and other cities, followed by a second lottery of equal size soon after.[77]

The arm of the Chinese state that generated the most relief monies over the famine year was most likely the Ministry of Communications, which, in addition to issuing famine relief postage stamps, applied famine surcharges on passenger and freight rates on the national rail system starting on October 11 (the surcharges were increased the following month).[78] By mid-December, each rail station along the Beijing-Hankou line was collecting on average 1,500 yuan a day in surcharges, which was projected to net almost 100,000 yuan from each station over the following two months.[79]

The ministry was thus able to waive roughly nine million yuan in transport fees for relief goods through the end of the famine relief campaign in May.[80] Since the onset of the food crisis in September, both official and extragovernmental agents seeking tax-free status for shipments of relief supplies such as grain, coal, and clothing were required to apply for freight passports from provincial authorities. On the whole, these relief supplies crisscrossed the country free of charge on the state rail network, with nearly half the remitted transport fees applied to goods moving down the Beijing-Shenyang line from the northeast.[81]

Freight volumes across China consequently soared, compared to previous years. In January 1921, for example, the Beijing-Shenyang rail line alone conveyed 65,350 tons, or 106,428,000 *jin*, of Manchurian grain—both for relief agencies and the general market—to Tianjin and other cities south of the Great Wall, a sixfold increase over the 9,541 tons and 10,434 tons on the same line in the two previous Januaries. The *North China Herald* observed in March 1921 that the managers of the Chinese rail system had even doubled an estimate that Herbert Hoover had recently made on the maximum capacity of the Chinese to move relief, based on his experience with American and European railways while overseeing American postwar relief in Belgium. The British newspaper added that "in performance records the managers have nothing of which to be ashamed."[82]

Throughout the fall and winter of the famine year, the money used to acquire relief grain in the northeast came from a variety of sources, including Zhili's district-level discount grain and soup kitchen operations described above and provincial and central relief agencies and charities based in Beijing and elsewhere. How, and to what extent, the central state ultimately procured the money required to acquire such volumes of grain is unclear. Plans such as the one announced in November by the Zhili Provincial Assembly to borrow five million yuan from Beijing and Tianjin banks for the purchase of grain from provinces along the Yangzi River and in Manchuria are a possibile explanation, but it is difficult to confirm that such loans were ever made.[83] Nonetheless, a relief infrastructure in the central government and that of Zhili province did take shape in mid-November, when the Beijing-based Government Relief Bureau set up distribution centers around the province (at Baoding, Ji, Shunde, and Daming), with a central depot at Tianjin, where the rail lines north to Manchuria and south to the Yangzi valley met.[84] In the case of one relief shipment the following month, the bureau and the Zhili provincial government were jointly responsible for the delivery of eleven million *jin* of relief grain to seven rail depots in eastern and western Zhili, which had a value of roughly 600,000 yuan.[85]

Conclusion

Foreign press and diplomatic reports over the famine year denied the surprising coordination between the rival militarists in relief and refugee movement. The three million yuan the *Peking & Tientsin Times* reported Zhang Zuolin to be demanding from the central government for military expenses in October 1920 corresponded exactly to what papers in the northeast were reporting that he was planning to raise there starting that month for famine relief south of the Great Wall, cabling the military governors of Jilin and Heilongjiang to launch fund-raising and ordering counties in Fengtian to raise monies according to the size of their fall harvests (a subject covered in chapters 8 and 9).[86] The figure would help account for the volumes of relief grain coming to the famine field from Manchuria through native societies two months later.

With the onset of famine conditions in September 1920, the *North China Herald* had condemned what it saw as Beijing's "characteristic attempt to push off the responsibility of action upon provincial officials," adding that what was "needed and what as yet we see no sign of is a coordinated effort, directed by the Government as a whole," to bring together the "present spasmodic efforts of individual persons and agencies."[87] The editors of the influential British weekly were correct in pointing out both the lack of a Qing-style central bureaucratic direction to relief operations in 1920 and the flowering of myriad aid efforts—both massive and modest—by individuals and agencies across the five-province famine belt. However, they failed to appreciate two key characteristics of the native relief efforts unfolding hundreds of miles from their offices in the treaty port of Shanghai: the vital degree of official coordination required to acquire and deliver grain across provincial jurisdictions, and the fact that many of these extragovernmental efforts were engineered by members of these same military establishments condemned for their supposed inaction in the face of a calamitous famine. In other words, in the absence of a solvent central state in 1920, and in light of the correspondingly low public faith in the integrity of cash-starved public institutions, many people in official circles put their resources and energies into the myriad quasi-governmental groups that had formed contemporaneously with formal state relief programs in the fall. Provincial and central government ministries, official relief agencies, and the Beiyang leadership in Beijing generally played a secondary role in the relief of rural Zhili, but one that appears no less crucial in ensuring its overall efficacy.

Ensuring the unhampered movement of railway stock and covering the expenses of relief transportation was the central government's most significant role in the famine mitigation effort. It should be stressed, though, that this did not merely entail the smooth running of the rail infrastructure connecting the North China drought areas with Zhangjiakou to the north, Taiyuan to the west, Hankou and Nanjing (at Pukou) to the south, and Mukden to the northeast. It also involved the coordination of the travel of famine migrants out of the disaster districts and the mobilization of vast amounts of resources between the domains of what had become de facto independent military regimes—those of the relatively autonomous military governor of Shanxi, Yan Xishan, and, most notably, Marshal Zhang Zuolin, who ruled the three provinces of Manchuria. To that region we now return.

CHAPTER EIGHT

Migrant Routes

In late September 1920, gendarmes garrisoned just beyond the walls of Beijing were tasked with cooking porridge for travelers passing through. In conjunction with the system of daytime soup kitchens that capital authorities had recently set up across the region, the garrison worked through the night, serving in one instance 130 refugees newly arrived by train from famine-ravaged Hejian prefecture in central Zhili. These men and women stayed only a few hours before, rested and fed, setting off early in the morning for Suiyuan and other parts of Inner Mongolia, where they intended to "eke out a living."[1] Garrison soldiers performed this task until at least the end of March.[2] For the eight months straddling the winter of 1920–21, adult members of such families on the move could deposit children at a transit shelter set up by the Ministry of Communications near Beijing's main rail station at Xizhi gate, where older relatives venturing north could return for them when returning to their home districts in the spring.[3]

In the summer of 1920, many farming families and other residents of the Yellow River basin headed in the opposite direction of incoming grain trains, following the transport links southward to the Yangzi River valley, northward through Beijing to the Mongolian plains, or northeast through Tianjin to the forested expanse of Manchuria. It would be meaningless to date the beginning of this outward movement, since it followed well-established seasonal migration routes. However, with the onset of famine conditions in late summer 1920, reports of travelers along these routes spiked in number. In August, before the formally recognized onset of famine conditions across the north, groups of families referred to in the press as coming from the ranks of the poor (*pinmin*) were already stopping in Beijing—in one case, having come from as far as southwest Shandong—with the intent of settling in Inner Mongolia.[4] But by late summer, with recognized disaster (*zaihuang*) unfolding in Zhili and other districts affected by the drought-famine, others, dubbed "calamity-stricken people" (*zaimin*) or "people in distress" (*nanmin*) in the press, joined this well-trod path northward beyond the Great Wall and through the mountain passes.

This main distinction in the Chinese press between different types of people in transit was essentially based on their level of desperation, rather than any political designation, such as being in a condition of exile or statelessness.[5] In the context of 1920s China, the use of the English term "refugee" in the strict sense is anachronistic, so the word is used here only descriptively; *zaimin* and *nanmin* are translated loosely, depending on the circumstances in which these people appear in the sources, to better recognize their agency: either as famine migrants (afflicted people on the move with relative autonomy) or refugees (arriving in a place beyond their home districts who receive state or charitable refuge or assistance in some form).

How were incoming flows of people received in neighboring military domains, in communities along the banks of the Yangzi or the Heilongjiang (Amur), or the grasslands leading to the Gobi? And how might have famine figured in the calculations of the leaders in a region increasingly dominated by Japanese interests? Vagrant populations have long been a source of fear and suspicion by China's ruling establishment and the communities through which they passed. The ubiquity of migrants and refugees in China's tumultuous modern period has led to their inevitable appearance in narratives of urban history and warfare. Yet little light has been shed by the literature on the communities along the routes they traveled.[6] Therefore, it is difficult to determine what precedents existed in terms of refugee relief in the 1930s and 1940s, when China's refugee crisis reached mammoth proportions.[7]

Chapter 2 examined refugee reception in and around the city of Beijing. Far more people were taken in, at least temporarily, by communities in Manchuria—possibly a million migrants out of the twenty to thirty million victims across North China, or somewhere between 3 percent and

5 percent of the people afflicted by famine.[8] While a very rough measure of movement to the northeast over the year, this is considerably higher than previous estimates.[9] In 1920, famine migrants were passing between the domains of autonomous military regimes—Cao Kun's and Wu Pei-fu's Beiyang regime and that of Marshal Zhang Zuolin, based in Feng-tian. Nonetheless, these domains were becoming increasingly intertwined in the politics of the Chinese capital, and their social and political ties would play an outsized role, relative to that of the rest of China, in the overall relief operation, both in terms of receiving refugees and dispatch-ing resources to the famine field. This chapter explores how strangers in flight were received elsewhere in China at the time. While at times re-stricted or banned, on the whole movement between the provinces and into major cities over the course of the 1920–21 crisis was free-flowing and subsidized by various levels of the state, despite occasional concerns about plague and other diseases that had only recently ravaged the sections of the northeast where a majority of famine migrants were headed. There-fore, the degree of official coordination about the transfer of migrants and relief goods in 1920–21 from the highest levels of government down to county magistrates and district officials is noteworthy. Much of the or-derliness of migrant settlement in Fengtian, Jilin, and Heilongjiang indi-cated the firm grip that Zhang's military administration had on society down to the local level in the three provinces.

To the Yangzi

The arrival of legions of men and women fleeing the northern drought districts in 1920 should be considered in the context of the prolonged, if spasmodic, civil war described in chapter 1. This fighting had brought Bei-yang armies southward through Hubei and into Hunan in previous years to dislodge rival regimes that were entrenching themselves in the south, at great cost to the local populations.[10] The reception of tens of thousands of northerners fleeing south into Hubei and beyond indicates that relief concerns among the public transcended the period's North-South factional divides, a fact echoed by the heavy presence of central and southern Chinese in the leadership of national relief organizations created for the north, as seen in chapter 5.

Residents of Henan and Shandong drought districts connected by rail to the Yangzi River valley fled south, growing to large numbers by the end of the summer of 1920. The Beijing-Hankou rail line added cars to its trains to convey them down to Hubei until the end of October, a free-of-charge policy of southward movement that was repeatedly extended by the Ministry of Communications through the fall.[11] Over the centuries, great numbers of people fleeing disaster appeared regularly in the great Yangzi port city of Hankou, which—together with adjacent Wuchang and Hanyang—formed a metropolis of trade and industry and hosted military stations. As recently as the 1880s, every year during the months of high water in fall and winter the city hosted thirty thousand refugees, a number that had reached two hundred thousand during the flood of 1848–49.[12]

The provisioning style of the region's elites in 1920, erecting sheds and dispensing porridge to incoming refugees, stretched back as far as the eighteenth century. By January 1921, "no less than 30,000" Henan refugees were camped in Hankou, the British consul wrote his superiors, "housed in matsheds" and "fed by the native charitable societies with rice and porridge."[13] Other estimates put the number of refugees in the city at forty thousand, a number that prompted municipal authorities to meet with the city's Chamber of Commerce and charities to step up relief efforts.[14]

Many of those arriving in the city performed acts of desperation similar to those performed in Beijing, begging from stores, offering their children for sale, or seeking to marry their daughters into local households.[15] Others held organized demonstrations about their condition. For example, several hundred men and women arrived in tattered clothes by train from Shandong, via Henan, one day in late December. Splitting into groups of several dozen, each led by a leader, they marched up and down the streets with red banners announcing their plight and appealing for food and cash at major stores. On Huangpi Street, the arrivals reportedly held an "especially insistent demonstration" before authorities blocked them from continuing. At nightfall, strangers directed them to the care of charities in the city.[16]

In 1920 in Hankou, two main types of groups appear to have been behind the organization of relief activity. The first, benevolent halls, were initially formed in the city by merchants in 1830, endowed with farmland and urban commercial property, and by the end of the century there were thirty-five of them.[17] In the late autumn of 1920, ten of these halls reportedly decided at a conference in the city to move up the date of their annual winter relief efforts in light of the migrants "streaming in" from the north.[18] The extent of their activity over the crisis is unclear, though. In some cases, after taking in refugees—including several hundred children from Henan, who arrived early one November morning—benevolent halls handed over their charges to a larger group called the Hankou Charity Society (Hankou cishan hui), which appears to have been an umbrella association of the city's charities.[19]

At its first famine fund-raising meeting, held in mid-September, the society raised an initial 137,000 *diao* (or strings of a thousand cash) in donations from twelve men, plus one thousand *bao*, or 160,000 *jin*, of bran.[20] The group used the money to take in refugee children, hire seamstresses to produce clothes for distribution to the city's poor, and take care of the corpses that appeared on the city streets in groups of two or three over the winter until they could be claimed by kin—a task the charity shared with the city police.[21] With a core staff of thirty, the society added these activities to existing services it performed for the public—it ran an orphanage, hospital, and river lifeboat service and provided assistance to households struck by fire—paid for by monthly contributions from city merchants, along with ticket surcharges collected by shipping and ferry companies.[22]

In many respects, the society's services did not differ from those that benevolent halls had long provided for Hankou's residents. However, the society had a quasi-official character, having been formed in the river city in the late 1910s with initial funding from members of the city's merchant and official circles, including Hubei's military and civilian governors and the president of the republic. In this sense, one of the more active groups involved in the assistance of famine refugees in 1920–21 in Hankou resembled the hybrid official-charitable nature of groups such as the Grain Relief Society in Beijing over the famine year.

More broadly, the central Chinese city provided a spectrum of relief activity across the famine zone similar to what the capital to the north did. Members of the merchant-gentry class active in the city's winter relief bureau sold grain at discount prices to the public, including forty thousand *shi* of Hunan rice in January;[23] the Dachang Tobacco Company funded the establishment of four soup kitchens in the city, jointly managed by the winter relief bureau;[24] twenty-one Hankou policemen provided several thousand *diao* raised from their annual Lunar New Year banquet to local relief efforts;[25] and individual philanthropists met with migrants on the streets, with one man in November handing out thirty *diao* to fifty-three newly arrived refugees seated on the front steps of a government office building.[26] And numerous relief groups were formed with the aim of mobilizing relief for districts up the rail line in Henan and Zhili in particular. These included a local chapter of Liang Shiyi's North China Relief Society (which had raised half a million yuan by early October), the Wuhan YMCA, and an assortment of smaller charities that together had raised 100,000 yuan by mid-December.[27]

Beyond the Wall

Those who trekked on their own or in small groups northward beyond the Great Wall did so at great risk. The numbers of deaths seemed to rise exponentially among unescorted travelers who went on foot or by cart instead of those moving by rail. In early November, multiple papers reported that nine hundred people lay dead in three feet of snow and "unusually frigid" weather on the roads leading over the passes into Inner Mongolia.[28] Amid windstorms and another two feet of snow, authorities in Wanquan county there dug mass graves and transported the thousand-odd bodies that had accumulated on the roadsides.[29] Into winter, travelers to Beijing reported seeing the frozen corpses of the poor lying in the snow drifts along the roads to Zhangjiakou (Kalgan).[30]

Up in the area around Zhangjiakou, an entrepôt for tea, furs, and other goods traveling between China and Russia, the military served only minor relief roles, dispensing monies there as early as September.[31] Refugee management in the area was largely performed by a relief society organized by the magistrate working in tandem with broader local society. On November 1, soup kitchens set up by the county were operating in the city of 63,000, after which members of the gentry, merchant, government, police, and education circles formed the Disaster Relief Society of Zhangjiakou (Zhangjiakou jiuzai hui) with the objective of caring for the ten thousand migrants who had already settled in the vicinity of the city.[32] By the middle of November, with migrants "still [arriving] in an endless stream," lodging had been set up; winter clothes had been distributed to over two thousand people; and the city soup kitchen was serving porridge twice daily—an operation for which county authorities would bring in an additional 255,898 *jin* of grain by rail the following month to supplement local supplies.[33]

However, Manchuria was the primary destination of migrants from Zhili and Shandong in particular. The fact that migrants chose the edge of Siberia instead of the rice-growing regions of the south showed the enduring strength of a migratory pattern established at least as early as the first decades of the Qing.[34] North China's main treaty port of Tianjin served as the main entrepôt for migratory movement into Manchuria, and there, as in Beijing, the authorities appear to have been at the forefront of refugee management. With thousands of men and women from Zhili pleading for assistance at the provincial government offices in Tianjin in the first few days of September, various police agencies collected 18,500 yuan for allocation of cash and grain to arriving refugees.[35] The police then hired twenty-four boats to convey them back to their home districts in time to sow winter wheat.[36] Repeated over the course of the first half of the autumn, these actions of course did not resolve immediate subsistence needs, and more and more people opted to go to the northeast.

Regardless of how people fled the famine districts to the neighboring domains of Manchuria—by boat or train or on foot—there was fear that plague or cholera would follow. Sixty thousand people had died in North China a decade earlier from an outbreak of pneumonic plague that swept down along the rail line from the northern fringes of Heilongjiang in 1910. In October 1920 an outbreak of pneumonic plague erupted in the northeast among seasonal fur-trapping communities on the Mongolian border in the extreme west of Heilongjiang, and the epidemic spread as far south as Shandong, claiming a total of nine thousand lives and 1.1 million yuan were needed to handle the medical crisis.[37]

Rather than serving as incoming carriers of disease, migrants heading northeast in 1920 were more likely to be heading into a hot zone of pneumonic plague, a disease endemic in particular to Heilongjiang's marmot populations, whose coats could pass for marten or sable fur—a fact exploited by migrant trappers seeking to meet high fur demand in Europe.[38] With thirteen reported dead of the plague (*shudu*) in February 1921 in Harbin (where the Chinese Red Cross had set up a clinic specifically for the treatment of epidemics in Harbin earlier in September), trains heading to the Siberian border town of Manzhouli (Manchurian Station) from the city were limited to one a day, and travelers heading in that direction were subject to three days' quarantine en route by the authorities, among other measures.[39]

In what thus amounted to a grave game of chase, with Tianjin police receiving and dispatching arriving famine migrants, while thousands of families that had been returned to their homes earlier in the fall by authorities had come back by November, some people perished on the roads, having found relief insufficient in their home districts. As late as September, police were urging officials in rural districts to join with members of the merchant-gentry class there to make it possible to provide relief at home for those afflicted by the famine.[40]

As migrants continued to move, it was announced that Zhili's military governor, Cao Kun, and his counterpart in the northeast, Zhang Zuolin, were negotiating about how to coordinate and cover the expenses of migrant transportation and resettlement in Zhang's domains.[41] Between them, the two men controlled eight Chinese provinces, maintaining a balance of power between them over the crisis year while creating an advisory role for themselves in the administrations of President Xu Shichang and the newly restored premier, Jin Yunpeng. It was an arrangement that gave Cao and Zhang a say over major appointments and national policy, both in and beyond their respective domains.

Xu was apparently behind an initiative to settle famine refugees permanently in the northeast. In October, he summoned the ministers of the interior and of agriculture and commerce to discuss the idea of establishing a state-funded program that would sponsor the settlement of able-bodied people among the calamity-stricken (*zaimin*) in frontier provinces to open up land for cultivation. Reports framed the proposal as a component of the broader famine relief effort. Beiyang authorities consulted with Zhang about establishing such a program in his Manchurian domains, a program that would be implemented in fits and starts over the famine year.[42]

To the Northeast by Train, Boat, or Foot

The timeline of negotiations at the highest levels roughly corresponded to that of the migrant policing carried out by local authorities. In the last few days of August, before full official encouragement of migration to the northeast, railroad authorities had already added extra cars to trains along the Beijing-Fengtian line to convey refugees bound northeastward out of Tianjin. By the tens of thousands, residents of western and southern Zhili and counties closer to Tianjin were arriving at the port with the stated aim of settling in regions north of the Great Wall—where, according to news reports, they planned to "open wasteland for cultivation" (*kaiken huangdi*).[43] Many arriving families were unable to pay for passage, and the railway assigned ten empty train cars to move them to Fengtian province free of charge at a rate of one train a day, a policy reportedly ordered by Zhili's governor, Cao Rui, on August 27. In the first weeks of autumn, tens of thousands of migrants had begun camping in districts around Tianjin.[44] Police began a general policy of offering them the option of going on to the northeast, with those deciding to do so each given several *jiao* (a *jiao* being one-tenth of a yuan) before they departed by rail for Shenyang (known also by its Manchu name of Mukden) in Fengtian (map 5). As late as December, trains continued to arrive on a daily basis in Tianjin from places in Zhili and Shandong, each with several cars designated for refugees headed beyond the Great Wall, and refugees were occasionally fed along the way by railway authorities such as the station officer who acquired 4,000 yuan to purchase several thousand *jin* of steamed buns for families awaiting transport in the railway depot at Tianjin.[45]

For the first half of the famine crisis, refugees transported by rail to Manchuria were apparently conveyed in open cars. One September report described the operation as involving twenty freight cars carrying sixty people each, for a total of 1,200 a day from Tianjin into Fengtian.[46] Trains to Fengtian were halted in November following the deaths of six passengers from cold. But cutting off the rail option in this case merely shifted deaths to the roads running parallel to the tracks into the northeast, on which an unspecified number of corpses were reported during these temporary stoppages.[47] Eventually, open train cars were "without exception" changed for covered ones on lines controlled by the Ministry of

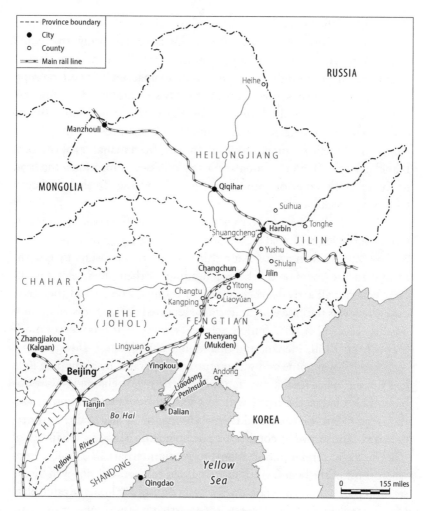

MAP 5. The three northeastern provinces (Manchuria).

Communications by order of its top leaders, according to one news source, on "humane" (*rendao*) grounds, although it apparently took until February for this change to be made.[48]

Migrants traveled to the northeast by sea as well, crossing the Bo Hai to ports on the Liaodong Peninsula. Over three days in early September, nine ships from Tianjin and one from the Shandong coast conveyed 6,400 famine migrants to Yingkou, a treaty port lying a dozen miles up from the mouth of the Liao River in the northeast corner of the Liaodong Sea. From there, halfway up the rail line from Dalian to Shenyang, they could continue by train up into the northeastern provinces. Within days, a steamship carrying another 2,000 migrants approached Yingkou, prompting a meeting between members of the city's Chamber of Commerce, police department, and a bureau called the Sanjiang gongsuo.[49] By the end of September, a relief society formed by these offices had distributed 6,000 yuan in relief—money sourced, in part, from managers of the local branches of the Bank of China and Bank of Communications, the head of the local chamber of commerce, and a Nanyang Brothers Tobacco Company executive.[50]

"No arrival of refugee boats is going unmet at the dock by representatives of the society," read an October report in a Jilin newspaper, whose readers were by then aware that a third of the stricken were, by government mandate (more on this below), heading for their province.[51] It is unclear whether all arrivals received aid, or if only "women and the aged" did, which was the case with at least one reported dockside distribution.[52] By early December sixty-four vessels had conveyed at least 100,000 migrants from Zhili, Henan, and Shandong to Yingkou.[53] These ships—each had its own name and was presumably operated by a shipping line; it is unclear what fees, if any, famine migrants were charged—were apparently loaded to the brim, with anywhere from one thousand to two thousand people on each, and there were reports of deaths due to illness onboard. The crowded conditions prompted the Yingkou Chamber of Commerce to send a public appeal to its counterpart in Tianjin, from where most of the boats sailed, insisting that refugees be conveyed by the steamship companies in a fashion that was not "against humane principles" (*fan rendao zhuyi*); follow-up reports on arriving vessels suggest that passenger numbers went unchanged.[54]

Along the sea route to the port of Yingkou, the threat of disease was even more recent and real. The arrival of shiploads of refugees over the autumn followed a cholera epidemic the year before that claimed ten thousand lives in the northeast, almost half in Harbin—and the disease was believed to have entered the region through the port of Yingkou. The completion of a quarantine hospital by the Chinese Plague Prevention Service at the port in 1920 may explain the city's willingness to accept that year's influx, since doctors could examine the arrivals.[55] The total expenditure for the group's anti-epidemic effort over the autumn is unclear, but it apparently exceeded 20,000 yuan and may well have reached twice that.[56] The northeastward flow of people on the rails via Tianjin, which continued to the spring of 1921, was also halted on occasion, often out of fear of disease or other concerns.[57] But stoppages to refugee movement at sea or over the rail system during the famine and larger crisis of 1920–21 were short and only occasional.

If it is possible to estimate the numbers of refugees traveling by train or ship, those on foot are another issue. They bypassed the port and rail stations of greater Tianjin altogether, which makes their numbers much more difficult to gauge. One American missionary described in his memoirs how the famine "brought countless thousands of refugees through Lingyuan," a city just over the border from today's Hebei in Liaoning, where he had resided as a child. "Christians and other volunteers cooked [grain] into a semi-liquid gruel and doled it out to those starving families as they went by," Robert Tharp remembered. "Two doors away from us up the street, Mr. He also set up some cookstoves in the street and fed hundreds more. . . . Hurriedly, other feeding places were set up throughout the city, and for weeks thereafter the thousands were fed, then encouraged to move on to make way for still more." There is no reason to imagine that Lingyuan's reception of these families—marching in "total silence," gleaning as they went, with an occasional emaciated donkey or wheelbarrow with children—was atypical among communities along the migrant trail.[58]

In the end, how many people made the journey along the network of paths through the agricultural districts of Fengtian and beyond into Jilin and Heilongjiang is not at all clear. Railroad traffic was the best documented form of movement in the period. Authorities had a better handle on the numbers moving under official sponsorship into the northeast on trains, making any estimate of the total number of people who moved into the region—or anywhere, for that matter—in 1920–21 merely a guess.

The Fengtian Leadership

In September 1920, after having agreed with Cao Kun that Zhili migrants could move into Manchuria, Zhang Zuolin held a planning and fundraising meeting at his Fengtian provincial offices in Shenyang with the military governors of Heilongjiang and Jilin, along with the heads of various civic and business organizations in the province.[59] Within two weeks, the plan was made public: 20 percent of incoming famine migrants would remain in Fengtian, the first and most populous of the provinces to the northeast of Zhili; 30 percent would continue on to and settle in Jilin, which was under the administration of Bao Guiqing (1865–1934), a man from the same village in southern Fengtian as Zhang; and the remaining 50 percent would go further along to Heilongjiang, where Sun Liechen (1872–1924), another ally and recent appointment of Zhang's, presided.[60]

Politics throughout the northeastern provinces was very much dominated by Zhang. The "tiny, frail-looking, mustachioed illiterate" man had gone from being a frontier bandit leader tapped to head a local garrison by a local prefect in 1903 to being in firm control of one of the country's most industrialized provinces by 1916. In the meantime, Zhang "first came to prominence," Gavan McCormack explains, "because of his role in crushing the republican revolutionaries in 1911–12," later giving "serious consideration" to the idea of setting up an "independent loyalist stronghold based in the old Manchu capital of Mukden [Shenyang]," a "staunchly monarchist position" Zhang held onto even after Yuan Shikai had "come to terms with the revolutionaries."[61]

Zhang had much to gain from using migrant labor to develop the land on the vast estates in his possession on the edge of Mongolia—part of the land, grain, railroad, pawnshop, and other business interests he owned at this time, which were estimated to be worth fifty million yuan.[62] But there may have been other reasons for Zhang's interest in refugee relief over the famine year, including the fact that precisely a century before his grandfather had fled to Fengtian from his village in Zhili during a famine.[63] Moreover, Zhang's Fengtian clique of political allies was mostly composed of first- or second-generation migrants from Zhili and Shandong.

Zhang's administration was able to manage such an influx of famine migrants in part because of the firm grip it had established on government structures in Fengtian, down even to the subcounty level. Since his rise to power in 1916, Zhang had imposed strict regulations against public protest, suppressing existing practices of official negotiation with the gentry over tax policy and other matters. "No place was left for the principles of mediation and accommodation even in the rhetoric of officials," Hans van de Ven writes, "let alone in practice. Local sub-county networks were effectively placed under martial law. The military and military solutions to social problems had won the day."[64] Ruthless and calculating toward his rivals, Zhang "maintained an effective peace" in his domains until his assassination by the Japanese in 1928, advancing his and his allies' interests "without goading their population to rebellion."[65] This level of state control on local governance helps explain the apparent adherence of local officials to decrees from Zhang's office on refugee reception over the famine year and the ability of the northeastern provinces to absorb such numbers of people in a relatively orderly manner.

The region under Zhang's rule was also under the heavy influence of the Japanese, who had annexed neighboring Korea only ten years before. In 1920, the Japanese had investments totaling 440 million yen in the South Manchurian Railway Company, based in Dalian—"a quasi-governmental corporation with many subsidiary enterprises beyond rail-roads and one of the largest research organizations in the world until 1945," in the words of Prasenjit Duara.[66] Having donated 60,000 yuan to an unspecified relief fund—possibly at the fund-raising meeting Zhang had held with business leaders at his headquarters the week before—the Japanese-controlled railway announced in early October that it too would transport refugees free of charge along its rail network and would transport relief supplies at half price, adding rail cars in December for their transport northward to Harbin.[67]

Migrants at Shenyang

Shenyang, the capital of Fengtian province and political seat of the three northeastern provinces, sat at the junction of the Chinese-owned North China railway (running northeast from Beijing) and the Japanese-owned South Manchurian Railroad (running north from Dalian). The rail station faced the western side of a ten-mile-long earthen rampart encircling the city, where 2,000–3,000 famine migrants a day converged in early September. Some left immediately for points beyond the city, and as they scattered throughout Fengtian, Zhang ordered all counties in the province to take in an initial 300–500 migrants each and raise sufficient funds to find a place for them to "settle down" (*anzhi*). County magistrates were also instructed to make head counts of the people arriving in their districts, tallying them by age and sex for the purpose of relief measures.[68] Considering its sparser population, Fengtian's eastern edge was meant to absorb a large part of the quota of 20 percent of all migrants earlier set for the province by Zhang, many of whom would be expected to open land for agriculture starting in the spring.[69]

Others stayed in Shenyang, at least for a while, at encampments restricted by the authorities to suburban land beyond the city's rampart. By the middle of the month, with several thousand people already camped out in huts constructed from mats made of reeds and other materials, some built at official expense, officials had handed out emergency relief at two sites in villages to the west of the city to prevent disorder and mass begging in the city.[70] Famine migrants were encouraged to seek out friends or relatives in the vicinity but were otherwise barred from entering the city center, which was encircled by a twelve-yard-high brick wall; nor were they permitted to beg in the suburbs in large groups. With offers of cash, however, authorities encouraged arriving migrants to eke out a living in the surrounding countryside until the fall harvest, after which all of them in the environs of Shenyang were to stay put in their lodgings as harvesting would be under way.[71]

Of course, people fleeing famine were arriving in a city with a population of resident poor, and it appears that official and charitable programs for them worked separately from those for refugees. The Shenyang police used seized gambling money in October to finance the annual winter opening of shelters for the poor in the city and assisted a local benevolent hall with its annual launching of winter housing and grain distribution for the city's population of beggars (*qigai*) and local poor (*pinmin*) generally. When official shelters eventually closed in late March, many residents were sent to this organization's shelters, which doubled as workhouses and trade schools for the indigent.[72]

More than 100,000 migrants had arrived in the area of Shenyang by the end of September, an estimated 70,000 of them from Zhili, and with the weather turning cold, police selected a temple compound and unused soldier barracks to erect more formidable refugee lodgings.[73] With an initial 10,000 yuan from Zhang's office, the police set up soup kitchens at the main encampment to dispense porridge twice a day, followed by a second officially sponsored encampment and soup kitchen in a nearby village.[74]

The relief efforts of Zhang's administration did not escape criticism in the Shenyang press. In October, the major Japanese-owned paper in the city, *Sheng jing shibao*, pointed out that the refugees still housed in sheds were particularly vulnerable to the cold, especially as they moved about for much of the day in search of supplementary food.[75] Coincidentally or not, within days Zhang's office instructed the municipal police and civil administration to purchase twenty thousand sets of old army clothes for distribution at these sites and to erect several more soup kitchen facilities inside and outside of the city. Zhang's reported plan also included the conversion of temples and vacant official facilities into shelters to operate until spring, when money would be raised to send refugees north to open lands for agriculture.[76]

Jilin Province

The twin cities of Changchun and Jilin shared a valuable news source, *Jichang ribao*, which—along with Shenyang's *Sheng jing shibao*—provided sufficient coverage of relief affairs to give a sense of refugee reception in rural communities. This includes identifying those people behind relief activity over the fall in half a dozen Jilin counties, some quite remote, and what relief and fund-raising methods they chose. During the republic, Jilin—the provincial capital, a river city of half a million famed for its buildings and shipbuilding industry that exploited the great timber reserves in the nearby mountains—was in the process of being eclipsed by the railroad community of Changchun some sixty miles to the west. The provincial capital under the People's Republic, Changchun already had a population of half a million and was a major market for soybeans on the rail line running up to Harbin.[77] Lying on a main route of migration, Changchun was instead the recipient of families in flight in groups of nearly a thousand people from each train through the fall, with some staying put while others continued north.[78]

The formal reception of refugees in Changchun began as early as September, when the circuit intendant (*daoyin*; a military position above that of the magistrate) with jurisdiction over the twin cities met with other officials and gentry to raise money for the establishment of a soup kitchen at a Buddhist temple in the western part of Changchun expressly for arriving refugees; at the same time, the intendant requested 5,000 yuan from Military Governor Bao for emergency relief measures.[79] A month later, managers of businesses in the city, determining that the temple facility was insufficient to meet the needs of the growing numbers passing through, raised funds for the opening of a similar service in a commercial district of the city.[80] The opening of two other facilities followed, each run by a local gentry household every year from winter to spring, one at a city wharf and the other at a city temple.[81] Similar to what we have seen in Beijing, these facilities became sites for the distribution of winter clothes and other relief goods to the threadbare by charitable individuals and businesses over the year.[82]

In late October a charity group called the Jilin Charity Relief Society (Jilin yizhen hui) had asked the provincial government to issue instructions to district intendants and county magistrates to work with local gentry to create subbranches of the society for relief fund-raising purposes and refugee reception.[83] Press reports shed light on the cases of a dozen counties that followed the order over the fall and winter. Rural district chiefs and local defense squads (baoweituan) in places such as Jilin county undertook to look out for incoming migrants, and magistrates and other local actors raised donations in their respective districts in Sipingjie and Lishu.[84] In October, the magistrate of Jilin reported to his superiors that he was dividing the eight hundred migrants who had just arrived in his jurisdiction evenly among the county's ten main districts and towns, and this practice of spreading arriving refugees and migrants evenly throughout districts appears to have been adopted by local officials generally.[85]

Some more detail is provided for Liaoyuan, just across the provincial border from Fengtian. The county had no rail line in 1920, and the migrants reaching there from as far away as Zhili, Shandong, and Henan arrived by cart or on foot. The Liaoyuan magistrate and police had reportedly failed to raise adequate relief monies by the middle of October, when a local army division commander teamed up with them and local merchants to hold five days of benefit theatrical performances at a large local playhouse and tea complex, with a bill of well-known actors. At first, the magistrate and commander used the proceeds to provide emergency relief to refugees as they moved to other locations in the region to eke out a living. But soon after Zhang's office issued instructions for all counties in the northeast to share the responsibility of taking in refugees, an additional two thousand were on their way to Liaoyuan, and the two men convened with the heads of the county merchant and agricultural associations, pooling money and grain for the refugees' arrival. The commander donated 5,000 yuan and the magistrate 200, with additional contributions from the district intendant, the local education bureau, and the merchant association—all managed by a relief bureau set up at the county level.[86] Liaoyuan's approach to fund-raising for refugee reception closely matched those of other counties in the region. For example, Changtu county over the border in Fengtian held a three-day benefit concert for which the magistrate bought up ten box seats at five yuan each and local businesses followed suit with purchases of 908 yuan in tickets to support the local refugee relief society (*zaimin jiuji hui*) set up by the circuit intendant.[87]

North of Liaoyuan lay the neighboring county of Yitong, whose magistrate in mid-October received a cable from the provincial governor informing him that seven hundred refugees from Zhili and Shandong were on their way to his jurisdiction—presumably by cart or on foot, since the county, some fifty miles south of Changchun, had no railroad. The governor reportedly instructed the magistrate to drum up contributions (*quanjuan*) from the public at once, after which the county chief assembled the local gentry to discuss raising funds—in part out of fear that the migrants would scatter all over his jurisdiction if nothing was prepared for their arrival. He then ordered his chief of police to secure the use of a facility downtown with thirty empty rooms for lodging and secured contributions of grain from the gentry, a local official, and a man at what appears to have been a benevolent hall in town, avoiding any disorder when the migrants arrived.[88]

Further to the northeast, just above Jilin city, lies the county of Shulan, also without a rail connection in 1920. There, in early November, the head of the tax office convened a hundred members of the area's merchant-gentry class at a local church, where he was elected relief fund-raising chief and collected 5,000 *diao* for remittance to the famine districts. Within days, five hundred migrants appeared in the area, half of whom

were assigned to work projects in the county, while the rest were sent to
reclaim arable land along the banks of a local river, according to a report
submitted by the magistrate to the province that found its way into Harbin's *Yuandong bao*.[89]

Harbin

In the republic, Harbin was a center of trade situated on the very northern edge of Jilin province. The city included a treaty port section hosting
the largest Western (mostly Russian) population in China, a community
that had seen an explosion of growth after the Russo-Japanese war of 1905.
At Harbin the rail line coming north from Changchun forked, with one
branch running eastward to the Russian border and the port of Vladivostok, while the other cut westward through the wheat and millet fields of
the northeast plain and over the Khingan Range to the Mongolian steppe
and onward to Lake Baikal and the city of Irkutsk (and, ultimately, Western Europe). Since in 1920 the city was the central distribution point for
trade and production originating in the vast forests and fields over the
provincial border in Heilongjiang, Harbin lay as much in the orbit of the
neighboring military governor headquartered 170 miles to the northwest
in the Heilongjiang capital of Qiqihar (Tsitsihar).

Adding another layer to the sources of authority in the city, Harbin
was the seat of government for the leased railway zone of the Chinese
Eastern Railway, a Russian concern that had also invested in the creation
of the most prominent Chinese-language daily newspaper in the region.
Yuandong bao was the main rival to Shenyang's *Shengjing shibao* in
terms of distribution and influence over the northeast. And each newspaper reflected the particular dynamic of its host city. Just as *Shengjing
shibao*'s Japanese ownership reflected Japan's dominance of the South
Manchurian Railway and commerce generally in the southern sections
of Manchuria, *Yuandong bao* was a hybrid creation of progressive voices
and commercial interests, ones that "mirrored the development of the
Sino-Russian border town itself in the early twentieth century," in the
words of Rudolph Ng.[90]

Yuandong bao was founded in Harbin in 1907 by a Russian railway
administrator using the presses of the defunct Shenyang-based Russian

newspaper *Shengjing bao*, which closed down after the Russo-Japanese War. Overseen by Russian Sinologists trained at the Oriental Institute in Vladivostok, the paper's content was produced together with a staff of Chinese journalists, and included sections in the vernacular geared toward a working-class readership. The paper's circulation of 5,000 placed it first among Manchuria's twenty Chinese-language newspapers in the late 1910s, reaching readers in the more densely settled South Manchuria, in the forested expanse of North Manchuria, and as far away as Outer Mongolia.[91]

As early as mid-September, famine migrants began appearing in Harbin's Chinese section, *Yuandong bao* reported, crowding the ticketing hall of the station and begging in the area, managing at times to collect substantial charitable donations.[92] Within the week, one man was observed handing out fifty yuan to Zhili refugees getting off a train from Changchun, which at local markets was enough to buy a half-*jin* of sorghum (the daily ration given out by relief societies) for 1,540 people.[93]

Refugee management in the Chinese section was an improvised partnership between municipal authorities and the merchant community. Publicly expressing concerns about potential disorder from the influx, police met arriving migrants at the station throughout the fall and escorted them to inns in the district or to points east of the city, at times transporting them in a fleet of carts that the police had mobilized. As winter approached, city officials and the merchant community together rented several large spaces to house the poor, soliciting donations from the public for winter distributions of clothes and food and to cover the travel expenses of refugees returning south in the spring.[94]

As was the case with the Beijing press, *Yuandong bao* provided moving coverage of the plight of famine migrants in its area, which likely prompted charitable reactions locally. In one representative news story from November, the male head of a newly arrived family lodging in a hostel in the Chinese district died of illness in front of his wailing wife and son, after which the local charity society (*cishan hui*) furnished a coffin and a burial plot.[95] Responding in early December to the sight of migrants offering their children for sale on the city streets, a prominent member of the Harbin gentry announced a plan to donate an unspecified but "large" amount of money and, along with other charitable individuals, urged the municipal government to join them in opening a home for child refugees and orphans.[96] Early in 1921, members of the merchant-gentry class set up a charity clinic in the Chinese section of the city to treat the

ailments of the growing numbers of poor.[97] Funding for the lodging of
arriving refugees and the setting up of soup kitchens was also generated
at a series of meetings held over September and October by Zhili,
Shandong, and Henan natives in the city.[98]

Efforts to meet the needs of famine refugees coincided with annual
efforts to provide food to the area's poor, which was customarily the undertaking of a motley set of official and charitable groups. In late October,
the Jilin provincial government set up a soup kitchen for refugees in
Binjiang district, which encompassed the Chinese section of Harbin, with
an initial 5,000 yuan in state funds.[99] Charities followed suit later in
the fall, starting with local members of the merchant-gentry class who
funded their own soup kitchens in the district with benefit theatrical
performances—one of which brought in 3,000 yuan. The city's charity
society set up a facility in a city temple, dispensing porridge twice daily to
as many as six thousand people (on one day in January), using donations
of grain from the public. The society also distributed flour and a thousand specially ordered items of clothing at the facility at the Lunar New
Year and brought in a physician to stress sanitation and health measures
after the appearance of unspecified illnesses among attendees.[100] Other
soup kitchens included one in the eastern suburbs run by a charity formed
by devotees of a religious group, the Lijiao sect, who solicited donations
of cash and grain in February.[101] Finally, as in Beijing, soup kitchen operations were supplemented by grain distributions both large and small
over the year, including a donation of one thousand *shi* of grain to refugees by one local resident just as winter set in.[102]

Heilongjiang

The ultimate destination for most of the migrants heading to Harbin was
Heilongjiang province to the north. Many intended on settling in the forested sections along the Chinese border with Russia. In anticipation, the
provincial government of Heilongjiang, based in the city of Qiqihar, prepared one set of barracks designed for prisoners of war and a second designed for garrison soldiers as temporary lodging and canteens, while local
charities reportedly raised funds for other unspecified relief measures.[103]

Over a period of apparent confusion in October migrants and refugees were crowding into Qiqihar and "idling away," while relief funds were slow to be disbursed to the counties.[104] At the start of November, Military Governor Sun dispatched the heads of the gold mining and forestry bureaus, both part of the provincial Ministry of Agriculture and Commerce, to Harbin to set up a reception facility for the processing of people there before assigning them to counties for settlement. Reports noted that the operation was following a set of instructions to the provincial government from Zhang at his headquarters in Fengtian.[105] The facility received advance cables with the age and sex breakdowns of migrants en route to Harbin, while municipal police and Binjiang district officials met them on arrival, as we have seen, apparently making sure they did not roam around Harbin.[106] By the beginning of December, the dispersal of migrants along the Chinese Eastern Railway to points in the interior was well under way, with, in one case, sixty rail cars passing through Harbin in mid-December and heading east on the line leading through an expanse of woodlands to the Russian border.[107]

Once they alighted and headed into the interior, migrants entered what was very much a frontier area. "There are no roads in North Manchuria," an American consular official wrote as late as 1926, "but overland traffic is carried over trails which existed prior to the construction of the Chinese Eastern Railway."[108] In some respects, it was a good time of year to convey such numbers of people to the northern fringes of the country, despite the cold. Travel by cart or car was best in winter when the ground was frozen and streams and swamps iced over, and the region had relatively little snow compared to neighboring regions.

However, refugees and migrants were not arriving in communities that lacked civic institutions or forms of social organization found further south. The charity society of Suihua county, for example, sixty miles due north of Harbin, reportedly expanded in September 1920 to include a sub-branch in Yong'an town in the county's western district. The following month, a member of the gentry of Tieli town to the northeast reportedly sent word to Suihua that he had followed suit by organizing a charity society there, using donated funds to set up a poor shelter and charity loan office, which presumably offered low-interest or interest-free loans to poor farmers or peddlers.[109]

Conclusion

In the first few days of 1921, a driver took a cart of grain southward over the frozen soil of Heilongjiang, down from the wheat and sorghum fields of the north Manchurian plain. Following the web of cart paths over which much of the province's foodstuffs and furs moved in the early republic, the driver soon descended to one of the region's many riverbanks, where goods continued by raft or sled—depending on the season—to the major market and rail hub at Harbin. A distance of six miles and the Sungari River lay between the driver and his destination. So did a hundred famine migrants from the south. The driver's load never made it to market in Harbin, but news of the assault on it did. Their "hunger unbearable," the migrants set upon the cart from all directions, making off with every last grain as the hapless driver returned punches and insults. "Soup kitchen servings had been cut off" before the migrants attacked, *Yuandong bao* explained. Provincial authorities had apparently reversed their policy of serving food to those fleeing the famine-stricken south, and many people in Heilongjiang, the frigid expanse north of the Sungari, were presumably left to fend for themselves.[110]

After a mostly uninterrupted movement of people over the four months since the start of the North China famine, Sun had cabled Zhang in Shenyang in late December 1920, asking him to cut off the flow of people into China's northernmost province. Sun's stated reason was that the bitter cold was threatening the lives of those en route, either on the icy roads or in the open boxcars used up to that point to convey refugees for free along the railroad. By January 1, the number of famine migrants in the northeast might have exceeded a million, many of whom had been divided among counties and districts across the three provinces of Fengtian, Jilin, and Heilongjiang through a quota system mandated by Zhang. While official and charity soup kitchens were active through the winter in the Chinese section of Harbin, official soup kitchen activity for newly arriving migrants appears to have been suspended further north in Heilongjiang, to eliminate the northward flow of migrants into the province. Sun's cable to Zhang was followed a few days later by a cable from Zhang to authorities in the south, instructing them to stop the migration of another 200,000 migrants reportedly poised to continue the journey into the northeast.[111]

From late August to the end of December 1920, the first four months of the famine, the regimes of Zhili and Fengtian had coordinated and subsidized a remarkably smooth transfer of people into the sparsely settled northeast. Several hundred thousand others had migrated elsewhere in the country, and while in cases local authorities defied provincial orders to allow migrants to stay in their districts, such acts appear to have been exceptional. By the first few days of 1921, Zhangjiakou at the edge of Mongolia was host to more than ten thousand famine migrants, Tianjin to more than forty thousand, and Hankou on the Yangzi to some thirty thousand. Thousands more had made it to Shanghai, where as early as November local benevolent halls had set up soup kitchens expressly for those fleeing the north. Charities had moved up the dates for starting their annual winter distributions of grain and clothing in light of their arrival, and police and benevolent halls had raised funds to finance their travel onward by boat or train to Jiangxi, Nanjing, and other parts of the country.[112]

Tracing the flows of people north and south from the famine field in 1920–21 has revealed several things. The first is that in places as disparate as Hankou, Zhangjiakou, and Harbin, both authorities and members of society generally followed similar practices when receiving and settling refugees over the year. Tracing the flows has also offered a window into a precise moment in regional and national politics. In each of the northeastern provinces, local crises competed for the attention of authorities and tested the capacity of society to deal with the inundation of people from the south. In Fengtian, an October hailstorm obliterated the crops of fifteen villages in the eastern outskirts of the capital, resulting in extra levies on surplus grain in unaffected districts as part of a gentry-run relief scheme.[113] In Jilin, hundreds of Korean guerrilla fighters—mostly "Korean farmers and students," according to the *North China Herald*—launched devastating raids from their base areas in Jilin on Japanese consulates and other interests in the same month.[114] And in Harbin, Russian refugees appeared in the city throughout the summer and fall—ten thousand in September alone—fleeing unrest and the relatively new Soviet regime in Russia. Most arrived with no job and little capital, and Russians developed a reputation, warranted or not, for fueling crime and prostitution in the city.[115] In addition, the Harbin chapter of the Chinese Red Cross was active over the summer of 1920, coming to the aid of Chinese nationals in trouble spots over the border in Siberia.[116]

It was in this context that official nods were given to this mass movement into China's northeast. What motivations lay behind both official policies and energies in the northeast related to the broader famine crisis affecting the North China Plain? And what underpinned the evident support of the public for the relief of refugees and the famine districts hundreds of miles to the south?

For the top leadership in the region (that is, Zhang's regime), Tokyo's designs on the region was presumably paramount.[117] Relief mobilization and refugee flight were occurring in the context of Korean guerrilla attacks on Japanese interests in Manchuria, which precipitated a punitive incursion into Chinese territory—with public objections but private nods from Zhang's government in Shenyang—by three thousand Japanese troops and air attacks against guerrilla positions that lasted until early 1921.[118] Japanese agents at the time were known to be fostering bandit activity in China's borderlands—for example, on the periphery of Japan's coastal possessions in Shandong, which Chinese authorities vigorously protested—to foment instability and portray Chinese leaders as incapable of governing their own territory.[119] A refugee crisis or plague outbreak in Manchuria posed similar opportunities for undermining Chinese sovereignty. As other studies of the period have shown, various Chinese regimes in the period between the Beiyang government and the Nationalists aimed to demonstrate the governability of the Chinese nation and establish the legitimacy of Chinese rule and sovereignty to the resident foreign powers in the treaty ports of Shanghai and Tianjin through the provision of effective policing and modern health regimes.[120] And while the sources used in this chapter do not reveal the thinking of relief administrators at the highest level, such as Zhang, in 1920, it is not at all improbable that security fears—such as the threat of a Japanese landgrab on the pretext of preventing a plague epidemic or humanitarian catastrophe—may have played a role in Zhang's relief and refugee calculations.

Hardly a pawn in the service of Japanese interests in the region, Zhang proved consistently recalcitrant and calculating in his dealings with

Tokyo, which were hardly straightforward and could be interpreted in any number of ways. Tokyo offered material and diplomatic assistance in matters concerning the northeast, where Zhang needed little help; meanwhile, Tokyo never delivered the support he so eagerly sought in his campaigns for political supremacy in China proper to the south.[121] According to some accounts, Sun Yat-sen, the Nationalist aspirant to the presidency then based in Canton, saw Zhang as deliberately thwarting the Japanese through his creation of rival industry and infrastructures in the region, and Sun would position himself closer to Zhang in the ensuing years.[122]

However, the responses by government and society throughout the northeast were so broad and, in many cases, so spontaneous as to suggest that they stemmed from deeper factors than political calculation and official mandates from on high. They appeared, instead, woven into the fabric of society from urban centers to the farthest reaches of Chinese territory along the Amur. They also reveal the powerful connections that people in the northeast felt for those experiencing famine in the areas of the north below the Great Wall, where many northeasterners traced their ancestry. Refugee reception was one form of social assistance that communities in the northeast performed over the year. The region also had abundant agricultural wealth for export, to which we now turn.

CHAPTER NINE

Manchurian Relief

People bringing in hundreds of dollars. All the front wall" of the mission station is "covered with names of donors," an American noted from the field in Shaanxi. "Bringing gifts from villages in all directions . . . rich and poor give freely."[1] Such observations by a woman traveling in the spring of 1921 through a remote section of China's northwest presents the possibility of famine relief between rural communities, not merely from urban centers to the countryside, as we have seen, for example, with Beijing's charitable relief of the Zhili famine field. This raises the question: how responsive were far-flung rural communities to the plight of their counterparts on the Yellow River plains? Chenggu county, not far from the borders of Gansu and Sichuan, had escaped the severe drought and famine conditions afflicting eastern Shaanxi. What relief sums was a district like Chenggu even capable of producing? Capturing the extent of giving to famine relief drives in remote Shaanxi, or anywhere else across the interior, is exceedingly challenging. Fortunately, the same local news outlets in Manchuria that shed light on the migrant trail in the northeast offered similarly detailed coverage of famine relief fund-raising, enough for us to follow aid mobilization in both cities and county towns spread across the northeast.

Refugee reception in China's northeastern provinces played an important role in containing overall mortality from famine conditions over the winter of 1920–21. But Manchuria's response to the national crisis was a two-way mobilization, involving contributions to the distant famine districts by communities north of the Great Wall just as the afflicted moved into their midst. This can be seen through sketching the desire and ability of residents of cities and towns in the northeast to dispatch relief to the famine districts of Zhili and elsewhere to the south. The subject warrants special attention here because our understanding of empire- or nationwide relief mobilization by Chinese society generally in the late Qing and early republic remains dominated by the experience of Jiangnan, or greater Shanghai, and is seen largely through the prism of the major Shanghai news daily, *Shenbao*.[2]

To illustrate just how incomplete the documentary record can be on the role of communities in Manchuria in providing disaster relief elsewhere in the country at the time, we turn to the summary report *The North China Famine of 1920–1921*. This was compiled and published after the famine by the main joint Chinese-foreign relief society in Beijing, the Peking United International Famine Relief Committee. Due to the decentralized character of disaster responses, the report is the closest thing to an exhaustive data set of overall relief monies generated by both native Chinese and international actors and agencies, and it has underpinned the empirical analyses of existing studies on the famine.[3] The only breakdown the report provides of Chinese relief contributions by city and province over the famine year is the summary of results of the National Famine Relief Drive launched in the middle of February 1921. The drive was organized at the height of famine conditions by a broad spectrum of civic, religious, and business groups, led by an international board that included the philanthropist couple Xiong Xiling and Zhu Qihui; the American minister to China, Charles Crane; the wife of the American philosopher and educational reformer John Dewey, who was in the country at the time on a lecture tour; and Beijing gendarmerie commander Wang Huaiqing. Of the drive's total revenue of 2,133,133 yuan, the largest share was 817,192 yuan from Beijing, where a door-to-door effort reportedly reached "every house in the city."[4] This was followed by Shanghai's 347,422 yuan, Hankou's 175,947 yuan, and Canton's 143,919 yuan. Shenyang, the seat of Zhang Zuolin's regime, contributed 9,256 yuan, and Jilin city, further to the north, gave 371 yuan, while the entire province of Heilongjiang contributed merely 161 yuan.[5] Judging by this, the society over which Zhang ruled in the northeast appears, at best, to have been cut off and unresponsive to the mass starvation unfolding elsewhere in the country.

There is much more to the story than what was reflected in the 1922 report and the English-language press generally. Over the year additional channels of relief ran parallel to those originating in or known to China's international circles at the time. In this chapter I aim to sketch the social and institutional networks that enabled the sourcing and mobilizing of vast amounts of grain purchased by the central state, charities, and other agents in Manchuria for the Yellow River famine field. I also examine the various strategies that charities, relief societies, and native-place associations used in the northeast to generate monies for the subsistence crisis in Zhili and elsewhere, from theatrical fund-raisers to mandatory deductions from state payrolls.

The Manchurian Connection

With Manchuria facing abundant harvests of corn, beans, and other crops in the autumn of 1920, Zhang's headquarters in Shenyang naturally received appeals from various quarters for assistance in relieving conditions in the famine field. The association of benevolent halls in Tianjin cabled Zhang in late August, just as people fleeing war and drought flocked to the city, to urge him to facilitate the acquisition of increased amounts of grain in the northeast for free transport southward.[6] Similarly, General Wu Peifu reportedly was assured by Zhang that he would relax controls on the movement of grain southward, after Wu made a special appeal to him for assistance in stabilizing the market south of the Great Wall—negotiations that are especially noteworthy considering Zhang's open disdain for Wu, touched upon in chapter 1, and their intensifying rivalry that would lead to war between them within two years.[7]

The northeast's famine response would build on war relief channels opened in July. At the end of the July war, Jilin province shipped two thousand *shi* of rice and five thousand *dai* of flour to Beijing as part of a larger effort by Zhang's regime to mobilize war relief grain among members of the merchant-gentry class in the three provinces under his rule. A mid-August news brief reported another five thousand *shi* of assorted relief grain was "sped" to the capital by Zhang, presumably for discount sale, and in early October, Zhang reportedly sent 10,000 yuan for the establishment of a discount grain office in Beijing to handle the increasing contributions from the northeast over the autumn months.[8]

In September, Zhang ordered that the surplus grain harvested in the northeast first be used as famine aid instead of being exported, and he instructed provincial and railroad officials to incentivize the movement of grain by remitting various fees and taxes.[9] Resources began to be mobilized in September under the auspices of the Zhili provincial government, which sent money via a native bank in Fengtian for Zhang's office to handle the purchase of twenty thousand *shi* of millet and sorghum for emergency assistance to send to soup kitchens operating in famine districts south of the Great Wall.[10] A delegate of Zhang's promptly had six thousand *shi* of grain sent to Tianjin, followed by a second shipment of 3,500 *shi* of millet the following week.[11]

In October, the Fengtian Province Drought-Famine Relief Society (Fengsheng jiuji hanzai xiehui) formally replaced the province's Relief Society for Zhili Warzone Victims (Zhili zhandi zaimin zhenji hui) created over the summer.[12] Earlier in the month, Zhang had formally permitted the purchase of five million *shi* of millet and sorghum in the northeast and ordered all districts in the three provinces to assess their harvests and determine the amount of grain each could mobilize.[13] According to one report, contributions from each county in the northeast with healthy harvests was set at 3,000 *shi*, 2,500 *shi*, or 1,500 *shi* of grain, based on county size.[14]

Five million *shi* appears to have been a feasible procurement, as it amounted to roughly half the total annual surplus of northern Manchuria—that is, production beyond the needs of the populations of Jilin and Heilongjiang.[15] News reports from Harbin confirm the October arrival there of agents from the central government in Beijing to coordinate the acquisition of relief grain for the North China Plain.[16] These agents continued to arrive into December, when a central depot was set up in Changchun with branches in Fengtian, Harbin, and Jilin city to handle the volumes of outgoing grain.[17] So much silver was flowing into Manchuria for these operations that the metal was soon trading at 145 coppers per silver yuan, down from 180 not long before, according to the British consul in Shenyang—who noted that this noticeably increased the cost of living for foreigners residing in the northeast.[18]

American and British opinions of this level of coordination between Chinese authorities diverged, and British intelligence even contradicted itself. "As [Zhang] insists on the Provincial contributions being given preference over the grain purchased by the joint Chinese and Foreign Famine Committee," Wilkinson, the British consul, wrote his superiors from the Manchurian capital on January 15, "there has been some dissatisfaction felt by the latter and the Governor has been quite wrongly accused of holding up cars for military and speculative purposes."[19] Three weeks later, an altogether different message made it into the British legation's annual report to Whitehall. "Only a mere fraction of the money would be expended on famine relief" if left in the hands of the Chinese, Britain's chief envoy to Beijing, Beilby Alston, wrote Earl Curzon, the British Foreign Secretary. "Relief committees were formed, mainly on foreign initiative," and "owing to the callous indifference of the military tuchuns [*dujun*], Generals Chang Tso-lin and Tsao Kun, railway traffic is considerably interfered with through wagons being held up."[20]

As British intelligence made its way up the chain of command, the Chinese leadership's decision to prioritize native relief operations was construed as callousness and corruption. Beijing responded with a sharp rejoinder to the circular logic of such charges in the treaty port press: "By red tape and obstruction you probably mean the inspection of goods transported over the Government railways for famine relief," Cabinet Secretary (Guowuyuan mishu) Xia Qingyi (1876– ?) explained in a letter to the editor of the *Peking & Tientsin Times* in the last days of 1920, "but such inspection has for its object the exercise of control to avoid profiteering and corruption suggested by you in the first quotation."[21] In Washington, meanwhile, the administration of President Woodrow Wilson received decidedly different accounts from its envoy in Beijing. "Railway facilities in north China now used almost exclusively for transportation of coal and free transportation of relief supplies," Charles Crane had cabled Washington in December. "Military uses at minimum. . . . Practically all moneys raised for this purpose reaches [*sic*] the actual sufferers."[22]

Semiofficial Relief Efforts in the Northeast

The abovementioned grain volumes were purchased by agents working on behalf of the myriad efforts south of the Great Wall: grain discount sales and/or soup kitchens in the Beijing metropolitan area as well as hundreds of counties to the south, and grain distribution programs managed by provincial and central government agencies, charities, native-place associations, and individuals. Manchurian grain was also commonly used over the famine year to provision the efforts run out of international societies, Christian missions, and the work-relief programs of the American Red Cross in Shandong and elsewhere, which are touched upon in our final chapter. The extent to which crops were either freely donated by producers or contributed according to quotas set by Zhang's regime is unclear. However, the press in the main northeastern cities of Shenyang, the twin cities of Changchun and Jilin, and Harbin covered a range of various ways through which contributions were generated for the North China Plain, from official circles down to rural communities as far away as the Siberian border. By mid-September, Zhang had committed to spending 700,000 yuan on the overall relief effort: 400,000 yuan to purchase sorghum and millet locally to send to the Zhili and Shandong famine districts, 200,000 yuan for the reception of refugees in the northeast, and 100,000 yuan on the relief of Fengtian counties afflicted by a recent hailstorm.[23] By October, with one million yuan in contributions already collected for the relief of Zhili and Shandong, Zhang's public fund-raising plan was revised upward to a goal of three million yuan, a large part of which was to come from officials working in the administrations of the three northeastern provinces.[24]

A few observations might be made about the fund-raising campaigns that appeared in the three major urban centers of the northeast. First, each saw the formation of semiofficial societies whose overall fund-raising strategy had a component that was meant to spread the burden among officials and civil servants on the state payroll. In this, they appear to mirror the fund-raising payroll percentage schemes being implemented in the same month of October in various ministries in Beijing (discussed in chapter 5). However, Zhang's efforts had a higher likelihood of success, considering the fact that, in contrast to the central government in Beijing, by 1920 Manchuria had become one of the most robust regional economies in China, and the governments of the three provinces of Fengtian, Jilin, and Heilongjiang were in a correspondingly healthy fiscal state. Second, in the case at least of the Fengtian and Harbin semiofficial societies, their formation appears to have coincided with Cao Kun and Zhang Zuolin's cabled request to the central government in October to send out circulars to all military and civil governors to have officials in their administrations raise monies and other resources for famine relief.[25] The fact that these semiofficial societies were launched in the wake of these circulars and around the same time that, for example, the military governor of Hunan issued a call to all military officials under his command to contribute to famine relief, suggests a coordination of fund-raising across a large section of the country's military establishment.[26]

Fengtian's province-wide relief effort was initiated by members of the Provincial Assembly at the end of October expressly for the relief of Zhili, Shandong, and Henan, as well as of communities hit earlier in the month by hailstorms in Fengtian itself.[27] One of the first fund-raising moves by the Fengtian Province Drought-Famine Relief Society was to announce a policy of docking 5 percent (or, according to another report, 10 percent) of the monthly salary of everyone on the provincial payroll, including the military, civil servants, and school employees.[28] This was accompanied by benefit performances at a Shenyang theater over five consecutive days in the autumn.[29]

However, Jilin's counterpart to Fengtian's semiofficial society, the Jilin Charity Relief Society, appeared to be considerably more active over the fall, and was formed nearly a month earlier. It was chaired by the military governor, Bao Guiqing, with vice chairs from the Chamber of Commerce and Provincial Assembly. At the group's inaugural meeting in early October, it too decided that all military officers and provincial officials would contribute from their salaries over three months, according to a progressive scale from 10 percent to 30 percent.[30] At a November meeting, provincial school administrators and teachers also agreed to donate a portion of their pay to the effort.[31]

The Chinese district in Harbin also had its counterpart to the semiofficial societies to the south, the Binjiang Charity Relief Society (Binjiang yizhen hui), which was founded by people from military, civil, education, police, gentry, and merchant circles in late October.[32] Revealing its closeness to the provincial administration, the society also arranged for the staff members of all provincial agencies to take pay cuts (*kouxin*) of 20 percent for the months of October through December to benefit famine relief.[33]

The three societies appeared to differ in their approach to generating funds from the wider public. Harbin's society urged gentry, merchants, farmers, workers, and others not on the state payroll to "donate at will" (*suiyi juanzhu*). The Jilin society appeared to be considerably more aggressive, turning first to the entertainment sector for contributions over the three-month campaign leading up to January, arranging for theater complexes in Changchun to contribute 1 percent of their monthly ticket sales, restaurants in the city to contribute 2 percent of their monthly income, and for second- and third-tier brothels to contribute 2.20 yuan and 2.10 yuan, respectively, for every 100 yuan of their monthly income. The county government and police were tasked with ensuring compliance.[34] And in December, the society acquired a list from the police that classified households in the city according to a three-tiered scale of perceived ability to contribute to the citywide fund: household heads were asked to bring to the society's offices 100 *diao*, 50 *diao*, or 10 *diao*—whatever had been determined as their "suggested contribution" (*renjuan*)—for which they would receive a receipt to prove payment if asked by society staff members.[35] As for Fengtian, official correspondence quoted in the provincial gazette indicates that famine relief contributions in at least one case, those remitted to the province from Kangping county, had been "raised through the police" (*jingsuo quanmu*).[36]

Official donation registers (*juance*) also offered a choice of relief campaigns to which subscribers could contribute. One submission from Jilin's Hailong county, which appeared to come entirely from small businesses there, designated 80 yuan (*xiaoyang*) for Beijing's poor (*jingshi pinmin*), 69 yuan for the northern famine zone (Huabei *zaiqu*), and 120 yuan for victims of the earthquake that had struck Gansu in December 1920.[37] In the case of a donation roster submitted in July 1921 by the staff of Fengtian's commissioner for foreign affairs (*jiaoshe yuan*), 13 yuan each were to be donated to the northern famine districts and the Gansu earthquake zone, with no money devoted to the "support of relief" (*zhenfu*) for Shaanxi's and Beijing's soup kitchens.[38]

Over the first three months of the fund-raising drive, the semiofficial societies dispatched relief monies and grains in a piecemeal fashion, either through their respective provincial governments or directly to the famine districts in cash or kind. The dispatch of monies from Changchun apparently began in late October, and the press reported three more remittances up to January totaling 80,000 yuan, sent to the field via the main international relief committee in Tianjin and to a native bank, and divided among the afflicted provinces—with Zhili receiving the largest share.[39] In contrast, the Fengtian and Harbin societies sent a combination of monies and trainloads of grain. By the end of December the Fengtian society had handed over 100,000 yuan in funds to the provincial government and also sent a team of ten men to accompany three thousand *shi* (or possibly 480,000 *jin*) of grain by train to western Zhili.[40] In December, Harbin's Binjiang Charity Relief Society remitted 30,000 yuan to the famine field—after unexplained delays that were criticized in the press—and spent another 40,000 yuan on food and clothing for arriving famine migrants.[41] Afterward, the group dispatched a hundred train cars of sorghum destined for all five afflicted provinces in the new year, when it began another round of fund-raising.[42]

It should be pointed out that throughout the famine year, independent charity relief drives at times produced sums rivaling those of the semiofficial societies mentioned above.[43] Over two days in November, for example, public high schools in Shenyang raised 10,000 yuan, which was remitted to the famine field through the provincial government.[44] And Shenyang's pharmacies decided at a convention the following month that each firm would contribute from 200 yuan to 20 yuan, according to the amount of its capital, and within days 17,000 yuan was remitted to the famine districts through the Chamber of Commerce.[45]

Native-Place Associations

"Coolie (*kuli*) takes pity on refugee," ran a headline in Harbin's *Yuandong bao* in mid-November 1920. The refugee was a woman roaming the city's Chinese district (the officially designated destination for those arriving from the distant famine districts), carrying an infant girl, towing along a young son, and stretching out her free hand to passersby. A young laborer stopped to ask where in the country she had come from. Zhili, she replied, and the man, reportedly "spurred with thoughts of his own native-place (*sangzi*)," handed the woman three yuan. With bystanders reportedly astonished by the exchange, the woman promptly kowtowed four times in thanks and took off, gripping enough cash to feed herself and her children for over a month.[46]

Aside from its poignancy, what should interest us about this anecdote is the role that native place played in a brief exchange between strangers hundreds of miles from the famine zone. Consumers of news in Harbin had learned only recently that Zhang had mandated that half of all famine migrants destined for the northeast would pass through Harbin and head to Heilongjiang province, where many would stay for good, opening up land on the forested frontier in the spring.[47] What would amount to close to a million people arriving in Heilongjiang through colonization programs by the spring would put upward pressure on local food prices, at least in the short term. Yet the Harbin public, and especially the city's poor, to which this "coolie" belonged, was already experiencing price hikes—an increase of 25 percent in the case of sorghum, a major relief grain, since the start of the crisis—as agents from the south put in orders for hundreds of millions of *jin* of Manchurian grain to compensate for the failed harvests in Zhili, Shandong, and elsewhere.[48] The fact that so many inhabitants of China's vast northeast could trace their origins to the two afflicted provinces of Zhili and Shandong should be borne in mind when considering refugee reception and relief mobilization in the region in 1920–21. As mentioned above, Zhang's own grandfather had left his village in Zhili amid famine in 1821 and come to the northeast. He had joined a mass migration of able-bodied men in good years and of whole households in disastrous ones that accelerated with the intensified crises of the late nineteenth and early twentieth centuries, just as the ailing Qing dynasty abandoned its preferred policy of limited Han migration to the imperial family's ancestral homeland.

Nearly half of the funds raised by the Binjiang Charity Relief Society came from Harbin's formidable community of Zhili natives.[49] In addition, the city's Zhili native-place association conducted relief efforts of its own, which included raising 12,000 yuan to send south twenty-two train cars' worth of assorted grains through the provincial government in January.[50] People also acted independently out of hometown sentiment. For example, one man in Heilongjiang used 5,000 yuan of his personal funds in November to buy millet for "the old and young facing starvation and the cold" in his native Zhuozhou, in central Zhili.[51]

The *huiguan* complexes where members of native-place associations held meetings and fraternized across the country and in Chinese communities overseas (discussed in chapter 5) were also sites where fund-raisers from outside groups could appeal for support. The visit by representatives of the Public Society for the Relief of Shandong (Shandong zhenzai gonghui), a quasi-governmental organization, gives a sense of the national reach of the networking behind particular campaigns. "One yuan saves a life!" was the slogan the group used to rouse support for their Shandong "compatriots" (tongbao) at a fund-raising event involving public entertainments at a Jinan park in mid-October.[52] Afterwards, its fund-raisers fanned out to Qingdao, Yantai, Beijing, Tianjin, Shanghai, Ningbo, and locations in Zhejiang, Hubei, Jiangxi, and elsewhere over the fall.[53] The campaign included Harbin's Shandong huiguan where two representatives of the group made an appeal in November, which the group's chair complemented with a cabled appeal for donations to a Harbin charity relief (yizhen) society.[54] The network generated an enormous amount: the society was responsible for a full half of the sixty-four million jin of relief grain moving on the railways into the famine districts of Shandong in December.[55]

Rural Fengtian, Jilin, and Heilongjiang

Occasionally, news reports offered vignettes of fund-raising at more remote locations. Zhang had instructed county magistrates to work with merchant associations, education bureaus, and other local bodies to pool contributions from the public, and the monies thus raised were to be remitted to the provincial government for the mass purchase of grain for the famine field—although it appears that monies were occasionally transmitted directly to the famine districts through other channels.[56] While it is especially difficult to determine the extent and volume of charitable activity beyond the region's main urban centers, one report from the banks of the Yalu River described how one of the two police bureaus in Andong (today's Dandong on the North Korean border) collected 1,120 yuan by the end of October, after which the city police chief, a native of Tianjin, generated another several hundred yuan in donations, and Chinese merchants added another 3,000 yuan, which they remitted to the famine zone in early December.[57]

Further north in Jilin's Yushu county, some twenty-five miles east of the main rail line running to Harbin, officials and merchants likewise convened in November in a local church building for a county fund-raising meeting attended by five hundred people. The county magistrate and the parish minister each donated 2,000 *diao*, the tax office chief donated 1,600 *diao*, two local men each gave 1,000 *diao*, and others contributed smaller amounts for a combined total of 26,192 *diao* (or 4,190 yuan), reportedly for immediate remittance to unspecified famine districts. Later that month, the magistrate's wife summoned the wives of policemen, merchants, and area gentry to a fund-raising meeting at the county's girls' school. Thirty-four people came, raising what appears to have been a disappointing 900 *diao*. Afterward, the magistrate's wife and the wife of a church minister visited gentry families who had neglected to send representatives to the meeting and pressed them for contributions.[58]

At Shuangcheng, the county magistrate assembled members of the merchant-gentry class at the Chamber of Commerce in October to form a temporary relief committee, which he chaired. A fortress town and one of the oldest communities in the area, located thirty-two miles south of Harbin, Shuangcheng had a sizable Russian community and a large number of its distilleries, cotton-cloth firms, and oil factories were owned by Zhili, Shanxi, and Shandong natives.[59] Twenty-four staff members of the relief committee were then sent to towns and villages around the county to raise monies from wealthy gentry in each district, according to a news report, which added that members of the community "took pleasure in doing good and valued giving away" (*leshan haoshi*).[60] While no figures were given for the county-wide effort, a report from December recounted that students at a public elementary school in Shuangcheng held a benefit performance that month at a teahouse, which received an "exceedingly enthusiastic" (*yichang yongyue*) response of 50,000 *diao* in ticket sales over three days.[61]

Fund-raising also appeared to take on the form of competition between communities. "With each province and each county in the country all mobilizing relief," asked one newly installed magistrate in his county a hundred miles east of Harbin along the Sungari River, "how can Tonghe be willing to fall behind (Tonghe *qi ken luo*)?" Together with merchant-gentry from the area, he organized a two-day charity benefit performance in November, with proceeds to be remitted to the famine field, and a fund-raising drive meant to benefit arriving refugees.[62]

Merchants, charity societies, and garrison commanders amassed grain and cash donations in other sections of Heilongjiang over the famine year.[63] But, curiously, some of the earliest famine relief fund-raisers reported in the regional press occurred in some of its remotest locations, some five hundred miles up the rail line from Harbin on the border with Siberia. There in October, at Manzhouli, the railway police and local military officers answered a fund-raising call from Military Governor Sun Liechen by organizing three days' worth of charity performances at a teahouse in the border town starting on November 7, with the proceeds headed for the famine zone.[64] Frontier police in Heihe, the border town three hundred miles due north of Harbin on the Amur River, responded with benefit performances of their own at two local theaters in November, raising 11,000 yuan over three days for relief of the famine districts.[65]

Conclusion

Of course, no report or collection of sources can offer complete and comprehensive totals for the relief activity that took place at all levels in response to any particular crisis. But what the Beijing international relief society's 1922 report credits to China's three northeastern provinces for spring relief and what, based on the region's news media, the region actually produced in 1920–21 suggest entirely different social landscapes. Substantial sums were mobilized for relief across the social strata of communities in the northeast as far apart as those on the Amur River facing Russian Siberia and the Mongolian steppe. Money was raised through benefit concerts, at fund-raising meetings, and, in some cases, by exacting contributions from district families based on household wealth. What motivations lay behind the volumes and variety of relief mobilization across the northeast for famine districts hundreds of miles away? Native-place ties or sentiment, as we have seen, certainly played a role. But unfortunately, news briefs in the region's papers quoted rarely, if ever, from the speeches given at fund-raisers. So it is difficult to say whether national shame over repeated natural disasters, fears of social disorder, ethical injunctions, pity, or a combination of motivations were foremost in the minds of those appealing to local residents to open their purses for those suffering in the famine districts south of the Great Wall.

But if the voices appearing in two major Jilin province newspapers are any indication, the logic and tenor of public appeals for relief mobilization in the Chinese communities of Changchun and Harbin were varied. The writer of a "current affairs" column in *Jichang ribao* repeatedly chose to shame his northeastern readers into donating to relief efforts for their compatriots (*tongbao*) by stressing the actions taken so far by members of the foreign community in China, particularly Europeans and Americans.[66] But more prominently placed editorials in the same pages of the paper left out such comparisons to foreigners or southern Chinese, instead seeking to mobilize Jilin residents by pointing out the roots that many northeasterners had in afflicted Zhili and Shandong or by making more straightforward emotional appeals.[67] *Yuandong bao*, the Harbin paper under Russian management, offered a similar variety of printed appeals to the Chinese public there, with some pieces comparing relief initiatives by Harbin's Chinese unfavorably with the dozen train cars of flour already dispatched to the famine field by members of the large Russian community in the city, while others attempted simply to pull at the heartstrings of readers on behalf of their stricken compatriots.[68]

Bryna Goodman has framed social welfare activity as an important legitimization strategy used by native-place associations (*tongxianghui*) as they modernized in the early twentieth century from the provincial lodges (*huiguan*) of the late imperial period.[69] These associations served as nodes of relief mobilization by Zhili and Shandong natives throughout the northeast. It should be noted that native-place associations were also operating in a period of heightening nationalism that shaped the broader context of the relief effort, and thus in their bid for political relevance, members were fully aware of the role that non-Chinese communities in the region had in relieving the famine districts to the south. This extended beyond the main international societies and missionary activity to Shenyang's Japanese community, whose contributions included 1,000 gold coins in Japanese currency (*rijin yuan*) from the Japanese Red Cross of Manchuria remitted to the Ministry of the Interior through Zhang's administration in early November and 4,000 yuan later that month from fund-raising by Japanese merchants in the city, again remitted through the provincial government.[70] Members of Harbin's large Russian community contributed additional resources, such as ten train-cars' worth of flour sent to unspecified parts of the famine field in October by a wealthy Russian merchant whose name appeared as Sikejieli in the Chinese press.[71] The following month, unidentified Harbin Russians sent 1,400 *bao* of relief flour (possibly 224,000 *jin*) down the South Manchurian Railway to Tianjin—where, unsure of which relief agency to entrust it to, they had it stored temporarily at the train station.[72] And over the fall, Russian musicians and dancing troupes in Harbin were also reportedly active in raising funds for the relief of North China's stricken provinces.[73]

Manchuria was an increasingly international space in the republic, whose residents experienced a combination of national and native-place sentiment that drove the mobilization of aid by both state and private actors for the drought-hit communities of the North China Plain and other relief needs. The spread and scale of this collective effort, over long distances and across contested boundaries, should be kept in mind as we turn to the most familiar area of relief in 1920–21: international aid.

CHAPTER TEN

International Relief

In the middle of October 1920, a spell of rain gave rise to a last-ditch effort to sow seeds of winter wheat in the fields of southern Zhili. It was a dramatic burst of activity in an otherwise lifeless landscape that had not seen precipitation in any form for at least a year.[1] The *Times* correspondent captured the scene for his readers across the world in Britain, writing that "several soaking rains" had recently fallen on a countryside where "only the hardier weeds" had survived, transforming the "whole aspect of the country, psychologically as well as physically. . . . The fields again show green," with sprouts of wheat already reaching four and five inches high. "In every corner and by every farmer" the last few "bits of clothes" and "sticks of furniture," and even children had been disposed of for the cash needed to buy seed, readers learned, and "wheat has been planted, and it is coming up gloriously." "But it is a forlorn, long-distant hope," the correspondent cautioned. There were seven months to go before the wheat ripened, and "the harrowing problem will be to live until June."[2]

To an early twentieth-century *Times* readership, it was a familiar Chinese scene: farmers who were scrambling in a desperate bid to sow crops for the spring were simply on their own, without their countrymen so much as extending a hand, while, the correspondent continued, "Tsao Kun, Governor of the Province" and "other generalisimi [*sic*] swagger with more multitudes of troops," clogging the vital rail lines from grain-rich parts of the country.[3]

But not an insignificant share of wheat seed planted by farmers in the region had been distributed at no charge by a Chinese aid group—the

Shunzhi Drought Disaster Relief Society—whose seed assistance program would have been familiar to the readers of any number of Chinese news dailies that same month. By the middle of October, counties in Daming prefecture in Zhili's extreme south and other nearby prefectures including Shen, Ji, and Baoding—a total of fifty counties—had seen the distribution of wheat seed worth 20,000 yuan to farmers too poor to acquire seed themselves, and the society was poised to distribute seed worth an additional 20,000 yuan that had been secured in Kaifeng, collectively enough seed to sow for seventy thousand average family farms in the region.[4] Oral legends about local sages scattering buckwheat seeds "to save the people from famine" were in fact "very popular" at the time across rural Zhili, according to the historian Cao Xinyu, and the group's leaders may well have known this.[5]

A month earlier, readers of newspapers across the country would have learned that the founding leaders of this aid group were natives of rural Zhili counties who served in military and official posts in the capital,[6] some of the men the *Times* correspondent had reported were "swaggering" about while farmers in south Zhili made a final attempt to have spring harvests. "There is a detached air of resignation in those who have not had a real meal for weeks that is incomprehensible to one from the West," another *Times* report read that autumn. "If they have no food they must die. They have no food, therefore they must die. That sums up their whole attitude. . . . I asked if the Government would help them. That question was received with amusement. I might as well have asked if the moon would help them. Help from the Government was an idea so alien that it had not even occurred to them."[7] To *Times* readers, no native relief structure existed at the outset of famine in 1920—"Chinese Resigned to Starvation—Death the Only Prospect" ran the headline—let alone one composed of members of the capital's ruling establishment, whose group had the distinction of being the first aid effort to reach over half of Zhili's ninety-seven afflicted counties that autumn.[8]

Such perceptions helped mobilize aid to China from overseas, particularly from the United States. Foreign newspapers and missionary literature consistently cast doubt on the willingness or ability of the Chinese state and urban society to intervene in cases of flood and drought in the interior and suggested that relief initiatives and agency within stricken Chinese communities were impossible.[9] The following pages explore the international dimension to the overall relief effort in 1920–21. This mainly consisted of the joint committees of foreigners and Chinese based in Beijing, Shanghai, and the capitals of the five affected provinces; the American Red Cross; and Catholic and Protestant missions spread across the famine field. Here we place the international effort on the timeline of the subsistence crisis. International aid did not materialize in any significant form until well into 1921, and the vast majority of Chinese who were assisted by international societies were reached only on the eve of the spring harvests in April and May 1921, in the last quarter of the famine year.

Back to the Fields

Having failed to negotiate control over the four-million-yuan famine loan secured in January 1921, the Beiyang regime and other agencies continued to cobble together relief sums into the new year. The Government Relief Bureau sent relief grain in batches of a million *jin* to sections of the Zhili disaster zone in January.[10] Around the same time, the Ministry of Finance released 60,000 yuan for relief distribution in Zhili and Governor Cao Rui sent an additional 200,000 yuan to Fengtian to acquire sorghum for the famine districts.[11] With banditry becoming an acute affliction in southern Zhili's Daming prefecture, the Ministry of the Interior released 300,000 yuan for distribution there, a sum *Zhongguo minbao* described, using a common expression, as "a cup of water tossed onto a bonfire" (*beishui chexin*) in an appeal to philanthropic groups for assistance.[12] Within weeks, two groups—the Zhili Charity Relief Society (Zhili yizhen hui) and the semiofficial Shunzhi Relief Support Office (Shunzhi zhuzhen ju)—managed to respond with a reported three million yuan in relief monies, distributing the funds to the region's famine-afflicted districts at a rate of two to four yuan for each affected household.[13] Relief capacities of the central government and society generally were even further stretched by an earthquake that struck the remote northwest of the country in the evening of December 16, collapsing cave dwellings and crushing granaries in the loess communities of Gansu and leading to the deaths of more than 200,000 people.[14]

As spring approached, and in anticipation of a healthy winter wheat harvest, a coordinated effort was launched to return home those who had fled their native districts throughout the north. In February, the Ministry of the Interior instructed Commandant Wang Huaiqing to have his gendarmes begin escorting famine migrants assembled in the metropolitan region down the Beijing-Suiyuan rail line to the rail hub at Fengtai, and from there to their homes; authorities managing the project were instructed to provide each refugee, irrespective of sex and age, with ten yuan in relief monies along the way.[15] At month's end, the Ministry of Communications instructed the Tianjin-Pukou rail line to add trains to the counties south of Tianjin and further into Shandong for this purpose.[16]

In light of warming weather leading into March, shelters in Beijing began clearing out their residents, and those camped outside the city gates were ordered to return to their homes.[17] In the garrison city of Baoding in central Zhili, Xiong Xiling's Relief Society for the Five Northern Provinces sent ninety-four men and women out of its shelter.[18] Meanwhile, various Beijing charities were reportedly raising money to help cover the expense of conveying people back to their home districts.[19] Two staff members from an unspecified charity soon fetched 532 men and women from Zhangjiakou for their return back to Tang county, in Zhili.[20] Groups of five hundred to one thousand people were escorted home on rail lines, roads, and canals from Beijing and Zhangjiakou during the late winter.[21] The sheer numbers of people en route in March overwhelmed authorities, and in one mid-month report officials of the Beijing-Suiyuan rail line, reportedly flooded with refugees, pled with central authorities to stem the flow.[22]

As vast an operation as was needed to return many thousands of refugee families to their home districts—in this case coordinated by central, provincial, and municipal authorities; native charities; and international relief societies—it did not require modern logistics or administrative capabilities. A method of luring farming families back to their fields was prescribed by Chinese texts on famine administration from as early as the Ming period, when so-called return allocations (*zisong*) were designed to encourage vagrant farmers to return to their home districts in times of crisis, as a first step toward rebuilding agricultural production and returning to some degree of normalcy. In a practice similar to what was done in 1921, imperial disaster administrators normally required that returning farmers follow a specific route, along which they would present a certificate entitling them to cash handouts at relief stations at various points on their way home, rather than receiving a lump sum at once.[23] As precarious conditions persisted for millions across the north in the late winter of 1921, the mass return in warming temperatures to fields with sprouts of winter wheat was at least a harbinger of the end to the crisis. Back on February 28, the officially designated starting date of the refugees' departure for home, Wang traveled to the rail hub at Fengtai, south of Beijing, to see off a group of 838 refugees, "men and women, old and young," that his gendarmes had escorted there, posing with them for a photograph to "mark the occasion" (*liu wei jinian*).[24]

International Societies

Members of the European and American communities in China had been in their summer retreats on the Zhili coast when talk of famine was first heard among their servants. With the forces of the Anhui political faction defeated by the Zhili and Fengtian forces in July, foreigners returned to the capital unmolested, and the 1,000 yuan left from a 1,600-yuan siege provision fund raised by the foreign community was put into an account dedicated to famine relief.[25] By mid-September, diplomats and missionaries in China's major cities had formed societies to prepare for the impending famine. The American minister to Beijing, Charles Crane, wired an impassioned appeal to President Woodrow Wilson, before combining foreign efforts into a relief committee representing eleven nationalities from Beijing's small foreign community, most of whom resided in the Legation Quarter just inside the main city wall in the North City.

At the end of September, Xiong had entertained members of the foreign delegations in the capital at his Beijing residence to begin discussing how to combine Chinese and foreign relief efforts.[26] Within days, representatives of various foreign and Chinese relief organizations filed into the *huiguan* meeting hall of the organization of Chinese who had studied in Europe or America, and the Peking United International Famine Relief Committee came into existence.[27] Delegates from a dozen foreign nations formed an executive committee chaired by G. Douglas Gray (a physician in the British legation), a body that in turn worked with a larger administrative council of prominent Chinese, including Xiong and Liang Shiyi. Also on the council sat H. C. Emery, representative of the American Advisory Committee, which had just been formed by Crane, a Wilson appointee who would help mobilize the first stage of millions of dollars for famine relief across the United States until his departure when Warren Harding became president in early 1921.

It makes sense that Xiong was the one to initiate and host joint efforts with members of the diplomatic community in the fall of 1920. As discussed in previous chapters, he was both politically well placed and a man whose family had a foot in several social circles. His wife, Zhu Qihui, was very active in charities in the capital, including various Chinese Red Cross institutions (discussed in chapter 4). She spoke no English, however, only Japanese and Chinese, and she walked with an impaired gait from having had bound feet as a child. The couple's daughter, Rose, recently returned from college in the United States, was likely to "dance very well, and in public," the "best example of the flapper style" that an American at the time said she had met in Beijing, with "bobbed and waved hair" and "excellent English."[28] Xiong had been instrumental in orchestrating the relief of millions during floods three years before and had a hand in multiple relief endeavors in 1920, but he took a much less prominent overall role, for reasons that are unclear. After shepherding eighteen Chinese relief societies in early October into a larger umbrella group under the auspices of Liang's North China Relief Society, Xiong worked behind the scenes, serving on various committees and advocating certain relief policies in the press or appealing for famine loans from overseas. But otherwise the era's most prominent activist for philanthropic causes mostly confined himself to work on an orphanage he had established in Beijing's Western Hills for six hundred refugee boys and girls from the 1917 flood.[29] This reduction in his prominence in relief efforts left a personality vacuum in the national relief effort of 1920, one that, at least in the foreign-language press, other, mostly foreign, figures filled.

It should be borne in mind that the overall numerical presence of foreigners across China was minuscule, even in major cities such as Beijing. Beyond those residing in the Legation Quarter, the city's foreign population numbered 1,524 in 1917, over a third of whom were Japanese and roughly a fifth were American—the second-largest foreign nationality in the capital.[30]

That said, institutionally, the foreign presence in China loomed large. The advisory and managerial roles that foreigners had filled since the last decades of the Qing (in the Maritime Customs Service, for example, or in major engineering works on the canal and river systems) positioned them well for the logistical challenges posed by large-scale disaster relief projects.[31] Since they began in the 1870s, foreign relief efforts in China, often led by missionaries, had largely run parallel to Chinese operations, receiving little recognition from the Qing state. It was not until 1906 that the first joint Chinese-foreign relief operation was formed, in Shanghai, to relieve flood and famine in nearby Jiangsu.[32] In 1920, foreigners played a semiofficial role as the seven international committees divided the five-province famine zone between them. The most prominent of these was the Peking United International Famine Relief Committee, which, based in the capital, both assumed responsibility for the western half of Zhili province, which was served by the Beijing-Hankou rail line, and acted as a quasi-official center for data on famine conditions and relief operations across the north.[33]

Under the International White Cross

In the months since their formation in the fall, the international societies had begun setting up the infrastructure required for the intensification of their respective relief efforts in the face of growing needs across the famine field. By the end of December, the Peking committee had established branches in its designated section of central and southern Zhili at the four prefectural seats of Baoding, Daming, Shunde, and Zhengding and had allocated 227,000 yuan and 7,500 items of clothing among them for distribution.[34] The group's investigative teams had also gathered intelligence from missionaries and other informants in the field and determined that at the same time in December slightly more than eight million people across Zhili were in a state of destitution and need of assistance if they were to survive to the spring harvest.[35] By early January, the Tianjin-based international society had begun bringing into its eastern section of Zhili grain instead of cash, relieving 217,305 people (or 8 percent of the destitute population in the section) with an average of fifty *jin* of grain each.[36]

Residents who had fled were returning to their home districts with several months remaining and no household grain reserves to tide them over just as peak prices appeared across much of the North China Plain—assuming that there would be a successful harvest of winter wheat in May. After beginning primarily with the distribution of cash in their first few months of operation, the international societies gave aid in the form of free relief grain for the remainder of the crisis, which was collected by villagers at stations set up in designated locations around the famine field. After foreign relief workers began making forays into the stricken interior under the adopted flag of the 1920–21 international relief effort in China—with a white cross on a blue background, the flag flew from grain carts and junks and at grain depots across the five-province famine field—Zhili authorities periodically issued orders to local militias and police to provide armed escorts for them, particularly in drought-struck areas with bandit activity or stray bands of marauding soldiers, such as southeastern Zhili and northern Henan.[37]

The detailed journal of an American field-worker provides a rare window into the day-to-day operations of the international effort in a corner of the east-central Zhili famine field. Arriving by cart from the railhead in nearby Cang county in mid-February, Harley Farnsworth MacNair relieved the two foreign men who had opened the station earlier in the year, 110 miles south of Beijing at the small market town of Shaheqiao, a cluster of clay homes with a "picturesque bridge uniting the two tiny sides of the town." Shaheqiao was in Hejian county near the junction of two small rivers coursing over the North China Plain to Tianjin: "Flat and dusty, dusty, dusty, endlessly dusty," noted MacNair, a graduate of Columbia University and the University of California, Berkeley, who would turn thirty that year. "Not one green thing."[38]

Upon assuming responsibility in November for providing relief to people in the eastern half of Zhili, an area of plains served by the rail line running south from Tianjin to Pukou on the Yangzi, MacNair's North China International Relief Society of Tientsin had published one of the earliest pieces of intelligence on the extent of crop failure and destitution across the entire famine field. Headed by the former Chinese foreign minister M. T. Liang, with the American consul in Tianjin, Stuart J. Fuller, as vice president, the society collected data on local social and ecological conditions from the Christian missions it contacted in all five provinces.

It estimated that 14,248,000 people were already threatened by famine as of November, more than half of whom resided in Zhili. From mid- to late autumn, the society launched relief operations in twenty-six counties in Zhili (and a few in Shandong), working with missionaries and local gentry to relieve 130,000 people using 400,000 yuan. During Mac-Nair's stint in the field, the number of people reached by the society in eastern Zhili would rise to 1.5 million.[39]

MacNair was one of nearly six hundred foreigners who contributed time to the societies in the field in all five provinces, almost all of whom were tapped from around forty-five missionary organizations. They were joined by some three thousand Chinese who also worked largely on a volunteer basis, as well as paid porters and other laborers.[40] Many of the Christian organizations that supplied volunteers for the international relief programs conducted their own relief efforts over the year—work that ranged from orphanages and medical clinics to mass grain distribution centers run out of parishes and mission stations—spending collectively more than two million yuan by the end of the crisis.[41] Despite a century of intense Protestant activity in China, it was not until a decade before the famine, at a conference of world Protestant missions in Edinburgh, Scotland, in 1910, that an effort was launched to coordinate the independent evangelical activity of the many dozen Protestant denominations across China, surveying each province and dividing it into discrete mission fields.[42] In September 1920, mission representatives convened in Beijing to orchestrate relief measures by the Christian communities spread across the stricken provinces, and their investigations on the extent of crop failure and human need in remote parts of the country began appearing regularly in both the Chinese and the foreign-language press.[43]

Christian relief activity crops up in numerous local historical accounts of famine over the year, often associated with particular Protestant denominations or dioceses of the Catholic Church.[44] MacNair's post lay in the mission district of the Anglican Diocese of Beijing, which, he explained, had "conducted much industrial and other relief work" in the county earlier in the famine year.[45] Mission workers were instrumental in the relief forays into the interior by the international societies, using their familiarity with local conditions to identify people in need, coordinate relief efforts with local officials and gentry, and distribute relief goods.

But relying on missionaries for this came at a cost. "Entrusting relief to missionaries" created "immense difficulties," the secretary of an international society explained in October 1920. "Many [non-Christians] are known to be holding back large sums, and others sending them to other organizations."[46] European and American mission leaders, both Catholic and Protestant, were also careful to include local elites in their aid activities to limit disputes over the fairness of distribution. "We insist that the gentry shall be asked to control these distributions," a priest from Yanshan county, on the coast of Zhili, explained to the bishop of Beijing in early September, "so that they may be witness to the equitable and impartial distribution as we intend to make of it."[47] "It must be kept in mind that the missionaries of the interior, as a matter of fact and experiences in southeast Chihli, cannot without immense difficulties, distribute millet soup to the needy," a Daming-based French Jesuit bishop explained in the autumn from his ecclesiastical jurisdiction of thirty-nine counties with eleven million inhabitants. "The ideal way of helping the starving population would be for the Government itself to furnish the markets of the interior with foodstuffs."[48]

Part of the reason for these complications was that the famine field remained a space for proselytization, despite the efforts by the committees to ensure that religious or political favor was not a factor in the allocation of relief goods.[49] The Tianjin-based North China International Society, chaired by United Methodist pastor Frank B. Turner, had related (emphasizing the point by using capital letters) in its November report that "NO RELIGIOUS DISTINCTION WHATEVER" was being made in its relief operations, "ABSOLUTE NEED BEING THE ONLY CRITERION." Nonetheless, evangelism continued to play a role in his denomination's independent relief projects: "Mrs. G. Purves Smith at Chu Chia addressing a crowd of famine folk waiting for grain," read a photo caption appearing after the famine in *The Missionary Echo of the United Methodist Church*. According to the caption "That day we gave away over 400 tracts."[50] "We did not lose sight of the special opportunity afforded us through this work to preach the gospel," one Lutheran mission worker explained of the work in western Henan. "The Lutherans of America donated large sums," Alfred E. Trued, an Augustana Synod (Swedish Mission in China) missionary, recorded in his memoirs. "They wanted the need on the Lutheran mission fields to be met first if possible." Ration "tickets were in reality tracts of a special kind," he explained, "so the ones who received them got both spiritual and physical food. In that way the gospel was also spread."[51] And the Beijing-based Buddhist Relief Fund-Raising Society sent in monks who could speak the local dialect to preach the dharma alongside their relief efforts in the famine districts of western Zhili and eastern Shanxi. There, the more orthodox beliefs and methods that these outside monks offered to transcend worldly suffering ran up against the more syncretic practices of their local counterparts, who incorporated folk or Daoist beliefs and "supernatural and superhuman powers, chants and incantations for the endurance of cold, hunger, and other types of deprivation," James Carter explains in his study of a monk from greater Tianjin who spent six months in Jingxing county in 1920–21.[52]

Altogether twenty foreigners were posted at MacNair's relief station in Hejian, seven of whom were members of the faculty at St. John's University in Shanghai, and all remained for five to six weeks at some point from early January to mid-May, when the station closed.[53] Although St. John's was part of the American (Episcopal) Church Mission in China, MacNair's account of the station's operation is notably secular in character. Working out of what had once been a coal merchant's family compound in the village center, MacNair and his team of native clerks and laborers were provisioned with sorghum brought in daily, often through violent dust storms, on eight or so carts from the railhead two counties to the east in Cang. Much of the work involved comparing arriving loads with relief logs. Carters were charged double the market rate for either losses or gains in their freight en route—any gain suggesting that grain had been deliberately weighted down with water or sand after grain had been stolen.[54]

Standing on a dike, the American could see fourteen villages from his headquarters, each of them set on "slight rises" with a ring of willow trees and the occasional peach or jujube orchard.[55] The county had been hit hard, with 60–90 percent of its population affected by the drought-famine, according to one estimate, and 90–100 percent stricken in adjacent Xian county to the south. Still, barking dogs, crowing roosters, and other signs of life met the stranger at each cluster of homes.[56] Chinese clerks first canvassed the district, categorizing households into three tiers of need, and village families then sent representatives, led by the village headman holding the village flag, to the relief station three times a month to collect ten days' worth of rations. On one day in February, for example, 15,589 *jin* of grain was distributed to seven hundred families, or just over half a *jin* per day for each member of a family of four.

The international committees had collectively decided to distribute roughly half a *jin* of grain per person per day. This amount was decided upon after nutritionists advised the committees that it was sufficient to sustain an idle adult until the spring harvest; it also roughly matched both the standard famine rations used by Qing famine administrators and the minimum grain serving stipulated earlier in November by the Ministry of the Interior for soup kitchens operating in the capital.[57] With the exception of young women, MacNair noted, every demographic group from children to the aged appeared to collect supplies at the relief station, which was guarded and kept in order by soldiers armed with bayonets. Mac-Nair also had a "limited supply" of padded coats, which he gave out regularly to the "most ragged" appearing at the depot.[58]

A colleague determined that for every dollar of relief money spent on the station, eighty-six cents went to food, eight to transportation, and six to general expenses.[59] The station's operating expenses came to two hundred yuan every two weeks, which included a daily "board allowance" of a yuan for each foreign supervisor plus the pay for the "clerks, cooks and coolies." In spite of the gravity of the operation, the workers unloading the arriving grain sacks were "an extraordinarily jolly, willing bunch. Always joking and laughing," MacNair observed. "If the carts from [the railhead in Cang] are delayed," in the event of a sandstorm or another incident pushing the workers' shift past dusk, "they don't protest but treat [unloading each 1.2-ton cartload in the dark] as a game."[60]

As station supervisor, MacNair chased down reports of fraud in the surrounding district. He recorded that in one case a letter sent to the station charged that, in a village six miles away, a wealthy family was partaking of relief grain and another nonexistent family was also on the rolls, to the benefit of the village chief. Upon investigation, MacNair found the "allegation apparently unbased on fact; the 'rich' family had every appearance of being extremely poor, in spite of not knowing ahead of time of our coming." The fictitious family "consist[ed] of one vociferous and voluble woman . . . who lives with her one son and two nephews," he determined. "They offered every evidence of being real—and of needing food."[61] Malfeasance was doubtless present in the famine field; but so, apparently, were old gripes and grievances, which presumably were behind such false accusations.

MacNair developed an admiration for the people in his famine district, "almost all" of whom were "most remarkably cheerful—in appearance," he noted. Despite their "jabbering and crowding" as they filed into the depot's courtyard, and despite telltale signs of malnutrition, stunted growth, and in some cases insanity induced by the horrors of famine, "most of the people around here are *very* bright and intelligent-looking, their faces showing real character. Some are distinguished in appearance with beautiful hands and eyes."[62] Not a few men from the region had recently returned from serving in the Labor Corps in France during World War I, and MacNair spotted pictures of the French city of Lyons tacked on the walls of two remote village homes.[63] After several weeks of touring his district—during which he went on what he called "orgies" of buying art from rich families selling off paintings and vases—MacNair again noted that "the inhabitants of this black famine-stricken area are, for the most part, smiling and cheerful in their attitude. A lot more will die, as many have died already, but, if they must, they will die smiling."[64] Such stoicism and good cheer, as we will see, appears to have been interpreted by some foreign observers as an unusually high Chinese tolerance for suffering, which, it was thought, contributed to general inaction by Chinese in times of such calamity.

The first rain of the season fell on the afternoon of February 28, MacNair noted, describing it as "not a heavy one, but enough to encourage the crops and lay the dust momentarily."[65] Over the border in Shandong a healthy dose of rainfall fell in the same week, promising a "bumper harvest" of winter wheat in May and June.[66] Fortuitously, February 28 was the same day the Ministry of the Interior had set for the return of migrants to their home districts, and the fresh rain no doubt brightened the homeward journey of many thousands of returning farmers. "The people are beginning to work in the fields now," MacNair noted on March 5.[67] "Left Shanghai one month ago tonight," he wrote nine days later. "A month of good experience. Not as harrowing as I had feared—mainly

on account of the stoical, and even smiling, sportsmanship of these remarkable people."[68]

However, many people had not gotten onto the rolls of MacNair's
relief operation, including those returning, after the canvassing of local
needs had already taken place, from places like the camps that had sprung
up on the outskirts of Tianjin and in Zhangjiakou by the Great Wall.
Such exclusions occurred all over the famine field due to the stretched
resources of the international societies, as the Peking committee noted
regarding its work in southern Zhili's Daming county, where out of a population of half a million the society "decided to omit certain villages
completely and the villages to be helped were selected from the government lists [of needy districts and households] by lot."[69] In Hejian, Mac-
Nair found such families in their homes mashing millet chaff, bark, and
leaves into six-inch cakes, which many people ate each day at midmorn-
ing and midafternoon. Some residents were insistent about getting onto
the lists. "Another onslaught of the 'monstrous regiment of women,'"
MacNair recorded one Saturday in mid-March.[70] Most of the women had
come from a dozen or so miles away, despite having tightly bound feet,
and in groups of ten to twenty they made "as confused and menacing an
uproar as a Shakespearian Roman mob" to get their families onto the
rolls.[71] Many of those who survived through the crisis succeeded in getting added to the relief registers of the international societies, while others
found their way into the hands of independent relief stations run by the
missions. And still others, if they did not simply fend for themselves, were
taken into the care of native relief efforts discussed in previous chapters.
Finally, there was the possibility of joining the various work relief programs that appeared across the disaster zone.

The American Red Cross and Work Relief

Americans were the largest group of foreigners active in famine relief in
China over the year, and their role played out in two different ways. Donors in the United States contributed millions of dollars to the operating
budgets of the various international relief committees, transmitted via the
American legation in Beijing. With the exception of a few minor projects,

these committees decided to devote the vast majority of their relief resources in the form of free relief.[72] In contrast, the American Red Cross operation, the only one of any significance to be run by members of a single foreign nationality, was exclusively based on work relief. This had been the favored policy of the civil engineer Charles Davis Jameson, who had been sent to China when the Americans first secured permission from the Qing to study central China's volatile Huai River system in 1911.[73] Nine years later, the agency's work was concentrated in nineteen counties in western Shandong over the winter and spring of 1920–21, and it spent nearly 2.5 million yuan over the famine year to hire local laborers to build roads suitable for cars, dig wells, and work on other infrastructural projects. Each worker was allowed five dependents who would be maintained along with him, and the group provided payments in grain that supported 928,000 people over the crisis.[74]

"The classes most useful to the province obviously would be the choice of any sociologist," the group reasoned in an end-of-crisis report. "This meant cutting off our lists the maimed, the halt and the blind, the diseased, paupers, and the aged without support. Vigorous men of family were to be the natural choice for laborers. But knowing the revulsion of feeling which Chinese would experience upon the bald announcement of such a policy," the report continued, the Red Cross "sought to have influential Chinese choose this policy of their own free will."[75] The group presumably had in mind men along the lines of China's foreign minister, Yan Huiqing, who had been leading negotiations about the famine loan. The great famine of 1920–21 marked "the first time in China that a trial was made with the principle of making the sufferers render some return in the form of labor for the relief they received," Yan later recalled in his memoirs. "At first a certain section of the public considered this type of relief as harsh and repugnant, but soon the reasonableness of it was appreciated and the principle had been gradually adopted by other philanthropic organizations."[76] The American Red Cross directors were joined by some Chinese who saw in these projects an intervention in a society where, as they understood it, relief in times of crisis customarily met immediate survival needs and nothing more. Their plan offered a "lesson of organization for the construction of public improvements" that the Chinese might learn, the group explained, just "as they have learned others which have been set by their Western friends."[77]

Yet work relief (*yigong daizhen*) had long been a key component of flood or famine relief programs at both the imperial and local levels. In Zhili under the Qing, it served not only to extend relief policy beyond stopgap measures of sustenance to longer-term solutions to the threat of flood or drought such as dike management, irrigation, and reforestation. It had also expanded the statutory beneficiaries of state disaster relief (the rent- and tax-paying sedentary agricultural population) to include those normally excluded from relief rolls—migrant laborers and other itinerants who were often seen as threats to social stability and, ultimately, the state. This, as historians have shown, lessened the chances of future disruptions to the food supply and state revenues while ensuring that relief recipients were rooted and occupied.[78] At times local elites embraced work-relief methods as well, and examples of their sponsorship of relief work on infrastructure in rural Zhili crop up in gazetteer biographies of local figures active in the late imperial period.[79]

Continuing this practice into the republic, multiple levels of the Chinese state undertook work relief projects in 1920–21, parallel to those of the American Red Cross. The Ministry of the Interior had reportedly raised six million yuan in 1920 (some of the money came from a two-million-yuan increase in monthly surtax revenue through the Ministry of Communications) for road and railroad relief projects, including the construction of two main routes—one between Shijiazhuang and Cang in Zhili, and the other between Yantai and Weifang in Shandong.[80] On a smaller scale, work-relief projects funded by the Ministry of the Interior included hiring refugees to dredge the Beijing city moat and enlisting two thousand attendees of Beijing soup kitchens for road and bridge repair in the suburbs.[81] Some magistrates in rural districts worked with local gentry over the course of the famine to hire the local destitute to work on maintenance of the city wall and county roads expressly as work relief.[82] Buddhist relief groups also sponsored road and street repairs as a form of work relief in sections of the famine field.[83] And the Beijing gendarmerie turned to such methods in its varied relief programs in the capital. These appeared eminently practical, such as tasking police officials with finding suitable locations for digging wells along the main roads into the capital, so refugees could make a living by peddling well water around the city.[84] Another plan, attributed to Wang Huaiqing, was designed to meet a deficit of three hundred suburban patrolmen by hiring 237 able-bodied refugees at shelters around the city to join patrol squads, a plan that employed them "in place of direct relief" (*yidai zhenji*).[85]

But Chinese work relief endeavors in 1920–21 were merely vestiges of the High Qing model. The famine had followed a steady nineteenth-century decline in the capacity of Chinese officialdom to restore "normalcy" after disasters, replaced by disaster governance aimed merely at saving lives.[86] What should be stressed is that commentators mistook this decline in Chinese capacity for a cultural aversion to the principle of work relief or to investment in preventive measures.[87] If the Americans did not introduce such a model to the Chinese relief repertoire, their presence in 1920–21 reinforced current trends among modernizers and state builders in China toward the use of coercive and punitive work regimes for the indigent and those stricken by disaster.[88]

It was perhaps no coincidence that, not long before, the American Red Cross had gone through a bitter change in leadership—one that radically altered its style of operation, if not its mission. In 1904, the organization had gone from being run out of the home of its founder, Clara Barton, and funded predominantly with small donations from the American public and designed to meet "any public need, not just war," into a semiofficial agency that received millions of dollars in funds from J. P. Morgan and other financial firms and was, under an act of Congress, closely aligned with the War Department.[89]

In her recent history of the American Red Cross, Julia Irwin charts the effort to "reinvent the ARC for the twentieth century" after Barton's ouster, "securing the association's special place in Progressive-Era foreign affairs" by "redefin[ing] the ARC's humanitarian assistance as a social scientific undertaking" staffed by professionals.[90] However, an examination of the stated rationale of what Irwin calls the group's forays into "preventative aid in China" reveals that the aims were as much pedagogical as practical, as much lessons in the virtues of industriousness to the Chinese farmer as they were a bid to pave or dig his way out of future subsistence crises.[91] "The principal value of the 'work' plan," the American Red Cross directors explained from China in 1921, "is to be found in the preservation of the moral tone of the community saved." Looking ahead, the American organization suggested expanding these methods to a wider demographic group than the one represented by the 160,000 adult males recruited over the course of the famine year. "All of the above deals with the employment of men," the directors noted. "While the employment of women offers some peculiar difficulties, there is no other reason why women and large children ought not to be required to do something to earn their food." Lamenting the lack of "mass employment" possible through "hairnet classes, straw weaving, and sewing groups," the directors noted that "a considerable portion of the rock on the Peking streets is broken by women and children. Thus the whole subject deserves study."[92]

By design, the Red Cross operation in Shandong and three other Chinese provinces in 1920 left sizable segments of the population to the care of local elites. These included not only the aged and infirm but also any surplus able-bodied men excluded from the Red Cross rolls once funds donated from the American public had been absorbed by labor and construction costs. Four family members per worker were fed by the organization, and since workmen were given twice the rations allotted to their "idle dependents," the system resulted in food costs that were one-sixth higher "on account of the 'work' feature." Overall, when including construction materials, "the 'work' plan is nearly 39% more expensive than the 'free' plan for an equal number of persons reached," the group determined in its end-of-crisis report, a sacrifice the Americans abroad deemed necessary to "eliminate the professional beggars, opium smokers, and all those who are crafty enough to fool the investigators."[93] The 850 miles of road and 3,572 wells constructed as Red Cross work projects over the course of the famine year, then, were at the expense of several tens of thousands of residents who were turned away from free assistance.

In the process, the American-run infrastructural projects in the Chinese interior risked assuming a starker character with the deployment of soldiers from the US Fifteenth Infantry, based in Tianjin, to serve as foremen on work sites in Shandong and elsewhere, a move by the American Red Cross that the State Department belatedly deemed "extremely inadvisable."[94] A flurry of correspondence followed in the winter between Washington and the legation in Beijing over fears that the Japanese, who had recently been awarded control of the Shandong coast by the Treaty of Versailles, were using rumor and pamphleteering to shift local suspicions away from Tokyo's own ambitions and to the intentions of US military personnel instead.[95]

American relief projects across the famine field served to reinforce a trend in the direction of pedagogical work-ethic programs for the indigent in China. As we have seen, work relief had long been part of local and central relief programs in China, but these programs were being shaped and understood within a discourse of work ethics and the usefulness of the poor and famine-stricken to the nation-state. Earlier in the 1920–21 famine, recipients of disaster relief had still largely been selected in a similar fashion to how they had been chosen in China's late imperial period, prioritizing females of all ages, old men, and boys in soup kitchens and village-level mutual aid programs, while excluding drug addicts and able-bodied men. But a new discourse began to affect the provision of relief during the 1920s, signaling an emphasis on productivity over unconditional assistance—what Janet Chen has called the criminalization of poverty and a valuation of people based on their contribution to state strengthening.[96]

Conclusion

Part of an American-led surge in global civilian relief interventions in the wake of World War I, the foreign contribution to China was crucial in 1920. But it was relatively slow to materialize. The total numbers of people who received relief goods or funds from the international societies across the five-province famine field rose from 461,000 in December 1920 to 3,259,627 in the following March and 7,731,611 at the end of May. Roughly a third of the north's famine-stricken were reached by the international efforts, and the majority of them were assisted only during the final two months of the crisis.[97] Of course, this delay is understandable considering the great distances that news and resources had to travel to and from overseas, chiefly the United States. But considering the timing of the foreign contribution, along with the role of the treaty powers in the three-month delay of the Maritime Customs famine loan over the same period, the international contribution to China's famine-fighting effort in 1920–21 appears more modest than the literature has since made it out to be. This raises questions about whether the international dimension should take center stage in narratives of China's greatest famine of the early twentieth century.[98]

Foreign relief workers were at a loss to explain the relatively low death toll over the preceding months. An American supervising well-digging projects for an international relief society in the southern Zhili famine field noted only a "pitiful little band of supplicants" waving tiny branches "for much of the year" in front of a "dingy and dilapidated" two-foot-high wood-and-plaster rain god figurine—but nothing in his published memoirs resembled native relief for the starving. "In contrast," he noted only "the action started by the [international] Famine Relief Commission to avert famine."[99]

With too few visible deaths to constitute calamity, prominent observers concluded that the media had in fact sensationalized the crisis. "I believe the American business public in China are almost unanimous in that the famine was muchly exaggerated in the American Press," Julean Arnold, the US commercial attaché, wrote Washington after having served as a field secretary for the American Red Cross over the famine year.[100] Others suspected that the Chinese were simply resistant to the effects of malnutrition. "It is beginning to look, now," in February 1921, "as if the amount of relief coming in and the surprising resisting powers of the Chinese people would prevent anything resembling debacle," John Earl Baker, director of American Red Cross China, wrote his superiors in Washington. "In fact, there seems to be disappointment, in some quarters, that thousands are not seen dead in the fields, as the trains rush through the country." "The Chinese people are inured to hardship," he continued, "and such people are hard to kill, under any conditions."[101] For a number of foreign observers, including the leaders of the international relief committee in Beijing over the year, the survival of so many Chinese since autumn was a mystery—explained by, among other things, the "surprising capacity of the Chinese" to live off tree bark and leaves and a "mild winter" (in fact, winter temperatures in the famine districts had generally been only slightly above average during the crisis).[102]

So what enabled some 95 percent of North China's more than twenty million destitute to survive until spring, keeping deaths to around half a million in the 1920–21 famine? One reason was that rain returned in 1921. The levels of the water table and river systems did not drop as profoundly in 1920–21 as they had, for example, after three rainless years in the late 1870s famine. Another factor was the successful containment of epidemic disease. This was spearheaded by the international societies, a success they credited to a combination of delousing of clothing at relief stations and the policy of keeping populations on relief scattered and close to their homes. These international efforts were joined by native ones, which included those conducted by the hospital of Shanghai's Society for Doing Good Far and Wide (Guangjihui), which sent medical teams to the famine field and was credited in one case with saving three thousand lives from an epidemic using a combination of Western and Chinese medicine.[103] This apparent efficacy of health measures was in stark contrast with the experience over the border in Russia, where typhus was a contributor to several millions deaths amid famine in 1921–22, despite extensive American interventions there.[104] Nor was opium cultivation the threat to Chinese food production that it had been in the 1870s, according to British intelligence—which credited the vigilance of local magistrates with the improvement.[105] And then there was the railroad, which in the 1870s had existed in China only in the area of Shanghai, and then only briefly before opponents had the tracks torn up for various reasons.[106] There is no doubt that, as the famine historian Cormac Ó Gráda has noted, "were it not for the construction of six thousand miles of railway line in the previous few decades, the Chinese famine of 1920–21 would have been much more deadly."[107]

But it should be stressed that technology is of course neutral in humanitarian terms; the nature of infrastructure of any sort depends on how it is used. The mere existence of a rail network in 1920–21 is not enough to explain events, which played out due to the rail network's smooth, subsidized operation over the course of the crisis, allowing for the scale and reach of native relief activity examined in chapters 1–9. How did the volume of native Chinese relief compare with overseas aid? Without anything close to a central clearinghouse of data on relief provisioning over the year, estimates for what it took to maintain over twenty million destitute residents for nine months are difficult to arrive at. Nonetheless, it is clear that not only were international relief efforts late in starting, but the international share in total relief expenditures was only a fraction of what the literature has made it out to be.

At the onset of famine, the main international society based in Beijing had offered a conservative projection that 120 million yuan would be needed to maintain twenty million people until the spring harvest (at a yuan per person per month).[108] At the end of the crisis, this same society estimated that only 37 million yuan had been made available for relief over the year—by all relief agencies, native and foreign, public and private—and that the foreign share of this relief total was 40 percent. A foreign contribution of between a third and a half of all relief needs in North China would indicate an enormous reliance on outside assistance. But of course the difference between 37 million yuan and the actual funds needed to carry tens of millions of people through the year is enormous. It is hardly surprising to learn that by its own admission the Peking committee's estimated total outlay of 37 million yuan on measures to avoid mass starvation was, in its own words, "merely a guess."[109] As we have seen in the past few chapters, the extremely decentralized nature of relief activity over the year—not only in Beijing, but in stricken districts, along the refugee trail, and in communities across Manchuria—put no single authority or agency in the position to gauge relief totals over the year. Even if we raise our estimate of total relief outlays to 60 million yuan— half of the initial estimate of 120 million yuan—then the foreign share would be closer to a fifth of overall relief expenditure in 1920–21 in China, giving relief operations in the crisis a decidedly less international and more indigenous character.

In light of the delayed arrival of the foreign contribution, the colonial overtones to Beijing's lack of tariff sovereignty and corresponding lack of control over relief financing, and the reinforcement of punitive work-relief trends by the American Red Cross operations, the foreign role in 1920–21 is considerably more mixed. When historians focus on the international dimension to relief in the Chinese Republic—in the form of the various joint Chinese-foreign charity relief societies (*huayang yizhen hui*)—this also privileges new and high-profile forms of relief organizations (ones resembling familiar patterns in North America and Western Europe) at the expense of indigenous developments and those inherited from the past. In other words, this focus on the cosmopolitan origins of relief flattens our perception of nonstate disaster responses to a single sphere of activity, one that was largely alien to the afflicted communities and their wider social networks. The extent to which layers of organized native relief activity have been elided in scholarship generally is worth noting, especially in light of the recent flurry of studies on Anglo-American humanitarian policy and the centrality given to Western actors and institutions in the "humanitarian discovery of hunger" and aid delivery at home or around the globe.[110]

CONCLUSION

Oh! she is good, the little rain!
And well she knows our need
Who cometh in the time of spring
to aid the sun-drawn seed;
She wanders with a friendly wind
through silent nights unseen,
The furrows feel her happy tears
and lo! the land is green!

Du Fu, "The Little Rain"

As late as June 1921, a community tucked into the mountains of Shanxi, reachable by mule train from the provincial capital, was still awaiting a decided return of spring rains and an end to famine conditions. From the village one afternoon, clouds seemed to caress the mountaintops up the valley as if taunting the sun-beaten spring wheat below. A bell tolled from the local temple in a constant vigil, as a rain goddess and then the Dragon King were hoisted onto the shoulders of the resident men, each in a sedan chair bedecked with willow branches. An American visitor that day watched the line of villagers snake up the path toward a shrine on the slope of a nearby mountain. Red-clad dancers led the way, acting as coquettes waving their fans to beckon the procession onward, wake the spirits ahead, and tease down the clouds in the distance. Actors brought up the rear, bringing traditional tales to life as the old and young members of the community lined the route, chanting mantras to the skies for rain. Just superstition—no, the visitor dismissed her first reaction. It did not do justice to the farmer's ritual. Authored by his forebears, the procession sustained him, she reasoned, providing an outlet for energy and emotion when despair had paralyzed everyone around. Then, within moments, a downpour rolled down the valley in sheets. The Dragon King returned carried on many shoulders "like a victorious football team." The temple swelled with bodies, bands played, firecrackers replaced the solemn bell, and on and off for weeks showers fell on the surrounding fields.[1]

The findings in this book complement reappraisals of Chinese society in the republican period but also slightly modify them. We have identified the projection of charity relief from the capital, Manchuria, and elsewhere into the North China Plain, which would seem to stem from the "civil-elite amalgam" that Mary Rankin has conceptualized in her study of self-government and localism in the early republic.[2] As Rankin points out, this "civil" sphere thrived in combination with a vibrant journalistic industry, which made it largely an urban phenomenon. Yet as we have seen, the varied forms of this civil sector—from confessional or sectarian groups such as Buddhist or redemptive societies to native-place organizations and professional associations—belied the official and military character of much of their initiatives and members. In this way, charity relief followed late imperial precedents of close official-elite management of welfare concerns.

We also examined the rural counterpart to this civil sphere, in the form of the long-distance provisioning and local operation of grain discount sales and soup kitchens in the famine districts. As this involved cooperation between gentry and officials on matters of public concern, this sphere was neither fully governmental nor autonomous from the state but rather part of what Philip Huang has called a "third realm" of activity positioned between the two.[3] To most farmers and other rural residents, this third realm was the state, hosting the lowest echelons of the bureaucratic relief system inherited from the imperial period. This state-society collaboration increased in the republic when, in the words of Philip Kuhn, a "positive value" was placed on local initiative—something that had been viewed with more suspicion under the Qing—as an "essential adjunct to bureaucracy" amid declining imperial capacities.[4] At certain times and in certain places relief campaigns involved mandatory contributions based on salary, occupation, or household wealth. In this respect, urban fund-raising methods resembled those of the countryside, where communities often based mutual aid contributions on household harvests or land ownership. In both the cities and rural communities, the devolution of famine relief strengthened the hands of elites of all levels—national, regional, and local—as they carved out clearer roles for themselves in local governance, or microcivic capacities, of which famine relief was part.

Yet how do we align the picture we have seen of gentry initiative in the famine field with the rural social disintegration, increased absentee landlordism, and heightened state exactions charted by historians over the course of this same period across Zhili—what Kuhn sums up as the "arbitrary exercise of power by rapacious local elites"?[5] The problem might be one of periodization. Although historians have identified structural changes that certainly reached down to the village level with the New Policy reforms in the last years of the Qing, empirical examinations of increased social tensions at the village level pertain to later in the republic and largely coincide with the mid-1920s Northern Expedition and subsequent Nationalist Nanjing Decade. "The actual workings of county government during the first two decades of the twentieth century is a large subject on which research has barely begun," Kuhn wrote in the mid-1970s.[6] In terms of community- or district-level disaster policy in the north—an increasingly crucial aspect of rural governance and social relations—the field has hardly advanced since. Despite the prominence of flood and famine in Zhili in the 1910s and 1920s, disaster policy does not figure at all in, for example, Liu Jianyun's focused study of the self-government movement in the province.[7] In Su Xinliu's book-length study of village life amid flood and drought in republican-era Henan, the 1920–21 famine is presented as occurring in a period of spiralling prices for basic goods, subsisting off of famine foods, selling of children, praying for rain, and refugee flight; there is no mention of gentry action, village mutual aid, or other relief measures. Instead, passing references to emergency relief, grain discount operations, and work relief by the Ministry of the Interior in 1920 are upstaged by the urban charity relief performed by the major international relief society in Henan, led largely by Canadian missionaries.[8] Xia Mingfang's study of rural society amid natural disaster in the republican period is the most empirically rich resource on the subject. But it is worth noting that his discussion of qualitative changes to village life—increased social conflict and the weakening of community bonds amid these calamities—is nearly entirely based on cases from the 1930s and 1940s.[9]

Part of this comes down to data—or the absence of it. One of the reasons that richer social histories exist for the Nationalist period is the far greater documentation of daily life produced under that regime. Before 1928, data on certain subjects can be so scarce as to be of little scientific value, making it difficult to determine the nature of village dynamics in the years before the Nationalist rise to power.[10] One must not assume, however, that observations about social relations in the better-documented 1930s apply to the previous decade. Based on what we have observed here of disaster responses around 1920, some tentative observations might be made on local governance and social relations in the remainder of the decade.

1924–25: China Transforms?

The wars that occurred in North and South China in 1924 appear to have inaugurated a new and heightened phase of what would become widely known as warlordism. The first phase, which had begun in 1916 with the death of President Yuan Shikai and the disintegration of his patronage networks into competing factions, was characterized by what one historian has called "itinerant militarists" financed by local or distant patrons for whom they carried out military campaigns in the chess game between the Beiyang regime in Beijing and secessionist regimes in central and South China. In the early 1920s, these roving commanders began acquiring a territorial base of their own through alliance or conquest, and the populations and resources of these territories increasingly became sources of extraction for the pursuit of further war and personal ambition and survival.[11]

By the end of the 1920s, Wang Huaiqing, the man who had presided over famine relief administration in the capital earlier in the decade, had fallen into obscurity, but not before he participated in one of the major political events of the time. The complicated nature of events that would pave the way for the Nationalist Northern Expedition against the Beiyang regime came down, in various ways, to money, and the seemingly mundane matter of soldiers' pay. With 1.5 million yuan in back pay owed to the thousands of men charged with policing and defending the capital in 1923, Wang and Feng Yuxiang (1882–1948), another general, had denounced the central leadership, going so far as to bring several hundred garrison soldiers to protest in front of the presidential palace and leading to the ouster of President Li Yuanhong.[12] The following year, Wang facilitated a coup staged by Feng, who was incensed because his soldiers' pay was six months in arrears when they were in command of the Second and Third Route Armies of Wu Peifu, a leader of the Zhili faction.[13] As

Wang's forces assisted Wu in holding Zhang Zuolin's Fengtian armies at bay in the area near the Great Wall in early autumn 1924, Feng's army swept down from the north into Beijing, where he deposed and arrested Cao Kun, who had assumed the presidency a year before by buying the required parliamentary votes, precipitating the fall of the Zhili clique.[14] More symbolically, Feng expelled the last members of the Qing court from the inner sections of the Forbidden Palace, where Puyi had resided since his abdication in 1912. By the end of the month, the last of the Qing emperors had sought refuge in the Japanese legation.[15] Wang, a man who had embodied the old guard in the famine of 1920–21, participated in giving the imperial house the coup de grâce.

The period from 1924 onward was marked by an increase in the frequency and intensity of war. Beyond the fighting in 1911–13 associated with the Xinhai revolution and after two relatively conflict-free years, each year in China between 1916 and 1930 saw on average eight "full-scale" wars, not counting "innumerable small-scale clashes" of troops, in the words of Diana Lary; in "the worst single year" of 1928 there were sixteen discrete wars in China.[16]

Equally significant to the scale of violence from the wars of 1924–25 onward was a newfound pervasiveness of the military in nearly all aspects of life, from the careers to which the elites aspired and cultural and social ideals more generally to industry and landownership. Beijing's military commanders in the 1910s and early 1920s, Jiang Chaozong and Wang, had both straddled social spheres and taken on multiple identities, including that of the classical scholar—an identity that was fast becoming antiquated.

War and state exactions had implications for the social and political dynamics at the most local levels: the district and village. Rural customs of mutual aid and charity, and the social relations underpinning them, did not die of inertia but at the hands of an increasingly intrusive state apparatus. Rural communities across the 1920–21 famine field that had experienced relatively limited deaths and desertion soon saw a debilitating cocktail of soaring taxes, ecological crises, and the incessant requisitioning of men and vital resources by warring provincial regimes, if they were not subjected to the ravages of war itself. Meanwhile, disruptions to the civilian food supply would become a standard weapon of war, affecting even coastal enclaves such as Shanghai.[17] These years were also when some of the most notorious figures of the period effectively established fiefdoms in both rural and urban sections of the country.[18] Even the policies of "model" governors with progressive reputations changed dramatically amid the heightened competition among their peers.[19]

Beyond their economic toll on the populace, these heightened state extractions came with a social cost, introducing the predatory position of the tax agent. This prompted the retreat of local elites en masse from village leadership roles, as entrepreneurial tax brokers with no personal investment in the welfare of local communities formalized antagonistic relationships within villages. The protective role that local elites had taken traditionally—for their own advantage as much as that of their neighbors—was increasingly supplanted by impersonal and extractive forces emanating from the cities where rural landowners increasingly settled.[20]

From the mid-1920s onward, conflicts increasingly tied up transport networks and, at times, brought them to total paralysis. The steady climb of rail freight volumes in Hebei and western Shandong from the early 1890s peaked in 1921, and then again in 1923, before a marked decline to 1929, after which it did not reach its early 1920s levels until the 1930s.[21] And the civil wars from 1924 on emptied entire districts of what had been essential modes of grain and relief transport within and between communities in earlier crises. In Dezhou, Shandong provincial officials had ordered county officials to secure over four thousand carts for military use in September 1924, "promising to pay 50 yuan for the horse and 100 for the groom if either was killed in battle." And "sometimes carts and men were simply seized at gunpoint," Arthur Waldron writes. In one location in the southwest of the province, "the order requisitioning 300 carts arrived at the farmers' busiest season, just as beans were being harvested and wheat planted," and the magistrate was promptly fired for not overruling the villagers' objections fast enough.[22] Similar mass mobilizations and disruptions to economic activity occurred in 1924 to the south in the Yangzi valley and to the north, where in greater Beijing "practically all motor cars owned by Chinese companies" were confiscated for military use.[23] In 1926, "while carts were being requisitioned" to carry military supplies for the Shanxi government, Henrietta Harrison explains, "almost all transport came to a halt since none of the carters dared go out."[24] The seizure of essential modes of transport in the countryside—not only trains but also farmers' carts—became standard practice across large sections of the country by the mid-1920s.

Sichuan offers the most extreme example of rural China's mid-1920s spiral into chaos. Large sections of the province of seventy million people had been ravaged by military contests over territory since the late 1910s. By 1924, the province had splintered into the domains of at least ten feuding militarists, many of whom required farmers to cultivate opium as a cash crop providing lucrative tax revenues, leading to dramatic declines in grain production when drought visited the province in 1924. In May of 1925, 80 of Sichuan's 146 counties were reportedly experiencing famine conditions unseen there since the establishment of the republic: 300,000 had already starved to death and another 200,000 had died of pestilence and disease, by one count, while 700,000 had been displaced.[25] In one county, Tongjiang, an estimated 70 percent of those afflicted by the famine had already died.[26] There were reports that cannibalism was rife in the north of the province—an indicator of considerably more extreme conditions than had existed in the five northern provinces in 1920–21.[27]

Despite leading to the deaths of 1.15 million people, by one count, the Sichuan famine of 1925 would become a footnote, at best, in historical works.[28] Societies were formed in the province and as far away as Shanghai for the relief of Sichuan's afflicted counties. But these were clearly overwhelmed, both because they were working in increasingly trying conditions in the famine field and because they were appealing to urban, coastal publics whose members were increasingly preoccupied with the revolutionary fervor of the May Thirtieth Movement and varied crises of their own.

Some of these changes (such as increased taxation) were more sudden in most places, while others (state penetration of village politics, for example) were culminations of developments originating in the late Qing. Nonetheless, the intensification of both physical and ideological conflict in the mid-1920s was combined with social and cultural changes more generally. This served to sap state and civic capabilities further while undermining public resourcing of welfare matters, creating the very conditions, as the decade wore on, for the normalization of disaster itself.

The China International Famine Relief Commission

With the sprouts of spring in 1921 and the abrupt end of famine conditions in the north, there remained millions of yuan in unspent donated funds in the hands of the various international relief organizations. Representatives of the seven international relief societies involved in the 1920–21 famine convened in Beijing in September 1921 to pool the two million yuan they collectively had left over and give the money to a single new organization, the China International Famine Relief Commission.[29] After a series of consultations in the United States in early 1922, managers of the American relief fund decided to use its surplus as an endowment for forestry and agriculture studies at Nanking and Peking Universities for the purpose of the "study and investigation of famine causes."[30]

Meanwhile, the Chinese government tried, and failed, to establish its own central famine relief and prevention organization. This Beijing had proposed doing with the remaining customs revenue generated by the famine surtax agreed to between Beijing and the four major treaty powers. In mid-May 1921, just as the long-awaited rains were falling on the northern famine districts, Chinese Foreign Minister Yan Huiqing had formally submitted to members of the Diplomatic Body Beijing's proposal to create a National Famine Prevention Commission within the Ministry of the Interior, using the remaining funds raised from the customs surtax imposed for the famine relief loan brokered earlier in the year.[31] By mid-July, a circular to the legations from the then dean, Batalha de Freitas, asked that the collective response agreed to by the Diplomatic Body rejecting the proposal be "sent by each Legation on the 21st instant" to the Chinese side. The American version of the note stated that because the proposal was "not provided for in the (initial) agreement" for the famine loan between Beijing and the powers, the idea was "not acceptable." The letter ended by asking that the customs surtax—which had been so far applied for only four and a half months of its year's validity—be instead terminated in advance "in accordance with the spirit" of the Chinese Ministry of Foreign Affairs' original request for the surtax in October 1920.[32]

In August Yan wrote the American legation with revisions to Beijing's original plan, proposing to spend a million yuan of the surtax surplus for the relief of flood victims in Shandong and Zhili with the remainder used "to organize a new Board of Control of the Famine Prevention Endowment Fund to be composed of both Chinese and foreigners who will have joint effective supervision and control."[33]

Yan's follow-up appeal was apparently ignored.[34] Instead, in October, the Diplomatic Body sought the formation of a foreign-controlled board to handle the customs surtax surplus before a decision was reached on what to do with it, and this body was created with Dwight W. Edwards of the Peking United International Famine Relief Committee at its head.[35]

Over the course of 1922, in the face of severe food shortages and rising prices in greater Beijing, the board responded positively to an appeal by Yan for an interest-free loan of half a million yuan from the customs surtax surplus to fund a poor relief committee in the region.[36] In 1923 there was a major improvement in food conditions nationwide, with "all parts of China" reporting "an excellent harvest of all crops," and the new dean of the diplomatic body, the Dutch minister, W. J. Oudendijk, proposed allowing the remaining famine loan funds to go to the China International Famine Relief Commission, an idea agreed to by the Chinese government, according to Edwards.[37]

By 1924, the last remaining major fund from the famine of 1920–21 was in the hands of the international relief commission. A tie-breaking foreign vote on its board kept the commission under foreign control, according to Walter Mallory, its executive secretary from 1922–27. This arrangement, he later explained, was designed to "block pressure" from Chinese officials who might wish to "allocate funds without regard to the severity of conditions" or spread "the commission's funds too thinly to be effective."[38] Edwards served as vice chair, while John Earl Baker, the American Red Cross's director in China, served on the executive committee. "Relief shall not tend to pauperise the population and to reduce it to a state of dependence," the commission determined at its inception, taking a similar approach to that of the American Red Cross. Except in the case of emergencies, relief would "be given only in exchange for a fair return of labor," largely on major engineering projects around the country, and spending would reach fifty million yuan over fifteen years amid the country's unfolding natural and man-made disasters.[39] In this way, the 1920–21 famine resulted in the creation of one of the largest disaster management organizations in the Chinese Republic. However, the commission would soon be overwhelmed by circumstances and the severity of the disasters striking the country.

The Northwest Famine of 1928–30

The China International Famine Relief Commission soon found itself facing one of modern China's most severe droughts and famines. In late May 1927 Buddhist monks held rituals in Beijing praying for rain to end the "continued drought" that was "doing untold damage to North China crops."[40] Within six years of the healthy harvests and replenished stocks in communities across the North China Plain in May 1921, famine loomed once again on the lower reaches of the Yellow River. In the spring, sections similar to the ones struck by drought in 1919–20, such as Shandong and Zhili, were affected, and famine conditions appeared in autumn of 1927, as they had in the fall of 1920. By the autumn of 1928, the concentration of drought and ensuing famine conditions shifted to the north and west, encompassing sections of Shanxi, Henan, Shaanxi, and Gansu before centering on the upper reaches of the Yellow River in Suiyuan and Chahar.[41]

Due to what it called the "disorganized conditions of travel" in increasing sections of the country since its creation following the 1920–21 famine, the various provincial branches of the commission came together only every three years.[42] Between April 1925 and May 1931, the commission convened as a whole only once. This was in mid-November 1928 in Tianjin, where it decided to take direct control of the subcommittees in the stricken provinces of the North China Plain and create additional ones in the isolated yet hardest hit northwest. "In the interest of economy," the committee had followed "the practice of not maintaining personnel in active service in the interim between famines."[43] The commission had no committees in Chahar, Suiyuan, or Gansu before 1929.[44]

In Gansu and neighboring Shaanxi, famine in the late 1920s was the "worst within living memory," in the words of the provincial committee, adding that the "politico-military situation has undoubtedly accentuated the distress . . . but the fact remains that the primary cause of the famine is due to drought" and the failure of three successive harvests.[45] The commission delivered a total of 10,345 tons of grain in 1929, with the majority (7,266 tons) going to Suiyuan. Shaanxi received 408 tons. None went to Gansu. The commission delivered only 2,419 tons the next year (handing out more cash instead), the bulk of it (1,848 tons) to Shaanxi, while finally setting up a system of soup kitchens in Gansu that served 10,000 people daily.[46]

By the end of 1930, 3–10 million residents of nine provinces stretching from coastal Shandong to inland Gansu would die of famine-related causes.[47] As an indicator of distress, land values dropped by 17 percent in the northwest in 1928 and did not return to their 1927 level until 1933. There had been no such drop in 1920–21.[48] The northwest famine of 1928–30 would become the iconic case of Chinese mass starvation that many Westerners would soon read about as they were introduced to Mao Zedong and the Shaanxi-based Communists in *Red Star over China* by the American journalist Edgar Snow, who visited Inner Mongolia in 1929.[49]

So what had changed in the area of disaster relief? Disentangling the numerous factors behind each of the famines is terribly difficult. Nonetheless, despite their similarities—striking roughly 300 rural counties across multiple provinces—there were fundamental differences between the two Chinese drought-famines that bookended the 1920s and resulted in an extraordinarily higher death toll in the later case. Probably most crucial was the difference in intensity of war. Earlier in the decade, military interference of relief work had been limited to banditry and roaming bands of defeated soldiers following the July war of 1920. In 1928–30, full-scale war between Nationalist troops and those of the military regimes in the north brought military activity to a majority of the districts afflicted by drought—eighty of ninety-two counties affected by famine, in the case of Zhili (Hebei).[50] This brought paralysis to the national rail system—only a tenth of the thousand locomotives in the North were reportedly in use at all in 1928—which drastically curtailed the transfer of resources from Manchuria and elsewhere in the country.[51]

Another major difference was back-to-back years of harvest failure in 1928–30 compared to a single year's subsistence crisis in 1920–21. The rains of spring 1921 returned healthy crops after a year's rainless skies in much of the north in 1919–20. In contrast, the three consecutive years of drought in 1927–29 came on top of a steady decline in harvests across the north since 1925, along with a major earthquake that hit Gansu in May 1927.[52] Another key difference was the proximity of the heart of the 1920–21 drought and famine zone to the political and commercial seats in Beijing and Tianjin, Manchuria, and the more affluent coast. At the end of the decade, drought was most severe in the remote interior, in Inner Mongolia and the loess regions of the northwest.

But the crucial factors of climate, geography, and paralyzed infrastructure do not tell the whole story behind the deaths of millions to starvation in the last years of the 1920s. Nor does the retreat of international assistance, for example, in the case of the American Red Cross—which refused to intervene in August 1929, citing disorder, disruptions to communications, taxation, and available reserves of food in China, which it said "did not conform to the popular American conception of the term 'famine.'"[53]

The organization's reasoning reflected fundamental social changes in China since its last major intervention in the Chinese famine field, a shift in political culture and attendant state priorities in the mid-1920s, between the great famines at each end of the decade. Warfare had also been normalized by the end of the 1920s. Waldron has identified 1924–25 as a "turning point" in China, not in the technologies and style of Chinese warfare, but in the understanding and uses of violence in Chinese society.[54] This process affected all levels of society, from the village to the nation, and involved the omnipresence of combat, the increased valorization of martial values in light of anti-imperialist and "national salvation" movements, and the increasingly exacting state-society relationship to attain the finances and manpower to wage the near-constant civil and anti-Japanese wars in the quarter-century from 1925 to 1950.

The millions of deaths from the 1928–30 famine were only the beginning of mass mortality amid a spiral of war and disaster. The greatest flood in modern history followed the famine when the Yangzi broke its banks and flooded an area the size of England and Wales in 1931, leading to the deaths of possibly a million people.[55] Data provided by Xia casts the first decade of Nationalist rule as the most environmentally disastrous of the republican era, with 20–70 million people stricken by drought, flood, or other natural disasters in each of the ten years from 1927 to 1936—even before the outbreak of eight years of total war with Japan.[56]

In this wider context, the relatively effective effort presided over by the Beiyang regime in 1920–21 takes on added significance.

National Salvation and Sacrifice

Changes appear to have coalesced within Chinese elite political culture in the years since the great famine of 1920–21. State strengthening involved predatory relationships with state agents that, at best, offset the benefits that the China International Famine Relief Commission and other agencies continued to provide. The extended political and economic reach of the Chinese state disrupted the peasant market economy in pursuit of fiscal targets while offering little to rural communities in return. Meanwhile, in the destabilized environment of civil war, absentee landlordism, and heightened fiscal demands, local leadership positions were increasingly taken up by those less inclined to maintain the reciprocal relationships and customary mutual aid that had marked social relations in rural communities earlier in the decade.

Illustrating this broad shift, Andrea Janku shows how attention to the famine in this sphere of debate varied widely. She argues in her study of media during the 1928–30 famine that a "powerful public sphere" pressured the Nationalist regime to commit state resources and energies and demonstrate its "responsibility for the welfare of this people." *Da gongbao*, the Tianjin daily formerly owned by the Beiyang regime, put the famine front and center of its coverage, while joining dozens of Beijing- and Tianjin-based charity and quasi-official relief groups in petitioning against work relief in favor of emergency relief in the famine districts. By contrast, "only a regular and conscientious *Shenbao* reader," Janku writes of the major Shanghai daily, "would have been aware of a major subsistence crisis in some part of the country by the end of 1928, let alone a national crisis." When the paper did turn to the famine in late 1929, rather than focus on the human toll, its editorials focused on the promotion of work-relief programs and other "constructive" aspects of the crisis the paper saw contributing to the Nationalist state-building project.[57]

This declining attention to disaster indicated two longer-lasting changes. The first was a focus on national strength vis-à-vis the imperialist threat of Japan and the Western powers, which explains the Nationalist Party's overlooking crises in the interior while holding national humiliation days throughout the year.[58] The second change was pursued to actualize this strength: a further reorientation of the Chinese state away from disaster-prone regions and toward coastal, urban, and industrial areas for the purposes of bankrolling the empowerment of state institutions.[59] In other words, there were structural changes under way in China that led to the increased vulnerability of communities in China's interior at the hands of the state. This was not a collapse in state capabilities; it was a shift in political prioritization.

In other ways, the weakening of the international character of disaster relief in China was a product of revolutionary activity over the 1920s. In the immediate aftermath of the May Fourth Movement triggered in 1919, the country had experienced a wave of anti-Christian activity. Much of this was spurred by charges that the faith was antiscience, but the actions against church schools and groups largely fizzled out by 1922. By the mid-1920s, however, half a dozen provinces experienced a resurgence of anti-Christian activity—especially in central and South China as the ideological groundwork was laid there before the arrival of Nationalist armies in the beginning stages of the Northern Expedition in 1924–25. By 1926, the Nationalist Party's second congress had deemed mission charities and schools the "throat, tongue, claws, and teeth" of imperialism, and the climate induced missionaries, Protestants in particular, to flee the country.[60] This was combined with a sharp fall in North Americans choosing careers in the mission field after 1924, and, by 1927, huge declines in revenues for the major mission boards in the United States relative to the peaks of the 1910s. By one estimate, the 6,500 Protestant missionaries in China at the beginning of 1927 had dropped around 40 percent to 4,000 by the middle of the following year.[61] The mission workers who had served as key data gatherers and facilitators for the international relief societies in 1920–21 were fast pulling out of the interior just as famine returned to the north.

The first order of business when the Nationalists took power was the restoration of Chinese sovereignty over the country's territory and affairs. In 1928, they revised the country's tariff regime with the United States, freeing Nanjing to fix its own customs taxes in late 1928, which it set between 7.5 percent and 27.0 percent—bringing an injection of revenue the moment famine flared in the northwest.[62]

But the regime's strategies for raising revenue from among the general rural population immediately conflicted with any stated intention to relieve distress in the disaster-prone sections of the north. The Nationalists began to remove vital fallback strategies widely used by families on the North China Plain to weather crises, such as earth salt production, which was criminalized in the late 1920s after being the means by which communities survived the 1920–21 famine.[63] By the 1930s, as Patricia Thornton has shown, the model local official was to take an antagonistic posture toward the community he was charged with administering in service of the state, even at the expense of poverty or famine alleviation.[64]

The increasingly extreme policies of the Nationalist government in the face of Japan's seizure of Manchuria in 1931 and its all-out invasion in 1937—including the breaking of the Yellow River dikes that made refugees of four million residents and killed as many as 900,000 others—were the culmination of a fundamental shift in political values that had found full traction in the mid-1920s.[65] This trajectory over the 1920s reveals much about the Chinese experience of modernity more generally. Recognizing the size and reach of China's late imperial civilian granary system (which extended into the republican period, as we have seen) "forces us to take more seriously the paternalistic welfare ideology of Confucianism," in the words of R. Bin Wong.[66] Increased demands on the population for the state-building project, together with the normalization of disaster, formed part of what Wong has dubbed "the twentieth century collapse of the Confucian agenda" and China's "imperial decline into modernity."[67] As Kathryn Edgerton-Tarpley argues in her comparison of the Yellow River flood of 1938–47 with the late Qing famine of the 1870s, the character of Chinese governance and political legitimacy experienced a fundamental change in the modern period from one based on paternalistic social welfare to one based on national defense and the sacrifice this required of the population.[68] Numerous scholars have examined how this sacrifice for national causes reached a horrifying peak in the People's Republic in the Great Leap Forward famine of 1958–62.[69] Evidence of the relatively robust performance of imperial and communal relief systems and codes over the 1920–21 famine suggests that we might more precisely locate this decline in the 1920s, during the struggle for national salvation amid imperialism that was soon heightened by total war with Japan.

EPILOGUE

The Toilet General

In the southwestern outskirts of Beijing, a few hundred yards from the twelfth-century Lugouqiao (Marco Polo Bridge) where skirmishes precipitated all-out war with Japan in 1937, I emerged from the Dajing subway station in search of a stone. What remained of Dajingcun in 2013 was a cluster of half-demolished storefronts and homes amid a great stretch of bulldozed rubble, all beneath a cliff-face of residential high-rises rising into a hazy canopy of sky. The residents I approached on the construction site's dirt tracks were migrants from elsewhere in the country; none of them had heard of a temple where a stone stele had been erected nearly a century before to memorialize the actions of the city's gendarmerie commander amid looting and famine. My only trace of the stone inscription was a digitized rubbing in the collections of the National Library of China downtown.

Over years of searching, I had grown accustomed to finding only traces of the fading historical footprint of a leading figure in the everyday life of the Chinese capital a century ago. It was down the bullet-train line in Tianjin where I found the most formidable of vestiges—the Western-style home that Wang Huaqing retired to in the years before his death in 1953, which had been converted into a multifamily complex in the Maoist period. There in 2013 the caretaker, kindly allowing a Chinese friend and me to a walk briefly through the shuttered building, had nothing to say of its former occupant, only to note, just before we left, the uniquely solid construction of the home's curved grand staircase. There was nothing compared to it among the neighborhood's other gated mansions, he observed, all of which were in varied stages of disrepair or conversion into the café bars and discos then taking over the quarter.

Wang had suffered the fate of a second-rate warlord, appearing only in passing in English-language accounts of military engagements or the biographies of leading generals from the period.[1] In one of his rare non-military appearances, Kenneth Pomeranz finds Wang dispatched to central Zhili to conduct rain prayer rituals on behalf of residents in 1924.[2] And Wang enjoys something of a cameo appearance in Jung Chang's family memoir, *Wild Swans*, passing through her grandfather's hometown in eastern Zhili in 1908 when Wang served as a unit commander in Manchuria. Admiring the calligraphy hanging above a temple gate, the future head of the capital military summons the man who created it, Chang's grandfather, and takes him on as his aide-de-camp.[3]

Cyberspace, along with the volumes of warlord biographies and sketches that line the shelves of mainland bookstores today, offer scattered mentions of Wang, though, casting him in an altogether different light. In one account from a 2007 collection of essays, Wang had installed a custom-built toilet in his Beijing office, the size of an office desk, heated by coal from below, with a desk mounted before its porcelain seat to meet the demands of a chronic bowel condition. In two- to three-hour sessions spread over each day, the account explains, Wang thus conducted the business of his various offices, his contraption always on hand, following him onto the battlefield through the 1920s.[4] The account can be corroborated by a similar, if briefer, passage in the recollections of Wang's Thirteenth Division staff advisor, Li Lunbo.[5] *China Daily* online later published a similar account with the rather circular title "Toilet General with a Special Liking for the Toilet."[6] In print as well as online, Wang had become "the toilet general" (*matong jiang jun*).

Revisiting my notes afterward, I could no longer picture the man presiding over Beijing's affairs without his porcelain perch—ordering thousands of ceramic bowls for the city soup kitchens one November afternoon in 1920, or disciplining his men after they doused people at a grain discount center with water one cold December day as a form of crowd control.[7] I was not sure what, if anything, this added dimension contributed—aside from a rather vivid illustration of how reductive a process historical memory can be.

APPENDIX

The Nankai Camp, Tianjin

China's largest assembly point of families fleeing drought-famine in 1920–21 was in the Nankai district of suburban Tianjin. In many ways, the camp was a microcosm of the nationwide famine fighting effort. The informal management of the camp, the timeline of its formation and dismantling, and the handling of famine-related diseases such as typhus there all capture the decentralized and hybrid character of refugee management and relief provisioning in much of China over the famine year.

Families had converged in roughly the same spot in Nankai where in 1917 tens of thousands of flood refugees—many from the same Zhili counties struck by drought in 1920—had waited until the floodwaters that had devastated much of the province receded. As early as September 1920, people started settling on a patch of open, uncultivated land in Nankai—with no objection from its owners, according to a report in the spring—building huts for themselves out of mud and scavenged materials.

The Nankai camp, surrounded by a freshly dug ditch and a raised mud wall, would not be the only refugee encampment in the environs of North China's main treaty port, but it was by far the largest, with fifty thousand residents at its peak. Most of them came from Zhili communities within a hundred miles of the city, according to one tally, but there were also families from more distant Shandong.[1] Initially, some 60 percent of the camp residents could, for the time being, fend for themselves on the outskirts of the city, according to an investigation in November, living by scavenging for food and for stalks and stubble for fuel.[2] Some pulled rickshaws or otherwise competed for menial jobs with Tianjin's resident poor, who had already been struggling with an economic slump and the effects of the region's drought as early as the summer. Four-fifths of the four hundred cotton-weaving workshops in Tianjin had closed in the past year, according to one local report, due in part to the plummeting purchasing power of residents in the region's famine districts. To meet rising food prices in August, the Tianjin Chamber of Commerce had brought in 30,000 *shi*, or 3.6 million *jin*, of grain from Anhui to be sold at a discount to the public.[3] As difficult as it was for people who were eking out an existence in the area, the remaining 40 percent of camp residents reportedly arrived dependent on aid to get through the months ahead, and for them "at a comparatively early date, viz. first of October, certain Chinese philanthropists began giving out a limited quantity of steamed bread," the Local Relief Board of the North China International Relief Society of Tientsin explained in a summary report, "An Account of the Nankai Refugee Camp Relief Work," published later in the spring.[4]

Over the camp's half-year existence, no single relief organization or government agency, including the police, would take charge of its management or oversight. Instead, the camp was run jointly by seven charities, each of which took on the management of at least one of the fourteen sections into which it was divided, in many cases paying refugees to erect huts of reed-mats and other materials. A single Chinese relief group sponsored six of the camp's sections, which collectively held 21,291 residents, or nearly half of the total population. Another six groups—four Chinese, one Chinese-Japanese, and one formed by the local relief board of Tianjin's international relief society—took on the maintenance of the remaining eight sections.

The Nankai camp attracted considerable media attention, such as to an autumn parade of military and school bands involving Chinese Boy Scouts and the YWCA to drum up support for relief there.[5] Meanwhile, systematic food distributions at the camp were undertaken by a variety of groups and individuals, both official and private. Some appeared to target the entire camp with their efforts. The first of these may have been a relief committee composed of members of the city's merchant-gentry class, prominently promoted by Yang Yide (1873–1944), a police official who had recently been put in charge of the presidential bodyguard.[6] The group dispensed food once every five days starting in the fall, using subscriptions from individuals and firms that totaled 40,000 yuan. Other groups limited their distributions to particular camp sections. In November, a relief society formed by the municipal police was reportedly giving out steamed buns daily in two sections of the camp and continuing its clothing and grain distributions through December, while another Chinese charity society distributed relief rations in another two sections.[7] Two soup kitchens were established jointly by Tianjin's international society and the city's Port Relief Affairs Office;[8] the Bank of Zhili organized sorghum flour handouts of 10 *jin* and 7.5 *jin* to "destitute" and "secondary poor" families, respectively;[9] and the police chief of a precinct from as far away as Shanghai arrived one day in early winter with 30,000 yuan for cash distributions.[10] In all, over sixty charities, firms, schools, and individuals were thanked in one summary report for supplying coal, building materials, straw mattresses, blankets, pipes for running water, medicine, salt packets, and other relief materials over the famine year.

As much as authorities and relief societies during the crisis endeavored to prevent the formation of high concentrations of refugees in or around the famine zone, the few officially sanctioned camps such as Nankai's offered a chance for medical reformers to test out and showcase methods in hygiene administration—in favor of which there was a movement sweeping government and elite circles in China at the time, a phenomenon Ruth Rogaski has studied in detail in the adjacent treaty port of Tianjin.[11] Some 95 percent of the 27,000 residents already encamped at Nankai in early December were deemed "uneducated" and "ignorant of hygiene methods," according to *Da gongbao*, the Beiyang government's newspaper, at the same moment that Tianjin's main international relief society was setting up teams of male and female hygiene workers in the camp.[12] Earlier in the year, teams sent by a Chinese relief society to investigate health conditions in the rural famine districts had reported that the lack of state funding was the primary reason district magistrates gave for the lack of progress in hygiene education and administration in the interior, where the construction of covered drains especially was desperately needed.[13]

Disease struck the camp in December in the form of smallpox. Although the state-run Plague Prevention Agency of Zhili vaccinated 14,683 camp residents, some 700 camp residents, mostly children, were moved to an isolation ward due to an appearance of the disease, from which 200 people had died by the end of the month.[14] But despite tens of thousands of people being crowded together on a mere three-sixteenths of a square mile of land so close to one of China's largest cities, outbreaks of disease in the area of the Nankai camp were otherwise kept under control over the duration of its existence.

Behind this success was a combination of official and extragovernmental disease management that took shape in cities around the region. Fearing continued outbreaks of smallpox in the area of Nankai, schools closed well before the Lunar New Year for students to return home early, and the Beiyang Anti-Epidemic Bureau set up a multiroom treatment clinic and dispensary by the camp to limit the spread of the disease.[15] Surprisingly, after a handful of students at a nearby Nankai school died of typhoid fever early in the fall, the nearby group of refugees was permitted to grow further. Local schools established ties with the camp, including a Nankai middle school that organized day classes in December for two groups of fifty refugee children, while a student from the newly opened Nankai University nearby organized classes for eighty-eight refugee children in the same week.[16] Significantly, in North China's largest single concentration of refugees in the famine year, there were no known cases of typhus, normally a common scourge and leading cause of death in the event of famine.

On February 17, 1921, Tianjin police announced that the camp at Nankai would be closed within five days and that all residents would receive fifteen days' worth of food and one yuan per adult (or 50 cents per child), although it is unclear in what fashion these monies were distributed. Refugees heading south or west into the respective relief fields of the two international relief committees operating in Zhili were required to walk three miles west of the city to collect relief tickets (for redemption by the committees upon arrival in their home districts) and were then escorted by police another ten miles beyond the city limits.[17] The closing of North China's largest encampment appeared to have been coordinated with the return of refugees to their home districts all over the north for the arrival of spring.

Chinese Characters

The entries are alphabetized letter by letter of the romanization, ignoring word and syllable breaks—with the exception of personal names, which are ordered first by surname and then alphabetically by given name. Major cities are excluded. Only former names of provinces are given. Chinese-language periodicals are listed in the bibliography instead of here.

Andong 安東
Anhui 安徽
anran wuyang 安然無恙
anwei 安慰
Anxin 安新
Anyang 安陽
Anyingcun 安營村
anzhi 安置

baihua 白話
bang 磅
banguan 半官
banshou banshe zhi yi 半售半施之意
bao 包
Bao Guiqing 鮑貴卿
Baoding 保定
baojia 保甲
baoquan 保全
Baoshantang 寶善堂
Baotou 包頭
baoweituan 保衛團
Beidaihe 北戴河

Beifang jizhen xiehui 北方急賑協會
Beijing pin'er yuan 北京貧兒院
Beijing-Wannan shisan xian jiuzai xiehui 北京宛南十三縣救災協會
beishui chexin 杯水車薪
Beiwusheng hanzai zhenji hui 北五省旱災賑濟會
Beiwusheng xieji hui 北五省協濟會
Beiyang 北洋
bian ke e bu si 便可餓不死
bianmin shichang 便民食廠
bilin deng bei 鄙吝等輩
bingcheng zhe "muxun" 秉承着母訓
bingzai 兵災
Binjiang 濱江
Binjiang yizhen hui 濱江義賑會
bujun tongling 步軍統領

caimai 採買
Cang 滄
can wu rendao 殘無人道
Cao Kun 曹錕

Cao Rui 曹鋭
chadianer qisi 差點兒氣死
Chaha'er 察哈爾
Changchun 長春
Changping 昌平
changpingcang 常平倉
Changtu 昌圖
Chen Delin 陳德霖
Cheng Daoyi 程道一
Cheng Qiyuan 程启元
chengbao zaihuang 呈報災荒
Chenggu 城固
cheng mu xun 乘母訓
chiqiong tuan 吃窮團
choujuan 抽捐
chu ji su liang wei zizhu su jin 出積粟量爲
　　資助粟盡
cipin 次貧
cishan hui 慈善會
cishan jia 慈善家
cishan xing 慈善性
cishan yinhang 慈善銀行
cungui 村規
cun zhang fu 村長副
cunzheng 村正
cun zi jiuji 村自救濟

Dachang 大昌
da cishan jia 大慈善家
dai 袋
da jie guo nian 大揭鍋年
Dajingcun 大井村
Dalian 大連
Daming 大名
dan 擔
Daowai 道外
daoyin 道尹
Datong 大同
Daxing 大興
de 德
dexing 德行
dezheng 德政
Dezhou 德州
dianzhu guyi diaonan 店主故意刁難

difangzhi 地方誌
Ding 定
Dingxian hanzai jiuji hui 定縣旱災救濟會
dongzhen 冬賑
dou 斗
Du Fu 杜甫
Duan Qirui 段祺瑞
duban 督辦
dujun 督軍
dun 頓

fang 坊
Fangshan 房山
fangzhao 仿照
fan rendao zhuyi 反人道主義
fei ba ta chiqiong buke 非把他吃窮不可
feitu 匪徒
Feng Gongdu 馮公度
Feng Guozhang 馮國璋
Feng Sizhi 馮司直
Feng Yuxiang 馮玉祥
Fengsheng jiuji hanzai xiehui 奉省救濟旱
　　災協會
Fengtai 豐台
Fengtian 奉天
feng wo muqin de ciming 奉我母親的慈命
Fojiao chouzhen hui 佛教籌賑會
Fojiao cibei hui 佛教慈悲會
Fojiao jiuying hui 佛教救嬰會
Fucheng 阜城
Fujiadian 傅家甸
Furu jiuji hui 婦孺救濟會
Fuyintang 福音堂

ganyan youyin 甘言誘引
gaoliang 高粱
Gaoyi 高邑
ge cishan tuanti 各慈善團體
Gong Yunfu 龔雲甫
gonggong shitang 公共食堂
gongzheng shishen 公正士紳
Gu Zhongxiu 谷鍾秀
Gu'an 固安
Guangjihui 廣濟會
Guangzong 廣宗

guan mi 官米
Guantao 館陶
Guanyin 觀音
gu chi migu 估吃米穀
guchui 鼓吹
Guide 貴德
Guowuyuan 國務院
Guowuyuan mishu 國務院秘書

Hailong 海龍
Haixing 海興
Hankou 漢口
Hankou cishan hui 漢口慈善會
Hanyang 漢陽
hanzai 旱災
he 合
He Zonglian 何宗蓮
Hebeiqu 河北區
Hedongqu 河東區
Heihe 黑河
Hejian 河間
Henan hanzai jiuji hui 河南旱災救濟會
Houhai 后海
Huabei jiuzai xiehui 華北救災協會
Huabei *zaiqu* 華北災區
Huai 淮
Huailai 懷來
Huailu 獲鹿
huanghan 荒旱
Huangpi 黃陂
Huangpu 黃埔
huayang 華洋
huayang yizhen hui 華洋義賑會
huiguan 會館
huojie suo 貨借所
hutong 胡同
huzhao 護照

Ji 冀
Ji Shaoquan 籍少荃
Jiading 嘉定
Jian Zhaonan 簡照南
Jiang Chaozong 江朝宗
Jiang Yanxing 蔣雁行
Jiang Yucheng 江宇澄

jiang jun 將軍
Jiangnan 江南
jianshang 奸商
jiao 角
jiaoshe yuan 交涉員
jiaoyu hui 教育會
jihuang 饑荒
Jilin 吉林
Jilin yizhen hui 吉林義賑會
jin 斤
Jin 晉
Jin Yunpeng 靳雲鵬
Jingji yidai shuizai hegong shanhou shiyi
　京畿一帶水災河工善後事宜
Jingji zhouchang choubanchu 京畿粥廠籌
　辦處
jingshi pinmin 京市貧民
Jingshi pinmin jiuji hui 京市貧民救
　濟會
jingsuo quanmo 警所勸募
Jingxing 井陘
jingzhao yin 京兆尹
Jingzhao zaihuang jiuji hui 京兆災荒
　救濟會
jinshi 進士
jinzhi 禁止
jipin 極貧
jipin hui 濟貧會
jiugui 舊規
jizhen 急賑
juance 捐冊
juanzhu 捐助
jun biao zancheng 均表贊成
junfa 軍閥
jun liang jiuji 均糧救急

Kaifeng 開封
kaiken huangdi 開墾荒地
kanghan 亢旱
Kangping 康平
Kangxi 康熙
kanluan 戡亂
kanluan youfang 戡亂有方
kouxin 扣薪
kuli 苦力

lai yi quanhuo 賴以全活
Laozi 老子
leshan haoshe 樂善好捨
leshan haoshi 樂善好施
Li 蠡
Li Chun 李純
Li Hongzhang 李鴻章
Li Qingfang 李慶芳
Li Yuanhong 黎元洪
Li Zhongkai 李鍾凱
Li Zhangtai 李長泰
liang 兩
Liang Shiyi 梁士詒
Liang Shuming 梁漱溟
Liangshi jiuji hui 糧食救濟會
Liang shi yixing 梁氏義行
liangxin shang zhuzhang ke ye 良心上主張
可也
Liao 遼
Liaodong 遼東
Liaoyuan 遼源
Lijiao 里教
Lingxue yaozhi yuanqi 靈學要誌緣起
Lingyuan 凌源
linren jie ji, wo he ren dubao 鄰人皆饑，我
何忍獨飽
linshi daizhu chu 臨時貸助處
Linshi wowotou hui 臨時窩窩頭會
Lishu 梨樹
Liu Hongsheng 劉鴻聲
Liu Qingtang 劉慶鐺
Liu Ruoceng 劉若曾
liuli shisuo 流離失所
liu wei jinian 留為紀念
longwang 龍王
Lü Haihuan 呂海寰
Lugouqiao 盧溝橋

Ma Fuxiang 馬福祥
Ma Jiping 馬冀平
Mancheng 滿城
Manzhouli 滿洲里
mao 毛
Mao Zedong 毛澤東
Mao'er hutong 帽兒胡同

matong jiang jun 馬桶將軍
mei feng xiongsui 每逢凶歲
Mei Lanfang 梅蘭芳
Mianyi zhuzhen hui 棉衣助賑會
mihuang 米荒
mingyu dongshi 名譽董事
minsheng 民生
mitan 密探
mi weiyuan 密委員
mixin 迷信
mu 畝

Nan'aocun 南坳村
Nankai 南开
Nanle 南樂
nanmin 難民
Nanpi 南皮
Nanyang 南洋
Nanyuan 南苑
nian xi xiang yi 念係鄉誼
Ningjin 寧晉
nuanchang 暖廠
Nü hongshizi hui 女紅十字會

Pan Jinong 潘吉農
pin 貧
Pingding 平定
pingmin gonggong shitang 平民公共食堂
pingmin shitang 平民食堂
pingtiao 平糶
pingtiao ju 平糶局
pinmin 貧民
Pinmin jiuji hui 貧民救濟會
pubao 鋪保
Pudong 浦東
Pukou 浦口
putong banfa 普通辦法
Puyi 溥儀

Qian 錢
Qian Chongkai 錢崇塏
Qianfosi 千佛寺
qiangpo 強迫
qigai 乞丐
Qing 青

Qinghe 清河
Qinglongqiao 青龍橋
Qingshi gao 清史稿
qi zhen 乞賑
qu 區
Quanguo Fojiao chouzhen dahui 全國佛
　教籌賑大會
quan huozhe shenzhong 全活者甚眾
quanjuan 勸捐
Qunfang zhuzhen hui 羣芳助賑會

Rehe 熱河
rendao 人道
renjuan 認捐
renmin shi bu fen nanbei de 人民是不分南
　北的
rexin 熱心
rijin yuan 日金元

Sa Zhenbing 薩鎮冰
sangzi 桑梓
Sanjiang gongsuo 三江公所
Sanqin gongmin jiu Shaan hui 三秦公民
　救陝會
Shaheqiao 沙河橋
Shandong zaiqu jiuji hui 山東災區救濟會
Shandong zaizhen gonghui 山東災賑公會
shang min dei yi wu yu 商民得以無虞
Shangqiu 商丘
shanshi 善士
shantang 善堂
Shanxi chouzhen hui 山西籌賑會
Shanyin 山陰
shaopin 稍貧
shecang 社倉
Shen 深
sheng 升
Sheng jing bao 盛京報
Shenze 深澤
shi 石
Shijiazhuang 石家莊
shiye jieshaosuo 失業介紹所
shourongsuo 收容所
shouwu 首務
shu 黍

Shuangcheng 雙城
shudu 鼠度
shuhui 贖回
Shulan 舒蘭
Shulu 束鹿
Shunde 順德
Shunping 順平
Shunzhi hanzai jiuji hui 順直旱災
　救濟會
Shunzhi zhuzhen ju 順直助賑局
shushi cishan benyi 殊失慈善本意
Sikejieli 斯克節里
Sipingjie 四平街
song de bei li 頌德碑立
su 粟
Suihua 綏化
suiyi 隨意
suiyi juanzhu 隨意捐助
Suiyuan 綏遠
Sun Liechen 孫烈臣
Sun Yat-sen 孫逸仙
Sun Zhenjia 孫振家
suoshou zhongzhong ku 所受種種苦
Sutian 蘇田
suyu 俗語
Suzhou 蘇州

taifei 太妃
taitai 太太
Tan Xiaopei 潭小培
Tang 唐
tebie banfa 特別辦法
Tian Wenlie 田文烈
Tieli 鐵驪
tishu 提署
tixu bing jian 體恤兵艱
Tong 通
tongbao 同胞
Tonghe *qi ken luo* 通河豈肯落
Tongjiang 通江
tongling 統領
tongling tixu pinmin 統領体恤貧民
Tongshanshe 同善社
tongxianghui 同鄉會
Tongxian linshi zhenji hui 通縣臨時賑濟會

tongzhi 同志
Tongzhou 通州

Wan 完
Wang Chenglin 王成林
Wang Daxie 汪大燮
Wang Hu 王瑚
Wang Huaiqing 王懷慶
Wang Maoyi 王懋宜
Wang Nimin 王尼民
Wang Zhanyuan 王占元
Wang Zhixiang 王芝祥
Wanping 宛平
Wanquan 完全
Wei 威
weibo 微薄
Weifang 濰坊
Weihui 衛輝
weisheng 衛生
Weisheng zongju 衛生總局
wei Zhongguoren xiu sha 爲中國人羞煞
wen 文
Wenshi ziliao 文史資料
wu 武
Wu Bihua 吳壁華
Wu Bingxiang 吳炳湘
Wu Peifu 吳佩孚
Wu'an 武安
Wuchang 武昌
Wuji 無極
Wuliucun 五柳村
wu li zhi jia 無力之家
Wuqiang 武強
Wuqing 武情
Wushanshe 悟善社

Xia Qingyi 夏清貽
Xian 獻
Xiangfangqiao Guanyin si 象坊橋觀音寺
xianggui 鄉規
xiangren 鄉人
xiangzu 鄉族
xian nü hou nan 先女後男
xiaokang 小康
xiaomai 小麥

xiaomi 小米
xiao qigai 小乞丐
xiaoyang 小洋
xiaoyi 孝義
Xie Yutang 謝玉堂
Xindiancun 辛店村
xin dou 新斗
xing cishan 性慈善
Xingtai 邢台
Xingye 興業
Xinhai 辛亥
Xinhe 新河
Xiong Xiling 熊希齡
xiren 西人
Xu Qian 徐謙
Xu Shichang 徐世昌
Xuanhua 宣化

yamen 衙門
Yan Huiqing 顏惠慶
Yan Xishan 閻錫山
Yang Chunting 楊春亭
Yang Dahong 楊大洪
Yang Tianji 楊天驥
Yang Xiaolou 楊小樓
Yang Xiuqin 楊秀琴
Yang Yide 楊以德
Yangcun 楊村
yangmin 養民
yangyuan 洋元
Yanshan 鹽山
Yantai 煙台
yaoji tongzhi gongyi 邀集同志公議
Ye Gongchuo 葉恭綽
Yi 易
yi 義
yicang 義倉
yichang yongyue 異常踴躍
yidai zhenji 以代賑濟
yigong daizhen 以工代賑
Yin Hongshou 殷鴻壽
Yingkou 營口
yinqi cishan xin 引起慈善心
yi ren 邑人
Yitong 伊通

yi wei minshi 以維民食
yiwen lei 軼聞類
yixing 義行
yi zai daci dabei, shi shiren daode 意在大
　慈大悲,使世人道德
yizhen 義賑
yi zhong minming 以重民命
yi zhong rendao 以重人道
Yong'an 永安
Yongding 永定
yong shi shishe zhi yi 用示施捨之意
you ce zhi xia zhe 尤策之下者
yuan 元
Yuan Shikai 袁世凱
Yuanshi 元氏
Yuetan 月壇
Yushu 榆樹

zaihuang 災荒
zaimin 災民
zaimin jiuji hui 災民救濟會
Zhang Hong 張宏
Zhang Jingyao 張敬堯
Zhang Jiusheng 張久盛
Zhang Shouyong 張壽鏞
Zhang Wensheng 張文生
Zhang Zhitan 張志潭
Zhang Zuolin 張作霖
Zhangjiakou 張家口
Zhangjiakou jiuzai hui 張家口救災會
Zhangjiazhuang 張家莊

Zhanhou zaimin jiuji hui 戰后災民救濟會
Zhao 趙
Zhao Erxun 趙爾巽
zhenfu 賑撫
Zhengding 正定
Zhenji 賑紀
zhenji youcha 賑濟有差
Zhenwuchu 賑務處
Zhenzai weiyuan hui 賑災務員會
Zhili 直隸
Zhili yizhen hui 直隸義賑會
Zhili zhandi zaimin zhenji hui 直隸戰地
　災民賑濟會
Zhi shen linshi pingtiao ju 直紳臨時
　平糶局
zhongchang 中昌
zhonghu yixia 中户以下
zhouchang 粥廠
Zhu Qihui 朱其慧
Zhu Yanyu 朱延昱
Zhuang Yunkuan 莊蘊寬
zhuangding 莊丁
zhubanren 主辦人
Zhuolu 涿鹿
Zhuozhou 涿州
zigu jiuhuang wu shance 自古救荒無善策
zisong 資送
zizhi hui 自治會
zongsiling 總司令
Zongwuchu 總務處
zuo daguan fa dacai 做大官發大財

Notes

Introduction

1. Amartya Sen's *Poverty and Famines* remains the standard analysis of the human and institutional causes of starvation.
2. For example, Arthur Waldron quotes Chen Duxiu, "Dao Junfa" (Down with warlords), *Meizhou pinglun*, 28 December 1918 ("The Warlord," 1080).
3. Sheridan, *Chinese Warlord*; Gillin, *Warlord*; A. Nathan, *Peking Politics*; Ch'i, *Warlord Politics in China*; McCormack, *Chang Tso-lin*; Wou, *Militarism in Modern China*.
4. Suleski, *Civil Government in Warlord China*, 190. This is not to say that understandings of military figures in the republic have not evolved. After spending decades as the "running dogs of imperialism" in the Maoist period, more than a few warlords enjoyed something of a rehabilitation as local heroes in the 1980s, even as "something close to national heroes," praised in the mainland Chinese press as "patriotic generals" for their roles in anti-Japanese resistance (Lary, foreword, vii–viii).
5. "Simply defined," in the words of McCord, "warlords are military commanders who, as a result of their control of military force, exert a significant degree of autonomous political power within weak and fragmented political orders" (*Military Force and Elite Power*, 50). He explains elsewhere that as a system "warlordism did not originate simply in the rejection of legitimate political authority by military commanders, but rather in the difficulty of defining which authority was legitimate" (*The Power of a Gun*, 310).
6. Taking the form of both academic study and more popular history, this continuing trend is summarized by Zhang Qiang and Weatherley, "The Rise of 'Republican Fever.'"
7. See Wakeman and Edmonds, *Reappraising Republican China*. Also see Dikötter, *The Age of Openness*.

8. van de Ven, "Public Finance and the Rise of Warlordism"; Waldron, *From War to Nationalism*.

9. Lary, *The Chinese People at War*; Lary and MacKinnon, *The Scars of War*; MacKinnon, Lary, and Vogel, *China at War*; Henriot and Yeh, *In the Shadow of the Rising Sun*.

10. Edgerton-Tarpley, *Tears from Iron*; Li Wenhai and Xia, *Tian you xiongnian*; Zhu, *Minbao wuyu*; Muscolino, *The Ecology of War in China*; Ristaino, *The Jacquinot Safe Zone*; Courtney, *The Nature of Disaster in China*.

11. Rowe, *Saving the World*; Will and Wong, *Nourish the People*; Rawski, *The Last Emperors*.

12. Lillian Li, *Fighting Famine in North China*; Simon, *Civil Society in China*.

13. Barnett, *Empire of Humanity*, 34.

14. Fassin, *Humanitarian Reason*, 3.

15. Devereux, *Theories of Famine*; Ó Gráda, *Famine*.

16. Notable exceptions to this are Ransmeier, *Sold People*; and Wang Di, *Street Culture in Chengdu*.

17. Dillon and Oi, *At the Crossroads of Empires*; Yeh, *Shanghai Splendor*; Rogaski, *Hygienic Modernity*; Lu Hanchao, *Beyond the Neon Lights*; S. Smith, *Like Cattle and Horses*; Goodman, *Native Place, City, and Nation*.

18. Chang Liu, *Peasants and Revolution in Rural China*; Huaiyin Li, *Village Governance in North China*; Philip Huang, *Peasant Economy and Social Change*; Esherick, *The Origins of the Boxer Uprising*; Perry, *Rebels and Revolutionaries in North China*; Johnson, *Spectacle and Sacrifice*; Dubois, *The Sacred Village*; Harrison, *Man Awakened from Dreams*.

19. For other works that focus on the international dimension of relief in 1920–21, see Kang and Xia, *20 shiji Zhongguo zaibian*; Lillian Li, *Fighting Famine in North China*; and A. Nathan, *A History of the China International Famine Relief Commission*.

20. Gates, *China's Motor*; Ransmeier, *Sold People*.

21. Kuhn, "Local Self-Government under the Republic"; Huang, *The Peasant Economy and Social Change*; Duara, *Culture, Power, and the State*.

22. Lillian Li, *Fighting Famine in North China*, chapter 9; Naquin, *Peking*, 651.

23. Barnett, *Empire of Humanity*; Vernon, *Hunger*, 17–40; Rodogno, *Against Massacre*; Moniz, *From Empire to Humanity*; Irwin, *Making the World Safe*; Shaw, *Britannia's Embrace*; Porter, *Benevolent Empire*.

24. Watenpaugh, *Bread from Stones*, 3 and 8 (emphasis added).

25. An important exception is Konishi, "The Emergence of an International Humanitarian Organization."

26. Pantuliano, foreword.

27. Bennett and Foley, *Time to Let Go*, 8 and 53.

28. Maxwell and Majid, *Famine in Somalia*, xiii–xiv.

29. De Ville de Goyet, "Stop Propagating Disaster Myths," 762. I thank Rony Brauman for bringing this article to my attention.

30. L. Wong, *Marginalization and Social Welfare in China*, 34; Ekbladh, *The Great American Mission*, 27–29.

31. On early modern charity organizations generally, see Liang, *Shishan yu jiaohua*.

32. *Da gongbao*, 2 October 1920; *Aiguo baihua bao*, 17 November 1920.

33. *Zhongguo minbao*, 12 September 1920; *Xiao gongbao*, 22 September 1920; *Laifu bao*, 26 December 1920.

34. Cabanes, *The Great War and the Origins of Humanitarianism*; Grant, *Philanthropy and Voluntary Action*; Porter, *Benevolent Empire*.

35. Estimates of Russian famine mortality in 1921–22 range anywhere from one to ten million. See Patenaude, *The Big Show in Bololand*, 196–97.

36. Green, "Humanitarianism in Nineteenth-Century Context."

37. Yang, *Tombstone*; Brown, *City versus Countryside*; Wemheuer, *Famine Politics in Maoist China*.

38. Kaplan, *The Stakes of Regulation*, 378. I thank Arnaud Orain for bringing this book to my attention.

39. Dikötter, *Mao's Great Famine*; Thaxton, *Catastrophe and Contention in Rural China*.

40. Unfortunately, the 1920–21 famine rarely appears in the issues of an important record of daily life in prerevolutionary China, *Wenshi ziliao* (Cultural and historical miscellany). It is hard to say why. One can only speculate that by the time *Wenshi ziliao* was first compiled in the 1960s, the 1920 famine had been overshadowed by the considerably more devastating warfare and ecological disasters of the Nationalist period.

41. David Strand notes that Beijing in the mid-1920s had "80 dailies [and] 30 evening papers" (*Rickshaw Beijing*, 324). In 1920, more than a hundred dailies had been established in the capital, according to Beijing's modern gazetteer (BJZH, *Beijing zhi*, 42–53).

42. Weston, "Minding the Newspaper Business," 4.

1. War in July

1. *Xiao gongbao*, 3 July 1920.

2. For a gazetteer's description of this delicate dynamic over the course of 1920, see *Jing XZ* 23a.

3. Snyder-Reinke, *Dry Spells*; Rawski, *The Last Emperors*, 220–30.

4. *North China Herald*, 4 September 1920.

5. Chinese Government Railways, *Guide to Peking*, 60.

6. Ting, *Government Control of the Press*, 51.

7. This figure is based on a tally taken for the Second World Press Conference in 1921. See Lin Yutang, *A History of the Press*, 117 and 124.

8. Allen, *Only Yesterday*, 77.

9. A. Nathan, *Peking Politics*, 15.

10. McCord, *The Power of a Gun*, 265.

11. See Rowe, *Saving the World*.

12. Wang Runze, *Zhang Liluan yu Da gongbao*, 30.

13. Wang Runze, *Beiyang zhengfu shiqi de xinwenye*, 376; Strand, *Rickshaw Beijing*, 57.

14. Quoted in Strand, *Rickshaw Beijing*, 57.

15. BJZH, *Beijing zhi*, 45.

16. Gamble, *Peking*, 508.

17. BJZH, *Beijing zhi*, 44 and 49.

18. *Shenbao*, 12 October 1920.

19. The cartoons appeared through the fall and winter of 1920–21 in *Shenbao*, *Shibao*, and *Yishibao*. The photo collage appears in *Shibao*, 17 October 1920.

20. By my own reckoning, five Chinese broadsheets have long served as the go-to news source for scholars of 1910s and 1920s China (Shanghai's *Shenbao* and *Shibao*, Beijing's *Shuntian shibao*, Tianjin's *Da gongbao*, and *Yishibao*, which had both Beijing and Tianjin editions). Coming in a distant sixth and seventh are Beijing's *Chenbao* and Shanghai's *Minguo ribao*. This is largely due to the accessibility of these papers in bound reprints in libraries or in digital form online. Many other newspapers from the early republic used in this study were short-lived, and for that reason (presumably, along with the destruction of the wars and cultural purges later in the century) they are exceedingly difficult to locate in libraries anywhere. Nonetheless they survive in particular collections, most notably in hard copies at the Peking University Library or on microfilm at the National Library in Beijing and the Shanghai Municipal Library.

21. Guo, *Wu Peifu da zhuan*, 140–43; Ch'i, *Warlord Politics in China*, 136.

22. McCormack, *Chang Tso-lin in Northeast China*, 50–52.

23. Wou, *Militarism in Modern China*, 24–28; McCord, *The Power of a Gun*, 260; Beasley, *Japanese Imperialism*, 117.

24. Wou, *Militarism in Modern China*, 22–24.

25. For an early episode of tension over the foreign construction of a rail line near Shanghai, see Pong, "Confucian Patriotism."

26. J. Buck, "Price Changes in China," 241.

27. Tan, *The Boxer Catastrophe*, 55.

28. *Shanghai Gazette*, 14 July 1920.

29. Egan, "Fighting the Chinese Famine," 46.

30. *North China Herald*, 17 and 24 July 1920; *Xiao gongbao*, 17, 19, and 20 July 1920.

31. Michael Tsin notes that the British military attaché considered Wu "one of the two most able soldiers" in China at the time (*Nation, Governance, and Modernity in China*, 56). See also *North China Herald*, 24 July 1920; *Shanghai Times*, 26 July 1920; Zhang Jungu, *Wu Peifu zhuan*, 279–82; Guo, *Wu Peifu da zhuan*.

32. Wou, *Militarism in Modern China*, 26.

33. McCord, "Burn, Kill, Rape, and Rob," 39.

34. *Shanghai Times*, 26 July 1920; McCord, "Burn, Kill, Rape, and Rob," 32.

35. Lary, *Warlord Soldiers*, 37.

36. *Shanghai Times*, 26 July 1920; McCord, "Burn, Kill, Rape, and Rob," 25.

37. McCord, "Burn, Kill, Rape, and Rob," 28 and 39.

38. Lary, *Warlord Soldiers*, 68.

39. *North China Herald*, 31 July 1920.

40. Ch'i, *Warlord Politics in China*, 81.

41. *North China Herald*, 31 July 1920; McCormack, *Chang Tso-lin*, 53.

42. McCord, *The Power of a Gun*, 272.

43. *Da gongbao*, 30 July 1920.

44. *Sheng jing shibao*, 31 September 1920.

45. Xiong Xiling, *Xiong Xiling xiansheng yigao*, 3799–824.

46. Zhou, *Xiong Xiling zhuan*, 429.

47. McCord, *The Power of a Gun*, 189; Xu Youchun, *Minguo renwu*, 50.

48. Liu Shoulin et al., *Minguo zhiguan nianbiao*, 59–60.

49. *Xiao gongbao*, 26 August 1920.

50. *Da gongbao*, 12 July 1920.

51. *Da gongbao*, 27 July 1920.

52. *Shihua*, 31 July 1920; *Shuntian shibao*, 10 and 12 August 1920.

53. *Shuntian shibao*, 10 August 1920.

54. *Shihua*, 31 August 1920.

55. Will and Wong, *Nourish the People*.

56. *Yishi bao*, 19 September 1920; *Xiao gongbao*, 19 September 1920.

57. *Shihua*, 30 August 1920; *Chenbao*, 30 August 1920.

58. *Aiguo baihua bao*, 2 September 1920.

59. *Chenbao*, 24 January 1921; Liu Shoulin et al., *Minguo zhiguan nianbiao*, 248.

60. *Zhuo XZ* 1:2:14a.

61. *Zhongguo minbao*, 6 August 1920.

62. *Shihua*, 17 August 1920.

63. *Xiao gongbao*, 17 August 1920.

64. *Shuntian shibao*, 29 August 1920.

65. *Shihua*, 24 August 1920.

66. McCord, "Burn, Kill, Rape, and Rob," 23.

67. *Da gongbao*, 12 July 1920.

68. Quoted in *Xiao gongbao*, 9 July 1920.

69. Quoted in *Shihua*, 25 August 1920.

70. Duara, *Culture, Power, and the State*, 31. Villages in North China each had a temple to the Dragon King, as did irrigation-gate communities that traditionally existed to manage and negotiate water use within farming communities.

71. Lillian Li, *Fighting Famine in North China*, 111–13.

72. *Da gongbao*, 5 July 1920.

73. Quoted in *North China Star*, 21 August 1920.

74. van de Ven, "Public Finance," 830.

75. *North China Star*, 21 August 1920.

76. *Da gongbao*, 30 July 1920.

77. See Elvin, *The Retreat of the Elephants*.

78. *North China Herald*, 31 July 1920.

79. Wou, *Militarism in Modern China*, 27–31.

80. Woodhead, *Adventures in Far Eastern Journalism*, 173.

81. Wou, *Militarism in Modern China*, 34–35; *Shanghai Gazette*, 2 August 1920; McCormack, *Chang Tso-lin*, 53.

82. A. Nathan, *Peking Politics*, 176.

83. Ch'i, *Warlord Politics in China*, 37.

84. A. Nathan, *Peking Politics*, 176.

2. Municipal Relief

1. Gamble, *Peking*, 30, 94, and 101.
2. Bredon, *Peking*, 15–29; Crow, *The Travelers' Handbook for China*, 204.
3. Gamble, *Peking*, 270.
4. Dray-Novey, "The Twilight of the Beijing Gendarmerie," 359; Gamble, *Peking*, 70–71.
5. *Beijing baihua bao*, 20 January 1921.
6. *Shihua*, 1 August 1920; *Xiao gongbao*, 6 August 1920.
7. Millet, a major relief grain, is variously called *shu*, *su*, and *xiaomi* in sources in the period (*Xiao gongbao*, 18 August 1920).
8. *Shihua*, 16 September 1920; *Chenbao*, 26 September 1920.
9. Dray-Novey, "The Twilight of the Beijing Gendarmerie," 352.
10. Dittmer, "An Estimate of the Standard of Living," 127.
11. *Yishi bao*, 22 September 1920. The authorities employed no absolute measure of standard of living to arrive at these estimates. Instead, poverty was a subjective case-by-case classification of need.
12. Gamble, *Peking*, 269.
13. *Shihua*, 27 August 1920.
14. Will, *Bureaucracy and Famine*, 186–99.
15. Ibid., 129–30.
16. *Shuntian shibao*, 23 September 1920.
17. Crow, *The Travelers' Handbook for China*, 28.
18. *Shihua*, 11 August 1920; *Xiao gongbao*, 19 August 1920.
19. *Shihua*, 28 August 1920; *Xiao gongbao*, 23 August 1920.
20. *Chenbao*, 25 January 1921; *Beijing baihua bao*, 2 February 1921.
21. *Beijing baihua bao*, 2 February 1921; *Shihua*, 10 March 1921.
22. Naquin, *Peking*, 662–63.
23. Dray-Novey, "The Twilight of the Beijing Gendarmerie," 362.
24. *Xiao gongbao*, 14 July 1920.
25. Xu Youchun, *Minguo renwu*, 50.
26. *Xiao gongbao*, 19 July 1920.
27. Xu Youchun, *Minguo renwu*, 401.
28. Rhoads, *Manchus & Han*, 256–57; Strand, *Rickshaw Beijing*, 13 and 297.
29. Rhoads, *Manchus & Han*, 256–57; Gamble, *Peking*, 67–70; Xu Youchun, *Minguo renwu*, 229.
30. *Xiao gongbao*, 20 July 1920; *Zhongguo minbao*, 6 August 1920; *Chenbao*, 10 and 19 August 1920; *Shihua*, 24 August and 15 November 1920; *Minyi ribao*, 4 October 1920; *Zhenzai ribao*, 6 November 1920.
31. *Xiao gongbao*, 19 July 1920.
32. *Chenbao*, 23 August 1920; *Shihua*, 23 August 1920; *Xiao gongbao*, 23 August 1920.
33. *Chenbao*, 29 August 1920; *Yishi bao*, 1 September 1920; *Shuntian shibao*, 16 September 1920.
34. *Zhongguo minbao*, 6 November 1920; *Shangye ribao*, 6 November 1920; *Zhenzai ribao*, 12 November 1920.

35. *Shihua*, 15 November 1920.

36. *Xiao gongbao*, 15 and 19 July 1920; *Shihua*, 28 and 29 July and 11 September 1920.

37. *Aiguo baihua bao*, 31 October 1920; *Beijing ribao*, 31 October 1920.

38. *Zhongguo minbao*, 3 October 1920; *Beijing ribao*, 14 October 1920; *Shihua*, 20 October 1920; *Da gongbao*, 30 October 1920.

39. *Xiao gongbao*, 20 and 22 July 1920; *Shihua*, 6 September 1920; *Yishi bao*, 28 September 1920.

40. *Shihua*, 28 August 1920.

41. *Xiao gongbao*, 18 September 1920.

42. *Chenbao*, 11 and 17 November and 14 December 1920; *Shuntian shibao*, 14 October 1920; *Zhongguo minbao*, 26 November 1920; *Zhenzai ribao*, 28 November 1920; *Shihua*, 5 December 1920; *Beijing baihua bao*, 28 January 1921; *Xiao minbao*, 21 March 1921.

43. *Chenbao*, 4 October 1920.

44. *Xiao gongbao*, 21 December 1920.

45. *Xiao minbao*, 13 January 1921; *Shihua*, 18 January 1921; *Beijing baihua bao*, 18 January 1921.

46. *Xiao minbao*, 23 January 1921.

47. Naquin, *Peking*, 651.

48. *Xiao gongbao*, 17 August 1920.

49. Yamin Xu, "Policing Civility on the Streets."

50. *Tianjin Zhongmei ribao*, 30 September 1920; *Zhongguo minbao*, 20 December 1920; *Chenbao*, 27 February 1921.

51. *Xiao gongbao*, 29 November 1920.

52. *Minyi ribao*, 12 December 1920; *Fengsheng*, 7 March 1921.

53. *Shihua*, 16 September 1920; *Shuntian shibao*, 26 September 1920; *Xiao gongbao*, 28 September 1920.

54. *Yishi bao*, 2 October 1920; *Shihua*, 20 October and 7 November 1920; *Xiao gongbao*, 20 October 1920; *Chenbao*, 25 November 1920; *Zhongguo minbao*, 20 December 1920.

55. *Chenbao*, 7 November and 21 December 1920; *Xiao gongbao*, 11 November 1920; *Shihua*, 25 November 1920.

56. Tong, "Social Conditions and Social Service," 79.

57. *Shihua*, 10 and 26 September 1920.

58. Examples of strangers intervening in suicide attempts by drowning appear in *Shihua*, 13 September and 21 October 1920; *Xiao gongbao*, 13 and 29 October 1920; *Beijing baihua bao*, 5 November 1920 and 29 January 1921; *Xiao minbao*, 28 January 1921; *Guobao*, 24 March 1921; *Fengsheng*, 10 April 1921.

59. *Shihua*, 2 December 1920.

60. Jingji zhouchang choubanchu, *Zhengxin baogao shu*, 79; *Chenbao*, 24 September 1920; *Shihua*, 26 September 1920; *Yishi bao*, 26 September 1920; *Xiao gongbao*, 8 October 1920.

61. Dray-Novey, "The Twilight of the Beijing Gendarmerie," 362; Lillian Li, *Fighting Famine*, 159.

62. *Xiao gongbao*, 4 October 1920; Gamble, *Peking*, 279.

63. *Shihua*, 24 September 1920.
64. *Xiao gongbao*, 26 September 1920.
65. *Xiao gongbao*, 21 and 26 September and 4 October 1920; *Zhongguo minbao*, 24 September 1920; *Shihua*, 26 September 1920; *Yishi bao*, 26 September 1920; *Shuntian shibao*, 13 October 1920; *Aiguo baihua bao*, 6 February 1921; *Zhengfu gongbao*, 13 June 1921.
66. *Shihua*, 24 October 1920; *Xiao gongbao*, 1 November 1920; *Zhongguo minbao*, 28 December 1920.
67. *Shihua*, 30 October and 1 November 1920; *Xiao gongbao*, 31 October and 4 November 1920.
68. *Shangye ribao*, 6 November 1920.
69. Jingji zhouchang choubanchu, *Zhengxin baogao shu*, 226, 238, 250, 274; Li and Dray-Novey, "Guarding Beijing's Food Security," 1019.
70. Gamble, *Peking*, 277.
71. *Chenbao*, 29 October, 1920.
72. *Chenbao*, 24 October 1920; *Xiao gongbao*, 14 November 1920.
73. *Chenbao*, 29 October 1920; *Shihua*, 29 November 1920; *Zhongguo minbao*, 29 November 1920.
74. *Xiao gongbao*, 21 September 1920.
75. Gamble, *Peking*, 276–77.
76. *Xiao gongbao*, 29 October and 3 and 7 November 1920; *Baihua guoqiang bao*, 2 November 1920; *Shuntian shibao*, 6 November 1920.
77. *Xiao gongbao*, 21 September 1920.
78. *Aiguo baihua bao*, 19 November 1920; *Xiao gongbao*, 19 November 1920; Jingji zhouchang choubanchu, *Zhengxin baogao shu*, 83.
79. Lillian Li records an "adult famine ration standard of .005 *shi* of husked grain per person per day" for the Qing period, which at 120 *jin* per *shi* and 2,250 calories per *jin* amounts to 1,350 calories per ration (*Fighting Famine*, 159). Pierre-Étienne Will similarly states that under the Qing "the typical ration of one-half *sheng* per day would represent . . . 420 grams of bleached rice, just barely a survival ration, for at about 3,300 kilocalories per kilogram, 420 grams provides less than 1,400 kilocalories" (*Bureaucracy and Famine*, 132).
80. Jingji zhouchang choubanchu, *Zhengxin baogao shu*, 73.
81. *Shihua*, 3 November 1920; *Minyi ribao*, 4 and 11 November and 1 December 1920; *Zhenzai ribao*, 9 November 1920.
82. Dray-Novey, "The Twilight of the Beijing Gendarmerie," 360; *Baihua guoqiang bao*, 17 November 1920; *Xiao gongbao*, 17 November 1920; *Zhenzai ribao*, 10 November 1920.
83. *Jiuzai zhoukan*, 7 November 1920; *Shihua*, 7 November 1920; *Xiao gongbao*, 7 November 1920.
84. *Shihua*, 22 December 1920.
85. *Xiao gongbao*, 27 December 1920.
86. *Aiguo baihua bao*, 7 December 1920.
87. Naquin, *Peking*, 642.
88. *Shihua*, 19 October 1920.

89. *Minyi ribao*, 26 October 1920; Gamble, *Peking*, 98; Crow, *The Travelers' Handbook for China*, 225; Naquin, *Peking*, 665.
90. *Yishi bao*, 18 January 1921.
91. *Beijing wanbao*, 26 March 1921; Gamble, *Peking*, 277.
92. Dray-Novey, "The Twilight of the Beijing Gendarmerie," 368; Strand, *Rickshaw Beijing*, 95–97.
93. Ding, *Guanli Beijing*, 57; Gamble, *Peking*, 69.
94. *Shihua*, 8 November 1920.
95. Strand, *Rickshaw Beijing*, 96.
96. Jingji zhouchang choubanchu, *Zhengxin baogao shu*, 129.
97. *Beijing ribao*, 3 October 1920.
98. *Shuntian shibao*, 23 September 1920.
99. *Shuntian shibao*, 28 October 1920; *Xiao gongbao*, 29 October 1920.
100. *Shihua*, 15 October 1920. For another example of fund-raising initiatives by garrison soldiers, see *Chenbao*, 19 December 1920.
101. *Shihua*, 11 November 1920; *Xiao gongbao*, 12 November 1920.
102. *Aiguo baihua bao*, 17 October 1920; *Shihua*, 17 October 1920.
103. This had the potential to raise a substantial amount of revenue: car imports to China had risen 65 percent in value in the previous year alone, to 3.569 million taels, or silver ounces, and hundreds of these were already on the streets of the capital (*Xiao gongbao*, 3 November 1920; McElroy, *Aims and Organization of the China Society of America*, 7; Bredon, *Peking*, 51; Gamble, *Peking*, 73).
104. *Shihua*, 7 November 1920.
105. *Chenbao*, 10 December 1920; *Xiao gongbao*, 10 December 1920.
106. *Beijing baihua bao*, 17 January 1921.
107. *Zhongguo minbao*, 9 November 1920; *Xiao gongbao*, 9 November 1920.
108. *Chenbao*, 13 October 1920; see also *Chenbao*, 28 November 1920; *Guobao*, 14 January 1921.
109. *Shihua*, 13 October 1920.
110. *Xiao gongbao*, 17 October and 11 November 1920; *Chenbao*, 19 October 1920; *Shihua*, 25 November 1920.
111. *Chenbao*, 24 September 1920; *Shihua*, 7 October 1920; *Xiao gongbao*, 17 October 1920; *Xiao minbao*, 28 January 1921.
112. *Zhenzai ribao*, 7 November 1920; *Minyi ribao*, 13 November 1920; *Zhongguo minbao*, 26 November 1920.
113. *Shihua*, 4 October 1920; *Xiao gongbao*, 10 October 1920.
114. *Yishi bao*, 18 December 1920; *Xiao gongbao*, 19 October 1920.
115. *Xiao gongbao*, 9 January 1921; *Zhengfu gongbao*, 13 June 1921; *Da gongbao*, 10 October and 5 and 9 November 1920; Xu Youchun, *Minguo renwu*, 2591–92.
116. *Aiguo baihua bao*, 24 December 1920; *Zhongguo minbao*, 17 December 1920.
117. Jingji zhouchang chobanchu, *Zhengxin baogao shu*, 33, 47.
118. *Shihua*, 30 September 1920.
119. *Fengsheng*, 16 October 1920.
120. *Minyi ribao*, 4 November 1920.
121. *Xiao gongbao*, 15 November 1920.

122. *Shihua*, 31 October 1920; *Xiao gongbao*, 11 November 1920 and 6 January 1921.
123. *Xiao gongbao*, 16 December 1920.
124. *Shihua*, 20 December 1920 and 26 February 1921.
125. Gamble, *Peking*, 220.
126. Ibid., 282.
127. *Chenbao*, 24 September 1920.
128. Will, *Bureaucracy and Famine*, 139.
129. Gamble, *Peking*, 281.
130. Will, *Bureaucracy and Famine*, 134 and 137.
131. *Shihua*, 21 November and 3, 12, and 24 December 1920, and 8 and 23 January, 24 February 1921; *Minyi ribao*, 10 and 21 November and 14 December 1920; *Chenbao*, 21 November 1920 and 25 February and 13 March 1921; *Zhongguo minbao*, 26 November 1920; *Xiao gongbao*, 30 November and 17 and 27 December 1920; *Beijing baihua bao*, 31 January and 6 and 15 February 1921; *Guobao*, 22 March 1921.
132. Ransmeier, *Sold People*, 4.
133. Edgerton-Tarpley, *Tears from Iron*, 161–210.
134. *Yishi bao*, 10 September 1920; *Shihua*, 1 October 1920; *Xiao gongbao*, 24 December 1920.
135. *Minyi ribao*, 13 November 1920.
136. *Yishi bao*, 7 December 1920.
137. Gamble, *Peking*, 277; see also 276 and 487.
138. *Wuqiang XZ* 410.
139. Gamble, *Peking*, 270 and 278.
140. Janet Chen, *Guilty of Indigence*, 67.
141. Ibid., 62.
142. *Xiao minbao*, 1 March 1921.
143. Ibid.
144. The categories were twenty Beijing *diao*, or two hundred coppers, for the destitute of young and old age; one hundred coppers for the young and old of moderately poor status; and fifty coppers for the "ordinary poor" (it is unclear whether this category included able-bodied adult men). These sums were no pittance: two hundred coppers could buy forty days' worth of half-*jin* famine rations at grain discount centers. See *Shihua*, 27 February 1921.
145. *Zhengxin baogao shu*, 75, BMA, J181-018-22110.
146. Dray-Novey, "The Twilight of the Beijing Gendarmerie," 367.
147. Crow, *The Travelers' Handbook for China*, 205.

3. Military Men

1. Strand, *Rickshaw Beijing*, 15.
2. Dong, *Republican Beijing*, 8.
3. Gillin, *Warlord*; D. Buck, *Urban Change in China*.
4. Dong, *Republican Beijing*, 87.
5. Shi, *At Home in the World*.

6. Ch'i, *Warlord Politics*, 42–43.
7. Zhao, "Wo suo zhidao de Wang Huaiqing," 177.
8. Li Lunbo, "Wang Huaiqing er san shi," 183.
9. *Shanghai Gazette*, 14 July 1920.
10. Zhao, "Wo suo zhidao de Wang Huaiqing," 177.
11. Slack, *Opium, State and Society*, 31.
12. *Xiao gongbao*, 23 October 1920.
13. BMA, J181-018-10687, "Baoan jingcha er dui baogao" [Report of Public Security Police Unit 2], case no. 57, March 1919, 1–9.
14. Strand, *Rickshaw Beijing*, 56.
15. Wang was squarely in the Zhili faction of Beiyang politics, sharing with its leader Cao Kun both provincial origins and an alma mater (the Beiyang Military Academy). Wu was a protégé of and came from the same county in central China as the leader of the Anhui faction, Duan Qirui. See Ch'i, *Warlord Politics*, 68–70.
16. Dray-Novey, "The Twilight of the Beijing Gendarmerie," 351–58.
17. Gamble, *Peking*, 71.
18. *North China Herald*, 15 June 1919, cited in Dray-Novey, "The Twilight of the Beijing Gendarmerie," 371.
19. Strand, *Rickshaw Beijing*, 314.
20. *North China Herald*, 24 July 1920.
21. Xu Youchun, *Minguo renwu*, 190, 618.
22. Chen Shanchang, "Wang Huaiqing songde bei."
23. Jerome Chen, "Defining Chinese Warlords and Their Factions," 594.
24. Zhang Zhaoyin, "Wang [Huaiqing] songde bei."
25. Wang Huaiqing, preface to Jingji zhouchang choubanchu, *Zhengxin baogao shu*, 3.
26. It is unclear what level of education Wang had attained, although he received a classical education in his youth. Powell and Tong, *Who's Who in China*, 212–13.
27. Dray-Novey, "The Twilight of the Beijing Gendarmerie," 366.
28. *Xiao gongbao*, 20 September 1920. This estimate is based on the daily famine ration of 1,500 calories stipulated by the Ministry of the Interior for all municipal soup kitchens later in November, which is discussed in more detail below.
29. Weston, *The Power of Position*, 205.
30. Patterson, "The Journalism in China," 50. The appearance of Patterson's study in a University of Missouri publication was no coincidence: Missourians were remarkably prominent in early twentieth-century journalism in China, from Thomas Millard, who founded Shanghai's *China Press* in 1911 and *Millard's Review* (later the *China Weekly Review*) in 1917, and Carl Crow, who set up United Press International's first China bureau, to Edgar Snow, author of *Red Star over China*. French, *Through the Looking Glass*, 99–106.
31. *Yishi bao*, 28 February 1921.
32. Liu Xiaolan and Wu, *Chuanjiaoshi zhongwen baokan*, 372–84.
33. Powell and Tong, *Who's Who in China*, 68–70. In November 1920 Xu had taken a position in the military government of Guangdong. See Xu Youchun, *Minguo renwu*, 1201.
34. Wang Runze, *Beiyang zhengfu shiqi de xinwenye*, 372.

35. *Shihua*, 1 March 1921.
36. The article appeared on 16 September 1920 in *Chenbao, Shihua, Xiao gongbao, Yishi bao*, and *Zhongguo minbao*, and on the following day in *Shuntian shibao*.
37. Zhao, "Wo suo zhidao de Wang Huaiqing," 174. See also Xu Youchun, *Minguo renwu*, 190.
38. Wang Huaiqing, preface to Jingji zhouchang choubanchu, *Zhengxin baogao shu*, 3.
39. *Shihua*, 30 September 1920.
40. *Shihua*, 11 November 1920; *Xiao gongbao*, 12 November 1920.
41. *Shihua*, 23 December 1920.
42. *Shihua*, 8 January 1921.
43. Sheridan, *Chinese Warlord*, 47; *North China Herald*, 27 September 1913.
44. P. Fuller, "Decentring International and Institutional Famine Relief," 882.
45. *Peking Leader*, 30 September 1919.
46. For a detailed study of a late imperial figure who exemplified such a combination of attention to security and social welfare measures, see Wei, *Ruan Yuan*.
47. Duara, "Of Authenticity and Woman," 342–43.
48. Despite its prominence in Beijing at the time, the society has been little studied. Shao Yong's *Zhongguo huidaomen*, possibly the most comprehensive study of these syncretic or redemptive societies, includes no apparent mention of the society, nor does it appear in Lu Zhongwei's *Zhongguo mimi shehui*. One of the few authors to mention it, Wing-tsit Chan (*Religious Trends in Modern China*, 165–66), appears to confuse it with the Six Sages Union True Dao Society (Liu shen chen dao tongyi hui), a group founded, according to Twinem, in Chengdu, Sichuan, in 1921. Twinem, "Modern Syncretic Religious Societies in China. II," 595.
49. This was the case in the altar room of the group's Nanjing chapter in 1925, according to Twinem ("Modern Syncretic Religious Societies in China. I" and "Modern Syncretic Religious Societies in China. II"). I am grateful to Xia Shi for bringing these articles to my attention.
50. Goossaert, *The Taoists of Peking*, 309 and 314.
51. Xu Youchun, *Minguo renwu*, 229; Morrison, *Correspondence of G. E. Morrison*, 599 and 612; Liu Shoulin et al., *Minguo zhiguan nianbiao*, 59–61.
52. Goossaert, *The Taoists of Peking*, 179.
53. *Shihua*, 17 August 1920.
54. Later, in 1924, when Cao and Wu Peifu, the victorious generals in the July 1920 war, formed a Buddhist group in the capital, Jiang was elected its honorary chairman. His relationship with Wu would last into the 1930s. See Lu Zhongwei, *Zhongguo mimi shehui juan 5*, 45–47.
55. [Illegible], "Jiang Chaozong dezheng bei."
56. Ibid.
57. *Xiao minbao*, 23 January 1921; Mei and Liu, *Yishi yutai*, 331; *Shanbao*, March 1919.
58. See Wang Juan, *Jindai Beijing cishan*; Janet Chen, *Guilty of Indigence*.
59. Merkel-Hess, *The Rural Modern*, 101–3; Alitto, *The Last Confucian*.
60. *Guobao*, 15 January 1921.
61. Ibid.

62. *Xiao gongbao*, 14 January 1921; *Beijing baihua bao*, 14 January 1921; *Chenbao*, 14 January 1921; *Shihua*, 14 and 30 January 1921.

63. *Beijing baihua bao*, 26 January 1921.

64. *Beijing baihua bao*, 18 January 1921; *Aiguo baihua bao*, 10 September 1920; *Xiao gong-bao*, 14 and 21 September 1920; *Zhenzai ribao*, 11 November 1920; *Shihua*, 8 January 1921; *Shuntian shibao*, 4 September 1920.

65. *Shihua*, 1 February 1921.

66. *Da gongbao*, 26 September 1920; *Shihua*, 23 November 1920; *Zhenzai ribao*, 11 November 1920.

67. *Shangye ribao*, 6 November 1920; *Shihua*, 24 October 1920.

68. Katz, *Religion in China and Its Modern Fate*, 11.

69. Goossaert, *The Taoists of Peking*, 312.

70. Ibid.; Katz, *Religion in China and Its Modern Fate*, 27, 38, and 41.

71. Zhao, "Wo suo zhidao de Wang Huaiqing," 177.

72. Li Lunbo, "Wang Huaiqing er san shi," 183–88.

73. Wang Jingfu, "Jiang Chaozong shilüe."

74. Li Lunbo, "Wang Huaiqing er san shi," 183.

75. A. Lin, "Warlord, Social Welfare and Philanthropy," 153. See also Goikhman, "Chen Jiongming."

76. Alitto, *The Last Confucian*.

4. Cigarettes, Opera, and Religious Sects

1. *Shihua*, 14 September 1920.

2. Bianchi, "The Representation of Victims of Disasters."

3. Edgerton-Tarpley, *Tears from Iron*, 189–210.

4. *Zhongguo minbao*, 18 December 1920.

5. Rankin, *Elite Activism and Political Transformation*; Wue, "Profits of Philanthropy"; Zhu, *Minbao wuyu*.

6. J. Smith, *The Art of Doing Good*, 45–49; Naquin, *Peking*, 651–53.

7. *Beijing baihua bao*, 23 December 1920; *Zhongguo minbao*, 29 December 1920.

8. Zhou, *Xiong Xiling zhuan*.

9. Strand, *Rickshaw Beijing*; Ren, *Jindai Tianjin de cishan*.

10. Wang Juan, *Jindai Beijing cishan shiye*.

11. Janet Chen, *Guilty of Indigence*.

12. Katz, *Religion in China and Its Modern Fate*, 4–5.

13. Lee, *Travel Talks on China*, 9, 49, 87–88, and 246.

14. Major works by East Asian scholars include Fuma, *Zhongguo shanhui*; Liang, *Shishan yu jiaohua*.

15. J. Smith, *The Art of Doing Good*, 1. The earlier book was Yue, *The Spirit of Chinese Philanthropy*.

16. For examples, see P. Fuller, "'Barren Soil, Fertile Minds.'"

17. *Da gongbao*, 30 October 1920; *Xin shenbao*, 1 November 1920; *Shihua*, 7 November 1920.

18. *Zhongguo minbao*, 22 November 1920.

19. Harrison, *The Making of the Republican Citizen*.

20. Sanger, *Advertising Methods in Japan, China and the Philippines*, 77.

21. Cochran, *Big Business in China*, 1–2 and 19.

22. Ramsay, *The Peking Who's Who, 1922*, 26 and 103; *Minyi ribao*, 21 October 1920.

23. *Zhongguo minbao*, 23 December 1920.

24. *Minsheng yuekan*, 5 May 1921.

25. *Chenbao*, 6 January 1921; Xu Youchun, *Minguo renwu*, 1761.

26. *Shangye ribao*, 20 November 1920; *Xiao gongbao*, 20 November 1920.

27. *Xiao gongbao*, 25 November 1920.

28. Jingji zhouchang choubanchu, *Zhengxin baogao shu*, 46.

29. *Chenbao*, 26 November 1920; *Minyi ribao*, 26 November 1920; *Xiao gongbao*, 26 November 1920; *Shihua*, 26 and 27 November 1920; *Zhenzai ribao*, 27 November 1920; *Zhongguo minbao*, 29 November 1920.

30. Jingji zhouchang choubanchu, *Zhengxin baogao shu*, 126; *Shihua*, 1 December 1920.

31. Jingji zhouchang choubanchu, *Zhengxin baogao shu*, 221.

32. Cochran, *Big Business in China*, 45 and 104.

33. Tsin, *Nation, Governance, and Modernity in China*, 89.

34. Cochran, *Big Business in China*, 54, 105, and 117.

35. Rowe, *Hankow*, 92–105; Tsin, *Nation, Governance, and Modernity in China*, 25 and 90; Cochran, *Big Business in China*, 66.

36. *Shishi xinbao*, 1 October 1920.

37. Cochran, *Big Business in China*, 114; *Hankou xinwenbao*, 2 October 1920.

38. *Shishi xinbao*, 1 October 1920.

39. *Yuandong bao*, 20 December 1920.

40. *Shuntian shibao*, 15 October 1920; *Beijing baihua bao*, 23 October 1920; *Zhongguo minbao*, 1 December 1920.

41. Tsin, *Nation, Governance, and Modernity in China*, 90; Cochran, *Big Business in China*, 66; *Minguo ribao*, 10 September 1920.

42. *Zhongguo minbao*, 24 October 1920; *Shangye ribao*, 16 November 1920.

43. *Zhenzai ribao*, 16 November 1920.

44. Cochran, *Big Business in China*, 1–2, 19, and 103–4.

45. *Jiuzai zhoukan*, 1 and 30 January 1921.

46. Shi, *At Home in the World*, 68–95.

47. Zhu's secretary and interpreter listed her occupations to an American visitor in the early 1920s as follows: chief director of the Chinese Women's Red Cross Society, director of a Red Cross hospital and a Red Cross obstetrical hospital, president of the Chinese and Foreign Women's Philanthropic Society of Peking, member of a Chinese and foreign famine relief association, director of the Women's Commercial Savings Bank, president of the Girls' School of Commerce, and chairman of the Preparation Committee of the Metropolitan Bank of Peking (Seton, *Chinese Lanterns*, 272).

48. Xu Youchun, *Minguo renwu*, 556.

49. *Beijing ribao*, 30 September 1920; *Yishi bao*, 20 October 1920.

50. *Chenbao*, 19 December 1920; *Xiao gongbao*, 22 December 1920.

51. *Xiao minbao*, 3 February 1921. The operation, sometimes called a "kitchen for the people's benefit" (*bianmin shichang*) and operating with an initial budget of 3,450 yuan in charitable donations, brought its own ingredients into the city, presumably to keep costs down (*Xiao gongbao*, 2 February 1921). In March, reports described men and women "who had not eaten their fill for days on end" lining up eagerly outside, and after two months of operation the committee of ten men who were running the initiative added two locations in the eastern suburbs (*Chenbao*, 1 March 1921). See also *Zhongguo minbao*, 24 January 1921; *Chenbao*, 2 February and 1 March 1921; *Qunbao*, 3 February 1921; *Fengsheng*, 7 March 1921.

52. *Shihua*, 7 December 1920; *Xin shehui bao*, 4 March 1921.

53. Hershatter, *Dangerous Pleasures*.

54. *Chenbao*, 5 November 1920; *Guobao*, 26 January and 20 April 1921.

55. Gamble, *Peking*, 260 and 480–81.

56. Li was already involved in the opening of a school for five hundred poor boys in the eastern suburbs in 1919 and a workhouse, funded with charitable donations, in the western suburbs, where famine migrants congregated at a main rail junction. The workhouse admitted males ages 17–30 from among both the local poor and refugees for factory work and boys ages 11–16 for training in construction and other skills. See *Shuntian shibao*, 12 August 1920; *Beijing ribao*, 5 October 1920; *Shihua*, 4 February 1920.

57. *Zhenzai ribao*, 25 November 1920.

58. *Xiao minbao*, 4 February 1921.

59. Gamble, *Peking*, 37 and 247.

60. *Zhongguo minbao*, 2 December 1920.

61. *Shibao*, 3 November 1920; *Zhenzai ribao*, 13 November 1920.

62. Shi, *At Home in the World*, 56.

63. Gamble, *Peking*, 226.

64. Zucker, *Chinese Theater*, 171.

65. *Xiao gongbao*, 21 September 1920; *Chenbao*, 24 September 1920.

66. *Minyi ribao*, 25 September 1920.

67. Li Zhongming, *Jing ju dashi*, 54.

68. Actors Chen Delin and Liu Hongsheng also performed on the day (*Zhongguo minbao*, 28 October 1920); Xu Youchun, *Minguo renwu*, 2122, 2807, and 2854.

69. *Beijing baihua bao*, 22 January 1921; *Xiao minbao*, 23 January 1921.

70. *Guobao*, 3 March 1921.

71. "Lingxue yaozhi yuanqi," 1. Appearing amid passages on eclectic spiritual and philosophical teachings and calligraphy are biographical entries of "righteous conduct" (*yixing*) in the same genre as those that appear in gazetteers in the late imperial and republican periods. In one case reported in the publication's inaugural issue, a female resident of a Beijing *hutong* is praised for paying for a neighbor's coffin, a customary act of charitable piety ("Liang shi yixing"). I am indebted to Matthias Schumann-Brandau for bringing this publication to my attention.

72. *Xiao minbao*, 7 January 1921; *Xiao gongbao*, 16 December 1920.

73. *Aiguo baihua bao*, 18 January 1921.

74. *Shihua*, 30 July 1920.

75. *Chenbao*, 19 October 1920; see also *Fengsheng*, 19 October 1920.
76. *Shihua*, 23 January 1921; *Xiao minbao*, 25 January 1921; *Beijing baihua bao*, 27 January 1921.
77. *Chenbao*, 21 January 1921.
78. *Fengsheng*, 15 February 1921.
79. *Chenbao*, 24 October 1920.
80. Gamble, *Peking*, 238.
81. *Yishi bao*, 20 October 1920.
82. Many dozen of people were credited with modest donations. The larger donations included 1,000 yuan from the wife (*taitai*) of a military general; 637 yuan from the Jiading County Chamber of Commerce outside Shanghai; 500 yuan from a British military official; 400 yuan from the Suzhou customs office; 300 yuan from the metropolitan branch of the Chinese Red Cross; 250 yuan from a woman named Qian; 111 yuan raised at the Zhili Province Finance Bureau; 372 yuan, 100 yuan, and 12 yuan raised by the magistrates of three contiguous and unafflicted counties northwest of Beijing by the Great Wall (Xuanhua, Zhuolu, and Huailai, respectively); 100 yuan from the Ministry of the Interior; 16 yuan from an anonymous woman; and 200 yuan from Jiang, the society's founder. See *Zhengfu gongbao*, 1 February 1921.
83. *Chenbao*, 21 November 1920.
84. *Minyi ribao*, 14 December 1920; *Chenbao*, 6 January 1921.
85. *Xiao gongbao*, 8 January 1921.
86. Henriot, "'Invisible Deaths, Silent Deaths,'" 409.
87. Asen, *Death in Beijing*, 5, 36, and 41.
88. *Zhongguo minbao*, 31 December 1920.
89. Dray-Novey, "The Twilight of the Beijing Gendarmerie," 360; *Shihua*, 3 and 12 December 1920 and 23 January 1921; *Minyi ribao*, 10 November 1920.
90. *Shihua*, 18 February 1921; *Chenbao*, 21 February 1921.
91. *Chenbao*, 12 January 1921; *Shihua*, 12 January 1921.
92. *Xiao gongbao*, 24 December 1920 and 5 January 1921; *Fengsheng*, 19 and 27 October 1920; *Chenbao*, 22 October and 1 December 1920; *Yishi bao*, 2 October 1920.
93. *Shihua*, 31 August 1920.
94. *Shihua*, 23 October 1920.
95. *Zhongguo minbao*, 29 November 1920.
96. *Xiao minbao*, 22 March 1921.
97. *Shihua*, 16 November 1920; *Aiguo baihua bao*, 22 November 1920; *Zhongguo minbao*, 29 November 1920; *Chenbao*, 20 November 1920.
98. *Aiguo baihua bao*, 20 November 1920; *Zhongguo minbao*, 30 November 1920; *Xiao gongbao*, 18 January 1921; *Beijing baihua bao*, 17 February 1921.
99. *Aiguo baihua bao*, 6 December 1920; *Chenbao*, 7 December 1920; *Xiao gongbao*, 18 December 1920.
100. *Chenbao*, 27 December 1920.
101. *Zhongguo minbao*, 1 October 1920; *Yishi bao*, 3 October 1920; *Beijing baihua bao*, 25 January 1920; *Shihua*, 24 February 1921.
102. Gamble, *Peking*, 214, 272, and 486.

103. *Aiguo baihua bao*, 19 August 1920.
104. *Aiguo baihua bao*, 25 November 1920; *Shihua*, 26 November 1920.
105. *Aiguo baihua bao*, 31 December 1920; Xu Youchun, *Minguo renwu*, 2123.
106. Janet Chen, *Guilty of Indigence*, 14 and 31–32. See also Dong, *Republican Beijing*, 214–28.
107. Goodman, *Native Place, City, and Nation*, 253–55; Belsky, *Localities at the Center*, 242–45; Shue, "The Quality of Mercy"; Rogaski, "Beyond Benevolence."
108. Goodman, "What Is in a Network?" Goodman bases her conclusion in large part on Kōhama Masako's study of the records of a shelter for the disabled founded in Shanghai in 1919 (ibid., 162–75).
109. Tsu, "Native Charities of Shanghai," 509.
110. On the same day that it was announced that the soup kitchen bureau had selected 2,000 attendees to do roadwork as work relief in the suburbs of the capital, Wang, together with the municipal police and metropolitan government bureaux, hired craftsmen to teach trade skills to both male and female refugees coming into the hands of authorities at official shelters and soup kitchen facilities until their closing the following April. *Zhongguo minbao*, 20 November 1920; *Chenbao*, 13 January 1920 and 8 April 1921; *Shihua*, 24 October 1920.
111. Janet Chen notes the lackluster nature of many of the workhouse institutions in republican Beijing: the Qing-era Capital Vagrant Workhouse "slid into insolvency" in the early republic, later to be "reincarnated as a division of the Nationalist government's municipal Relief Home" (*Guilty of Indigence*, 32).
112. On late imperial traditions of spirituality and merit ledgers as they related to charity, see Brokaw, *The Ledgers of Merit and Demerit*; Janku "Sowing Happiness."
113. *Xiao gongbao*, 4 November 1920; *Shihua*, 21 November 1920.
114. *Chenbao*, 21 November 1920; *Zhongguo minbao*, 26 November 1920.
115. *Yishi bao*, 3 September, 1920; *Chenbao*, 20 November 1920; *Zhongguo minbao*, 26 November 1920.
116. *Guobao*, 25 March 1921.
117. *Chenbao*, 15 October 1920.
118. *Shihua*, 28 September 1920.
119. *Xiao gongbao*, 7 October 1920; *Yishi bao*, 20 October 1920; *Baihua guoqiang bao*, 5 November 1920; *Zhongguo minbao*, 28 December 1920.
120. Naquin, *Peking*, 603; Goodman, *Native Place, City, and Nation*, 217–57.
121. Goodman, "What Is in a Network?" 159.
122. Naquin, *Peking*, 557.

5. City Charities and the Countryside

1. *Shihua*, 17 October 1920.
2. *Shihua*, 3 October 1920.
3. *Shihua*, 13 October 1920.
4. *Zhongguo minbao*, 24 October 1920.
5. *Guobao*, 27 January 1921.
6. *Chenbao*, 21 February 1921.

7. *Shihua*, 1 October 1920.

8. *Shihua*, 10 October 1920.

9. *Beijing baihua bao*, 23 October 1920; Twinem, "Modern Syncretic Religious Societies in China. I," 464–67.

10. Naquin, *Peking*, 603–8; Goodman, *Native Place, City, and Nation*.

11. *Chenbao*, 28 September 1920; *Shihua*, 1 October 1920; *Xiao gongbao*, 17 December 1920.

12. *Jiuzai zhoukan*, 6 March 1921.

13. *Zhongguo minbao*, 18 September 1920; *Jingbao*, 24 September 1920; Xu Youchun, *Minguo renwu*, 2294.

14. Xu Youchun, *Minguo renwu*, 319, 671; ZGDAG, *Zhonghua minguo shi dang'an ziliao huibian*, 3:384–90.

15. *Zhenzai ribao*, 1 November 1920. Only the November issues of this daily could be located for this study (they are in the library of Peking University). See also *Shuntian shibao*, 9 October 1920; *Chenbao*, 27 October 1920.

16. *Jingbao*, 24 September 1920; *Shihua*, 16 and 20 September 1920; *Shuntian shibao*, 22 September 1920.

17. *Shunping XZ* 17 and 651.

18. *Ningjin XZ* (1929) 1:63b; see also *Ningjin XZ* (1999) 525; *Shuntian shibao*, 20 October 1920; *Da gongbao*, 16 and 25 November 1920.

19. *Zhenzai ribao*, 12 November 1920.

20. *Qiu XZ* 26; Xu Youchun, *Minguo renwu*, 82.

21. *Wei XZ* 16:46a.

22. *Haixing XZ* 25.

23. Other initiators of the group and their home counties in Zhili included a former army officer, Jiang Yanxing (1875–1941, Fucheng), and Liu Ruoceng (1860–1929, Yanshan). See *Shihua*, 9 September 1920; *Xiao gongbao*, 12 September 1920; *Yuandong bao*, 18 September 1920; *Xibei ribao*, 21 September 1920; Xu Youchun, *Minguo renwu*, 708, 2248, and 2466. The Central Park fund-raiser was reported in *Beijing ribao*, 9 October 1920; *Shihua*, 15 October 1920.

24. *Shuntian shibao*, 15 October 1920; *Zhenzai ribao*, 16 November 1920.

25. Xu Youchun, *Minguo renwu*, 708.

26. *Yuandong bao*, 18 September 1920; Xu Youchun, *Minguo renwu*, 28.

27. The founders included four Zhejiang natives and a man from Shanghai. The effort apparently grew out of a poor relief society (*jipin hui*) funded by interest on gold deposits that had been in the planning stages earlier in August by the same men together with three other Zhejiang natives and Ye Gongchuo (1881–1968), the minister of communications through the crisis and a native of Guangdong. See *Shihua*, 30 August 1920; *Shuntian shibao*, 16 September 1920; Xu Youchun, *Minguo renwu*, 55, 365–66, 616, 796, 809–10, 887, 989–90, 1256, and 1530; *Zhengfu gongbao*, 13 June 1921.

28. *Beijing ribao*, 18 September 1920. The founders of this group were Liu Qingtang, Zhang Shouyong (1876–1945), and Zhu Yanyu (1885– ?). See also *Shuntian shibao*, 19 September 1920; *Zhenzai ribao*, 25 November 1920; Xu Youchun, *Minguo renwu*, 339, and 1870.

29. *Shuntian shibao*, 26 October 1920; *Xiao gongbao*, 27 October 1920; Xu Youchun, *Minguo renwu*, 87 and 490.

30. McCord, *The Power of a Gun*, 311.

31. Ibid., 253–66.

32. *Shihua*, 2 March 1921. See also *Hankou xinwen bao*, 26 September 1920.

33. *Shuntian shibao*, 13 September 1920; *Xiao gongbao*, 22 September 1920; Xu Youchun, *Minguo renwu*, 1717 and 716.

34. *Zhengfu gongbao*, 8 October 1920; Liu Shoulin et al., *Minguo zhiguan nianbiao*, 24 and 52.

35. *Minguo ribao*, 14 September 1920; *Yishi bao*, 18 September 1920; *Zhengfu gongbao*, 8 October 1920.

36. Seton, *Chinese Lanterns*, 272.

37. Zhou, *Xiong Xiling zhuan*, 409–11.

38. Of the readily traceable attendees at the first national Buddhist relief fund-raising meeting (Quanguo Fojiao chouzhen dahui), one hailed from Hubei, one from Zhejiang, two from Jiangsu, and two from Fujian. This group should not be confused with Shanghai's Buddhist Compassion Society (Fojiao cibei hui; founded in Shanghai during the 1917 Zhili floods), which had a subsociety for sponsoring infants in the 1920 famine zone, the Buddhist Foundling Relief Society (Fojiao jiuying hui). See *Shuntian shibao*, 15 September 1920; *Shihua*, 16 September 1920; *Shibao*, 9 November 1920; *Zhongguo minbao*, 1 October 1920; Yu, *Xiandai Fojiao renwu*, 398, 927, 1066, 1267, and 1580; Cai Hongyuan, *Minguo renwu bieming*, 89, 259; Xu Youchun, *Minguo renwu*, 806; *Zhengfu gongbao*, 8 October 1920.

39. Kiely and Jessup, introduction, 5–7.

40. *Graphic*, 6 July 1878; Edgerton-Tarpley, *Tears from Iron*, 2.

41. *Celestial Empire*, 27 November 1920; *Xiao gongbao*, 8 October 1920.

42. *Zhongguo minbao*, 18 December 1920; *Minyi ribao*, 28 October 1920.

43. *Celestial Empire*, 19 March 1921.

44. Egan, "Fighting the Chinese Famine," 46.

45. *Shengjing shibao*, 14 October 1920; *Hankou zhongxi bao*, 8 December 1920; *Celestial Empire*, 5 March 1921.

46. Rankin, *Elite Activism and Political Transformation*; Rowe, *Hankow*; Strand, *Rickshaw Beijing*. See also Huang, "'Public Sphere'/'Civil Society' in China?"

47. Simon, *Civil Society in China*, 113; Brook and Frolic, "The Ambiguous Challenge of Civil Society," 12. It is worth noting that Simon's discussion of the Beiyang period focuses on the Nationalist-controlled sections of South China. Brook and Frolic's case study for what they call "autonomous group formation, or auto-organization" in the republic is Shanghai ("The Ambiguous Challenge of Civil Society," 12). The closest study to this one in terms of context is David Strand's *Rickshaw Beijing*, in which he notes that "the pre-industrial Chinese city supported a rich variety of public activities" in halls and guild chambers of various types that "sustained a tradition of debate and discussion," especially during times of crisis (167).

48. PUIFRC, *The North China Famine*, insert.

6. Village Mutual Aid

1. *Nanpi XZ* 6:48b.

2. Xia, *Minguo shiqi zaihai*, 79 and 395–403.

3. Initially, in October, official figures indicated that Shandong was the most affected of the five provinces, with twelve million destitute in 107 counties. Then, within a week, Shandong's main semiofficial relief society lowered the estimate of the destitute to four million in 60 counties, an estimate—presumably based on stricter definitions of need, that was later shared by the main international relief societies. See Wang Lin, *Shandong jindai zaihuang shi*, 182–83; *Shanxi tongzhi*, 221–22; PUIFRC, *The North China Famine*, 11.

4. *Zhengfu gongbao*, 6 October 1920; PUIFRC, *The North China Famine*, 11; *Minguo ribao*, 12 September 1920; *Shihua*, 29 September 1920.

5. *Zhengfu gongbao*, 13 June 1921. This chart for December 1920, published in the wake of the famine, was the only one on the crisis to appear in such detail in the Beiyang government's weekly gazette.

6. *Zhengfu gongbao*, 13 June 1921.

7. Seventy-five yuan a ton was the going price charged relief agencies for grain in Tianjin; the ration is the one used by major international relief societies over the year.

8. *Zhengfu gongbao*, 13 June 1921.

9. *Zhengfu gongbao*, 28 April 1921.

10. Lillian Li, *Fighting Famine in North China*, 250–82.

11. Mallory, *China*, 3; A. Nathan, *A History of the China International Famine Relief Commission*; Lillian Li, *Fighting Famine in North China*, 295–303.

12. J. Buck, *Land Utilization in China*, 108–11.

13. Pietz, *The Yellow River*, 59–69.

14. J. Buck, *Land Utilization in China*, 34; Lillian Li, *Fighting Famine in North China*, 90–101.

15. Lillian Li, *Fighting Famine in North China*, 94 and 102.

16. J. Buck, *Land Utilization in China*, 194–97.

17. Huaiyin Li, *Village Governance in North China*, 27–33.

18. J. Buck, *Land Utilization in China*, 186–90 and 209; Lillian Li, *Fighting Famine in North China*, 99; PUIFRC, *The North China Famine*, 15.

19. Mann, *Precious Records*, 143–77; Lillian Li, *Fighting Famine in North China*, 317–18; Huaiyin Li, *Village Governance in North China*, 29–30; Huang, *The Peasant Economy and Social Change*, 63.

20. Thaxton, "State Making and State Terror," 342.

21. Thaxton, *Salt of the Earth*, 115 and 249.

22. Pomeranz, *The Making of a Hinterland*; Esherick, *The Origins of the Boxer Uprising*, 173–81.

23. Lillian Li, *Fighting Famine in North China*, 84 and 103.

24. Chang Liu, *Peasants and Revolution in Rural China*, 12.

25. J. Smith, *The Art of Doing Good*.

26. Huang, *The Peasant Economy and Social Change*, 15. See also Duara, *Culture, Power, and the State*. For a focus on taxation based on the uniquely rich records of Zhili's Huailu county, see Huaiyin Li, *Village Governance in North China*.

27. Xia, *Minguo shiqi zaihai*; Su, *Minguo shiqi Henan shui han zaihai*.

28. Arkush, "The Moral World of Hebei Village Opera," 95–96.

29. *Shuntian shibao*, 14 October 1920; *Jingxing XZ* 15:9b and 15:23a; *Aiguo baihua bao*, 17 November 1920.

30. Billingsley, *Bandits in Republican China*, 40–69; *Shihua*, 2 October 1920; *Zhenzai ribao*, 12 November 1920; *Zhongguo minbao*, 27 December 1920.

31. Perry, *Rebels and Revolutionaries in North China*, 3.

32. PUIFRC, *The North China Famine*, survey map enclosure.

33. *Qinghe XZ* 14:6a.

34. *Shihua*, 9 October 1920.

35. MacNair, *With the White Cross in China*, 50.

36. A comprehensive list of items ingested during the famine is given in *Xiao gongbao*, 22 January 1921. See also PUIFRC, *The North China Famine*, 13.

37. According to one estimate, a quarter of China's 1,800 counties operated nurseries in 1920, including those in the Zhili drought zone, spending a quarter of a million yuan in forestry work and planting around one hundred million saplings (Reisner, *Reforesting China*, 3–15). See also Pomeranz, *The Making of a Hinterland*, 123–28.

38. The price of farm carts in one section of Zhili dropped in one year by 55 percent (J. Buck, "Price Changes in China," 240).

39. PUIFRC, *The North China Famine*, 15.

40. Ibid.

41. J. Buck, *Land Utilization in China*, 332.

42. Chang Liu, *Peasants and Revolution in Rural China*, 8 and 12.

43. *Qinghe XZ* 14:6a.

44. Whelan, *The Pawnshop in China*.

45. Huaiyin Li, *Village Governance in North China*, 12.

46. *Zhaicheng cunzhi* 86.

47. *Nanpi XZ* 9:78a.

48. Will, *Bureaucracy and Famine*, 139. Another example from the eighteenth century appears in *Cang XZ* 8:131b.

49. PUIFRC, *The North China Famine*, survey map.

50. *Wei XZ* 16:46a.

51. *Wei XZ* 16:43b, 16:44b, and 11:18ab.

52. *Wei XZ* 16:39ab.

53. *Wei XZ* 16:40a.

54. *Nangong XZ* 16:25b and 24:60b–62a; *Qinghe XZ* 16:46a and 11:12b.

55. *Qinghe XZ* 14:6a.

56. *Shihua*, 27 August 1920.

57. Edgerton-Tarpley, *Tears from Iron*, 134–37. See also Brokaw, *The Ledgers of Merit and Demerit*.

58. *Laifu bao*, 10 October 1920; Xu Youchun, *Minguo renwu*, 2048.

59. *Da gongbao*, 24 December 1920; *Jiuzai zhoukan*, 6 March 1921.
60. Huaiyin Li, *Village Governance in North China*, 148.
61. *Laifu bao*, 10 October 1920.
62. J. Smith, *The Art of Doing Good*, 55 and 88.
63. *Laifu bao*, 10 October 1920.
64. Two and three *he* of millet, being one-fifth and three-tenths of a *sheng* (pint), respectively, contained roughly 900 and 1,350 calories based on the following conversions: a *sheng* of grain corresponded to approximately two *jin*; and each *jin* (whether of corn, kaoliang, or millet) contained an average of 2,250 calories, according to the American Red Cross in 1921 (Baker, *Report of the China Famine Relief*, 18 and 222).
65. Lillian Li records an "adult famine ration standard of .005 *shi* of husked grain per person per day" for the Qing period, which, at 120 *jin* per *shi* and 2,250 calories per *jin*, equals 1,350 calories per ration (*Fighting Famine in North China*, 159). Will similarly states that under the Qing "the typical ration of one-half *sheng* per day would represent . . . 420 grams of bleached rice, just barely a survival ration, for at about 3,300 kilocalories per kilogram, 420 grams provides less than 1,400 kilocalories" (*Bureaucracy and Famine*, 132).
66. *Laifu bao*, 10 October 1920.
67. The categories were fairly well off (*xiaokang*), middle class (*zhongchang*), slightly poor (*shaopin*), secondarily poor (*cipin*), and destitute (*jipin*). Joanna Smith identifies a similar system of classifying poorer social strata whose members received aid from food-relief programs in the lower Yangxi region of the 1600s (*The Art of Doing Good*, 88), as does Lillian Li for eighteenth-century Zhili (*Fighting Famine in North China*, 224). See also *Jiuzai zhoukan*, 20 February 1920.
68. *Laifu bao*, 7 November 1920.
69. Ibid.
70. The source specifies that recipients would get "one *sheng* [pint] of the new *dou* [peck] measurement," equivalent to "four *he* of the old *dou* measurement," which is slightly more than rations of two or three *he* in Feng's plan.
71. Hsu, *Study of a Typical Chinese Town*, 9; Gamble, *Ting Hsien*, 156.
72. P. Fuller, "Struggling with Famine in Warlord China," 109–14.
73. *Shuntian shibao*, 9 October 1920. See also Xu Youchun, *Minguo renwu*, 2048.
74. Kuhn, "Local Self-Government under the Republic," 284.
75. Duara, *Culture, Power, and the State*, 5; see also 11, 16, and 56–67.
76. M. Barbour, "One Corner of the China Famine Field," 5.
77. Hsu, *Study of a Typical Chinese Town*, 5; Gamble, *Ting Hsien*, 4.
78. Hershatter, *Gender of Memory*, 32–64.
79. *Ci XZ* 17:15a.
80. *Qing XZ* 14:27b; Xu Youchun, *Minguo renwu*, 2628. In some cases, the biographies of widows credited them with directly assisting neighbors with grain grants in 1920 (*Wei XZ* 11:34a).
81. For examples from the late 1870s, see P. Fuller, "Decentring International and Institutional Famine Relief," 879.
82. Harrison, *The Man Awakened from Dreams*, 75; see also 24, 65, and 99.

83. The size of Qian Chongkai's contribution of several hundred thousand *jin* was not unique to aid moving between rural residents. In a nearby county a member of the local gentry was credited with handing out 1,000 *shi* of wheat and 5,000 silver coins in his village in 1920 (*Haixing XZ* 804). Another notable private distribution of grain and money in the countryside in 1920 can be found in *Qinghe XZ* 11:21a.
84. Harrison, "Newspapers and Nationalism in Rural China," 190 and 204.
85. For an interesting account of how the transport of relief at the local level was arranged in the period through completely unrelated institutions, see Zhang, *Social Transformation in Modern China*, 96–100.
86. *Da gongbao*, 30 November 1920.
87. Chinese Eastern Railway, *North Manchuria and the Chinese Eastern Railway*, 9; see also 74.
88. Tharp, *They Called Us White Chinese*, 108–9.
89. Waln, *The House of Exile*, 17–18.
90. See Ransmeier, *Sold People*, 191–96.
91. PUIFRC, *The North China Famine*, insert.
92. *Wuji XZ* 3:9a.
93. Baker, "Report of the China Famine Relief," 196–97.
94. For an excellent discussion of family and gender dynamics during the great North China famine of 1876–79, see Edgerton-Tarpley, *Tears from Iron*, 161–88.

7. Bureaucratic Relief

1. A. Nathan, *Peking Politics*, 68.
2. Bergère, "Une crise de subsistence en Chine," 1380.
3. Austin, *Saving China*, 193.
4. Kang and Xia, *20 shiji Zhongguo zaibian*, 59–80; Lillian Li, *Fighting Famine in North China*, 295–303.
5. *Wanxian xinzhi* 9:22a.
6. In 1920–21, this was the case in such Zhili counties as Jin, Shenze, Guangzong, Li, Baoding, Ningjin, Xian, Anxin, Mancheng, and Xinhe. See *Da gongbao*, 12 August, 18 September, 31 October, 3 and 14 and 16 November, and 1 December 1920; *Minguo ribao*, 18 September 1920; *Mancheng XZ* 18; *Xinhe XZ* (1929) 1:22a.
7. *Xinhe XZ* (2000) 21.
8. *Wei XZ* 7:32b–34a.
9. *Dingzhou shizhi* 19.
10. It should be mentioned that even within this one county, regulations appear to have varied according to locality. For example, the local annals for one village in the district describe a different regime for its charity granary, established in 1914: there, households with less than fifty *mu* of land were exempted from contributing, and families above this threshold were divided into three tiers, contributing seven *he* per *mu*, five *he* per *mu*, or three *he* per *mu*, respectively. This difference in policy from what appeared to prevail in the county in 1920 might have been a function of local preferences, or it might have reflected differences in policies implemented dur-

ing crisis versus more normal times. As for loans of grain, this presumably involved farmers returning an equivalent amount of grain to the granary after the next harvest. See *Ding XZ* 3:11b–12a; *Zhaicheng cunzhi* 84–86.

11. *Tianjin zhongmei ribao*, 31 August 1920; *Xiao gongbao*, 3 July 1920; *Da gongbao*, 7 and 21 July, 12 August, and 26 September 1920; *Guangzong XZ* 1:15a.

12. *Xiao gongbao*, 20 November 1920.

13. *Zhongguo minbao*, 10 November 1920. Today, Wu'an is located in Hebei province.

14. The "(?)" appears in the original text, perhaps the addition of an incredulous copy editor. *Celestial Empire*, 27 November 1920.

15. Weights and measures varied considerably across provinces and even localities. The above grain total was expressed in four ways: 5,183,600 *jin*, 10,220 *dun* (tons, or 1,680 *jin* each), 879,280 *shi* (which was normally converted by the Ministry of Communications in 1920–21 to 160 *jin* each but could range as low as 100 *jin*), and 1,903,770 *bao* (normally converted by the ministry to 160 *jin* each but could also range as low as 100 *jin*). ZGDAG, *Zhonghua minguo shi dang'an ziliao huibian*, 388; *Shuntian shibao*, 8 and 13 October 1920. See also *Da gongbao*, 21 July and 18 and 26 September and 6, 10, 13, 24, and 31 October and 3, 5, 9, 14, 16, and 30 November and 1 December 1920.

16. This estimate is based on the middle of the above spread—392,942,500 *jin* of grain brought into seventy-four Zhili counties for discount sale by the middle of November 1920 since the beginning of such efforts in August—divided by 16,567,164 people over three months. (Seventy-four of Zhili's 134 counties, if roughly broken down proportionally, would have held a little over half—16,567,164—of the province's thirty million people.)

17. S. Fuller and Liang, *Statement of Aims and Report on Famine Conditions*, 11.

18. Wong, "Qing Granaries," 481; see also the other chapters in Will and Wong, *Nourish the People*.

19. *Zhengfu gongbao*, 28 October 1920; *Shuntian shibao*, 28 October 1920; *Beijing ribao*, 28 October 1920.

20. This calculation is based on a purchase price of five coppers per *jin* of millet at grain discount centers and a diet of famine rations of a half-*jin* per day.

21. P. Fuller, "Decentring International and Institutional Famine Relief."

22. *Zhengfu gongbao*, 28 October 1920.

23. PUIFRC, *The North China Famine*, survey map.

24. *Da gongbao*, 8 December 1920; see also *Wan XZ* 9:22a.

25. *Shuntian shibao*, 1 January 1921; *Mancheng XZ* 18; *Jiuzai zhoukan*, 5 December 1920.

26. *Da gongbao*, 20 November 1920.

27. *Tianjin zhongmei ribao*, 31 August 1920; *Da gongbao*, 20 November and 1 December 1920.

28. *Zhongguo minbao*, 15 December 1920; *Jiuzai zhoukan*, 7 November 1920; *Da gongbao*, 21 November 1920.

29. Quoted in *Celestial Empire*, 5 February 1921 (emphasis added).

30. *Xingtai shizhi* 964. See also *Zhengfu gongbao*, 13 June 1921.

31. S. Fuller and Liang, *Statement of Aims and Report on Famine Conditions*, 9.

32. *Xinhe XZ* (1929) 4:11a–12b.

33. Ibid. 4:56b–57a. The estimate of people fed is based on a low daily ration of 1,500 calories and a price of five coppers (or fifty cash) per *jin*, which was what the American Red Cross paid for its relief grain in a nearby part of the famine zone.

34. *Guangzong XZ* 1:15a, 14:20a; *Jiuzai zhoukan*, 20 February 1921.

35. *Da gongbao*, 11 December 1920.

36. Guangzong *XZ* 14:20a; see also *Da gongbao*, 24 and 31 October and 11 December 1920.

37. *North China Herald*, 21 February 1921.

38. *Zhongguo minbao*, 4 November 1920.

39. *Da gongbao*, 20 December 1920.

40. *Zhongguo minbao*, 16 September 1920; *Shuntian shibao*, 16 September 1920.

41. McCord, *The Power of a Gun*, 260.

42. A. Nathan, *Peking Politics*, 75–76.

43. *Da gongbao*, 30 August 1920.

44. *Wei XZ* 16:29b.

45. Wang and Xiong, letter to Pastor, 22 September 1920, SD 893.48g/30.

46. Pastor, letter to Wang and Xiong, 23 September 1920, SD 893.48g/30.

47. Boorman, *Biographical Dictionary of Republican China*, 50–52.

48. Yan, letter to Crane, 1 October 1920, SD 893.48g/15. See also Zarrow, *China in War and Revolution*, 83.

49. Davis, telegram to Crane, 29 December 1920.

50. Ker, letter to Pastor, 29 December 1920, SD 893.48g/117.

51. Crane, telegram to Colby, 5 January 1921, SD 893.48g/81.

52. Alston, report entitled "Foreign Mission Heads as of January 31, 1921," 7 February 1921, FO 405/230/168.

53. "All Foreign Loan and Indemnity obligations secured on the Customs Loan including the Service of the Reorganization Loan have been fully met," read a news brief in March 1921, after which the foreign inspector general "released" over twenty-three million Shanghai silver taels to the central government in Beijing (*Celestial Empire*, 5 March 1921). See also Feuerwerker, *The Chinese Economy*, 82–85; A. Nathan, *Peking Politics*, 75.

54. Iriye, *After Imperialism*, 14.

55. Presumably from Yan, the letter bears only the ministry's seal and is not signed. Chinese Ministry of Foreign Affairs, letter to Pastor, 10 January 1921, SD 893.48g/159.

56. A. Nathan, *Peking Politics*, 67. "The factions agreed in viewing foreign relations as essentially a technical problem in which all Chinese shared the same interests," Nathan explains (ibid.).

57. *Peking & Tientsin Times*, 8 October 1920.

58. *Peking & Tientsin Times*, 25 October 1920.

59. Cheng, *Banking in Modern China*, 164–65. See also Morrison, *The Correspondence of G. E. Morrison*, 606–12.

60. Xu Youchun, *Minguo renwu*, 434.

61. *North China Herald*, 25 September 1920.

62. McCormack, *Chang Tso-lin*, 301.

63. Fuller, letter to Crane, 3 November 1920, SD 893.48g/260; *Peking & Tientsin Times*, 25 October 1920; *North China Herald*, 18 September 1920; Waldron, *From War to Nationalism*, 45.

64. *Zhongguo minbao*, 4 August 1920.

65. Crane, telegram to Colby, 22 January 1921, SD 893.48g/97; Obata, letter to Pastor, 4 December 1920, SD 893.48g/108. The four banks were the (British) Hong Kong and Shanghai Banking Corporation, Banque de l'Indo-Chine, Yokohama Specie Bank, and the (American) International Banking Corporation.

66. Crane, telegram to Colby, 4 February 1921, SD 893.48g/113; Yan, letter to Pastor, 19 January 1921, SD 893.48g/144; Greaves, letter to Ker, 3 December 1920, SD 893.48g/117; Evans, letter to Fuller, 17 January 1921, SD 893.48g/133.

67. The Maritime Customs Surtax Loan was ultimately allocated in seven parts to international relief societies: the Beijing Metropolitan District and western Zhili (790,000 yuan); eastern Zhili (720,000 yuan); Henan (880,000 yuan); Shandong (540,000 yuan); Shaanxi (540,000 yuan); Shanxi (400,000 yuan); and Shanghai, together with Gansu, where a massive earthquake had struck in mid-December 1920 (160,000 yuan). See PUIFRC, *The North China Famine*, 22.

68. *Yishi bao*, 15 September 1920.

69. Quoted in *Xiao gongbao*, 18 October. See also *Xiao gongbao*, 1 November 1920.

70. *Jingbao*, 25 September 1920.

71. *Chenbao*, 1 November 1920.

72. Morrison, *The Correspondence of G. E. Morrison*, 805.

73. *Zhongguo minbao*, 2 October 1920.

74. Ibid.

75. *Zhongguo minbao*, 3 October 1920; *Zhenzai ribao*, 6 November 1920.

76. *Xiao gongbao*, 19 August 1920.

77. *Shihua*, 21 December 1920; *Beijing ribao*, 15 October 1920; *Yuandong bao*, 1 December 1920 and 30 January 1921; *Da gongbao*, 2 December 1920.

78. *Chenbao*, 20 November 1920; *Zhongguo minbao*, 2 October 1920; *Zhenzai ribao*, 7 November 1920.

79. *Chenbao*, 13 December 1920.

80. PUIFRC, *The North China Famine*, 26. This amount also included fees for relief workers and telegraph use.

81. Ibid., 175.

82. *North China Herald*, 5 March 1921.

83. *Da gongbao*, 21 November 1920.

84. *Da gongbao*, 20 and 21 November 1920.

85. *Da gongbao*, 26 November and 28 December 1920; *Yishi bao*, 6 December 1920; *Zhengfu gongbao*, 13 June 1921.

86. *Peking & Tientsin Times*, 8 October 1920; *Yuandong bao*, 26 October 1920.

87. *North China Herald*, 25 September 1920. "In spite of past experience the Government finds itself with no better machinery for dealing with the situation than that which must be hastily improvised," the paper determined on October 9, and on October 16 it saw "no ground for supposing that Peking [would] surpass itself in anything but culpable negligence."

8. Migrant Routes

1. *Shihua*, 30 September 1920.

2. *Chenbao*, 11 December 1920 and 24 March 1921; *Xiao minbao*, 7 January 1921.

3. Established in mid-October by Ye Gongchuo—who, as head of the Ministry of Communications, was in charge of the country's rail network—the facility was open for boys ages 6–15 and girls ages 6–12. Several weeks after the shelter opened, with increasing numbers of underclothed infants arriving at the station, a ministry official sent a staff member to buy fifty sets of cotton baby clothing for arriving refugees. Considering the sheer numbers in transit, this single facility could have benefited only a small fraction of the children passing through the capital. The initiative may have been related to the fact that Ye, together with former gendarmerie commandant Jiang Chaozong, had served as honorary trustee of the Beijing Poor Children's Home, at a temple in the North City. See *Shihua*, 20 October 1920; *Minyi ribao*, 6 November 1920; *Shanbao*, March 1919.

4. *Shihua*, 13 August 1920.

5. The modern term "refugee" was first used by an international body in the same year as the 1920–21 famine, when the League of Nations applied it to Russians in flight from the Soviet Union—many of whom continued to reside in or pass through Manchuria as Chinese fled there from the drought districts. However, any clear distinction between a migrant and a refugee is a function of the international codification of the protective status afforded certain groups or individuals in the decade after World War II. Long, "When Refugees Stopped Being Migrants," 9. See also Gatrell, *The Making of the Modern Refugee*.

6. Pierre-Étienne Will offers an interesting but brief chapter on vagrancy in his study of state relief in eighteenth-century Zhili (*Bureaucracy and Famine*, 38–49), while outward famine migration is addressed only in passing in Lillian Li's work on famine in Zhili (*Fighting Famine in North China*, 301 and 321).

7. Schoppa, *In a Sea of Bitterness*; Dillon, "Politics of Philanthropy." The chapter on refugees in James Reardon-Anderson's study on migration into Manchuria also focuses on the Nationalist period (*Reluctant Pioneers*, 147–59).

8. Harbin's *Yuandong bao* (30 December 1920) put the number of famine migrants arriving in the three northeastern provinces at a million by the end of 1920. Although clearly a rounded number, this reflects a considerable increase compared to previous years. (Spread over the five months since the declaration of famine in August, this would have averaged out to 6,666 migrants a day into the northeast, by train or boat or on foot.) Of course, many of them returned south after the crisis ended, yet they were followed by several hundred thousand migrants participating in state-run settlement programs in Heilongjiang in the spring.

9. Cao Shuji puts the average annual immigration into Heilongjiang from 1918–22 at 141,000 and into Fengtian at 170,000 from 1912–21, while the official numbers he gives for Jilin are considerably smaller (*Zhongguo yimin shi*, 505–8). Thomas Gottschang and Diana Lary give higher estimates for migrants traveling to the northeast from Hebei and western Shandong alone, at 427,000 for 1920 and 277,000 for 1921 (*Swallows and Settlers*, 171). The same migration data appear in Reardon-Anderson,

Reluctant Pioneers, 100. Ma Ping'an cites six different sources and concludes that average migration to the areas north of the Great Wall or into the northeast was 200,000 a year from 1912–23, curiously with no great spike in 1920–21—although he emphasizes how difficult it is to generate accurate statistics for the period (*Jindai Dongbei yimin yanjiu*, 42–48). All these studies indicate a clear increase in migration to Manchuria over the course of the 1920s. Yet it should be stressed that, as Gottschang and Lary point out, until 1923 the "only systematic data on the movement of people between North China and Manchuria" was taken by the Chinese Maritime Customs Service regarding sea traffic into and out of Yingkou and other treaty ports (*Swallows and Settlers*, 36). (This is corroborated by the fact that migration statistics begin only for 1923 in a report published by the Nationalist government in 1930.) The Chinese railway authority "did not keep complete passenger records" for its section of the rail line leading into Fengtian, while the Japanese-owned South Manchurian Railway began processing migration numbers on any extensive scale only in 1927, after which it published three consecutive studies in 1928–30. The growth in migration seen in the late 1920s, then, may well be a function of the closer attention to migrant numbers in those years by the Japanese authorities—who, after the establishment of Manchukuo in 1932, would include a system of labor certificates that would further strengthen state oversight of migrant numbers. See also Tsao, *Chinese Migration to the Three Eastern Provinces*, 35.

10. McCord, "Victims and Victimizers."
11. *Da gongbao*, 29 September 1920; *Chenbao*, 2 December 1920.
12. Rowe, *Hankow*, 228–29.
13. "Hankow Intelligence Report, December Quarter, 1920," 24 January 1921, FO 228/3282/125.
14. *Hankou zhongxi bao*, 30 December 1920 and 1 January 1921; *Da Hanbao*, 31 December 1920.
15. *Hankou zhongxi bao*, 13 and 24 December 1920.
16. *Hankou zhongxi bao*, 28 December 1920.
17. William Rowe relates that salt merchants in neighboring Hanyang city founded the area's first benevolent hall in 1823, and that a charitable group providing such services as lifeboats on the Yangzi and burials was formed by a broader group of merchants in 1830 in Hankou (*Hankow*, 107 and 125).
18. *Hankou zhongxi bao*, 8 December 1920.
19. *Da Hanbao*, 2 November 1920.
20. *Hankou xinwen bao*, 18 September 1920.
21. *Hankou zhongxi bao*, 1 December 1920 and 4 January 1921; *Da Hanbao*, 5 December 1920.
22. *Hankou zhongxi bao*, 9 November 1920; *Da Hanbao*, 20 December 1920.
23. *Hankou zhongxi bao*, 29 January 1921.
24. *Hankou zhongxi bao*, 4 January 1921.
25. *Hankou zhongxi bao*, 16 and 23 January 1921.
26. *Da Hanbao*, 2 November 1920.
27. *Guomin xinbao*, 2 October 1920; *Da Hanbao*, 19 November and 15 December 1920; *Zhengfu gongbao*, 13 June 1921; *Hankou zhongxi bao*, 22 December 1920.

28. *Zhongguo minbao*, 6 November 1920; *Shihua*, 6 November 1920; *Chenbao*, 6 November 1920; *Baihua guoqiang bao*, 6 November 1920.

29. *Chenbao*, 11 December 1920.

30. *Shihua*, 28 December 1920.

31. *Zhongguo minbao*, 20 September 1920.

32. *Da gongbao*, 16 and 30 November 1920.

33. *Zhengfu gongbao*, 13 June 1921.

34. As Will explains, "Immigration was encouraged until 1688, tacitly tolerated until 1740, and continued thereafter despite restrictions that, although quite severe in principle, were easily relaxed whenever a calamity struck North China" (*Bureaucracy and Famine*, 45).

35. This included 5,000 yuan from the police chief's office; 1,000 yuan each from city police precincts; 2,000 yuan from the police investigative bureau; 2,000 yuan from the Bank of Communications and Zhili Bank; and 500 yuan from a man surnamed Hu. See *Da gongbao*, 2 September 1920; *Tianjin zhongmei ribao*, 14 September 1920.

36. *Da gongbao*, 17 and 30 September, 17 October, and 1 November 1920.

37. C. Nathan, *Plague Prevention and Politics in Manchuria*, 10 and 65–66.

38. *Da gongbao*, 9 September 1920.

39. *Yuandong bao*, 21 September 1920; *Shihua*, 28 February 1920.

40. *Da gongbao*, 2 September 1920.

41. *Yuandong bao*, 4 September 1920.

42. *Zhongguo minbao*, 3 October 1920; *Fengsheng*, 4 October 1920; *Beijing ribao*, 10 October 1920.

43. *Zhongguo minbao*, 3 October 1920.

44. *Chenbao*, 2 November 1920; *Shihua*, 8 October 1920.

45. *Tianjin zhongmei ribao*, 31 August 1920; *Shihua*, 30 August 1920; *Chenbao*, 30 August 1920; *Da gongbao*, 30 August and 27 December 1920.

46. *Yishi bao*, 17 September 1920.

47. *Shibao*, 13 November 1920.

48. *Qunbao*, 4 February 1920.

49. *Jichang ribao*, 16 and 23 September 1920.

50. *Zhongguo minbao*, 29 September 1920; *Jichang ribao*, 26 September 1920.

51. *Jichang ribao*, 3 October 1920.

52. *Yuandong bao*, 21 September 1920.

53. *Jichang ribao*, 7 December 1920.

54. Quoted in *Da gongbao*, 2 October 1920.

55. C. Nathan, *Plague Prevention and Politics in Manchuria*, 64.

56. *Sheng jing shibao*, 8 October 1920; *Jichang ribao*, 27 October 1920.

57. *Da gongbao*, 10 November 1920.

58. Tharp, *They Called Us White Chinese*, 108–9.

59. *Jingbao*, 25 September 1920.

60. *Jingbao*, 6 October 1920; *Jichang ribao*, 6 October 1920; McCormack, *Chang Tso-lin*, 34; Xu Youchun, *Minguo renwu*, 1539 and 2637.

61. McCormack, *Chang Tso-lin*, 9–10, 15, 17, and 26.

62. *North China Herald*, 2 October 1920; McCormack, *Chang Tso-lin*, 201 and 301.

63. McCormack, *Chang Tso-lin*, 15.

64. van de Ven, "Public Finance and the Rise of Warlordism," 863–65.

65. McCormack, *Chang Tso-lin*, 9.

66. Duara, *Sovereignty and Authenticity*, 48.

67. *Shengjing shibao*, 2 October 1920; *Chenbao*, 3 October 1920; *Yuandong bao*, 5 December 1920.

68. *Shibao*, 7 November 1920; *Yuandong bao*, 5 October and 7 November 1920.

69. *Yuandong bao*, 31 October 1920; *Shengjing shibao*, 15 January 1921.

70. *Jichang ribao*, 15 September 1920.

71. *Yuandong bao*, 4 September 1920; *Jichang ribao*, 9 September 1920.

72. *Shengjing shibao*, 5, 20, and 30 October 1920 and 24 and 26 March 1921; *Yuandong bao*, 5 December 1920.

73. *Yuandong bao*, 19, 29, and 30 September 1920.

74. *Jichang ribao*, 22 and 30 September 1920; *Yuandongbao*, 1, 20, and 27 October 1920; *Da gongbao*, 6 October 1920; *Shengjing shibao*, 20 October 1920.

75. *Shengjing shibao*, 12 October 1920.

76. *Shengjing shibao*, 5, 20, and 30 October 1920; *Yuandong bao*, 5 December 1920; *Jichang ribao*, 22 October 1920.

77. Imperial Japanese Government Railways, *An Official Guide to Eastern Asia*, 79.

78. *Jichang ribao*, 20 October 1920; *Yuandong bao*, 29 October 1920.

79. *Jichang ribao*, 23 and 24 September 1920.

80. *Jichang ribao*, 20 October 1920.

81. *Jichang ribao*, 26 November and 1 December 1920.

82. *Yuandong bao*, 28 November 1920; *Jichang ribao*, 19 December 1920.

83. *Jichang ribao*, 31 October 1920.

84. *Shengjing shibao*, 22 and 31 October 1920 and 1 January 1921; *Yuandong bao*, 31 October 1920 and 29 January 1921.

85. *Jichang ribao*, 19 and 30 September and 31 October 1920.

86. *Shengjing shibao*, 22 and 24 October 1920, 1 January 1921.

87. *Fengtian gongbao*, 26 April 1921.

88. *Shengjing shibao*, 15 October 1920.

89. *Jichang ribao*, 11 and 14 November 1920; *Yuandong bao*, 18 November 1920.

90. Ng, "A Chinese or a Russian Newspaper?" 103.

91. Ng, "A Chinese or a Russian Newspaper?" 104 and 109. See also Carter, *Creating a Chinese Harbin*, 28 and 32.

92. *Yuandong bao*, 14, 16, and 29 September 1920.

93. The grain was selling for 1.3 yuan per *dou* in local markets that week. See *Yuandong bao*, 21 and 24 September 1920.

94. *Shengjing shibao*, 29 October 1920; *Yuandong bao*, 9 and 31 October and 12 December 1920.

95. *Yuandong bao*, 27 November 1920.

96. *Yuandong bao*, 4 December 1920.

97. *Yuandong bao*, 21 January 1921.

98. *Yuandong bao*, 24 September and 2 and 13 October 1920; *Jichang ribao*, 2 October 1920.
99. *Shengjing shibao*, 31 October 1920.
100. *Yuandong bao*, 19 November 1920 and 1, 7, 18, 22, 23, 25, 26, 28, and 30 January and 15 February 1921; *Jichang ribao*, 24 November 1920.
101. The sect was founded by two men in 1913 in Beijing, according to Shao Yong, with the aim of promoting abstinence from tobacco and alcohol and works of charity. It spread to other cities in the country but was most prevalent in the north and northeast. A YMCA study in 1920 found thirty-one Lijiao organizations in Beijing and determined that most members were from the city's lower classes (*Zhongguo huidaomen*, 165–66). See also *Yuandong bao*, 6 February 1921.
102. *Yuandong bao*, 23 December 1920 and 5 January 1921.
103. *Shuntian shibao*, 6 October 1920; *Jingbao*, 6 October 1920.
104. *Yuandong bao*, 19 October 1920.
105. *Jichang ribao*, 2 November 1920; *Yuandong bao*, 2 November 1920.
106. *Yuandong bao*, 17 November 1920; *Jichang ribao*, 16 November 1920.
107. *Yuandong bao*, 2 and 12 December 1920.
108. Arnold, *China*, 673.
109. *Yuandong bao*, 24 September and 12 October 1920.
110. *Yuandong bao*, 7 January 1921.
111. *Yuandong bao*, 28, 30, and 31 December 1920.
112. *Shibao*, 2 November 1920; *Zhenzai ribao*, 14 and 26 November 1920.
113. *Shengjing shibao*, 3 October 1920.
114. "Guerrilla Warfare in Manchuria—Korean Successes—Japanese Regiment Annihilated" ran the *North China Herald* headline. Japanese authorities had reportedly suppressed news of the events. *North China Herald*, 18 December 1920. See also *Shengjing shibao*, 3 October 1920; McCormack, *Chang Tso-lin*, 41–42.
115. *Shihua*, 5 September 1920; *Yishi bao*, 11 September 1920; *Yuandong bao*, 25 November and 7 December 1920.
116. *Shihua*, 30 July 1920.
117. Dunscomb, *Japan's Siberian Intervention*, 141–43 and 155–56.
118. Ibid., 141–42.
119. Billingsley, *Bandits in Republican China*, 215–25.
120. Wakeman, *Policing Shanghai*; Rogaski, *Hygienic Modernity*.
121. Matsusaka, *The Making of Japanese Manchuria*, 271 and 302.
122. McCormack, *Chang Tso-lin*, 64.

9. Manchurian Relief

1. Taylor, "Mrs. Howard Taylor's Trip and Journal," n.p., SOAS.
2. Zhu Hu, *Minbao wuyu*; Rankin, *Elite Activism*; Wue, "The Profits of Philanthropy"; Edgerton-Tarpley, *Tears from Iron*, 131–55.
3. PUIFRC, *The North China Famine*. See also Mallory, *China*, 2–3; A. Nathan, *A History of the China International Famine Relief Commission*; Kang and Xia, *20*

shiji Zhongguo zaibian tushi, 75–80; Lillian Li, *Fighting Famine in North China,* 295–302.

4. PUIFRC, *The North China Famine,* 36.

5. Ibid., 32–39.

6. *Da gongbao,* 24 August 1920.

7. *Xiao gongbao,* 22 September 1920.

8. *Xiao gongbao,* 19 August 1920; see also *Shihua,* 28 July 1920; *Yuandong bao,* 2 October 1920.

9. *Yishi bao,* 14 September 1920.

10. *Yuandong bao,* 21 September 1920.

11. *Jichang ribao,* 22 September 1920; *Yuandong bao,* 1 October 1920.

12. *Shengjing shibao,* 30 October 1920.

13. *Yuandong bao,* 3 October 1920.

14. *Jichang ribao,* 27 October 1920.

15. Grain production in Jilin and Heilongjiang beyond the needs of their populations was around a million tons, or 1.68 billion *jin,* in 1920. See *Shibao,* 22 December 1920; Chinese Eastern Railway, *North Manchuria,* 66.

16. *Yuandong bao,* 9 and 16 October 1920.

17. *Yuandong bao,* 16 and 17 December 1920.

18. Wilkinson, "Mukden [Shenyang] Intelligence Report for March Quarter, 1921," 31 March 1921, FO 228/3290/67.

19. Wilkinson, "[Shenyang] Intelligence Report for December Quarter, 1920," 15 January 1921, FO 228/3290/43.

20. Alston, "Annual Report, 1920," FO 1423/1423/10, quoted in Jarman, *China Political Reports,* 455.

21. *Peking & Tientsin Times,* 3 January 1921; Xu Youchun, *Minguo renwu,* 1141.

22. Crane, telegram to State Department, 17 December 1920, SD 893.48g/66.

23. *Jichang ribao,* 15 September 1920.

24. *Yuandong bao,* 26 October 1920.

25. *Zhongguo minbao,* 14 October 1920; *Minyi ribao,* 29 October 1920.

26. *Da Hanbao,* 5 and 10 November 1920.

27. *Shengjing shibao,* 30 October 1920.

28. *Yuandong bao,* 30 October 1920; *Zhenzai ribao,* 22 November 1920.

29. *Yuandong bao,* 28 and 30 November 1920.

30. Monthly salaries of over 30 yuan would be docked 10 percent; salaries over 100 yuan would be docked 20 percent; and salaries over 200 yuan would be docked 30 percent. See *Jichang ribao,* 3 October 1920; *Yuandong bao,* 5 October 1920; *Shengjing shibao,* 14 October 1920.

31. Those receiving monthly salaries exceeding 30 yuan would also contribute 10 percent of their pay, with a limit of a one yuan contribution for anyone below that threshold. See *Yuandong bao,* 5 November 1920.

32. *Shengjing shibao,* 27 October 1920; *Yuandong bao,* 29 October 1920.

33. *Yuandong bao,* 28 October 1920; *Shengjing shibao,* 29 October 1920.

34. *Yuandong bao,* 24 November 1920.

35. *Jichang ribao,* 5 December 1920.

36. Quoted in *Fengtian gongbao*, 4 April 1921.
37. The yuan in this particular account were given in *xiaoyang*, or silver coins worth 10 to 20 cents each. See *Fengtian gongbao*, 24 April 1921.
38. *Fengtian gongbao*, 26 July 1921.
39. In one case the breakdown was 8,000 yuan to Zhili, 7,000 to Shandong, 3,000 to Henan, and 2,000 to Shanxi. See *Shengjing shibao*, 20 and 31 October 1920; *Da gongbao*, 23 November and 2 December 1920; *Yuandong bao*, 18 December 1920.
40. *Yuandong bao*, 19 December 1920; *Shengjing shibao*, 1 January 1921.
41. *Yuandong bao*, 30 November and 17 December 1920; *Jichang ribao*, 3 December 1920.
42. *Yuandong bao*, 13, 14, and 20 January and 1 February 1921.
43. *Jichang ribao*, 16, 26, and 30 September and 2 and 16 October 1920; *Yuandong bao*, 26 October and 5, 9, 13, and 14 November 1920; *Shengjing shibao*, 5 and 20 October 1920.
44. *Yuandong bao*, 13 and 30 November 1920.
45. *Yuandong bao*, 21 and 22 December 1920.
46. *Yuandong bao*, 12 November 1920.
47. *Yuandong bao*, 5 and 7 October 1920.
48. *Yuandong bao*, 1 December 1920.
49. *Yuandong bao*, 10 and 14 November and 18 December 1920.
50. *Yuandong bao*, 7 January 1921.
51. *Zhenzai ribao*, 19 November 1920.
52. At one of the earlier fund-raising meetings in Jinan, the military governor donated 40,000 yuan, a second man gave 10,000 yuan, and "people in the countryside" (*xiangren*) donated several thousand each. *Beijing ribao*, 12 October 1920. See also *Minyi ribao*, 11 November 1920; *Zhongguo minbao*, 10 November 1920.
53. ZGDAG, *Zhonghua minguo shi dang'an ziliao huibian*, 3:384.
54. *Yuandong bao*, 18 November and 5 December 1920.
55. *Zhenzai ribao*, 19 and 28 November 1920; *Da gongbao*, 24 November and 10 December 1920; *Zhengfu gongbao*, 13 June 1921.
56. *Shengjing shibao*, 8 October 1920; *Yuandong bao*, 20 November and 2 December 1920.
57. *Shengjing shibao*, 23 and 30 October 1920; *Jichang ribao*, 7 December 1920.
58. This above purchase estimate is based on the assumption that *diao* in this part of Jilin were strings of 100 coppers each, the traditional Chinese standard. There were some exceptions to this, such as the Beijing *diao*—which was a tenth of the value, worth only 10 coppers. See *Jichang ribao*, 3 and 21 November 1920.
59. Imperial Japanese Government Railways, *An Official Guide to Eastern Asia*, 61.
60. *Shengjing shibao*, 26 October 1920.
61. *Yuandong bao*, 11 December 1920; see also *Jichang ribao*, 11 and 18 November 1920.
62. Quoted in *Yuandong bao*, 23 November 1920.
63. *Yuandong bao*, 3 December 1920 and 18 January 1921.
64. *Jichang ribao*, 28 October 1920; *Shengjing shibao*, 30 October 1920.
65. *Yuandong bao*, 23 November 1920.
66. *Jichang ribao*, 19 and 23 September and 28 October 1920.

67. *Jichang ribao*, 22 and 23 September 1920.
68. *Yuandong bao*, 1 and 7 October, 5 and 6 November, and 9 December 1920.
69. Goodman, "What Is in a Network?"
70. *Zhongguo minbao*, 10 November 1920; *Yuandong bao*, 28 November 1920.
71. *Yuandong bao*, 13 October 1920.
72. *Da gongbao*, 21 November 1920.
73. *Da gongbao*, 10 October 1920; *Yuandong bao*, 1 December 1920.

10. *International Relief*

1. *Shihua*, 9 October 1920.
2. *Times*, 27 November 1920. "Famine in China—Starvation, Cholera, and Bandits—Children Sold for a Few Shillings," ran the headline. The report was mailed from China on 9 October.
3. Ibid.
4. Each of the group's 20,000-yuan purchases acquired two thousand *shi* of seed, according to reports, and each *shi* was presumably 160 *jin*. Coordinators of a different seed aid distribution earlier in Zhili estimated that each *jin* of wheat seed was sufficient to sow two *mu* of land. The calculation is based on an average farm size of eighteen *mu*. See *Zhongguo minbao*, 4 August 1920; *Shihua*, 15 October 1920; *Shuntian shibao*, 15 October 1920; *Beijing ribao*, 16 October 1920.
5. In his study of sectarian religion in Hebei, Cao Xinyu notes that these legends were recorded in stone steles in the region as late as 1937 ("From Famine History to Crisis Metaphor," 159).
6. *Shihua*, 9 September 1920; *Yishi bao*, 11 September 1920; *Shuntian shibao*, 11 September 1920; *Xiao gongbao*, 12 September 1920; *Zhongguo minbao*, 12 September 1920; *Minguo ribao*, 18 September 1920; *Yuandong bao*, 18 September 1920; *Tianjin zhongmei ribao*, 19 September 1920; *Xibei ribao*, 21 September 1920; Xu Youchun, *Minguo renwu*, 28, 407–8, 109–10, 706, 731, 1377, and 1429.
7. *Times*, 16 November 1920.
8. *Xiao gongbao*, 17 September 1920.
9. See P. Fuller, "'Barren Soil, Fertile Minds.'"
10. *Da gongbao*, 15 January 1921.
11. *Aiguo baihua bao*, 6 January 1921; *Da gongbao*, 12 January 1921.
12. *Zhongguo minbao*, 27 December 1920; see also *Chenbao*, 16 January 1921.
13. *Xiao gongbao*, 19 January 1921; *Beijing baihua bao*, 20 January 1921.
14. *Jiuzai zhoukan*, 13 March 1921.
15. *Aiguo baihua bao*, 18 February 1921; *Shihua*, 18 February 1921; *Yishi bao*, 19 February 1921.
16. *Zhongguo minbao*, 28 February 1921.
17. *Xiao minbao*, 28 February 1921.
18. *Guobao*, 3 March 1921.
19. *Chenbao*, 15 February 1921.
20. *Aiguo baihua bao*, 13 March 1921.
21. *Chenbao*, 15 and 16 March 1921.

22. *Zhongguo minbao*, 11 March 1921.
23. Will, *Bureaucracy and Famine*, 229.
24. *Shihua*, 2 March 1921.
25. Egan, "Fighting the Chinese Famine," 46.
26. *Shuntian shibao*, 30 September 1920.
27. *Xiao gongbao*, 3 October 1920.
28. Seton, *Chinese Lanterns*, 215, 270, and 272.
29. Zhou, *Xiong Xiling*, 414–19; *Zhongguo minbao*, 4 October 1920.
30. *China Sun*, 20 November 1920.
31. van de Ven, *Breaking with the Past*; Stross, *The Stubborn Earth*.
32. Darroch, *Report of the Central China Famine Relief Fund Committee*, 3 and 24.
33. The North China International Relief Society of Tientsin covered Zhili's eastern section. Relief in the remaining four provinces was undertaken by the American Red Cross (western Shandong); the International Auxiliary of the Shantung Famine Relief Committee of Tsinanfu (the rest of Shandong); and committees in Kaifeng, Taiyuan, and Xi'an for Henan, Shanxi, and Shaanxi provinces, respectively. In addition, a famine relief committee in Shanghai composed of prominent Chinese and foreigners operated independently in selected parts of the famine field.
34. *Da gongbao*, 28 December 1920; PUIFRC, *The North China Famine*, 20.
35. PUIFRC, *The North China Famine*, survey map insert.
36. *Da gongbao*, 10 January 1921.
37. *Da gongbao*, 3 and 28 November 1920.
38. MacNair, *With the White Cross*, 50.
39. PUIFRC, *The North China Famine*, 18 and 20.
40. Ibid., 41–47.
41. Ibid., 25. The source gives an "incomplete" figure of 2,021,178.90 yuan, adding that some missions had not responded to requests for their accounts.
42. Stauffer, *The Christian Occupation of China*, 299–300.
43. *Zhongguo minbao*, 19 September 1920; *Shihua*, 21 September 1920; *Jingbao*, 23 September 1920.
44. Sometimes the Christian activity that appears in records is more difficult to distinguish from the work of native groups, and at least in the case of the Protestants, the work does not simply follow the pattern drawn up in Edinburgh of designated mission fields. For example, this was the case in Wan county, located in the field of the American Presbyterian Mission, where the 13,393 bags of sorghum, valued at 80,358 yuan, distributed by the Gospel Hall (Fuyintang; literally the hall of fortunate sound or good news), located downtown by the county government and Chamber of Commerce, was by far the largest contribution listed in its account of relief originating from outside the county. The Fuyintang was a missionary institution in the style of a benevolent hall that appeared in relief capacities across the 1920–21 famine field, from Shaanxi province to east Beijing's Horse Market. In central Zhili's Wuji county, the Fuyintang established poor workhouses in two villages for locals to learn skills, as well as a village soup kitchen serving the old and infirm once a day. In Guangzong county, a hundred-room orphan home established by a resident of a village there was funded with some 3,000–4,000 yuan a year in American missionary

funds from the Fuyintang in neighboring Wei county. See *Wanxian xinzhi* 4:25ab, 8:1b–2a, and 9:22a; *Shunping XZ* 17; *Guangzong xian jiuzhi jiaozhu* 543; *Da gong-bao*, 13 December 1920; *Jiuzai zhoukan*, 5 December 1920; *Beijing baihua bao*, 13 February 1921.

45. MacNair, *With the White Cross*, 27.
46. Quoted in *Celestial Empire*, 30 October 1920.
47. Quoted in *Celestial Empire*, 16 October 1920.
48. Quoted in *Celestial Empire*, 30 October 1920.
49. PUIFRC, *The North China Famine*, 53.
50. *The Missionary Echo of the United Methodist Church*, 234.
51. Trued, "The Famine," 109 and 112.
52. Carter, *Heart of Buddha, Heart of China*, 92–93.
53. MacNair, *With the White Cross*, 37 and 42.
54. Ibid., 54 and 56.
55. Ibid., 41.
56. Ibid., 73, 101, and 115.
57. Baker, *Report of the China Famine Relief*, 18.
58. MacNair, *With the White Cross*, 45–48.
59. Ibid., 93.
60. Ibid., 69.
61. Ibid., 90–91.
62. Ibid., 48, 57, and 62.
63. Ibid., 46, 56, and 61.
64. Ibid., 86. A foreign visitor to the famine field elsewhere in Zhili expressed similar admiration. "There was a courtesy, tact, gentleness, and for the most part an honesty, which surprised me," Mansfield Freeman wrote in a May 1921 issue of *Millard's Review of the Far East*, an American news magazine published in Shanghai. Writing from Tang county—where, with half of the population affected by drought, local gentry had been setting up one soup kitchen for every two villages in the county in December, as discussed in chapter 6—Freeman added: "Village chiefs in some remote spot in the mountains received us with the grace and naturalness of cultured gentlemen. Even the children knew how to meet strangers and there was a spontaneity about their courtesy the secret of which many American children have not learned" ("Observations on Famine Relief Work," 621).
65. MacNair, *With the White Cross*, 68.
66. *Aiguo baihua bao*, 17 March 1921.
67. MacNair, *With the White Cross*, 85.
68. Ibid., 97.
69. PUIFRC, *The North China Famine*, 128.
70. Ibid., 108.
71. MacNair, *With the White Cross*, 57 and 106–9.
72. PUIFRC, *The North China Famine*, 67–77.
73. "There are a great many beggars and loafers," Jameson explained. "The crops are uncertain; famine relief is certain; and they are satisfied to sit down and wait for it" (quoted in Stross, *The Stubborn Earth*, 61).

74. Baker, *Report of the China Famine Relief,* 93–96.
75. Ibid., 14.
76. Yan Huiqing, "Yen Hui-ch'ing," 194, HIA.
77. Baker, *Report of the China Famine Relief,* 211–12. Some donors in the United States objected to the use of their money in work projects. "We understand that part of the relief fund sent to that section [of China] is used for digging ditches for irrigation," Mary Tuthill wrote in a letter she sent along with a check for $150 contributed by the "teachers and scholars of the Chinese Sunday School of Metropolitan Memorial N.E. Church" in Washington, "but we earnestly desire that this fund go *directly* to the people and be used for buying them food." The State Department relayed instructions to the American legation in Beijing to turn over the sum to "some local organization for the relief of famine sufferers." See Tuthill, letter to Colby, 10 November 1920; Adee, letter to Crane, 15 November 1920, SD 893.48g/32.
78. Will, *Bureaucracy and Famine,* 255–58; Lillian Li, *Fighting Famine in North China,* 53–55.
79. *Wei XZ* 16:39b, 19:25a; *Handan XZ* 10:44b.
80. *Zhongguo minbao,* 3 October and 9 December 1920 and 26 January 1921; *Zhengfu gongbao,* 3 October 1920; *Aiguo baihua bao,* 6 October 1920; *Xiao gongbao,* 21 October 1920.
81. *Shihua,* 22 September and 30 November 1920; *Fengsheng,* 24 October 1920.
82. *Laifu bao,* 21 November 1920.
83. *North China Herald,* 12 March 1921.
84. *Yishi bao,* 15 September 1920.
85. *Chenbao,* 29 November 1920; see also *Shihua,* 19 September and 28 November 1920.
86. Lillian Li, *Fighting Famine in North China,* 250–82.
87. As one foreign correspondent explained from Henan, "The Chinese believe in direct giving whereas foreigners generally believe in instituting public works, with giving as a corollary" (*Peking & Tientsin Times,* 23 November 1920).
88. Janet Chen, *Guilty of Indigence,* 74.
89. Dulles, *The Red Cross,* 19 and 66–69.
90. Irwin, *Making the World Safe,* 29–30 and 32.
91. Ibid., 45.
92. Baker, *Report of the China Famine Relief,* 211–12.
93. Ibid.
94. Davis, telegram to Crane, 29 December 1920, SD 893.48g/73. See also Crane, telegram to Colby, 28 December 1920, SD 893.48g/73.
95. Crane, telegram to Colby, 13 January 1921, SD 893.48g/89; Gauss, letter to Crane, 21 January 1921, SD 893.48g/160.
96. Janet Chen, *Guilty of Indigence.* By the end of the decade, the poor would become a national shame, Zwia Lipkin has argued in a study of poverty in Nationalist Nanjing, "deviants" amid the nation-building project and a social problem to hide (*Useless to the State,* 7; see also 61–79).
97. By January 1, 1921, the Tianjin-based international relief group for which MacNair worked had mobilized 16 percent of the 3,232,069 yuan the group would spend by

the end of the crisis in May. This pattern held true for all of the six main joint foreign-Chinese relief organizations, each of which spent roughly nine-tenths of its total relief monies for 1920–21 in the second half of the famine. See PUIFRC, *The North China Famine*, 18 and 20; S. Fuller and Liang, *Statement of Aims and Report on Famine Conditions*, 6–16.

98. See Lillian Li, *Fighting Famine in North China*, 295–300; Kang and Xia, *20 shiji Zhongguo zaibian tushi*, 75–80.

99. Barbour, *In China When . . .* , 26–27. Through the spring of 1921 George Barbour had been directing work relief in Shunde, where some nine thousand people had been fed daily at one gentry-run soup kitchen (discussed in chapter 7), and where one observant foreign relief team had found "independent societies for relief" organized by Chinese "in many places" (*Celestial Empire*, 5 February 1921).

100. Arnold, letter to the director of the Bureau of Foreign and Domestic Commerce, 3 June 1921, SD 893.48g/229. See also Shavit, *The United States in Asia*, 16.

101. Baker, letter to the director of American Red Cross foreign operations, 14 February 1921, SD 893.48g/726.

102. PUIFRC, *The North China Famine*, 21; see also Chu, Lee, and Chang, *The Temperature of China*, 4, 86, 89, 90, and 541.

103. *Zhongguo minbao*, 17 January 1921; PUIFRC, *The North China Famine*, 78–84; *Shihua*, 8 October 1920; *Da gongbao*, 15 November and 4 December 1920; *Shibao*, 25 December 1920.

104. Patenaude, *The Big Show in Bololand*, 197 and 238.

105. "The whole province of Shansi is free from the growth of poppy," an informant wrote the British consul in Tianjin (secretary of the International Anti-Narcotic Association of China, Shansi Branch, letter to Ker, 10 May 1920, FO 674/232). "It would be hopeless for anyone to try and grow [poppy] anywhere around here," another reported from southern Zhili, "as through the total lack of rain, no crops are growing of any kind," and this informant added that the local magistrate had ruined the few local attempts at poppy growing (Meech, letter to Ker, 3 May 1920, "Tientsin: 1920: Dossier 13: Opium Narcotics," FO 674/232).

106. Pong, "Confucian Patriotism."

107. Ó Gráda, *Famine*, 157.

108. PUIFRC, *The North China Famine*, 16. In October, the Peking United International Famine Relief Committee revised its estimate upwards to 210 million yuan (twenty million people for seven months at 1.50 yuan per person per month), while the North China International Relief Society of Tientsin arrived at 200 million yuan. See Gauss, letter to Crane, 9 September 1920, SD 893.48g/29; United International Famine Relief Committee, letter to the Chinese president, 26 October 1920, FO 228/3029/211; *Peking & Tientsin Times*, 5 November 1920.

109. PUIFRC, *The North China Famine*, 25. It had been "impossible to procure a statement" from what the Peking Committee called the "distinctly Chinese Societies" on the "amount of relief done by them," the report noted. "This was asked for, but received little response. The fact was that there were a large number of such societies and that they handled considerable sums of money." Instead, the report offered a summary table of "the amount of funds from all sources which were available in

the past famine. In some cases of course, these are simply estimates and in the instance of the amount contributed by the Chinese societies merely a guess." It was based on this that compilers estimated a total of eight million yuan contributed "through Chinese societies" out of its total estimated relief expenditure from all sources—official and private, Chinese and foreign—of thirty-seven million yuan in 1920–21. See PUIFRC, *The North China Famine*, 25–26.

110. Vernon, *Hunger: A Modern History*, 17; see also Cabanes, *The Great War and the Origins of Humanitarianism*; Moniz, *From Empire to Humanity*; Porter, *Benevolent Empire*; Shaw, *Britannia's Embrace*; Watenpaugh, *Bread from Stones*. An exception to this that focuses on Greek Catholic and Orthodox relief initiatives in Beirut is Tanielian, *The Charity of War*, 173–98.

Conclusion

1. The anecdote is from Brooks, "The YMCA Government of China," 71–74, NYPL. Similar rituals in a nearby section of Shanxi are described in Harrison, *The Man Awakened from Dreams*, 28–29. The translation of the verse by Du Fu (712–770), which came to Brooks's mind as she recalled the procession, is from Cranmer-Byng, *"Lute of Jade,"* 32.
2. Rankin, "State and Society in Early Republican Politics," 19.
3. Huang, "'Public Sphere'/'Civil Society' in China?," 228–32.
4. Kuhn, "Local Self-Government under the Republic," 259.
5. Ibid, 257; see also Huang, *The Peasant Economy and Social Change in North China*; Duara, *Culture, Power, and the State*; Thaxton, *Salt of the Earth*.
6. Kuhn, "Local Self-government under the Republic," 277.
7. Liu Jianyun, *Ni suobushi de Minguo mianxiang*.
8. Su, *Minguo shiqi Henan shui han zaihai*, 35, 48, 53, 60, 67, 71, 116, 140, 150, 165, 169, and 177.
9. Xia, *Minguo shiqi zaihai*, 255–73.
10. On the empirical challenges faced by the historian looking at this period, see Bianco, "Numbers in Social History."
11. Hsi-Sheng Ch'i, *Warlord Politics*, 47.
12. A. Nathan, *Peking Politics*, 206–8 and 233; Sheridan, *Chinese Warlord*, 126; Xu Youchun, *Minguo renwu*, 2046.
13. Waldron, *From War to Nationalism*, 127, 199, and 201; Sheridan, *Chinese Warlord*, 132.
14. Sheridan, *Chinese Warlord*, 132; Waldron, *From War to Nationalism*, 95 and 102.
15. A. Nathan, *Peking Politics*, 211–19; Sheridan, *Chinese Warlord*, 136.
16. Lary, *Warlord Soldiers*, 5.
17. Grain prices in Beijing rose almost 50 percent in the three months of the nearby Battle of the Great Wall; and earlier, in August, rice prices in Shanghai had jumped the same amount in just two days during the two-month Jiangsu-Zhejiang war, fought between the Zhili faction's regional allies there against Zhejiang, the last remaining province held by the Anhui clique. With the city's rice supply from up the Yangzi in Jiangsu cut off by military strategists there, the million-plus popula-

tion of China's most dynamic commercial center had been reduced to a tactical calculation. Meanwhile, the grain that did pass through the river and canal blockades leading into the metropolis had a "special military supply tax" imposed on it (Waldron, *From War to Nationalism*, 137–38).

18. "Although Tsinin had lived under warlords since 1916," David Buck writes in his study of the Shandong capital, "it was not until [Zhang Zongcang] became military governor in 1925 that the full force of warlordism descended upon the city" (*Urban Change in China*, 125).

19. The marked change to the state-society relationship in the mid-1920s applied even to the domains of provincial leaders with reputations for progressive policies. "Up to 1925 the tax burden was endurable," Henrietta Harrison writes in her biographical study of a member of the rural gentry there, "but then Shanxi's governor, Yan Xishan, entered national politics," which meant joining the fray ravaging the North China Plain to the south, and taxes in the province more than doubled again between 1925 and 1928 (*The Man Awakened from Dreams*, 126 and 131–32).

20. In the case of central Zhili's Huailu county, taxes shot up in 1925–26 when the main land tax doubled, and in the same year the province began collecting the following year's main land tax in advance. See Duara, *Culture, Power, and the State*, 217; Huaiyin Li, *Village Governance in North China*, 37.

21. Gottschang and Lary, *Swallows and Settlers*, 53.

22. Waldron, *From War to Nationalism*, 144–49.

23. *North China Herald*, 18 October 1924, quoted in Sheridan, *Chinese Warlord*, 132. See also Lincoln, *Urbanizing China*, 60–71.

24. Harrison, *The Man Awakened from Dreams*, 132; see also 126 and 131.

25. *Shenbao*, 30 June 1925.

26. *Shenbao*, 27 May 1925.

27. Xia, *Minguo shiqi zaihai*, 509.

28. A rare mention of the 1925 Sichuan famine is Xia, *Minguo shiqi zaihai*, 395.

29. Lamont, letter to American Advisory Committee, 15 September 1921, SD 893.48g/239. CIFRC, *Fifteenth Anniversary Book*, 3–12.

30. Lamont, letter to American Advisory Committee, 10 March 1922, SD 893.48g/258.

31. Yan, letter to Crane, 19 May 1921, SD 893.48g/217; Edwards, letter to Crane, 14 May 1921, SD 893.48g/207.

32. Dean's circular no. 128 to legations, 16 July 1921, SD 893.48g/231; Ruddock, letter to Yan, 21 July 1921, SD 893.48g/231.

33. Yan, letter to Ruddock, 12 August 1921, SD 893.48g/243.

34. Schurman, letter to the secretary of state, 26 October 1921, SD 893.48g/243.

35. de Freitas, letter to Yan, 12 October 1921, SD 893.48g/243.

36. Yan, letter to de Freitas, 3 May 1922, SD 893.48g/270; Schurman, letter to the secretary of state, 10 May 1922, SD 893.48g/268; de Freitas, letter to Yan, 4 May 1922, SD 893.48g/270.

37. CIFRC, *Annual Report 1923*, 1; Oudendijk's circular no. 318, 20 December 1923, SD 893.48g/284; Edwards, letter to Oudendijk, 15 December 1923, SD 893.48g/284.

38. Quoted in A. Nathan, *A History of the China International Famine Relief Commission*, 12.

39. CIFRC, *Fifteenth Anniversary Book*, 5; A. Nathan, *A History of the China International Famine Relief Commission*, 49.
40. *North China Standard*, 24 May 1927.
41. Godement, "La famine de 1928 à 1930," 10; CIFRC, *Annual Report 1928*, 1.
42. CIFRC, *Annual Report 1927*, 11.
43. CIFRC, *Fifteenth Anniversary Book*, 34; CIFRC, *Annual Report 1926*, 10; CIFRC, *Annual Report 1927*, 10–12; CIFRC, *Annual Report, 1928*, 5–10 and 13.
44. CIFRC, *Annual Report 1928*, 2; CIFRC, *Annual Report 1929*, 4; Godement, "La Famine de 1928 à 1930," 21.
45. CIFRC, *Annual Report 1929*, 42.
46. Godement, "La Famine de 1928 à 1930," 94–95; CIFRC, *Annual Report 1929*, 4; CIFRC, *Annual Report 1930*, 3.
47. According to the CIFRC, 3–6 million perished in the northwest alone. See also Xia, *Minguo shiqi zaihai*, 395; CIFRC, *Annual Report 1929*, 43; CIFRC, *Annual Report 1930*, 6.
48. J. Buck, *Land Utilization in China*, 332.
49. Snow, *Red Star over China*, 205–10.
50. Lillian Li, *Fighting Famine in North China*, 304.
51. Godement, *"La Famine de 1928 à 1930,"* 90–93.
52. Ibid., 10.
53. CIFRC, *Famine in China's Northwest*, 3.
54. Waldron, *From War to Nationalism*.
55. Courtney, *The Nature of Disaster in China*.
56. Xia, *Minguo shiqi zaihai*, 384–99.
57. Janku, "From Natural to National Disaster," 228, 235–36, and 43.
58. Zheng, *Never Forget National Humiliation*, 71–94.
59. Pomeranz, *The Making of a Hinterland*.
60. Quoted in Murdock, *Disarming the Allies of Imperialism*, 118–19 and 163.
61. Latourette, *A History of Christian Missions in China*, 768–69 and 821–22.
62. Spence, *The Search for Modern China*, 361.
63. Thaxton, *Salt of the Earth*, 115 and 249.
64. Thornton, *Disciplining the State*, 86–87. See also Strauss, *Strong Institutions in Weak Polities*, 89.
65. Muscolino, *The Ecology of War in China*.
66. Wong, "Qing Granaries," 497–98. This point has wider implications for the understanding of the evolution of the state in general. "The dominant logic in many accounts of state formation stresses two aspects of power," Wong writes—control over territory and extraction of wealth. "The Chinese case suggests that preindustrial states could do much more" (ibid., 505–6).
67. "Confucian Agendas," 321. Wong adds that "it remains easy—because of our reliance on European models—to ignore the larger edifice of political structure and ideology within which local government and social order issues were constructed in late imperial times and which informed the range of possibilities for post-imperial politics" (ibid., 324).
68. Edgerton-Tarpley, "From 'Nourish the People' to 'Sacrifice for the Nation.'"

69. Yang, *Tombstone*; Wemheuer, *Famine Politics in Maoist China and the Soviet Union*; Brown, *City versus Countryside in Mao's China*.

Epilogue

1. Zhang Jungu, *Wu Peifu zhuan*, 64–79; Meng and Meng, *Feng Yuxiang*, 103; Waldron, *From War to Nationalism*; A. Nathan, *Peking Politics*; Sheridan, *Chinese Warlord*.
2. Pomeranz, "Water to Iron," 92.
3. Jung Chang, *Wild Swans*, 33.
4. Wu Shizhou, *Minguo renwu chuohao zatan*, 179–82.
5. Li Lunbo, "Wang Huaiqing er san shi," 183.
6. "Dui matong qingyou duzhong de matong jiangjun," *China Daily*, 17 August 2010.
7. *Shihua*, 7 November 1920; *Chenbao*, 20 December 1920.

Appendix

1. Other notable encampments were in Tianjin's Hedongqu and Hebeiqu districts. *Da gongbao*, 7 November 1920.
2. *Shibao*, 13 November 1920.
3. *Da gongbao*, 24 August 1920.
4. *North China Star*, 26 April 1921.
5. *Da gongbao*, 1 November 1920.
6. Xu Youchun, *Minguo renwu*, 2126.
7. *Da gongbao*, 15 and 19 November and 23 December 1920.
8. *Da gongbao*, 24 November 1920.
9. *Da gongbao*, 1 December 1920.
10. *Da gongbao*, 27 December 1920.
11. Rogaski, *Hygienic Modernity*.
12. *Da gongbao*, 1 December 1920.
13. *Chenbao*, 10 October 1920.
14. *Da gongbao*, 25 December 1920.
15. *Chenbao*, 25 December 1920; *Da gongbao*, 27 December 1920.
16. *Da gongbao*, 6 and 9 December 1920.
17. *North China Star*, 26 April 1921.

Bibliography

The following abbreviations are used in the notes and bibliography.

BJZH   Beijing shi difang zhi bianzuan weiyuan hui
BMA   Beijing Municipal Archives
CIFRC   China International Famine Relief Commission
FO   Foreign Office Archives, Kew, London
HIA   Hoover Institute Archives, Stanford
NLC   National Library of China, Beijing
NYPL   New York Public Library
PUIFRC   Peking United International Famine Relief Committee
SD   Records of the Department of State relating to internal affairs of China
         (microfilm)
SOAS   School of Oriental and African Studies Archives, London
XZ   *xianzhi* (county/district gazetteer)
ZGDAG   Zhongguo dier lishi dang'an guan

Gazetteers

Cang XZ 1933
Ci XZ 1941
Ding XZ 1934
Dingzhou shizhi 1998
Guangzong XZ 1933
Guangzong xian jiuzhi jiaozhu 2001
Haixing XZ 2002
Handan XZ 1939
Jing XZ 1932
Jingxing XZ 1934

Mancheng XZ 1997
Nangong XZ 1936
Nanpi XZ 1932
Ning jin XZ 1929
Ning jin XZ 1999
Qing XZ 1931
Qinghe XZ 1934
Qiu XZ 2001
Shunping XZ 1999
Wan XZ 1934
Wanxian xinzhi 1934
Wei XZ 1929
Wuji XZ 1936
Wuqiang XZ 1996
Xingtai shizhi 2001
Xinhe XZ 1929
Xinhe XZ 2000
Zhaicheng cunzhi 1925
Zhuo XZ 1935

Periodicals

Aiguo baihua bao 愛國白話報 (Beijing)
Baihua guoqiang bao 白話國強報 (Beijing)
Beijing baihua bao 北京白話報
Beijing ribao 北京日報
Beijing wanbao 北京晚報
Celestial Empire (Shanghai)
Chenbao [The Morning Post] 晨報 (Beijing)
China Daily (Beijing)
China Sun (Tianjin)
Da gongbao [L'Impartial] 大公報 (Tianjin)
Da Hanbao 大漢報 (Hankou)
Fengsheng 峰聲 (Beijing)
Fengtian gongbao (Shenyang)
Graphic (London)
Guobao [The Nation] 國報 (Beijing)
Guomin xinbao [The National Gazette] 國民新報 (Hankou)
Hankou xinwenbao 漢口新聞報
Hankou zhongxi bao 漢口中西報
Jichang ribao 吉長日報 (Changchun and Jilin)
Jingbao [The Peking Press] 京報 (Beijing)
Jiuzai zhoukan [Famine Relief Weekly] 救災周刊 (Beijing)
Laifu bao 來復報 (Taiyuan)
Lingxue yaozhi 靈學要誌 (Beijing)

Minguo ribao 民國日報 (Shanghai)
Minsheng yuekan 民生月刊 (Beijing)
Minyi ribao 民意日報 (Beijing)
North China Herald (Shanghai)
North China Standard (Beijing)
North China Star (Tianjin)
Peking Leader (Beijing)
Peking & Tientsin Times (Tianjin)
Qunbao [Social Reports] 羣報 (Beijing)
Shanbao 善報 (Beijing)
Shanghai Gazette
Shanghai Times
Shangye ribao 商業日報 (Beijing)
Shenbao [Chinese Daily News] 申報 (Shanghai)
Sheng jing shibao 盛京時報 (Shenyang)
Shibao [Eastern Times] 時報 (Shanghai)
Shihua [The Daily Truth] 實話 (Beijing)
Shishi xinbao 時事新報 (Shanghai)
Shuntian shibao 順天時報 (Beijing)
Tianjin zhongmei ribao 天津中美日報
Times (London)
Xiao gongbao 小公報 (Beijing)
Xiao minbao 小民報 (Beijing)
Xibei ribao 西北日報 (Xi'an)
Xin shehui bao 新社會報 (Beijing)
Xin shenbao 新申報 (Shanghai)
Yishi bao [Social Welfare] 益世報 (Tianjin and Beijing)
Yuandong bao 遠東報 (Harbin)
Zhengfu gongbao 政府公報 (Beijing)
Zhenzai ribao 賑災日報 (Beijing)
Zhongguo minbao 中國民報 (Beijing)

Other Primary Sources

Arnold, Julean. *China: A Commercial and Industrial Handbook.* Washington: Government Printing Office, 1926.

Baker, John Earl, ed. *Report of the China Famine Relief, American Red Cross, October 1920–September, 1921.* Shanghai: Commercial Press, 1921.

"Baoan jingcha er dui baogao" [Report of Public Security Police Unit 2], case no. 57, March 1919. Jingshi jingcha ting [Municipal Police Bureau], BMA J181-018-10687.

Barbour, George B. *In China When . . .* Cincinnati, OH: University of Cincinnati Press, 1975.

Barbour, Margaret Hart. "One Corner of the China Famine Field." In *A St. Mary's Teacher in the Famine District of China,* 5–16. Hartford, CT: Church Missions Publishing Company, November 1932–January 1933.

BJZH. *Beijing zhi: baoye, tongxun she zhi* [Gazetteer of Beijing: newspapers and communications). Beijing: Beijing chuban she, 2005.

Bredon, Juliet. *Peking: A Historical and Intimate Description of Its Chief Places of Interest.* Shanghai: Kelly and Walsh, 1922.

Brooks, Rachel. "The YMCA Government of China, with a preface by Bertrand Russell." Unpublished manuscript, typescript 394, box 185 [1934]? NYPL.

Chen Shanchang. "Wang Huaiqing songde bei [Stele extolling the virtue of Wang Huaiqing]." 1920. NLC online digital catalogue, *guji* [Ancient Documents], *beitie jinghua* [Stele Transcriptions]. Accessed 2 December 2018. http://mylib.nlc.cn/web/guest /search/beitiejinghua/medaDataDisplay?metaData.id=609411&metaData.lId =613892&IdLib=40283415347ed8bd013483503a050012

Chinese Eastern Railway. *North Manchuria and the Chinese Eastern Railway.* Harbin: C.E.R. Printing Office, 1924.

Chinese Government Railways. *Guide to Peking: Peking-Hankow and Peking-Suiyuan Lines, 1920.* Peking: Bureau of Engraving and Printing, 1920.

CIFRC. *Annual Report 1923.* Peiping [Beijing]: CIFRC, 1924.

———. *Annual Report 1926.* Peiping [Beijing]: CIFRC, 1927.

———. *Annual Report 1927.* Peiping [Beijing]: CIFRC, 1928.

———. *Annual Report 1928.* Peiping [Beijing]: CIFRC, 1929.

———. *Annual Report 1929.* Peiping [Beijing]: CIFRC, 1930.

———. *Annual Report 1930.* Peiping [Beijing]: CIFRC, 1931.

———. *Famine in China's Northwest: American Red Cross Commission's Findings and Rejoinders Thereto.* Peiping [Beijing]: CIFRC, June 1930.

———. *Fifteenth Anniversary Book, 1921–1936.* Peiping [Beijing]: CIFRC, 1936.

Crow, Carl. *The Travelers' Handbook for China (Including Hong Kong).* 3rd ed. Shanghai: Carl Crow, 1921.

Darroch, J. *Report of the Central China Famine Relief Fund Committee.* Shanghai: North China Daily News and Herald, 1907.

Dittmer, C. G. "An Estimate of the Standard of Living in China." *Quarterly Journal of Economics* 33, no. 1 (November 1918): 107–28.

"Dui matong qingyou duzhong de matong jiangjun" [Toilet general with a special liking for the toilet]. *China Daily,* 17 August 2010. Accessed 17 September 2011. http:// www.chinadaily.com.cn/hqpl/yssp/2010-08-17/content_719783_2.html.

Freeman, Mansfield. "Observations on Famine Relief Work." *Millard's Review of the Far East,* 21 May 1921, 621.

Fuller, Stuart, and M. T. Liang, eds. *Statement of Aims and Report on Famine Conditions and How They Are Being Met, with Map of the Famine Region.* Tianjin: Tientsin Press for the North China International Society for Famine Relief cooperating with the Chinese Foreign Relief Committee, Shanghai, 1920.

Gamble, Sidney D. *Peking: A Social Survey.* New York: George H. Doran, 1921.

———. *Ting Hsien: A North China Community.* New York: Institute of Pacific Relations, 1954.

Hsu, Leonard S. *Study of a Typical Chinese Town: What Survey Revealed in Ching Ho, North China, Which Was Taken as Example.* Peiping [Beijing]: Leader Press, 1929.

[Illegible]. "Jiang Chaozong dezheng bei" [Stele commemorating the virtuous governance of Jiang Chaozong]. 1918. NLC online digital catalogue, *guji* [Ancient Documents], *beitie jinghua* [Stele Transcriptions]. Accessed 2 December 2018. http://mylib.nlc.cn /web/guest/search/beitiejinghua/medaDataDisplay?metaData.id=612352&metaData .IId=616833&IdLib=40283415347ed8bd013483503a050012

Imperial Japanese Government Railways. *An Official Guide to Eastern Asia: Transcontinental Connections between Europe and Asia.* Vol. 1: *Manchuria and Chosen.* Tokyo: Imperial Japanese Government Railways, 1913.

Jarman, Robert L., ed. *China Political Reports, 1911–1960.* Vol. 1: *1911–1921.* Chippenham, UK: Anthony Rove, 2001.

Jingji zhouchang choubanchu. *Zhengxin baogao shu* [Report of receipts and expenditures]. BMA J181-018-22110.

Lee, Frederick. *Travel Talks on China.* Washington: Review and Herald Publishing Association, 1926.

Li Lunbo. "Wang Huaiqing er san shi" [Two or three things about Wang Huaiqing]. *Wenshi ziliao xuanji, hedingben* (2010): 183–88.

"Liang shi yixing" [The righteous acts of Ms. Liang]. *Lingxue yaozhi,* September 1920, *yiwen* [anecdotes of excellence]: 8–9.

"Lingxue yaozhi yuanqi" [The origins of Lingxue yaozhi]. *Lingxue yaozhi,* September 1920, 1.

MacNair, Harley Farnsworth. *With the White Cross in China: The Journal of a Famine Relief Worker with a Preliminary Essay by Way of Introduction.* Beijing: Henri Vetch, 1939.

McElroy, Robert. *Aims and Organization of the China Society of America.* China Society Pamphlets, no. 1. New York: China Society of America, 1923.

Mei Souzhu, and Liu Yizhi. *Yishi yutai: Minguo chunian Beijing shenghuo baitai* [*Yishibao* extracts: Life in Beijing in the early years of the republic]. Beijing: Beijing daxue chubanshe, 2014.

Missionary Echo of the United Methodist Church. Vol. 20. London: Henry Hooks, 1922.

Morrison, George E. *The Correspondence of G. E. Morrison.* Vol. 2: *1912–1920.* Edited by Lo Hui-Min. Cambridge: Cambridge University Press, 1978.

Patterson, Don. "The Journalism in China." *University of Missouri Bulletin* 23, no. 34 (December 1922): 36–58.

Powell, John Benjamin, and Hollington Kong Tong, eds. *Who's Who in China.* Shanghai: Millard's Review, 1920.

PUIFRC. *The North China Famine of 1920–21 with Special Reference to the West Chihli Area.* Beijing: PUIFRC, 1922. Reprint. Taipei: Ch'eng Wen, 1971.

Ramsay, Alex. *The Peking Who's Who, 1922.* Beijing: Tientsin Press, 1922.

Sanger, J. W. *Advertising Methods in Japan, China and the Philippines.* Special Agents Series No. 209, U.S. Department of Commerce. Washington: Government Printing Office, 1921.

Seton, Grace Thompson. *Chinese Lanterns.* New York: Dodd, Mead and Company, 1924.

Shanxi tongzhi juan 35: Minzheng zhi [Shanxi annals, vol. 35: Civil governance]. Taiyuan: Zhonghua shuju, 1996.

Stauffer, Milton, ed. *The Christian Occupation of China: A General Survey of the Numerical Strength and Geographical Distribution of the Christian Forces in China.* Shanghai: Special Committee on Survey and Occupation, 1918–1921, China Continuation Committee, 1922.

Taylor, Mrs. Howard. "Mrs. Howard Taylor's Trip and Journal—Last Visit to China." Typescript, CIM/PP/482 Box 25 1919–23, SOAS.

Tharp, Robert. *They Called Us White Chinese: The Story of a Lifetime of Service to God and Mankind.* Charlotte, NC: Delmar Printing and Publishing Co, 1994.

Tong, Y. L. (Tang Yueliang). "Social Conditions and Social Service Endeavor in Peking." *Chinese Social and Political Science Review* 7:3 (1923): 75–93.

Trued, Alfred. "The Famine." In *Our Second Decade in China, 1915–1925: Sketches and Reminiscences by Missionaries of the Augustana Synod Mission in the Province of Honan,* Augustana Synod Missionaries, 107–13. Minneapolis: Board of Foreign Missions, 1925.

Tsu, Y. Y. "Native Charities of Shanghai." In *China Missionary Yearbook 1917,* edited by E. C. Lobenstine, 503–11. Shanghai: Christian Literature Society for China, 1917.

Waln, Nora. *The House of Exile.* Boston: Little, Brown, 1935.

Wang Huaiqing. Preface to Jingji zhouchang choubanchu, *Zhengxin baogao shu* [Report of receipts and expenditures]. BMA J181-018-22110, 3.

Wang Jingfu. "Jiang Chaozong shilüe [A historical sketch of Jiang Chaozong]." *Zhonghua wenshi ziliao wenku,* no. 9 (1996): 656–66.

Woodhead, H. G. W. *Adventures in Far Eastern Journalism: A Record of Thirty-Three Years' Experience.* Tokyo: Hokuseido Press, 1935.

Xiong Xiling, *Xiong Xiling xiansheng yigao: diangao yi* [Posthumous writings of Mr. Xiong Xiling: telegrams, volume I]. Shanghai: Shanghai shudian chuban she, 1998.

Yan Huiqing. "Yen Hui-ch'ing." Unpublished manuscript, box 1, folder "Yen, W.W. Chapters VI-XI," HIA.

ZGDAG. *Zhonghua minguo shi dang'an ziliao huibian* [Compilation of archival materials from the Chinese Republic]. Vols. 2 and 3. Nanjing: Jiangsu guji chuban she, 1991.

Zhang Zhaoyin. "Wang [Huaiqing] songde bei [Stele extolling the virtue of Wang (Huaiqing)]." December 1920. NLC online digital catalogue, *guji* [Ancient Documents], *beitie jinghua* [Stele Transcriptions]. Accessed 2 December 2018. http://mylib .nlc.cn/web/guest/search/beitiejinghua/medaDataDisplay?metaData.id =609614&metaData.lId=614095&IdLib=40283415347ed8bd013483503a050012

Zhao Shixian. "Wo suo zhidao de Wang Huaiqing" [The Wang Huaiqing I knew]. *Zhonghua wenshi ziliao wenku,* no. 9 (1996): 174–79.

Secondary Sources

Alitto, Guy. *The Last Confucian: Liang Shuming and the Chinese Dilemma of Modernity.* Berkeley: University of California Press, 1979.

Allen, Frederick Lewis. *Only Yesterday: An Informal History of the Nineteen-Twenties.* New York: Harper and Brothers, 1931.

Arkush, David. "The Moral World of Hebei Village Opera." In *Ideas across Cultures: Essays on Chinese Thought in Honor of Benjamin I. Schwartz,* edited by Paul A. Cohen and Merle Goldman, 87–107. Cambridge, MA: Council on East Asian Studies, Harvard University, 1990.

Asen, Daniel. *Death in Beijing: Murder and Forensic Science in Republican China*. Cambridge: Cambridge University Press, 2016.

Austin, Alvyn J. *Saving China: Canadian Missionaries in the Middle Kingdom, 1888–1959*. Toronto: University of Toronto Press, 1986.

Barnett, Michael. *Empire of Humanity: A History of Humanitarianism*. Ithaca, NY: Cornell University Press, 2011.

Beasley, W. G. *Japanese Imperialism, 1894–1945*. Oxford: Oxford University Press, 1987.

Belsky, Richard. *Localities at the Center: Native Place, Space, and Power in Late Imperial China*. Cambridge, MA: Harvard University Asia Center, 2005.

Bennett, Christina, and Matthew Foley. *Time to Let Go: Remaking Humanitarian Action for the Modern Era*. London: Overseas Development Institute, 2016.

Bergère, Marie-Claire. "Une crise de subsistence en Chine (1920–1922)." *Annales. Histoire, Science Sociales* 28, no. 6 (November–December, 1973): 1361–402.

Bianchi, Alice. "The Representation of Victims of Disasters in Ming and Qing Paintings." Paper presented at the Comparative Study of Disasters and Upheavals: Perceptions and Responses Conference, Southwest University for Nationalities, Chengdu, China, 18 October 2015.

Bianco, Lucien. "Numbers in Social History: How Credible? Counting Disturbances in Rural China (1900–1949)." In *The Study of Modern China*, edited by Eberhard Sandschneider, 255–83. London: Hurst, 1999.

Billingsley, Phil. *Bandits in Republican China*. Stanford, CA: Stanford University Press, 1988.

Boorman, Howard L. *Biographical Dictionary of Republican China*. Vol. 2. New York: Columbia University Press, 1968.

Brokaw, Cynthia J. *The Ledgers of Merit and Demerit: Social Change and Moral Order in Late Imperial China*. Princeton, NJ: Princeton University Press, 1991.

Brook, Timothy, and B. Michael Frolic. "The Ambiguous Challenge of Civil Society." In *Civil Society in China*, edited by Timothy Brook and B. Michael Frolic, 3–16. Armonk, NY: M. E. Sharpe, 1997.

Brown, Jeremy. *City versus Countryside in Mao's China: Negotiating the Divide*. Cambridge: Cambridge University Press, 2012.

Buck, David D. *Urban Change in China: Politics and Development in Tsinan, Shantung, 1890–1949*. Madison: University of Wisconsin Press, 1978.

Buck, J. Lossing. *Land Utilization in China: A Study of 16,786 Farms in 168 Localities, and 38,256 Farms, in Twenty-Two Provinces in China, 1929–1933*. Chicago: University of Chicago Press, 1937.

———. "Price Changes in China: The Effects of Famine and the Recent Rise in Prices." *Journal of the American Statistical Association* 20, no. 150 (June 1925): 238–41.

Cabanes, Bruno. *The Great War and the Origins of Humanitarianism, 1918–1924*. Cambridge: Cambridge University Press, 2014.

Cao Shuji. *Zhongguo yimin shi* [A history of migrants in China]. Vol. 6. Fuzhou: Fujian renmin chuban she, 1997.

Cao, Xinyu. "From Famine History to Crisis Metaphor: Social Memory and Cultural Identity in Chinese Rural Society." *Chinese Studies in History* 44, nos. 1–2 (Fall 2010–Winter 2010–11): 156–71.

Carter, James H. *Creating a Chinese Harbin: Nationalism in an International City, 1916–1932*. Ithaca, NY: Cornell University Press, 2002.

———. *Heart of Buddha, Heart of China: The Life of Tanxu, a Twentieth-Century Monk*. Oxford: Oxford University Press, 2011.

Chan, Wing-tsit. *Religious Trends in Modern China*. New York: Columbia University Press, 1953.

Chang, Jung. *Wild Swans*. London: Flamingo, 1993.

Chen, Janet Y. *Guilty of Indigence: The Urban Poor in China, 1900–1953*. Princeton, NJ: Princeton University Press, 2012.

Chen, Jerome. "Defining Chinese Warlords and Their Factions." *Bulletin of the School of Oriental and African Studies* 39, no. 3 (1968): 563–600.

Cheng, Linsun. *Banking in Modern China: Entrepreneurs, Professional Managers, and the Development of Chinese Banks, 1897–1937*. Cambridge: Cambridge University Press, 2003.

Ch'i, Hsi-Sheng. *Warlord Politics in China, 1916–1928*. Stanford, CA: Stanford University Press, 1976.

Chu, Coching, John Lee, and Pao-Kun Chang. *The Temperature of China*. Nanjing: National Research Institute of Metereology, Academia Sinica, 1940.

Cochran, Sherman. *Big Business in China: Sino-Foreign Rivalry in the Cigarette Industry, 1890–1930*. Cambridge, MA: Harvard University Press, 1980.

Courtney, Chris. *The Nature of Disaster in China: The 1931 Yangzi River Flood*. Cambridge: Cambridge University Press, 2018.

Cranmer-Byng, L., trans. *"Lute of Jade": Being Selections from the Classical Poets of China*. London: J. Murray, 1911.

De Ville de Goyet, Claude. "Stop Propagating Disaster Myths." *Lancet* 356 (August 26, 2000): 762–64.

Devereux, Stephen. *Theories of Famine*. New York: Harvester Wheatsheaf, 1993.

Dikötter, Frank. *The Age of Openness: China before Mao*. Berkeley: University of California Press, 2008.

———. *Mao's Great Famine: The History of China's Most Devastating Catastrophe, 1958–62*. London: Bloomsbury, 2010.

Dillon, Nara. "The Politics of Philanthropy: Social Networks and Refugee Relief in Shanghai, 1932–1949." In *At the Crossroads of Empires: Middlemen, Social Networks, and State-Building in Republican Shanghai*, edited by Nara Dillon and Jean C. Oi, 179–205. Stanford, CA: Stanford University Press, 2008.

Dillon, Nara, and Jean C. Oi, eds. *At the Crossroads of Empires: Middlemen, Social Networks, and State-Building in Republican Shanghai*. Stanford, CA: Stanford University Press, 2008.

Ding Rui. *Guanli Beijing: Beiyang zhengfu shiqi jingshi jingchating yanjiu* [Managing Beijing: the municipal police force during the Beiyang era]. Taiyuan: Shanxi renmin chuban she, 2013.

Dong, Madeleine Yue. *Republican Beijing: The City and Its Histories*. Berkeley: University of California Press, 2003.

Dray-Novey, Alison J. "The Twilight of the Beijing Gendarmerie, 1900–1924." *Modern China* 33, no. 3 (July 2007): 349–76.

Duara, Prasenjit. *Culture, Power, and the State: Rural North China, 1900–1942*. Stanford, CA: Stanford University Press, 1988.

———. "Of Authenticity and Woman: Personal Narratives of Middle-Class Women in Modern China." In *Becoming Chinese: Passages to Modernity and Beyond*, edited by Wen-hsin Yeh, 342–64. Berkeley: University of California Press, 2000.

Dubois, Thomas. *The Sacred Village: Social Change and Religious Life in Rural North China*. Honolulu: University of Hawai'i Press, 2005.

Dulles, Foster Rhea. *The Red Cross: A History*. New York: Harper and Brothers, 1950.

Dunscomb, Paul E. *Japan's Siberian Intervention, 1918–1922: "A Great Disobedience against the People."* Lanham, MD: Rowman and Littlefield, 2011.

Edgerton-Tarpley, Kathryn Jean. "From 'Nourish the People' to 'Sacrifice for the Nation': Changing Responses to Disaster in Late Imperial and Modern China." *Journal of Asian Studies* 73, no. 2 (May 2014): 447–69.

———. *Tears from Iron: Cultural Responses to Famine in Nineteenth-Century China*. Berkeley: University of California Press, 2008.

Egan, Eleanor Franklin. "Fighting the Chinese Famine." *Saturday Evening Post*, 9 April 1921.

Ekbladh, David. *The Great American Mission: Modernization and the Construction of an American World Order*. Princeton, NJ: Princeton University Press, 2010.

Elvin, Mark. *The Retreat of the Elephants: An Environmental History of China*. New Haven, CT: Yale University Press, 2004.

Esherick, Joseph. *The Origins of the Boxer Uprising*. Berkeley: University of California Press, 1987.

Fassin, Didier. *Humanitarian Reason: A Moral History of the Present*. Berkeley: University of California Press, 2012.

Feuerwerker, Albert. *The Chinese Economy, 1870–1949*. Ann Arbor: University of Michigan, Center for Chinese Studies, 1995.

Flath, James, and Norman Smith, eds. *Beyond Suffering: Recounting War in Modern China*. Vancouver: University of British Columbia Press, 2011.

French, Paul. *Through the Looking Glass: China's Foreign Journalists from Opium Wars to Mao*. Hong Kong: Hong Kong University Press, 2010.

Fuller, Pierre. "'Barren Soil, Fertile Minds': North China Famine and Visions of the 'Callous Chinese' Circa 1920." *International History Review* 33, no. 3 (September 2011): 453–72.

————. "Decentring International and Institutional Famine Relief in Late Nineteenth Century China: In Search of the Local." *European Review of History/Revue Européene d'Histoire* 22, no. 6 (July 2015): 873–89.

————. "Struggling with Famine in Warlord China: Social Networks, Achievements and Limitations, 1920–21." PhD diss., University of California, Irvine, 2011.

Fuma Susumu. *Zhongguo shanhui citing shi yanjiu* [A history of Chinese charities and benevolent halls]. Beijing: Shangwu yinshu guan, 2005.

Gates, Hill. *China's Motor: A Thousand Years of Petty Capitalism.* Ithaca, NY: Cornell University Press, 1996.

Gatrell, Peter. *The Making of the Modern Refugee.* Oxford: Oxford University Press, 2013.

Gillin, Donald. *Warlord: Yen Hsi-shan in Shansi Province, 1911–1949.* Princeton, NJ: Princeton University Press, 1967.

Godement, François. "La famine de 1928 à 1930 en Chine du Nord et du Centre." MA thesis, Université Paris VII, 1970.

Goikhman, Izabella. "Chen Jiongming: Becoming a Warlord in Republican China." In "State, Society and Governance in Republican," special issue, *Berliner China-Hefte* 43 (2013): 77–101.

Goodman, Bryna. *Native Place, City, and Nation: Regional Networks and Identities in Shanghai, 1853–1937.* Berkeley: University of California Press, 1995.

————. "What Is in a Network? Local, Personal, and Public Loyalties in the Context of Changing Conceptions of the State and Social Welfare." In *At the Crossroads of Empires: Middlemen, Social Networks, and State-Building in Republican Shanghai*, edited by Nara Dillon and Jean C. Oi, 155–78. Stanford, CA: Stanford University Press, 2008.

Goossaert, Vincent. *The Taoists of Peking, 1800–1949: A Social History of Urban Clerics.* Cambridge, MA: Harvard University Asia Center, 2007.

Gottschang, Thomas R., and Diana Lary. *Swallows and Settlers: The Great Migration from North China to Manchuria.* Ann Arbor: University of Michigan, Center for Chinese Studies, 2000.

Grant, Peter. *Philanthropy and Voluntary Action in the First World War.* London: Routledge, 2014.

Green, Abigail. "Humanitarianism in Nineteenth-Century Context: Religious, Gendered, National." *Historical Journal* 57, no. 4 (2014): 1157–75.

Guo Jianlin. *Wu Peifu da zhuan* [A biography of Wu Peifu]. Beijing: Tuanjie chubanshe, 2012.

Harrison, Henrietta. *The Making of the Republican Citizen: Political Ceremonies and Symbols in China, 1911–1929.* Oxford: Oxford University Press, 2000.

————. *The Man Awakened from Dreams: One Man's Life in a North China Village, 1857–1942.* Stanford, CA: Stanford University Press, 2005.

————. "Newspapers and Nationalism in Rural China 1890–1919." *Past and Present* 166 (2000): 181–204.

Henriot, Christian. "'Invisible Deaths, Silent Deaths': Bodies without Masters in Republican Shanghai." *Journal of Social History* 43, no. 2 (Winter 2009): 407–37.

Henriot, Christian, and Wen-hsin Yeh, eds. *In the Shadow of the Rising Sun: Shanghai under Japanese Occupation*. Cambridge: Cambridge University Press, 2004.

Hershatter, Gail. *Dangerous Pleasures: Prostitution and Modernity in Twentieth-Century Shanghai*. Berkeley: University of California Press, 1997.

———. *The Gender of Memory: Rural Women and China's Collective Past*. Berkeley: University of California Press, 2011.

Huang, Philip C. C., ed. "Paradigmatic Issues in Chinese Studies," special issue, *Modern China* 19, no. 2 (April 1993).

———. *The Peasant Economy and Social Change in North China*. Stanford, CA: Stanford University Press, 1985.

———. "'Public Sphere'/'Civil Society' in China? The Third Realm between State and Society." In Philip C. Huang, ed., "Paradigmatic Issues in Chinese Studies," special issue, *Modern China* 19, no. 2 (April 1993): 216–40.

Iriye, Akira. *After Imperialism: The Search for a New Order in the Far East, 1921–1931*. Cambridge, MA: Harvard University Press, 1965.

Irwin, Julia F. *Making the World Safe: The American Red Cross and a Nation's Humanitarian Awakening*. Oxford: Oxford University Press, 2013.

Janku, Andrea. "From Natural to National Disaster: the Chinese Famine of 1928–1930." In *Historical Disasters in Context: Science, Religion, and Politics*, edited by Andrea Janku, Gerrit Jasper Schenk, and Franz Mauelshagen, 227–60. London: Routledge, 2011.

———. "Sowing Happiness: Spiritual Competition in Famine Relief Activities in Late Nineteenth-Century China." In "Disasters and Religion," special issue, *Minsu quyi/Journal of Chinese Ritual, Theatre and Folklore* 143 (March 2004): 89–118.

Johnson, David. *Spectacle and Sacrifice: The Ritual Foundations of Village Life in North China*. Cambridge, MA: Harvard University Asia Center, 2009.

Kang Peizhu, and Xia Mingfang, eds. *20 shiji Zhongguo zaibian tushi* [A history of Chinese disasters of the twentieth century]. Fuzhou: Fujian jiaoyu chuban she, 2001.

Kaplan, Steven L. *The Stakes of Regulation: Perspectives on* Bread, Politics and Political Economy *Forty Years Later*. London: Anthem Press, 2015.

Katz, Paul. *Religion in China and Its Modern Fate*. Waltham, MA: Brandeis University Press, 2014.

Kiely, Jan, and J. Brooks Jessup. Introduction to *Reconsidering Buddhism in Modern China*, edited by Jan Kiely and J. Brooks Jessup, 1–33. New York: Columbia University Press, 2016.

Konishi, Sho. "The Emergence of an International Humanitarian Organization in Japan: The Tokugawa Origins of the Japanese Red Cross." *American Historical Review* 119, no. 4 (October 2014): 1129–53.

Kuhn, Philip A. "Local Self-Government under the Republic: Problems of Control, Autonomy, and Mobilization." In *Conflict and Control in Late Imperial China*, edited by Frederic Wakeman Jr., and Carolyn Grant, 257–99. Berkeley: University of California Press, 1975.

Lary, Diana. *The Chinese People at War: Human Suffering and Social Transformation, 1937–1945.* Cambridge: Cambridge University Press, 2010.

———. Foreword to David Bonavia, *China's Warlords*, vii–viii. Oxford: Oxford University Press, 1995.

———. *Warlord Soldiers: Chinese Common Soldiers, 1911–1937.* Cambridge: Cambridge University Press, 1985.

Lary, Diana, and Stephen MacKinnon, eds. *The Scars of War: The Impact of Warfare on Modern China.* Vancouver: University of British Columbia Press, 2001.

Latourette, Kenneth Scott. *A History of Christian Missions in China.* New York: Macmillan, 1932.

Li, Huaiyin. *Village Governance in North China, 1875–1936.* Stanford, CA: Stanford University Press, 2005.

Li, Lillian. *Fighting Famine in North China: State, Market, and Environmental Decline, 1690s–1990s.* Stanford, CA: Stanford University Press, 2007.

Li Wenhai and Xia Mingfang, eds. *Tian you xiongnian: Qing dai zaihuang yu Zhongguo shehui* [Heaven sends terrible years: Qing-era disasters and Chinese society]. Beijing: Sanlian shudian, 2007.

Li Zhongming. *Jing ju dashi: Mei Lanfang* [Master of Beijing opera: Mei Lanfang]. Beijing: Minzhu yu jianshe chubanshe, 2011.

Liang Qizi. *Shishan yu jiaohua: Ming Qing de cishan zuzhi* [Dispensing charity and culture: Philanthropic organization in the Ming and Qing]. Shijiazhuang: Hebei jiayu chuban she, 2001.

Lin, Alfred H. Y. "Warlord, Social Welfare and Philanthropy: The Case of Guangzhou under Chen Jitang, 1929–1936." *Modern China* 30, no. 2 (April 2004): 151–98.

Lin Yutang. *A History of the Press and Public Opinion in China.* New York: Greenwood Press, 1968.

Lincoln, Toby. *Urbanizing China in War and Peace: The Case of Wuxi County.* Honolulu: University of Hawai'i Press, 2015.

Lipkin, Zwia. *Useless to the State: "Social Problems" and Social Engineering in Nationalist Nanjing, 1927–1937.* Cambridge, MA: Harvard University Asia Center, 2006.

Liu, Chang. *Peasants and Revolution in Rural China: Rural Political Change in the North China Plain and the Yangzi Delta, 1850–1949.* London: Routledge, 2007.

Liu Jianyun. *Ni suobushi de Minguo mianxiang: Zhili difang yihui zhengzhi, 1912–1928* [What you don't know about the republic: Zhili local government assemblies]. Guilin: Guangxi shifan daxue chuban she, 2009.

Liu Shoulin, Wan Renyuan, Wang Yuwen, and Kong Qingtai, eds. *Minguo zhiguan nianbiao* [A chronology of official republican posts]. Beijing: Zhongguo shuju, 1995.

Liu Xiaolan, and Wu Chao. *Chuanjiaoshi zhongwen baokan shi* [A history of Chinese missionary periodicals]. Shanghai: Fudan University Press, 2011.

Long, Katy. "When Refugees Stopped Being Migrants: Movement, Labour and Humanitarian Protection." *Migration Studies* 1, no. 1 (2013): 4–26.

Lu Hanchao. *Beyond the Neon Lights: Everyday Shanghai in the Early Twentieth Century.* Berkeley: University of California Press, 2004.

Lu Zhongwei. *Zhongguo mimi shehui juan 5: Minguo huidaomen* [Chinese secret societies volume 5: Republican societies]. Fuzhou: Fujian renmin chuban she, 2002.

Ma Ping'an. *Jindai Dongbei yimin yanjiu* [Modern migration into the northeast]. Jinan: Qilu shushe, 2009.

MacKinnon, Stephen, Diana Lary, and Ezra F. Vogel, eds. *China at War: Regions of China, 1937–45*. Stanford, CA: Stanford University Press, 2007.

Mallory, Walter H. *China: Land of Famine*. New York: American Geographical Society, 1926.

Mann, Susan. *Precious Records: Women in China's Long Eighteenth Century*. Stanford, CA: Stanford University Press, 1997.

Matsusaka, Yoshihisa Tak. *The Making of Japanese Manchuria, 1904–1932*. Cambridge, MA: Harvard University Asia Center, 2001.

Maxwell, Daniel, and Nisar Majid. *Famine in Somalia: Competing Imperatives, Collective Failures, 2011–12*. London: Hurst, 2016.

McCord, Edward A. "Burn, Kill, Rape, and Rob: Military Atrocities, Warlordism, and Anti Warlordism in Republican China." In *Scars of War: The Impact of Warfare on Modern China*, edited by Diana Lary and Stephen MacKinnon, 18–47. Vancouver: University of British Columbia Press, 2001.

———. *Military Force and Elite Power in the Formation of Modern China*. New York: Routledge, 2014.

———. *The Power of a Gun: The Emergence of Modern Chinese Warlordism*. Berkeley: University of California Press, 1993.

———. "Victims and Victimizers: Warlord Soldiers and Mutinies in Republican China." In *Beyond Suffering: Recounting War in Modern China*, edited by James Flath and Norman Smith, 130–52. Vancouver: University of British Columbia Press, 2011.

McCormack, Gavan. *Chang Tso-lin in Northeast China, 1911–1928: China, Japan, and the Manchurian Idea*. Stanford, CA: Stanford University Press, 1977.

Meng Xianxi and Meng Jing. *Feng Yuxiang*. Beijing: Zhongguo wenshi chuban she, 2011.

Merkel-Hess, Kate. *The Rural Modern: Reconstructing the Self and State in Republican China*. Chicago: University of Chicago Press, 2016.

Moniz, Amanda B. *From Empire to Humanity: The American Revolution and the Origins of Humanitarianism*. Oxford: Oxford University Press, 2016.

Murdock, Michael G. *Disarming the Allies of Imperialism: The State, Agitation, and Manipulation during China's Nationalist Revolution, 1922–1929*. Ithaca, NY: Cornell University, East Asia Program, 2006.

Muscolino, Micah. *The Ecology of War in China: Henan Province, the Yellow River and Beyond, 1938–1950*. Cambridge: Cambridge University Press, 2015.

Naquin, Susan. *Peking: Temples and City Life, 1400–1900*. Berkeley: University of California Press, 2000.

Nathan, Andrew. *A History of the China International Famine Relief Commission*. Cambridge, MA: East Asian Research Center, Harvard University, 1965.

———. *Peking Politics. 1918–1923: Factionalism and the Failure of Constitutionalism*. Berkeley: University of California Press, 1976.

Nathan, Carl. *Plague Prevention and Politics in Manchuria, 1910–1931*. Cambridge, MA: East Asian Research Center, Harvard University, 1967.

Ng, Rudolph. "The Yuandongbao 遠東報: A Chinese or a Russian Newspaper?" In *Entangled Histories: The Transcultural Past of Northeast China*, edited by Dan Ben-Canaan, Frank Grüner, Ines Prodöhl, 101–18. New York: Springer, 2014.

Ó Gráda, Cormac. *Famine: A Short History*. Princeton, NJ: Princeton University Press, 2009.

Pantuliano, Sara. Foreword to Christina Bennett and Matthew Foley, *Time to Let Go: Remaking Humanitarian Action for the Modern Era*, 3. London: Overseas Development Institute, 2016.

Patenaude, Bertrand M. *The Big Show in Bololand: The American Relief Expedition to Soviet Russia in the Famine of 1921*. Stanford, CA: Stanford University Press, 2002.

Perry, Elizabeth. *Rebels and Revolutionaries in North China, 1845–1945*. Stanford, CA: Stanford University Press, 1980.

Pietz, David. *The Yellow River: The Problem of Water in Modern China*. Cambridge, MA: Harvard University Press, 2015.

Pomeranz, Kenneth. *The Making of a Hinterland: State, Society, and Economy in Inland North China, 1853–1937*. Berkeley: University of California Press, 1993.

———. "Water to Iron, Widows to Warlords: The Handan Rain Shrine in Modern Chinese History." *Late Imperial China* 12, no. 1 (June 1991): 62–99.

Pong, David. "Confucian Patriotism and the Destruction of the Woosung Railway, 1877." *Modern Asian Studies* 7, no. 4 (1973): 647–76.

Porter, Stephen R. *Benevolent Empire: U.S. Power, Humanitarianism, and the World's Dispossessed*. Philadelphia: University of Pennsylvania Press, 2017.

Rankin, Mary Backus. *Elite Activism and Political Transformation in China: Zhejiang Province, 1865–1911*. Stanford, CA: Stanford University Press, 1986.

———. "State and Society in Early Republican Politics, 1912–18." In *Reappraising Republican China*, edited by Frederic Wakeman Jr. and Richard Louis Edmonds, 6–25. Oxford: Oxford University Press, 2000.

Ransmeier, Johanna S. *Sold People: Traffickers and Family Life in North China*. Cambridge, MA: Harvard University Press, 2017.

Rawski, Evelyn. *The Last Emperors: A Social History of Qing Imperial Institutions*. Berkeley: University of California Press, 1998.

Reardon-Anderson, James. *Reluctant Pioneers: China's Expansion Northward, 1644–1937*. Stanford, CA: Stanford University Press, 2005.

Reisner, John H. *Reforesting China: Permanent Famine Prevention versus Famine Relief*. New York: China Society of America, 1921.

Ren Yunlan. *Jindai Tianjin de cishan yu shehui jiuji* [Charity and social relief in modern Tianjin]. Tianjin: Tianjin renmin chuban she, 2007.

Rhoads, Edward. J. M. *Manchus & Han: Ethnic Relations and Political Power in Late Qing and Early Republican China, 1861–1928*. Seattle: University of Washington Press, 2000.

Ristaino, Marcia R. *The Jacquinot Safe Zone: Wartime Refugees in Shanghai*. Stanford, CA: Stanford University Press, 2008.

Rodogno, Davide. *Against Massacre: Humanitarian Interventions in the Ottoman Empire, 1815–1914.* Princeton, NJ: Princeton University Press, 2012.

Rogaski, Ruth. "Beyond Benevolence: A Confucian Women's Shelter in Treaty-Port China." *Journal of Women's History* 8, no. 4 (Winter 1997): 54–90.

———. *Hygienic Modernity: Meanings of Health and Disease in Treaty-Port China.* Berkeley: University of California Press, 2004.

Rowe, William. *Hankow: Conflict and Community in a Chinese City, 1796–1895.* Stanford, CA: Stanford University Press, 1989.

———. *Saving the World: Chen Hongmou and Elite Consciousness in Eighteenth-Century China.* Stanford, CA: Stanford University Press, 2001.

Schoppa, R. Keith. *In a Sea of Bitterness: Refugees during the Sino-Japanese War.* Cambridge, MA: Harvard University Press, 2011.

Sen, Amartya. *Poverty and Famines: An Essay on Entitlement and Deprivation.* Oxford: Oxford University Press, 2013.

Shao Yong. *Zhongguo huidaomen.* Shanghai: Shanghai renmin chuban she, 1997.

Shavit, David. *The United States in Asia: a Historical Dictionary.* New York: Greenwood Press, 1990.

Shaw, Caroline. *Britannia's Embrace: Modern Humanitarianism and the Imperial Origins of Refugee Relief.* Oxford: Oxford University Press, 2015.

Sheridan, James E. *Chinese Warlord: The Career of Feng Yu-Hsiang.* Stanford, CA: Stanford University Press, 1966.

Shi, Xia. *At Home in the World: Women and Charity in Late Qing and Early Republican China.* New York: Columbia University Press, 2018.

Shue, Vivienne. "The Quality of Mercy: Confucian Charity and the Mixed Metaphors of Modernity in Tianjin." *Modern China* 32, no. 4 (2006): 411–52.

Simon, Karla. *Civil Society in China: The Legal Framework from Ancient Times to the "New Reform Era."* Oxford: Oxford University Press, 2013.

Slack, Edward. *Opium, State and Society: China's Narco-Economy and the Guomindang, 1924–37.* Honolulu: University of Hawai'i Press, 2010.

Smith, Joanna Handlin. *The Art of Doing Good: Charity in Late Ming China.* Berkeley: University of California Press, 2009.

Smith, S. A. *Like Cattle and Horses: Nationalism and Labor in Shanghai, 1895–1927.* Durham, NC: Duke University Press, 2001.

Snow, Edgar. *Red Star over China.* New York: Random House, 1938.

Snyder-Reinke, Jeffrey. *Dry Spells: State Rainmaking and Local Governance in Late Imperial China.* Cambridge, MA: Harvard University Asia Center, 2009.

Spence, Jonathan D. *The Search for Modern China.* New York: Norton, 2013.

Strand, David. *Rickshaw Beijing: City People and Politics in the 1920s.* Berkeley: University of California Press, 1989.

Strauss, Julia. *Strong Institutions in Weak Polities: State Building in Republican China, 1927–1940.* Oxford: Clarendon Press of Oxford University Press, 1998.

Stross, Randall E. *The Stubborn Earth: American Agriculturalists on Chinese Soil, 1898–1937.* Berkeley: University of California Press, 1986.

Su Xinliu. *Minguo shiqi Henan shui han zaihai yu xiangcun shehui* [Drought and flood disasters and rural society in republican Henan]. Zhengzhou: Huanghe shuili chu-banshe, 2004.

Suleski, Ronald Stanley. *Civil Government in Warlord China: Tradition, Modernization and Manchuria.* New York: P. Lang, 2002.

Tan, Chester C. *The Boxer Catastrophe.* New York: Norton, 1971.

Tanielian, Melanie S. *The Charity of War: Famine, Humanitarian Aid, and World War I in the Middle East.* Stanford, CA: Stanford University Press, 2018.

Thaxton, Ralph A., Jr. *Catastrophe and Contention in Rural China: Mao's Great Leap Forward Famine and the Origins of Righteous Resistance in Da Fo Village.* Cambridge: Cambridge University Press, 2008.

———. *Salt of the Earth: The Political Origins of Peasant Protest and Communist Revolution in China.* Berkeley: University of California Press, 1997.

———. "State Making and State Terror: The Formation of the Revenue Police and the Origins of Collective Protest in Rural North China during the Republican Period." *Theory and Society* 19, no. 3 (1990): 335–76.

Thornton, Patricia M. *Disciplining the State: Virtue, Violence, and State-Making in Modern China.* Cambridge, MA: Harvard University Asia Center, 2007.

Ting, Lee-hsia Hsu. *Government Control of the Press in Modern China, 1900–1949.* Cambridge, MA: East Asian Research Center, Harvard University, 1974.

Tsao, Lien-en. *Chinese Migration to the Three Eastern Provinces.* Shanghai: Ministry of Industry, Commerce and Labor, 1930.

Tsin, Michael. *Nation, Governance, and Modernity in China: Canton, 1900–1927.* Stanford, CA: Stanford University Press, 1999.

Twinem, Paul de Witt. "Modern Syncretic Religious Societies in China. I." *Journal of Religion* 5, no. 5 (September 1925): 463–82.

———. "Modern Syncretic Religious Societies in China. II." *Journal of Religion* 5, no. 6 (November 1925): 595–606.

van de Ven, Hans. *Breaking with the Past: The Maritime Customs Service and the Global Origins of Modernity in China.* New York: Columbia University Press, 2014.

———. "Public Finance and the Rise of Warlordism." *Modern Asian Studies* 30, no. 4 (1996): 829–68.

Vernon, James. *Hunger: A Modern History.* Cambridge, MA: Harvard University Press, 2009.

Wakeman, Frederic, Jr. *Policing Shanghai 1927–1937.* Berkeley: University of California Press, 1995.

Wakeman, Frederic, Jr., and Richard Louis Edmonds, eds. *Reappraising Republican China.* Oxford: Oxford University Press, 2000.

Waldron, Arthur. *From War to Nationalism: China's Turning Point, 1924–25.* Cambridge: Cambridge University Press, 1995.

———. "The Warlord: Twentieth-Century Chinese Understandings of Violence, Militarism, and Imperialism." *American Historical Review* 96, no. 4 (October 1991): 1073–100.

Wang, Di. *Street Culture in Chengdu: Public Space, Urban Commoners, and Local Politics, 1870–1930*. Stanford, CA: Stanford University Press, 2003.

Wang Juan. *Jindai Beijing cishan shiye yanjiu* [Charitable organizations in modern Beijing]. Beijing: Renmin chuban she, 2010.

Wang Lin. *Shandong jindai zaihuang shi* [A history of disasters in modern Shandong]. Jinan: Qilu shushe, 2004.

Wang Runze. *Beiyang zhengfu shiqi de xinwenye ji qi xiandaihua, 1916–28* [News organizations and their modernization during the Beiyang period, 1916–28]. Beijing: Zhongguo renmin daxue chuban she, 2010.

———. *Zhang Liluan yu Da gongbao* [Zhang Liluan and *Da gongbao*]. Beijing: Zhonghua shuju, 2008.

Watenpaugh, Keith David. *Bread from Stones: The Middle East and the Making of Modern Humanitarianism*. Oakland: University of California Press, 2015.

Wei, Betty Peh-T'i. *Ruan Yuan, 1764–1849: The Life and Work of a Major Scholar-Official in Nineteenth Century China before the Opium War*. Hong Kong: Hong Kong University Press, 2006.

Wemheuer, Felix. *Famine Politics in Maoist China and the Soviet Union*. New Haven, CT: Yale University Press, 2014.

Weston, Timothy B. "Minding the Newspaper Business: The Theory and Practice of Journalism in 1920s China." *Twentieth-Century China* 31, no. 2 (2006): 4–31.

———. *The Power of Position: Beijing University, Intellectuals, and Chinese Political Culture, 1898–1929*. Berkeley: University of California Press, 2004.

Whelan, T. S. *The Pawnshop in China: Based on Yang Chao-yü, Chung-kuo tien-tang yeh (The Chinese Pawnbroking Industry), with a Historical Introduction and Critical Annotations*. Ann Arbor: University of Michigan, Center for Chinese Studies, 1979.

Will, Pierre-Étienne. *Bureaucracy and Famine in Eighteenth Century China*. Translated by Elborg Forster. Stanford, CA: Stanford University Press, 1990.

Will, Pierre-Étienne, and R. Bin Wong. *Nourish the People: The State Civilian Granary System in China, 1650–1850*. Ann Arbor: Center for Chinese Studies, University of Michigan, 1991.

Wong, Linda. *Marginalization and Social Welfare in China*. London: Routledge, 1998.

Wong, R. Bin. "Confucian Agendas for Material and Ideological Control in Modern China." In *Culture and State in Chinese History: Conventions, Accommodations, and Critiques*, edited by Theodore Huters, R. Bin Wong, and Pauline Yu, 303–25. Stanford, CA: Stanford University Press, 1997.

———. "Qing Granaries and Late Imperial History." In *Nourish the People: The State Civilian Granary System in China, 1650–1850*. Pierre-Étienne Will and R. Bin Wong, 475–506. Ann Arbor: Center for Chinese Studies, University of Michigan, 1991.

Wou, Odoric Y. K. *Militarism in Modern China: The Career of Wu P'ei-Fu, 1916–39*. Folkestone, UK: Dawson, 1978.

Wu Shizhou. *Minguo renwu chuohao zatan* [Nicknames and miscellaneous talk about republican figures]. Zhengzhou: Henan renmin chuban she, 2007.

Wue, Roberta. "The Profits of Philanthropy: Relief Aid, *Shenbao*, and the Art World in Late Nineteenth Century Shanghai." *Late Imperial China* 25, no. 1 (2004): 187–211.

Xia Mingfang. *Minguo shiqi zaihai yu xiangcun shehui* [Disasters and rural society in the republican period]. Beijing: Zhonghua shuju, 2000.

Xu, Yamin. "Policing Civility on the Streets: Encounters with Litterbugs, 'Nightsoil Lords,' and Street Corner Urinators in Republican Beijing." *Twentieth-Century China* 30, no. 2 (April 2005): 28–71.

Xu Youchun, ed. *Minguo renwu da cidian* [Biographical dictionary of republican figures]. Shijiazhuang: Hebei renmin chuban she, 1991.

Yang Jisheng. *Tombstone: The Great Chinese Famine, 1958–1962.* New York: Farrar, Straus and Giroux, 2012.

Yeh, Wen-Hsin. *Shanghai Splendor: Economic Sentiments and the Making of Modern China, 1843–1949.* Berkeley: University of California Press, 2008.

Yu Lingbo, ed. *Xiandai fojiao renwu cidian* [Biographical dictionary of modern Buddhism]. Sanzhong: Foguang chuban she, 2004.

Yue, Tsu Yu. *The Spirit of Chinese Philanthropy: A Study in Mutual Aid.* 1912. Reprint. New York: AMS Press, 1968.

Zarrow, Peter. *China in War and Revolution, 1895–1949.* London: Routledge, 2005.

Zhang Jungu. *Wu Peifu zhuan* [Biography of Wu Peifu]. Beijing: Tuanjie chubanshe, 2006.

Zhang, Qiang, and Robert Weatherley. "The Rise of 'Republican Fever' in the PRC and the Implications for CCP Legitimacy." *China Information* 27, no. 3 (2013): 277–300.

Zhang Xin. *Social Transformation in Modern China: The State and Local Elites in Henan, 1900–1937.* Cambridge: Cambridge University Press, 2000.

Zheng Wang. *Never Forget National Humiliation: Historical Memory in Chinese Politics and Foreign Relations.* New York: Columbia University Press, 2012.

Zhou Qiuguang. *Xiong Xiling zhuan* [Biography of Xiong Xiling]. Tianjin: Baihua wenyi chubanshe, 2006.

Zhu Hu. *Minbao wuyu: Zhongguo jindai yizhen (1876–1912)* [Compatriots above all: modern charity relief in China (1876–1912)]. Beijing: Renmin chubanshe, 2012.

Zucker, A. E. *The Chinese Theater.* Boston: Little, Brown, 1925.

Index

Crane, Charles, 50, 166, 201, 204, 219, 220
credit programs. *See* loans
crime: in Harbin, 197–98; thefts by
refugees, 196. *See also* bandits;
corruption
Cultural and Historical Miscellany
(*Wenshi ziliao*), 85
customs: and famine loan, 165–68;
foreign control, 153, 164; under
Nationalist government, 252; revenues,
164, 166; surtax, 153, 165–66, 168,
246–47, 294n67. *See also* Chinese
Maritime Customs Service

Dachang Tobacco Company, 91, 179
Da gongbao, 24, 38, 251, 259
Dajingcun, 73, 255
Dalian, 187
Daming, 171, 221, 224
Daoism, 79, 80
debt. *See* loans
de Freitas, Batalha, 246
de Ville de Goyet, Claude, 10
Dewey, John, wife of, 201
Dikötter, Frank, 13
Ding County Drought-Disaster Relief
Society (Dingxian hanzai jiuji hui), 154
Diplomatic Body, 164–67, 168, 246–47
Disaster Relief Council (Zhenzai
weiyuan hui), 163
disaster relief policies, Qing, 4–5, 42,
48–49, 54, 63–64, 127–28, 133, 230
Disaster Relief Society of Zhangjiakou
(Zhangjiakou jiuzai hui), 179–80
disasters: earthquakes, 207, 217, 250;
frequency, 133; hailstorms, 197, 205,
206; mortality, 125; in 1920s, 245;
scholarship on, 3–4, 6–7; woodblock
prints, 87. *See also* famines; floods
diseases: cholera, 180, 184–85; plague,
176, 180–81; prevention efforts, 235,
259–60; smallpox, 259–60; typhoid
fever, 260; typhus, 12, 235, 257, 260.
See also medical clinics
Dodge & Seymour car dealership, 118

Dong, Madeleine Yue, 68
Door of Hope, 97
Dragon King, 19, 37, 239, 273n70
Dray-Novey, Alison J., 66–67
droughts: effects, 19–20; in 1919 and
1920, 19–20, 125–26, 131–32, 134–36,
234–35, 249–50; in 1927–29, 248–50; in
Sichuan (1924), 245
Duan Qirui, 27–28, 31, 35, 39, 116, 164,
279n15
Duara, Prasenjit, 79–80, 146, 187

earthquakes, 207, 217, 250
earth-salt production, 131–32, 253
ecological degradation, 1, 39, 130
Edgerton-Tarpley, Kathryn Jean, 253
Edwards, Dwight W., 247
elites: in Beijing, 111; charities, 8, 121,
179–80; donations, 50, 55, 167–68, 178;
famine relief efforts, 50–51, 240; palace
women, 55; social networks, 34, 117;
virtues, 78; wealth, 8, 168. *See also*
benevolent halls; gentry; merchants;
military officials; philanthropists; rural
gentry
Emergency Relief Society for the North
(Beifang jizhen xiehui), 115, 286n27
Emery, H. C., 220
employment assistance, 89, 96, 106,
283n56, 285n110
entertainment industry: amusement
parks, 100; Beijing opera, 98–99;
benefit performances, 89, 98–99, 190,
194, 206, 211–12; village opera, 134;
women, 97–98
Esteemed Goodness benevolent hall
(Baoshantang), 110

families, 64, 131, 147. *See also* children;
kinship networks
famine (1920–21): areas affected, *21*, 37,
38–39; causes, 1, 37–38, 39; deaths, 1–2,
5–6, 64, 101–2, 125, 150–51, 234;
drought and harvest failures, 20,
36–38; end of, 246, 249–50; individual

Index 337

commemorating, 82. *See also* Society for Awakening Goodness
Jiangsu province: famine relief (1906), 221; governors, 35, 49, 115, 163–64, 168; natives in Beijing, 115, 118
Jiangsu-Zhejiang war, 307–8n17
Jiangxi *huiguan*, 114
Jiangxi provincial government, 33–34
Jichang ribao, 189, 213
Jilin Chamber of Commerce, 206
Jilin Charity Relief Society (Jilin yizhen hui), 190, 206, 207
Jilin city: donations to famine relief, 201; grain purchases for famine relief, 203; newspaper, 189
Jilin province: cities, 189–90; fundraising for famine relief, 201, 205–6, 207, 211–12, 213; grain harvests, 203, 300n15; Hailong county, 207; Jilin county, 190; Korean guerrillas, 197; Liaoyuan county, 190–91; map, *183*; migration to, 295n9; military governor, 171, 185–86, 190, 206; newspapers, 184, 213; refugees in, 184, 185–87, 189–92; relief efforts, 189–92, 194; Shuangcheng county, 211; Shulan county, 191–92; Tonghe county, 211–12; war relief, 202; Yitong county, 191; Yushu county, 211; Zhang Zuolin regime, 176. *See also* Harbin; Manchuria
Jin Yunpeng, 40, 61, 169, 181
Jinan, 210, 301n52
Jiuzai zhoukan (*Famine Relief Weekly*), 95, 116

Kalgan. *See* Zhangjiakou
Kaplan, Steven L., 13
Katz, Paul, 84, 89–90
kinship networks, 90, 138
Korean guerrillas, 197, 198
Kuhn, Philip A., 240–41

labor. *See* employment assistance; migrant workers; work relief
Laifu bao, 141–45, 163

land sales, 137
land taxes, 38
Lary, Diana, 243
Li Chun, 168
Li Hongzhang, 70
Li, Huaiyin, 138
Li, Lillian, 4, 127, 132
Li Lunbo, 70, 84–85, 256
Li Qingfang, 96, 97, 99, 283n56
Li Yuanhong, 80, 116, 242
Li Zhangtai, 115
Liang, M. T., 222
Liang Shiyi, 116, 121, 179, 220
Liang Shuming, 85
Liaodong Peninsula, refugees in, 183–85
Lijiao sect, 194, 299n101
Lin, Alfred H. Y., 85
Lingxue yaozhi, 99, 283n71
Lingyuan, 185
Liu Hongsheng, 283n68
Liu Jianyun, 241
livestock, 60, 83–84, 136. *See also* mule carts
loans: bonds issued by county governments, 154; charity, 82–83, 195; from Chinese banks, 170, 171; foreign, 153, 164–68, 233, 246–47, 294n67; forgiveness, 139–40, 146; of grain, 291–92n10; from provincial governments, 145; village mutual aid, 137, 138–40
lotteries, 114, 170
Lü Haihuan, 112

Ma Fuxiang, 71
Ma Jiping, 117–18
MacNair, Harley Farnsworth, 222, 223, 225–28
magistrates: in Fengtian, 188; fundraising for famine relief, 113, 210, 211–12; in Jilin, 190–91; native-place ties of, 113; relief administration, 153–54, 155, 157, 158, 161, 163, 179, 188, 190–91; work relief projects, 230
Mallory, Walter, 247
Manchukuo, 295–96n9

Ministry of Agriculture and Commerce, 38, 169–70

Ministry of Communications: free refugee transportation, 177, 182–83; minister, 286n27, 295n3; rail transport of relief goods, 114, 126–27; relief fund-raising of, 170; returning refugees to homes, 218; transit shelters, 174. *See also* railroads

Ministry of Education, 169

Ministry of Finance, 60, 115, 164, 169, 170, 217

Ministry of Foreign Affairs, 165, 167, 169, 246

Ministry of Justice, 169

Ministry of the Interior: cash assistance, 217; discounted grain sales records, 155; famine prevention efforts, 246; famine records, 158; funding, 115, 213; liquor distillation bans, 47; lottery, 170; negligence during famine, 152; returning refugees to homes, 218, 227; shelters and, 97; soup kitchens and, 54–55, 56, 58, 61, 93, 162–63, 226; statistics, 101–2; work relief projects, 230, 241. *See also* police

Ministry of War, 59, 72. *See also* Beijing gendarmerie

missionaries: accounts of famine relief, 147, 185; American, 147, 185, 224–25, 252, 303–4n44; association with imperialism, 252; Canadian, 20, 241; Catholic, 75, 224; coordinated activity, 223; declining number of, 252; disaster relief efforts, 221; famine relief efforts, 219, 222, 223–25, 241; famine relief in 1870s, 107; French, 224; newspapers, 75; proselytizing activity, 224–25; Protestant, 20, 223, 224, 252, 303n44; views of Chinese, 90; in Zhili province, 221

Missionary Echo of the United Methodist Church, The, 224

moral values, 82, 107. *See also* virtue

Morgan, J. P., 231

mosques, soup kitchens, 54, 55, 58, 65

Mukden. *See* Shenyang

mule carts, 1, 128, 149, 155, 244–45

Muslims, 25, 58, 147. *See also* mosques

mutual aid. *See* village mutual aid

Nanjing Decade, 6, 85, 241

Nankai camp, Tianjin, 257–60

Nanyang Brothers Tobacco Company, 91, 93–95, 96, 184

Nanyuan, 30, 32, 82

Naquin, Susan, 51

Nathan, Andrew, 23, 40, 152, 167

National Citizens' Convention, 40

National Famine Relief Drive, 201

Nationalist government: in Canton, 28, 31, 40, 199; disasters, 250, 251–52, 253; local officials, 253; Nanjing Decade, 6, 85, 241; social welfare policies, 251, 253; state-building, 251, 253; tariffs, 252

Nationalist Party (Guomindang): civil wars, 249; leaders, 70; Northern Expedition, 241, 242, 252

native-place associations (*tongxianghui*), 105–6, 108, 111–12, 209, 213. *See also* provincial lodges

native-place ties, 110, 111–15, 208–10, 211, 212, 213

navy, clothing distribution, 62, 63

Newchwang. *See* Yingkou

New Policy reforms, 72, 101, 142, 241

news media: advertising, 26–27, 91; American journalists, 279n30; coverage of corpses in streets, 101; coverage of famine (1920–21), 14, 22, 24, 37, 101, 107–8, 234; coverage of Northwest famine (1928–30), 251; coverage of poverty, 24–25, 107; coverage of relief efforts in Beijing, 25–27, 69, 75, 83; coverage of relief efforts in Manchuria, 189, 193, 205, 212–13; coverage of relief efforts in Zhili, 158, 162; diversity, 22, 23; drought reports, 22, 38; editorials, 213; foreign, 171–72, 204, 215, 216, 234;

Soup Kitchen Provisioning Bureau
(Jingji zhouchang choubanchu), 55, 62,
74, 77, 93, 102
soup kitchens (*zhouchang*): in Beijing, 47,
51, 54–60, 65, 74, 92–93, 94–95; central
government orders, 162–63; in
Changchun, 190; compared to grain
distribution, 158; in Fengtian, 95;
funding, 55, 59–60, 92, 159, 162–63; in
Hankou, 179; in Harbin, 194, 196; news
coverage, 162; oversight, 56–59, 65, 74,
93, 226; portion sizes, 54, 55–56, 93,
159–60, 226; private sponsors, 92–93,
94–95, 100, 157–60, 161, 162; of religious
groups, 194; in rural areas, 115, 147,
157–62; in Shanghai, 197; in Shenyang,
188–89; in Zhangjiakou, 179–80; in
Zhili, 65, 113, 152, 157–62, 303n44
South Manchurian Railway Company,
187, 192, 214, 295–96n9
Soviet Union: border with China, 181,
192, 194, 195, 198, 212; epidemics, 235;
famine (1921–22), 12, 235, 271n35;
refugees from, 197–98, 295n5
Spain, minister to China, 164–65
Standard Oil, 118
State Department, US, 232, 305n77
St. John's University, Shanghai, 75, 106,
165, 225
Strand, David, 68, 89
student demonstrations. *See* May Fourth
Movement
Su Xinliu, 241
suicides and suicide attempts, 53–54, 109
Suiyuan province: drought and famine
(1927–28), 248, 249; government,
33–34; refugees in, 174
Sun Liechen, 186, 195, 196, 212
Sun Yat-sen, 28, 75, 85, 199
Sun Zhenjia, 58–59
syncretic societies, 79–80, 84, 225.
See also religious groups

taitai women, 69
Tan Xiaopei, 99

taxes, 38, 59, 60, 164, 170, 244, 308n20.
See also customs
telegraph, 23–24
Temple of the Moon (Yuetan), 102
Temporary Relief Society of Tong County
(Tongxian linshi zhenji hui), 35
Temporary Steamed Corn Bread Society
(Linshi wowotou hui), 27, 82, 99
Tharp, Robert, 185
Thaxton, Ralph A., Jr., 13, 131–32
theaters. *See* entertainment industry
Thornton, Patricia M., 253
Thousand Buddha Temple (Qianfosi),
82
Tian Wenlie, 116
Tianjin: American military forces, 232;
benevolent halls, 36–37, 202; Chinese
Red Cross chapter, 34, 159, 161; floods,
117; food supplies, 170, 214, 258;
foreign concessions, 39; international
relief societies, 221, 222–23, 224,
303n33; lotteries, 170; Nankai camp,
257–60; newspapers, 24, 26, 251;
police, 180, 181, 259, 260; refugees in,
180, 181, 182, 197, 228, 257–60; relief
efforts, 168, 180, 258–59; ships leaving
from, 183, 184; as treaty port, 73; US
consul, 222; Wang Huaiqing's home
in, 255–56
Tianjin Chamber of Commerce, 37, 168,
184, 258
Times, 215, 216
tobacco companies, 91–95, 118
Tongzhou, 32, 41, 73
transportation: automobiles, 60, 118, 244,
277n103; canal boats, 149–50; mule
carts, 1, 128, 149, 155, 244–45; ships,
183–84. *See also* railroads
treaty ports: Harbin, 192; military
leaders' escapes to, 72–73; scholarship
on, 6; Yingkou, 183–85, 295–96n9.
See also Shanghai; Tianjin
treaty powers: diplomats, 164–67, 168,
177, 203–4, 246–47; loan request,
164–68, 233, 246–47, 294n67. *See also*

Harvard East Asian Monographs
(most recent titles)

Harvard East Asian Monographs

Harvard East Asian Monographs

Harvard East Asian Monographs

Harvard East Asian Monographs